The Moral Foundations of the American Republic

BENJAMIN R. BARBER

WALTER BERNS

JAMES W. CEASER

JOSEPH CROPSEY

ROBERT A. DAHL

MARTIN DIAMOND

ROBERT A. GOLDWIN

RICHARD HOFSTADTER

ROBERT H. HORWITZ

WILSON CAREY McWILLIAMS

WILL MORRISEY

HERBERT A. STORING

GORDON S. WOOD

MICHAEL P. ZUCKERT

The
MORAL
FOUNDATIONS
of the
AMERICAN
REPUBLIC

THIRD EDITION

Edited by Robert H. Horwitz

University Press of Virginia
Charlottesville

THE UNIVERSITY PRESS OF VIRGINIA

Third Edition 1986   *Second Printing 1987*

Benjamin R. Barber, "The Compromised Republic: Public Purposelessness in America," © 1976 by Benjamin R. Barber. Martin Diamond, "Ethics and Politics: The American Way," © 1976 by Martin Diamond. Joseph Cropsey, "The United States as Regime and the Sources of the American Way of Life," © 1975 by The American Political Science Association, published by permission. Robert H. Horwitz, "John Locke and the Preservation of Liberty: A Perennial Problem of Civic Education," © 1976 by Robert H. Horwitz. Wilson Carey McWilliams, "On Equality as the Moral Foundation for Community," © 1976 by the (then) Kenyon Public Affairs Forum, Kenyon College. Will Morrisey, "The Moral Foundations of the American Republic: An Introduction," and James W. Ceaser, "In Defense of Republican Constitutionalism: A Reply to Dahl," both copyright © 1986 by the Kenyon Public Affairs Conference Center, Kenyon College.

Robert A. Goldwin, "Of Men and Angels: A Search for Morality in the Constitution," first appeared in the *Congressional Record*; Gordon S. Wood, "The Democratization of Mind in the American Revolution," © 1974 by Gordon S. Wood, first appeared in *Leadership in the American Revolution*, Library of Congress, Washington, D.C., 1974; Walter Berns, "Religion and the Founding Principle," © 1975 by Walter Berns, first appeared in *The First Amendment and the Future of American Democracy* (New York: Basic Books, 1976), where it was published in a somewhat different form; Herbert J. Storing, "Slavery and the Moral Foundations of the American Republic," first appeared in *The College*, St. John's College, Annapolis, Md., July 1976.

The editor and publisher are grateful for permission to reprint the following: Richard Hofstadter, "The Founding Fathers: An Age of Realism," from *The American Political Tradition and the Men Who Made It*, by Richard Hofstadter, copyright 1948 by Alfred A. Knopf, Inc., reprinted by permission of the publisher; Michael P. Zuckert, "John Locke and the Problem of Civil Religion," has been published as Bicentennial Essay number six in the publication series of *Novus Ordo Seclorum*, the Bicentennial of the Constitution Project of The Claremont Institute for the Study of Statesmanship and Political Philosophy, and is here reprinted with permission; *Novus Ordo Seclorum* is supported by a grant from the National Endowment for the Humanities; Robert A. Dahl, "On Removing Certain Impediments to Democracy in the United States," reprinted with permission from the *Political Science Quarterly* 92 (Spring 1977): 1–20; from "The Black Cottage" from *The Poetry of Robert Frost* edited by Edward Connery Lathem. Copyright 1930, 1939, © 1969 by Holt, Rinehart and Winston. Copyright © 1958 by Robert Frost. Copyright © 1967 by Lesley Frost Ballantine. Reprinted by permission of Holt, Rinehart and Winston, Publishers.

Publication of this volume is sponsored by the Kenyon Public Affairs Conference Center, Kenyon College, Gambier, Ohio. The authors alone are responsible for the opinions expressed and any policies recommended in their respective papers. The Kenyon Public Affairs Conference Center is a nonpartisan educational program and as such takes no position on questions of public policy.

CIP information appears on the last page.

Printed in the United States of America

This work is dedicated
to the memory of our colleagues,
Martin Diamond and Herbert J. Storing,
whose lives were devoted to
understanding and strengthening
the moral foundations of our Republic

Contents

Preface to the Third Edition

THE meaning of the moral foundations of the American regime has been sharply debated throughout the two centuries of our independent political life. Such questions were placed conspicuously—and permanently—on the agenda of American political debate with the signing of the Declaration of Independence, whose revolutionary doctrines marked a radical break with prior understandings of the bases of political legitimacy and morality. The Declaration proclaims as self-evident truths "that all men are created equal," that they are endowed "with certain unalienable rights," and that, if government is to be legitimate, it must be based on such principles as the consent of the governed and representation.

Having joyfully celebrated the two hundredth anniversary of the signing of the Declaration of Independence, Americans are now preparing a properly thoughtful celebration of the bicentennial of our Constitution in 1987. The next few years will be marked by many probing discussions of the meaning of our Constitution in particular and of constitutionalism in general. Among the many questions that will be placed on the agenda is the relationship of the principles of the Declaration to the Constitution. Does the former enunciate the moral foundations of our nation while the latter embodies them in a viable framework of government? Do these two extraordinary political documents form a harmonious whole, or do they differ, or even contradict one another, on fundamental issues, as some believe? Does the Constitution of 1787 continue to provide an adequate framework of government in the late twentieth century or has "history" or societal change rendered it obsolete in significant respects? If the latter, then how should Americans achieve such changes as they believe are required in our fundamental law? Should these changes be effected chiefly through the time-consuming and rather cumbersome amendment process provided in the Constitution itself, or should they be initiated by the Supreme Court or even by the executive power of a strong president? To what extent can Americans today be guided by the principles of the Constitution in dealing with such deeply divisive issues as the relationship between politics and religion? These and a host of related questions are discussed in the essays that follow.

The editing of this book follows the design of the preceding volumes in this series. I have sought to present the views of authoritative spokesmen writing from a broad variety of perspectives. All of these positions are thoughtfully and responsibly stated, but they are of such variety that no one can reasonably agree with all of them. My intention has been to place the reader in the midst of these controversies, both practical and scholarly, and thus to oblige him to consider the conflicting arguments and to draw his own conclusions.

Since publication of the first edition of this volume in 1977, I have added additional essays designed to broaden and strengthen its coverage. In this new edition the reader will find a pair of essays by Robert A. Dahl and James Ceaser, a new essay by Michael P. Zuckert linked with an excellent earlier essay by Walter Berns, along with a thoroughgoing Introduction written by Will Morrisey. It is strongly recommended that the reader peruse this Introduction in order to gain an overview of the contents of the volume and the relationships among its thirteen essays.

This volume, like its twenty or more predecessors, has been produced by the Public Affairs Conference Center Program of Kenyon College, a program initiated at the University of Chicago in 1961 by Robert A. Goldwin and brought to Kenyon by him in 1967. In recent years it has been ably directed by Fred Baumann of Kenyon's Department of Political Science.

I am indebted to many individuals and organizations for assistance in preparing this new edition, particularly to Will Morrisey, who cheerfully undertook the arduous task of writing the Introduction. He also shared major responsibilities with me at every step in preparation of the text and seeing the book through the press. It can quite truthfully be said that without his generous and skillful assistance this new edition would never have been brought to completion. I am also deeply indebted to Fred Baumann for his unfailing helpfulness, generosity, and enthusiasm. Finally, I want to thank the George Gund Foundation which, acting upon a recommendation of the Ohio American Revolutionary Bicentennial Advisory Commission, provided generous financial assistance toward initial publication of this book. I also was given substantial support from the National Endowment for the Humanities and the Earhart Foundation. This assistance afforded me the opportunity to prepare my own essay and to carry out editorial work on successive editions and printings of the book since 1977. The Kenyon College Faculty Affairs Committee provided financial support for typing, editing, word-processing and the like which greatly facilitated preparation of the volume for the press. To all of the foregoing I gratefully acknowledge the invaluable assistance that has been received; I alone am responsible for errors or other inadequacies in the volume.

ROBERT H. HORWITZ

Gambier, Ohio

The Moral Foundations of the American Republic

The Moral Foundations of the American Republic: An Introduction

Will Morrisey

IT is a resounding title, *The Moral Foundations of the American Republic*. What does it mean?

Each of us knows "the American republic," more or less. We grew up here; we felt the meaning of the word *American* long before we started to think seriously about it. Hearing such phrases as "American democracy," "the American way," or "the American dream," we associated them with what we eventually learned to call "liberty." We knew we had, for the most part, the right to speak and act as we wanted, without government interference. At the same time, we knew that because we were free we were also responsible before the law and before each other; we had no one to blame but ourselves if we said or did the wrong thing. We also learned, or at least came to feel, that our liberty depends upon a kind of equality. Although you and I may differ in tastes and abilities, we are equal as American citizens. You can't stop me from voting as I choose or from saying what I think about politics, as long as I do it on my own time. Nor can I stop you. These political facts of liberty and equality influence us in many ways, giving us those character traits recognized as "American" by friends and enemies throughout the world.

This Americanness goes well with our "republic." By *res publica* the ancient Romans meant, literally, "public thing." They distinguished republican Rome from Rome under the Caesars. Republican Rome meant Rome *as* a public entity, a country belonging to, ruled by, its citizens. This Rome was no democracy—a word of Greek origin, meaning rule by the *demos*, "the many who are poor." Republican Rome was what the classical political thinkers call a mixed regime. The few rich and the many poor shared political authority, each group with its own prerogatives and institutions. Together those institutions formed a government in which the claims of the few and the many could be balanced. This regime ended with the rule of the Caesars, who transformed Rome from a public thing into a private one "belonging" to the emperor. Rome then became at times a monarchy, at times a tyranny.

The founders of the American republic opposed a monarch, George III, who acted tyrannically against the colonies. "No taxation without representation" was the famous slogan. While demanding such representation, *by* demanding *representation*, the founders rejected pure democracy. In the greatest defense of the American Constitution, *The Federalist Papers*, James Madison calls pure democracy "a society consisting of a small number of citizens, who assemble and administer the government in person." "Such democracies have ever been spectacles of turbulence and contention," regimes "as short in their lives as they have been violent in their deaths" (*Federalist* No. 10). By *republic* Madison means a government to which citizens elect representatives, instead of attempting directly to conduct public affairs. Republican government "derives all its powers directly or indirectly from the great body of the people, and is administered by persons holding their offices during pleasure for a limited period, or during good behavior" (*Federalist* No. 39). Although our constitution displays a mixture of what might be called the monarchic (the presidency), the aristocratic (the Superme Court), the oligarchic and the democratic-republican (the Senate and House of Representatives, respectively), all of these institutions directly or indirectly derive their authority from "the great body of the people." The American republic thus differs from the Roman republic, as our constitution requires us to "mix" the different social and economic classes politically even as we elect our representatives.

This kind of mixing gives our republic a more democratic character than that of the Roman republic.[1] "American republic" means a government reflecting what Madison called "the genius of the American people"—not the ancient Romans or the Europeans of his day. This "genius" consists of a character that demands political liberty and the political equality such liberty implies. Today we see in ourselves much the same character Madison saw in his own contemporaries, although most of us cannot claim the English ancestry that predominated among Madison's Americans. Republican-

---

[1] The extent to which the United States Constitution establishes a *democratic*, as distinguished from a *"mixed,"* republic can only be determined by a careful assessment of the document itself, the writings of its Framers, and their speeches, particularly those delivered at the Constitutional Convention. In this volume differing positions on this important issue may be seen in the essays by Hofstadter, Diamond, and Wood.

ism conforms to the "genius of the American people," but other peoples can in turn conform themselves to that genius as immigrants and the descendants of immigrants. Conversely, other peoples can conform republicanism to their own genius, on their own land. Peoples who have replicated aspects of the American experiment in republicanism include the Japanese, the Indians, the Israelis, and most West Europeans.

Of course, republics constitute a small minority of the governments in the world. Tyrannies, oligarchies, and combinations thereof dominate most of the nations today, as they have throughout history. That such regimes now so often call themselves "people's republics" may be regarded as a sort of unintentional tribute to the attractions of modern republicanism. Contemporary tyrants and oligarchs want to be praised as the truest republicans—more, the truest democrats—of all.

Yet the American republic invites criticism by true and false democrats alike. While admitting the Founders' practical reasons for refusing to establish a pure democracy here, many of our contemporaries question the morality of this refusal. The liberty that enables America to be not only a republic but a *commercial* republic, with its attendant toleration of some economic inequalities, further provokes such critics. John Dewey, probably the most celebrated American philosopher of this century, insisted that the cure for the ills of democracy is not less but more democracy. The presence of this familiar and powerful opinion requires us to examine "the moral foundations" of the American republic, for this is where we can see the same fundamental issues we face today, stated in their purest form.

The term *foundations* suggests the firm underpinnings of a group of buildings. The American republic may be understood as a kind of city. Can a city's "foundations" be described as moral, even if we speak metaphorically? This question has perplexed human beings for millennia. The most authoritative guide to morality known to Americans, the Bible, depicts the founder of the first city on earth as a fratricide. The Book of Genesis tells us that after Cain murdered his brother, Abel, he "went away from the presence of the Lord, and dwelt in the land of Nod, east of Eden." There "he built a city, and called the name of the city after the name of his son, Enoch" (Genesis 4: 16, 17). Nor is it encouraging to read that Rome itself was founded by Romulus, who before that founding murdered his twin brother, Remus. The Roman historian Livy blamed the twins' "shameful rivalry" on "the lust for rule" (*History of Rome*, I, 6–7). These and other incidents related by historians much impressed the shrewd Florentine writer Niccolò Machiavelli. Not only did he teach that all cities are necessarily founded in crime and bloodshed, but he based his political philosophy on the belief that conquest—the conquest of other human beings and the conquest of nature itself—is the highest human ambition.

Americans find unvarnished Machiavellianism morally repulsive. We point instead to our own Founding, which culminated in a voluntary social compact, our Constitution, established by peaceful debate, not terrorist bloodletting. This is of course true, as far as it goes. But we also half-remember another aspect of our early history. The Founders failed to correct certain injustices committed by earlier settlers, including the destruction and exile of the continent's original inhabitants and the enslavement of a portion of its new inhabitants who were imported for the express purpose of chattel slavery. Our very act of founding occurred during a revolutionary war that the British and the American tories regarded as an extended act of fratricide. Perhaps we should admit, as some critics insist, that the American Founding, like so many others, rests on *im*moral foundations. We can and have built many good works upon these foundations. We tell the edifying myths Socrates called "noble lies," partially concealing the Founders' crimes. But we can never candidly deny the occurrence of those crimes.

Nonetheless, most Americans would find these criticisms offensive and unfair. On the issue of the alleged fratricide during our revolutionary war, they could appeal to the words of one of our most candid and honored Founders, Thomas Jefferson: "The tree of liberty must be refreshed from time to time with the blood of patriots and tyrants. It is its natural manure" (letter written from Paris, July 2, 1787). The killing and dying in our revolutionary war had a clear purpose and justification: the defense of liberty against what Jefferson's Declaration of Independence characterizes as "a long train of abuses and usurpations." The Declaration denies that the Americans sought a revolution, arguing rather that King George III and his ministers had rebelled against the colonists by assaulting the "unalienable rights" with which all human beings are "endowed by their Creator." The Founders' virtue, courage, served an end that itself served a moral end, the re-establishment of liberty.

This observation raises another fundamental issue. Obviously, a given course of action must have some end, some purpose, to justify it. But does a worthwhile end justify *any* means, that is, *any* course of action?[2] Alternatively, while an end may justify *some* means, if not any means, how does a given end limit our selection of means? Are there certain means that ultimately damage the ends they are intended to serve? The Founders confronted this problem and so do we, whenever we consider the major public issues of our time. Should young men and women serve, or be required to serve, in the armed forces? Should our government use the device of "positive discrimination" to improve the relative position of women and various minorities as they seek education and employment? How, why, and to what extent, if any, should the government's power be used to redistribute the nation's wealth? Should abortion be sanctioned by the government, or outlawed? As they consider such problems of ends and means, Americans often find themselves referring to the standards stated or implied in our Constitution, that is, to the legal foundations of the American republic. Because any law commands that one *should* or *should not* act in a certain way, we search our fundamental law for its underlying moral and political principles.[3]

2 Several twentieth-century political founders insisted that a sufficiently noble end does justify the use of any means that could achieve it. During the Russian Civil War, V. I. Lenin stated, "It does not matter if three-quarters of mankind is destroyed; all that counts is that ultimately the last quarter should become Communists" (cited in René Fuelop-Miller, *Fyodor Dostoevsky: Insight, Faith, and Prophecy* [New York: Charles Scribner's Sons, 1950], p. 105). According to Lenin, the vanguard of the proletariat, the class *in whom* the future greatness of humanity exclusively resides, must *therefore* triumph by any means necessary.

On the extreme Right, Adolf Hitler replaced Marxist-Leninist "class-consciousness" with "race-consciousness." He replaced Lenin's proletariat with the "Aryan race"; Jews and other so-called races served the same function in his demonology as the bourgeoisie did in Lenin's. Hitler therefore shared Lenin's extremism with regard to means, writing that "a philosophy of life is never willing to share with another," and thus will "not collaborate in an existing regime which it condemns, but feels obligated to combat this regime and the whole hostile world of ideas with all possible means" (*Mein Kampf*, vol. 2, chap. 5).

Notice that both Marxist-Leninist "class" and Hitlerian "race" are *embodied ideals.* That is, both ideologies insist that the favored "class"/"race" is both *necessary* for human *survival* and also the vessel of the *highest* form of humanity. This unification of the real and the allegedly ideal enables the ideologue to proclaim that any means are justifiable if they succeed. Thanks to the examples of Lenin, Hitler, and others, today even those who still endorse a communitarian vision of some future utopia, Left or Right, often hesitate to assume that the hatred one needs to destroy so many will not find new objects of hatred after its initial victims disappear.

3 This fact should not be confused with a very different assertion, namely, that the moral is identical to the legal. Although this assertion has had its defenders, a

Clearly, the phrase "moral foundations," though formidable, refers to deeply ingrained mental habits.

Mental habits, precisely because they are habits, invite and indeed require careful study by those who want to think for themselves and advance beyond the world of received opinion. In 1970 only about one in ten Americans over the age of 25 had attended college for four years. Today, the number is close to one in five; in your generation (if you are an American college student), it will be about one in four. College studies can challenge our habitual opinions, including those about the American republic and its Constitution. Among this book's essays you will find several such challenges. To intelligently defend or criticize our Constitution, our legal and moral foundations, one must learn to think and know, not merely opine and believe. This effort will require studying the intentions of the American Founders and the meaning of their work.

This book of essays can serve as one guide to the beginning of such study. It is a form of study that presents unique difficulties. The study of political things differs from the study of languages, mathematics, or the natural sciences. Understanding political things contrasts with knowing the principles of geometry, for example. Differences of opinion concerning a geometrical problem are susceptible to precise solution, to demonstration. No political dispute, not even a dispute over the stated intentions of politicians, resolves itself so neatly and finally. Politics presents words arranged as arguments, not numbers arranged as theorems. Numbers answer the question How many? They do not tell us Why. Even the numbers tabulated and sometimes manipulated by pollsters, even the authoritative numbers generated on election day, reflect judgments, not computations. One may calculate the effects of many proposals, but only in order to choose according to those nonnumerical criteria "better" and "worse." We come to know political things by considering speeches or arguments and the actions that confirm or belie those speeches.

This book contains thirteen essays—speeches of a sort—in which able historians and political scientists make various arguments about

---

single example will show its problematic character. In Hitler's Third Reich, Jews and other minorities were legally deprived of German citizenship, forced to identify themselves by wearing badges, deprived of jobs and housing, sent to concentration camps, and finally murdered. Many if not all of these actions met the formal standards of law—that is, they were duly enacted by the sovereign power, promulgated, and enforced. These laws were, moreover, in conformance with the Nazi moral code. But that of course did not make them genuinely moral.

the American republic and its moral foundations. Three pairs of essays precede the book's central essay, which is followed by three more pairs. This pairing suggests twinship; you will find it to be a twinship along a somewhat more civilized model than that provided by Romulus and Remus. Nevertheless, you will find serious disagreements between many of these "twins." One essayist will often contradict the other. Each essayist presents an explicit or implicit understanding of morality. Some differentiate between political and other forms of morality. All of these forms imply a given understanding of human nature, itself a matter of dispute. Depending in large measure on the answers to questions such as these, the moral foundations of the American republic are judged as good, bad, or as some mixture thereof. As you study the contradictions among these argued judgments, you will begin to see strengths and weaknesses in each essay. Everyone "has opinions," but if you follow these arguments with care, testing them for logic and accuracy, you can discover a world of thought beyond the familiar grab bag of received opinions. From this new perspective, you should see those opinions more clearly.

Although many collections of essays are themselves little more than grab bags of opinions, this one is not. Essays prepared for two major conferences on "The Moral Foundations of the American Republic" have been supplemented by essays selected because they provide additional, important arguments. At first reading, most of your effort must necessarily go into understanding individual essays. Some of them will strike you as rather complex, for the authors tersely express carefully measured arguments. For this reason you may not immediately see the overall structure of the book and the many relationships among the essays. The remainder of this introduction provides an overview.

The first two essays introduce several of the major themes of the book. The authors confront us with the problem of ends and means. In his "search for morality in the Constitution" Robert A. Goldwin discovers a combination of "noble principle and self-interest." This intentional conjunction of apparently opposed principles does not amount to hypocrisy. Rather, the Founders "looked at Americans and decided that it would be fruitless and impractical, and perhaps even morally wrong, for the new nation to strive to become spotlessly moral." The Founders sought to avoid the moral purism or utopianism that would strenuously cleanse human beings of every fault. They saw that to encourage such exertions would require the destruction of the political and economic liberty they had sought to win through their revolution, a liberty without which other natural rights are indefensible.[4] In this century we have witnessed repeatedly the correctness of the Founders' judgment. Whether these moral purists approach us from the Right (as in the case of Mussolini, Hitler, and others), or from the Left (Lenin, Mao, Pol Pot, and a legion of others), they invariably sneer at liberty while exalting some new "consciousness" that will, they assure us, bring not tyranny but "true freedom."[5] These attempts to achieve spotless morality often result in the application of what Machiavelli accurately described as "inhuman cruelty," usually followed by corruption far worse than the milder vices tolerated in the commercial republics.

Goldwin quotes with approval the first systematic political scientist, Aristotle, who wrote that lawmakers "make the citizens good by training them in habits of right action." The Constitution, Goldwin writes, "seeks to train us in habits of restraint and moderation," not by imposing them on us "from above" but by leaving individuals at liberty to compete with, and thus check, one another's ambitions. This cannot yield simple equality, although it has led to a very considerable degree of equality. Nor can it yield a perfectly harmonious balance, although it has led to what may be termed a form of dynamic balancing.

Benjamin R. Barber counterargues that while the Founders' regime succeeded in its time, circumstances have changed radically. The Founders expected "that from the clash of opposites, of contraries, of extremes, of poles, [would] come, not the victory of any one, but the mediation and accommodation of them all." But today, Barber contends, circumstances dictate limits, particularly limits on economic growth. The inequalities that do exist should no longer be tolerated because we cannot claim that they are merely temporary, soon to be overcome by economic expansion. In this new era of

[4] Many of the Founders were familiar with the writings of the English philosopher John Locke, who writes that "I have no reason to suppose that he, who would *take away my Liberty*, would not when he had me in his Power, take away everything else. . . . he who attempts to get another Man into his Absolute Power, does thereby *put himself into a State of War with him*; It being to be understood as a Declaration of a Design upon his Life" (*An Essay concerning Civil Government*, chap. 3).

[5] On this, compare Mussolini's fascist definition of totalitarianism—"everything for the State, nothing against the State"—with Fidel Castro's Communist slogan—"Everything inside the revolution, nothing outside the revolution."

limits, "speculation and entrepreneurship are no longer virtues."
The resulting alienation of those excluded from power can only be
remedied by "periodic redistricting in accordance with crucial demographic and economic developments," a perpetual, deliberate redistribution of political-economic power, thereby insuring direct citizen participation in government rather than the election of mere
representatives.

Although Barber writes of an *era* of limits, it would be wrong to
believe that he regards his argument as valid only in a certain historical period. In the closing pages of his essay, Barber makes it clear
that he strongly disapproves of economic speculation and entrepreneurship generally. He deplores the "hubris" of modern science's attempt to conquer nature, an attempt he regards as the fundamental
cause of alienation. He is thereby led to attack the moral-intellectual
foundations of commercial republicanism. He criticizes the work of
the American Founders not only for our time but for all time. His
argument concerning the limits of growth is less a description than a
prescription.

The second pair of essays explores the theme of ends and means as
reflected in human nature and in the character of modernity. The
historian Richard Hofstadter argues that the Founders combined a
nonmodern, "vivid Calvinistic sense of human evil and damnation"
with a modern desire for economic and political liberty. Their "distrust of the common man and democratic rule" resulted in strict
limits on popular participation in politics. Because he regards the
Constitution as undemocratic, Hofstadter believes it "curious" that
the agrarian Democratic-Republicans who gained power after 1800
respected the very institutions that restricted their power and, more
generally, restricted democracy. Writing in the late 1940s, he also
finds continued respect for the underlying principles of the Constitution somewhat curious, claiming that "no man [today] who is as well
abreast of modern science as the [Founding] Fathers were of eighteenth century science believes any longer in unchanging human
nature." In the decades since Hofstadter wrote, some scientists have
come to consider human nature less changeable than many scientists of Hofstadter's generation believed it to be. The matter has
again become controversial.[6] Be that as it may, whereas Barber would

6 See, for example, the debate over "sociobiology" provoked by Edwin O.
Wilson's *On Human Nature* (Cambridge: Harvard Univ. Press, 1978). Wilson and
his colleagues have been accused of conservatism, but consider also the writings
of Noam Chomsky, no conservative, on linguistics: *The Logical Structure of*

revolutionize the American republic by attempting to change our opinion concerning modern science, Hofstadter would revolutionize the American republic by "revolutionizing" *us*—by changing, or at least awaiting the changing of, human nature itself.

At this point Martin Diamond enters the debate. Thinking of the Aristotelian teaching cited by Goldwin, Diamond explains the relation of ethics and politics as understood by Aristotle and as presented (rather differently) by the American Founders.

Lawmakers make the citizens good by training them in habits of right action. Founders are not ordinary lawmakers; they prescribe a constitution, the "supreme law of the land." A constitution shapes the citizens' opinions and patterns of behavior, particularly their political behavior. A regime is the ruling order of the polity; it consists of those individuals and, secondarily, those institutions regarded as authoritative by the citizens—and therefore as models or guides for citizens' behavior. Each regime will tend to encourage the development of certain kinds of human beings and discourage the development of other kinds. For example, the entrepreneur is a common American type; not so in Maoist China, where other types were encouraged.

The American Founders understood the relation of ethics to politics in a somewhat non-Aristotelian way. The Americans would agree with Aristotle that different regimes influence the formation of different kinds of human beings, but they avoid trying to use political power for the direct formation of character. Insofar as they uphold liberty, not authority, they insist on indirect means to develop the type of citizenry required for the modern republican order. They consistently emphasize institutions more than direct moral education—which in any event can take place in churches, homes, and schools. Properly designed institutions regulate human selfishness by allowing its expression in certain ways carefully framed or channeled by law. In modernity, *government* tends to replace *regime*, as large areas of human life (including religion, education, poetry and other arts, the family, and day-to-day economic activity) are depoliticized, liberated from the direct effects of political authority. Government regulates these more or less private, often competing, forces; it does not rule them.

Diamond illustrates these observations by discussing Madison's analysis of faction, a perennial political phenomenon regarded by

Linguistic Theory (New York: Plenum Publishing, 1975) and *Language and Mind* (New York: Harcourt Brace Jovanovich, 1972).

Madison as a reflection not merely of economic circumstance but of human nature. Like Goldwin, Diamond finds the work of the American Founders brilliant but not entirely satisfactory. He ends his essay by exploring the possibilities for more direct means of forming a more elevated citizen-character, insofar as those means will strengthen, not undermine, the American republic.

The third pair of essays explores the problem of character formation as it relates to the intellectual formation of those who govern. Historian Gordon S. Wood writes of the Founders: "Somehow for a brief moment ideas and power, intellectualism and politics, came together—indeed were one with each other—in a way never duplicated in American history." The Founders exemplified a recognizable social-political type: the gentleman. Wood argues that these men—prosperous, learned, animated by both political ambition and by a sense of political responsibility—unintentionally "helped create the changes that led to their own undoing" by leading the American revolution, whose "transforming democratic radicalism" exceeded the Founders' expectations. The resulting "egalitarian culture" and "democratic society" yielded the "separation between ideas and power" that persists to this day.

Perhaps the most important of Wood's observations concerns the character of the Founders' ideas, which at least partly determined the way they used power. Professed egalitarianism does not itself require the separation of ideas from power. Lenin had ideas, as do hundreds of American demagogues (called, aptly enough, ideologues), some of whom wield considerable power. But the ideas of the Founders caused them to spurn militancy, to defend moderation.[7] Wood in effect remarks the Founders' moderation by saying that their rhetoric served reason. Nonetheless, the newly empowered majority increasingly preferred the sort of politician who presented himself as (in one instance) the "log cabin and hard cider" candidate. Wood may or may not be right to contend that the Founders anticipated none of this, but none can deny that it happened.

Robert H. Horwitz explicitly takes up this theme. He observes that although the more conservative founders lost their political rank, they won the economic argument. America resembles Alex-

[7] Despite Wood's preliminary statement that in the Founding "moment" ideas and power "were one with each other," the Founders never imagined that ideas could be embodied, that practice could unite with theory. A constitution, made of words meant to be obeyed, is not a blueprint, made of geometrically precise drawings meant to be embodied.

ander Hamilton's commercial republic much more than Thomas
Jefferson's agrarian republic. But whatever the domestic victories
and defeats they suffered, "neither the Federalists nor the Anti-Federalists provided an adequate analysis of the character and place of
civic virtue in the American Republic and the need for some form of
civic education." Without character formation for civic virtue, including patriotism and courage, a commercial republic may fall prey
to the military power of foreign governments that find riches tempting. A writer who did treat this problem thoroughly was also the
political philosopher who most influenced the Founders: John
Locke. Accordingly, Horwitz examines Locke for the arguments resulting from Locke's insistence that, in Horwitz's words, "a republic
based essentially on the pursuit of private interest can still develop
those virtues that are ultimately indispensable to the maintenance
of liberty."

Locke is, of course, a modern political philosopher. He stresses
individual liberty, not authority, and calls for the conquest of nature, not its imitation. He nonetheless shares at least one insight
with Aristotle: that laws are not sufficient to insure virtue. For that,
Locke would utilize what he calls "the law of opinion," whereby individuals are guided by the praise and blame of those around them
and, particularly, those to whom they look for guidance in social-
political matters. Writing for Englishmen, Locke would have the
gentleman class *privately* educated in such a way as would provide
a humane and prudent governing stratum, competent to guide the
nation's political affairs and deserving of the nation's deference.
"These people provide the standards of behavior and opinion by
which others are guided." Clearly, this is much the same class of
people whose American counterparts provided almost all of our
Founders.

Although Locke shares with Christianity the insight that individuals have a natural tendency toward selfishness, even tyranny,
he shows small interest in healing with the balm of Christian precepts the moral diseases to which flesh is heir. Locke would rechannel or redirect the passions, not attempt to suppress or replace them
with others. Even humane liberality can be taught by the means of
self-interest. By rewarding children with praise, in their sinful pride
they can be brought to compete in kindness. Patriotism too, Locke
believes, can be manufactured from these materials with these tools.

Horwitz admires the ingenuity of Locke's educational writings,
although he stops short of endorsing them. There is, perhaps a ten-

sion between "rugged individualism" and the human sensitivity to the "law of opinion." A more immediate problem concerns applicability: "Is such an educational program possible today, and, if so, by whom would it be developed and who would be its proper recipients?"

In the seventh, central, essay, Joseph Cropsey provides a magisterial assessment of the book's principal themes. Understand Cropsey's essays and the others, before and after, should fall more easily into place.

Cropsey makes the same distinction Diamond makes between classical regime and modern government, without using exactly the same words. He describes the American regime as imperfect because it is "complemented or completed by thought," which is private, not *of* the regime yet decisive to the regime's well-being. Thought—or rather "a medley of thoughts old and modern"—inclines us toward dissatisfaction with our regime, thereby threatening its very existence. This is especially true of thoughts intended as a critique of the political and philosophic principles of the very Constitution that guarantees protection of criticism. Publicly guaranteed *private* liberties have public results.

Cropsey traces this tension between the public and the private to modern political philosophy. The "hard" modernity of Machiavelli, "inspiriting, reminding man of his earthbound solitude and presenting the world as an opportunity for greatness of some description," struggles with the "soft" modernity of Hobbes and Locke, "pointing toward survival, security, and freedom to cultivate felt predilections." "The United States is an arena in which modernity," "hard" and "soft," public and private, can be seen to be "working itself out."

Cropsey describes and assesses the principal variants of modernity and concludes that even those elements of American life that did not originally partake of modernity (religion and natural philosophy) have been "transformed into, or been made ministerial to, the mollifying or indolent"—that is, they have been corrupted by "soft" modernity. Moreover, "the self-criticism of modernity is an episode in the continuous self-criticism of western [modern and premodern] man." This formulation again poses the problem of means and ends in its comprehensive form; criticism, a means to an end, can, if too corrosive, endanger the very end it seeks. "Perhaps the highest task of political philosophy is to understand, as the highest task of statesmanship is to govern, the relation of political life to thought." While stressing the danger of ungoverned thought to any political regime or quasi regime, Cropsey suggests that the political could not rule thought unless we united practice with theory. He does not suggest that this is possible or desirable, much less likely.

The American insistence on the privacy of religion reflects a Lockean understanding of the place of religion in a well-ordered regime. At the same time, religion is in many ways *the* repository of morality in human life; its public significance is therefore undeniable. The fourth pair of essays explores this significance.

Michael Zuckert clarifies Locke's subtle and discreet argument on "the reasonableness of Christianity." Reacting to decades of civil wars and centuries of religious persecution caused by men's religious passions, Locke intends to tame "Christianity's hitherto rather uncivil character." Americans today, accustomed to a "soft," Lockean Christianity characterized by peaceableness and love, may still see remnants of the old Christian militancy in various church-sponsored grassroots movements, both Left and Right. Locke and, to a somewhat lesser extent, the American Founders confronted a more formidable religiosity. Locke blames Christian incivility partly on the monotheism it shares with Judaism but mostly on its strong adherence to articles of faith as sufficient for salvation. The doctrine of salvation by faith alone weakens the importance of works, or acts, and thereby "renders religion a much less clear support for civil society" than before. The Protestant emphasis on predestination undermines this support still further. The doctrines of monotheism, salvation by faith alone, and predestination all tend to undermine moderation.

In the artfully tortuous argument of his *On the Reasonableness of Christianity*, Locke defends adherence to only one article of faith as sufficient for salvation. The article is that Jesus is the Messiah. Locke then argues that repentance is as important as faith, thereby reconnecting divine sanctions with works. Finally, and most radically, Locke pretends that Christianity is "reasonable," that is, that it incorporates the law of nature into its "law" of works—so recently resurrected by Locke himself. The extent to which Locke believes Christianity truly reasonable may be seen in the fact that those preeminently reasonable men, the philosophers, discover neither Jesus nor even morality by reason alone. Not only does Locke note this fact, but in his *Discourse of Miracles* he argues that the truth of no religion can be established by reason.

Zuckert suggests that Locke's proposed solution to the religious problem suffers from much the same defect as his solution to the educational problem. It might even be thought that the insufficiency of his educational reform reflects the insufficiency of his religious reform: the tension between individualism and the "law of opinion" reflects the tension between the Lockean philosopher's rationality and the political need for some support of morality. At the same time, the fact that mainline American Christianity today does tend toward talk of peaceableness and love reveals the success of Locke's attempt to tame religious passion. It also begins to reveal the tendency toward "the mollifying and the indolent"—toward an incapacity to defend the very liberty "reasonable" religion needs for its continued existence.

Walter Berns shows how this Lockean counsel came into practice in America. He presents evidence that the Founders "agreed that our institutions do not presuppose a providential Supreme Being" but agreed that preservation of those institutions does require such belief. Jefferson, for example, observed that religion can strengthen the modern doctrine of natural rights among the many who might otherwise not accept the doctrine. However, to support what Jefferson believed to be the scientific, rational truth of natural rights, "Christianity had to be made reasonable." Berns notes that "the origin of free government in the modern sense coincides and can only coincide with the solution of the religious problem," a solution that "consists in the subordination of religion." This subordination is not imposed, as in the totalitarian regimes, but induced by the lure of commercial activity, which does not so much force men to abandon religion as it encourages them to relegate it to a subordinate place in their lives. Still, it must be remarked that a tamed religion remains a religion, and the churches here have tended toward patriotism because clerics have seen that Christianity with civility yields less violent sins than Christianity without civility.

Berns exphasizes an important point now much overlooked. Religious toleration can rest only on what is regarded as a political truth. Without a belief in the modern doctrine of natural rights, the basis of religious toleration dissolves. In Berns's view, Jefferson tolerated differences of religious opinion while refusing to tolerate political heresy. He went so far as to advocate the teaching of certain American state papers as a political catechism—as did Abraham Lincoln in his famous "Address before the Young Men's Lyceum of Springfield, Illinois." Our contemporary advocates of a universal toleration extended to the political and moral realms perhaps have not reflected sufficiently upon the basis of, much less the justification for, such toleration. What moral and political foundations can replace those of the Founders' regime? Should those foundations be replaced? It has become very easy to ask such radical questions, but discovering answers superior to those of the Founders has proved difficult.

These difficulties become clear in the fifth pair of essays, a polemical but instructive exchange between two political scientists who have written extensively on American institutions. Robert A. Dahl would remove what he calls "impediments to democracy" in the American polity. He contends that different and conflicting "historical commitments" have resulted in these "impediments." The five major "commitments" he identifies are the Constitution; democratic agrarianism, industrialism, or "corporate capitalism"; the welfare state, and the "large military establishment."

The Constitution impedes democracy because it establishes a representative government and thereby fails to protect sufficiently certain minorities from "privileged" minorities. Moreover, what democracy we have finds itself channeled, as in the democratic agrarianism of Andrew Jackson, into the office of the president, our one nationally elected office-holder. This serves to empower not the people but the president, and thus stands as an instance of "pseudo-democratization." Dahl reserves his most vehement criticisms for the business corporations, which have, he believes, illegitimately transferred the traditional property rights of the small, agrarian landowners to their own very different capitalistic enterprises. Finally, the welfare state "has not done much to alter the hierarchical structures of corporate government" and the military establishment has given us "still another hierarchy."

Dahl would replace "corporate capitalism" and indeed many if not all of the constitutional offices with "procedural democracy," whereby all adults would make "collective decisions" on all major politicoeconomic issues. Dahl's immediate formal vehicle for these decisions appears to be a kind of parliamentary socialism, but parliamentarism would probably give way to the direct democracy advocated earlier by Barber. Dahl lists five criteria of "procedural democracy": political equality, effective participation, "enlightened understanding" (requiring equal and "adequate" access to information), "inclusiveness" (requiring "full citizenship" for all adults obliged to obey the laws), and "popular sovereignty." The list's most striking feature is the similarity, not to say redundancy, of the first two criteria and the last two—all virtual synonyms. Only the central criterion, "enlightened understanding," significantly differs from the others.

The criterion of enlightened understanding represents Dahl's attempt to solve a problem familiar both to the American Founders and to others who think seriously about democracy: How does democratic rule, rule by the majority, protect minority rights and make wise decisions? Put another way, how does majority rule restrain itself from majority tyranny? Dahl suggests that a system of "quasi experts" could be instituted; certain citizens would make it their business to understand and interpret the technical knowledge of experts to ordinary citizens. Perhaps because knowledge is neither wisdom nor justice, Dahl does not leave matters there. He goes so far as to suggest that "human consciousness" itself "will change profoundly" in coming centuries, thus solving the problem of reconciling justice, wisdom, and democratic consent, a problem no regime has fully solved in the course of human history so far. One might say that Dahl, like Hofstadter, pays the Founders an unintended compliment; he tacitly admits that the Founders' work could only be revolutionized if the very nature of the human beings the Founders knew were radically transformed.

James Ceaser criticizes Dahl's assumption that pure democracy would necessarily remove the injustices we deplore while preserving the considerable benefits of our existing polity. To take the simplest example, a democrat of course must regret the hierarchy of a large military establishment. But a democrat must also consider how to defend the country in a world where several dozen wars rage in any given year. "It may not be so clear," Ceaser writes, "that we should prefer more procedural democracy to our continued existence as a free nation, however imperfect." Once again we encounter the problem of ends and means. Ceaser argues that by abstracting various ideals or aspirations from the concrete circumstances in which all human beings must act, Dahl tends toward utopianism.

Ceaser extends his criticism to Dahl's very criterion of democracy itself. He raises the question of whether increased democratization of every aspect of our polity would really improve matters without exception. "To make such judgments would require abandoning the modern prejudice that equates the good exclusively with the democratic." As the first step toward abandoning that prejudice, we must ask: Are equality and liberty, the first and second principles, so to speak, of democracy, always unqualifiedly good? The volume's final two essays address this question, which may be regarded as *the* question confronting the citizens of modern republics.

Wilson Carey McWilliams praises equality but rejects what he regards as the modern misunderstanding of it. Modern egalitarians resent being ruled and secretly desire to rule. They demand equal treatment by others but scheme for advantage. Individualists, they make equality "dependent on assessments of its utility"—specifically, its utility in promoting the "civil peace and order" that enables them to conquer nature by economic and scientific means. These false egalitarians may call themselves capitalists or socialists. Whatever their ideology, they refuse to regard themselves as genuinely equal to others. To the American Founders, for example, "liberty and interest were primary in nature, and affection should only follow and assist."

McWilliams contrasts this with "civic equality," whose partisans demand an equal share in ruling *and* an equal right to be ruled. Civic equality reflects "concern for the good of the whole." This concern is not private and individual but communitarian. It reflects, albeit dimly, philosophic concern for "the whole" par excellence—the cosmos itself, "governed by a single law." As fully as possible in the particular, nonideal political realm, human beings should act in accordance with their "essential humanity," which "naturally seeks knowledge and the good life." *This* equality entails the distributive justice of the classical Greek philosophers as McWilliams interprets them. Such justice does not foolishly impose equal obligations on unequals. It rather "demands more of the powerful [defined broadly to include those of exceptional talents and virtues] for the good of the weak."

Scholars may dispute the accuracy of McWilliams's characterization of classical political philosophy. But for our purposes it must suffice to ask, Why should the powerful act for the good of the weak (particularly if "power" can mean talent and virtue)? In what way can service to the political whole obligate the best human beings within that whole? Can and should they truly care about those who finally are not their equals? It is one thing to say that insofar as we are human we *seek* "knowledge and the good life." But surely results count too, and the best must (by definition) seek more intensely and more successfully than others. Do the best human beings find communitarian politics worthwhile?

The American Founders rank among the best statesmen, and

perhaps the best human beings simply, of our history. They did not found a communitarian regime. But their reputation as "the best" of Americans must survive highly critical scrutiny in any case. In Herbert J. Storing's words, "It is a common opinion today . . . that, admirable as the American Founders may be in other respects, in their response to the institution of Negro slavery their example is to be lived down rather than lived up to." One may define equality in an unconventional way, as McWilliams does, then convict the founders of inegalitarianism. But Negro slavery fits no definition of equality, modern or ancient.

Storing defends the Founders against the "gross calumny" that they denied the humanity of blacks. "All of the Constitutional provisions relating to slaves . . . refer to them as persons." The Founders "carefully withheld any indication of moral approval" of slavery, insisting that slavery (a word they refused to put into the Constitution) only existed in conventional or positive law, not in natural law or right. Storing agrees with the assessment of that magnanimous former slave Frederick Douglass, who called slavery only "the scaffolding" of the Founders' work, "to be removed as soon as the building was completed." Although some of the Founders themselves owned slaves, "these masters knew that they were writing the texts in which their slaves would learn their rights."

Having refuted the charges of doctrinaires, Storing makes a more thoughtful criticism. "The problem is not that [the Founders] betrayed their principles . . . the problem lies rather in the principles themselves." The principle of individual liberty "contains within itself an uncomfortably large opening toward slavery" because such liberty tends to reduce constraints on self-interest to "merely prudential" calculations. He discerns a tendency "for justice to be reduced to self-preservation, for self-preservation to be defined as self-interest, and for self-interest to be defined as what is convenient and achievable." If slavery exists and its abolition looks inconvenient, then slavery will likely remain. This in turn causes a severe tension "between the doctrine of individual rights and the necessary moral ground of any government instituted to secure those rights." The tension becomes even more severe insofar as the government partakes of democracy, whereby the majority rule, not "the best." "Prejudice—arbitrary liking and trust and, of course, also disliking and mistrust—is inherent in political life, and its role is greater as the polity is more democratic."

Storing's argument focuses our attention on liberty as a means to the end of self-preservation, not on liberty as a means to another means, the pursuit of happiness. Jefferson's view of happiness evidently transcended mere self-gratification, but the word remains vague in the Constitution itself and can easily be made to mean self-gratification, the enjoyment of material property. Storing hopes, with W. E. B. DuBois, that black Americans themselves may offer a counterweight to "the political and moral defects of mere individualism."

McWilliams examines the defects of modern egalitarianism; Storing examines the defects of modern libertarianism. One might be tempted to make equality and liberty correct one another. To a considerable extent they already do. Whenever some Americans call for enforcing equality with state power, other Americans warn us of the threat this would pose to our liberty. Whenever some Americans misuse their liberty to exploit the weak, other Americans demand "fairness," by which they mean equality. Republicans and Democrats, conservatives and liberals, praise certain liberties and decry elitism. A sort of balance obtains.

To leave it at that, however, would be to complacently overlook the deeper problems with equality and liberty. To put it bluntly, equality and liberty alone can satisfy only a certain kind of soul, a soul that would neither ardently seek community, nor rule it, nor subvert it. But souls that want more than to be left alone—those that wish to commune with others, rule them, or injure them—will not leave the regime or quasi regime of equality and liberty alone. *Their* pursuit of happiness, or rather of what they take to be happiness, requires either a true regime or anarchy, not a quasi regime.

Those who wish to injure others and subvert community are often criminals and sometimes tyrants. Citizens animated by the principles of equality and liberty find themselves vulnerable to the depredations of criminal and tyrannical souls. Lovers of equality too generously assume that such souls need little more than some kind of sympathetic therapy, after which they will stand revealed as fellow lovers of equality, "the same as you and me." Lovers of liberty may regard such souls with more suspicion, but often find themselves powerless to act forcefully against them. Lovers of equality and liberty must hope that equality and liberty will seduce their enemies, who are not easy to defeat with the uncertain force lovers of equality and liberty can muster.

In extreme circumstances, when tyrannical souls gain sufficient power to threaten them seriously, lovers of equality and liberty need statesmen, who distinguish themselves from ordinary citizens by their skill at dealing with criminals and tyrants. This volume concentrates on the virtues and vices of ordinary citizens in the American republic. Necessarily incomplete for that reason, it must be supplemented by consideration of statesmanship, the virtues (and vices) of the politicians who preserve and sometimes transform the character of political life in a given place and time. The distinction between citizens and statesmen appears in the Declaration of Independence. Although the signers declare America's independence "by the Authority of the good People of these Colonies," they pledge not to the people but *"to each other"* their lives, fortunes, and "sacred Honor." To regard honor as sacred goes well beyond ordinary citizen virtue in a commercial republic. Nor did the Founders intend this superiority to be confined to the Founding period. In *Federalist* No. 71, Hamilton writes:

When occasions present themselves in which the interests of the people are at variance with their inclinations, it is the duty of the persons whom they have appointed to be the guardians of those interests to withstand the temporary delusion in order to give them time and opportunity for more cool and sedate reflection. Instances might be cited in which a conduct of this kind has saved the people from very fatal consequences of their own mistakes, and has procured lasting monuments of gratitude to the men who had courage and magnanimity enough to serve them at the peril of their displeasure.[8]

The presidency most obviously, but also the Senate, the Supreme Court, and even the House of Representatives (whose members, in Madison's words, shall "refine and enlarge the public views") all must exhibit such courage and magnanimity. To be sure, "enlightened statesmen will not always be at the helm," as Madison so accurately predicted. But they had better be at the helm on certain occasions, and in their enlightenment they must distinguish honor from popularity. To do so, they will need to guide their actions by principles beyond equality and liberty. To discover these principles of statesmanlike action, we must study the writings and actions of the statesmen themselves.

Finally, those who wish to commune deeply with others require

[8] Alexander Hamilton, *The Federalist Papers*, No. 71 (New York: New American Library, 1961), p. 432.

nothing less than religion, although sometimes they do not see this. McWilliams suggests this in the closing sentence of his essay: "If our nature yearns for a love and worth more perfect than even that which abounds in nature, it may be that it *is* our nature to seek a love and a worth beyond nature itself." Unless we imagine a deified humanity, this can only mean God. We have seen that the Founders sought to limit the fanaticism and discord religion tends toward. But we should also recall the questions raised by that prudent French statesman Alexis de Tocqueville: "Despotism may govern without faith but liberty cannot. . . . How is it possible that society should escape destruction if the moral tie is not strengthened in proportion as the political tie is relaxed? And what can be done with a people who are their own masters if they are not submissive to a Deity?"[9] Judging from our Declaration's several references to God and providence, the Founders prudently cultivated religious sentiments even as they domesticated them. To discover the principles at issue, we must study the religious and philosophic writers who examine the theologicopolitical question. We have seen that Locke is one; others include Augustine, Thomas Aquinas, Calvin, Spinoza.

In threatening equality and liberty, criminals and tyrants often force lovers of equality and liberty to discipline themselves in defense of their principles. Statesmen who defend equality and liberty as means to some nobler end often displease and may even threaten lovers of equality and liberty. But the latter could not survive for long without statesmen. The communalism of religious groups can easily threaten equality and liberty, but without some sense of community, a sense transcending the shifting interests of individuals, the well-being and defense of any country becomes at best problematic.

Clearly, the moral foundations of the American republic are more complex, and indeed problematic, than most Americans realize. But to point only to complexity and problems would unfit us for action in a world where the simple choices can be harder than the complicated ones. (How many sophisticates imagined they could overcome Hitler with diplomatic finesse? How many today continue to make the same mistake, albeit with different tyrants?) The moral and political foundations of the American republic, complex and

[9] Alexis de Tocqueville, *Democracy in America*, trans. Henry Reeve, Francis Bowen, and Phillips Bradley (New York: Random House, 1945), vol. 1, chap. 17, p. 318.

problematic though they are, also stand firmer than any similar foundations in the modern world. That is a simple fact. As you turn to the study of those foundations with the guidance of the writers here, you will need thoughtfulness to respond to complexity. But we should, I think, also turn to such study with gratitude for the simple fact of our foundations' endurance. That endurance, after all, helps make the study possible.

Of Men and Angels: A Search for Morality in the Constitution

Robert A. Goldwin

Several Cautions to the Reader

Do not be misled by the theological tone of the title of this essay. Despite the reference to angels, and despite the unlikelihood that any serious political inquiry can progress very far without encountering theological questions, it is my intention to present my argument in terms wholly secular, or at least as secular as political discourse can be.

The title speaks of men and angels, and doesn't mention women. As you shall see, the title refers to a sentence in *The Federalist*, the great commentary on the proposed Constitution written in 1787, principally by James Madison and Alexander Hamilton, under the pen name Publius: "If men were angels, no government would be necessary." I cannot, of course, take liberties with a famous sentence from a Great Book, but no one should think that women are being excluded. Publius would surely have conceded the full equality of women, as I do, in this respect, and in very many others, and would have agreed that women, every bit as much as men, are not angels.

Another caution: I read the sentence "If men were angels, no government would be necessary" as two linked assertions: one, that men are not angels, and, two, that government is necessary. I know, and I point out to the reader, that the sentence does not say that in so many words.

A final caution: I mean very seriously, as the subtitle indicates, that this essay is meant to be a search. What I am searching for is morality in the American constitution. Immediately three questions present themselves:

1. Why do we have to look for it?
2. What is meant by the constitution?
3. What morality is possible and appropriate for America?

I

Why must we look for and worry about morality in the constitution? For two good reasons. First, because so many immoral actions have besmirched our behavior in the recent past. We have had assassinations, Watergate, tawdry congressional sex scandals, corporation bribery on a worldwide scale, labor union murders, grain inspection frauds, mishandling of receipts of food stamps, cheating by medical laboratories, scandals in the management of guaranteed student loans, and so on and on in a seemingly endless list that convinces many that no part of the American community is uncorrupted, that immorality is ingrained in us as a national trait, that we are hopelessly immoral. That is one reason for searching for morality in the constitution.

A second reason is that we are a morally judging people who make moral judgments all the time. Sometimes we judge ourselves much too high and sometimes much too low. For example, wartime rhetoric made it seem that we had no selfish national interests in the world wars and their aftermaths, that unlike every other nation, including our allies, we fought for altruistic and idealistic reasons only.

But when we are not judging ourselves too generously, we are often very severe, some would say too severe, on ourselves. During the two years of the Watergate revelations, Europeans were confused by what they called our naive reaction to government behavior that they considered just what one must expect of government officials anywhere. One intelligent and thoughtful Englishwoman told me that the American public's reaction to Watergate revelations confirmed what she had long believed about Americans, that we suffer from "moral greed." Europeans generally thought we were denigrating ourselves excessively. Even now, when the facts are known, dismal as they are, many still think so.

The fact of evildoing and the discovery of it, and our unfailing national shock, and the widespread, vehement, public condemnation that follows, are evidences of two equally significant points: not only that we are capable of immorality, that is, that we are not angels; but also that we set very demanding moral standards of political behavior, approaching the angelic, and truly expect and demand politicians and other leaders to live up to them.

I belabor this duality because it is very important for the survival of political liberty and decency in the world that we Americans have a true appraisal of ourselves. In national matters, as in personal matters, to know yourself is as important to survival as it is to happiness. And to know yourself, as we all learn from study and from experience, is one of the most difficult tasks men and women face in life. If we do not know ourselves and hence judge ourselves by inappropriate standards, all kinds of false judgments result, too lenient or too harsh, but just right only rarely—and then only by accident.

The national danger is that by condemning ourselves or excusing ourselves unjustly, that is, by false standards, we will weaken the very forces in the world that are almost alone capable of upholding the principles of decency we love and seek to live by.

Americans are moral judgers, and severe judgers at that. More, we judge no one as severely as ourselves. This may not always have been the mass phenomenon that it is today, but elements of it have always been present in us.

That does not mean that we always, or even regularly, do the right or good thing. It means that when we do not, or when we do the wrong or evil thing, for whatever reasons of necessity, or convenience, or advantage, or whim, or passion, or ignorance, there are almost always, and almost always promptly, voices raised in self-criticism and self-condemnation. And those morally condemning voices have listeners.

Moral principle has weight and force in American political discourse. Even if we assume—as we must assume if we remember that men and women are not angels—that people act in politics primarily in pursuit of interests that are advantageous to them, and usually not advantageous, or even disadvantageous to others, nevertheless, in America individuals and groups are greatly strengthened if they can connect their cause to moral principles. And if that connection is a true one, and if decent, disinterested people can see that connection readily, the case is strengthened even more, even to the extent that supporters will be enlisted whose interests might otherwise not make them allies, or might otherwise even make them opponents.

One massive example comes readily to mind, and that is the great civil rights movement of the fifties and, especially, the sixties. The principles of justice and equality had been available for generations to all American interest groups seeking to pursue their own advantage through political action. The fact that individual leaders like Martin Luther King and interest groups like the NAACP and CORE and the Urban League could add to their otherwise insufficient political strength by connecting themselves, not only in words but in concerted actions, to the most powerful moral principles of the

American polity added to their strength fivefold, and more.

This combining of noble principle and self-interest, a foundation of American politics, is not hypocrisy, in my judgment. To show that black citizens gained material advantages by the legislation and court orders they obtained through moral arguments does not, I think, demean or debase the principles; it ennobles the interests. That is one way to understand Tocqueville's phrase "self-interest rightly understood"—that it is possible for selfishness to be ennobled, if not sanctified.

So seriously do Americans take morality, so politically powerful are the principles of justice and equality, that no policy, domestic or foreign, political or economic or military, can be successful, can get support, can be sustained, can survive setbacks, that does not have a clear and acceptable moral content, visible and meaningful to the Congress, the press, and above all to the American people. No matter how adroitly scheming, calculating, and self-serving individuals or groups may be, unless their suggested policies can be clothed in fitting moral garb, they will not have and hold for a sustained period the indispensable element for practical success—public support.

We can see America's moral standing more clearly in the context of a rough catalogue of varieties of moral postures of nations. For example, there are countries where a moral resignation prevails, where immoral practices are known and condoned; accepted, not resisted. There have been civil societies, of course, where morality was almost completely destroyed, so that when severe abuses of human decency occurred, the populace was not aroused in opposition, and could not be aroused. There have even been societies in which almost the entire populace was eager to join in acts of cruelty and depravity.

But even in Nazi Germany, perhaps the worst example in history of an entire civilized nation being corrupted and enlisted in the cause of evil, the leaders seemed not to be sure of the thoroughness of popular commitment to evildoing, and so they endeavored to keep secret the mass murders in the gas ovens. And apparently they were right that many Germans, even after a decade of indoctrination, would have found it impossible not to condemn such immorality, if it had been known to them.

Thus even when we contemplate the depths of human viciousness there is reason to believe that there is in human nature a strong inclination to what is morally right—something of the angel in us—and a strong aversion to what is morally wrong. There is also reason to believe that it is very difficult, but perhaps not impossible, to eliminate in almost all of us those tendencies toward what is morally right.

There are also many societies where practices that are of a lesser order of immorality, like bribery, or tax evasion, or nepotism, or other forms of cheating, not only occur, as they do in this country, but are accepted as part of "the way things are done." Revelations of such immoral practices don't shock the people of those countries. They simply comment, "Of course. Everybody does it."

There is probably less bribery and corruption in this country than in most others, but very far from an absence of them. In this country, however, if they are exposed, they are definitely not approved or condoned. When immoral practices are discovered and publicized, the highest-ranking officials, in and out of government, will resign or will be forced out of office. However many times examples of corruption in political or business or labor or even charitable activities are exposed, we seem never to lack the moral fervor to attack and condemn, and usually to prosecute.

I will add only one more variety of national moral posture to the brief, and surely incomplete, catalogue of societies: very moral civil societies. Some such may actually have existed for a time, and some may have existed only in fiction or utopian writings; in either case, I mean civil societies where there is no corruption, no bribery, no favoritism or self-seeking, no putting self-interest ahead of the public interest—societies that might be said to be thoroughly moral in act as well as in principle.

As I understand the Framers of our Constitution, on the evidence in *The Federalist* and in the debates of the Constitutional Convention, they looked at America and Americans and decided that it would be fruitless and impractical, and perhaps even morally wrong, for the new nation to strive to become spotlessly moral.

Liberty was their first principle and also their first goal. (Prosperity was their second goal.) A people that universally would put the public good ahead of private good every time would have to be regimented, ordered, disciplined, indoctrinated, preached to, and exhorted. Obvious institutional consequences would follow: state religion, uniform education, universal military discipline, diminution of family household influence, and curbs on commerce.[1]

[1] Plutarch tells us how Lycurgus transformed Sparta by limiting landholdings (which brought about economic equality); by making lead the official currency (which put an end to retail and foreign trade); and by decreeing that meals could

The Framers knew that such a society would have to put duties first and relegate rights and everything else that is private—both low and high—to a strictly subordinate place. Self-enrichment in such a society would be scorned and replaced by concern for the moral and economic strength of the civil society as a whole. I doubt that the Framers ever gave serious thought to making a nation of men and women who would be devoid of private ambition[2] as we are told is generally the case in present-day China, for example—but if they had given thought to it, they would have rejected it, in the name of liberty and plenty.

Their own moral concern and their awareness of the character of the American people made two things clear to the Framers: first, that political liberty and economic energy unavoidably engender some immorality, some cheating and selfish advancement of private good at the expense of the public; second, that the American people are unrelenting moral judgers. The two basic American moral facts are that immorality is unavoidable and unacceptable.

II

The Framers did not seek devices or measures to prevent all immorality, but rather to control its abuses, as consistent with the American character, consistent with the principles of liberty and equality of rights, consistent with the diversity of American ethnic origins and the multiplicity of religious sects, and consistent with the entrepreneurial energy they sought to encourage.

The reader will surely have noted that several times I have spoken of American character as the Founders perceived it, as if the nation had already been formed before its founding. To a large extent I think that was the case. Consider a little simple arithmetic. If we take 1619, the date of the establishment of the Virginia House of

---

no longer be eaten at home, but only in eating clubs (which ended the influence of mother and kitchen). These three changes reconstituted Sparta, almost at a stroke.

2 For those who wish to ponder this subject more thoroughly, I suggest reading the discussions of salary for public officials in *The Records of the Federal Convention of 1787*, ed. Max Farrand, 4 vols. (New Haven: Yale University Press, 1911–37). See Index: salaries of congressmen, salary of executive, salary of judges. See also *The Federalist*, No. 72.

Burgesses, the first American legislative body, as a starting point, it was 170 years later that the Constitution was ratified. That means that it was not until 1959, not too many years ago, well within the lifetime of most of us now old enough to be concerned about morality in politics, that Americans had as long a political experience on this continent since the Constitution as before it. If you have a feeling for how long ago 1789 was, you can feel how long a time the American people had to develop a character of their own before the written Constitution.

That character derived from many factors, including religion (most of the sects were dissenters); experience in self-government (the legislatures of many colonies had considerable power, including power of the purse); political doctrines emphasizing liberty and equality (from John Locke pre-eminently); and unusual, even unprecedented economic conditions.

Consider the economic conditions for a moment. Adam Smith describes tellingly, in *The Wealth of Nations*, published in 1776, the consequences of placing cultured Europeans, especially cultured in agriculture, on a vast and fertile continent, almost uninhabited, and pretty much free for the taking. His chapter on "Causes of the Prosperity of New Colonies," begins thus: "The colony of a civilized nation which takes possession either of a waste country, or one so thinly inhabited, that the natives easily give place to the new settlers, advances more rapidly to wealth and greatness than any other human society." In Seventeenth- and Eighteenth-Century America, labor was in short supply relative to demand. Wages were high, and conditions were favorable to the worker. It was hard to hold on to hired hands because it was so easy for them to save enough in a short time to move off to start their own enterprise, usually farming their own piece of land, and plenty of open space to move on to.

The situation was favorable for the flowering of respect for the free individual's rights, because those who were not slaves had to be treated well to keep them on the job, since they had so many opportunities everywhere. Where every hand is valuable, if you can't enslave him or her, you have to pay a high price for that person's labor. And what you pay dearly for, you value highly. But even if an employer did treat employees or indentured servants well, he was likely to lose them in a fairly short time, a few years usually, because it was so easy for newcomers with ambition to strike out on their own. In such circumstances, where the demand for labor exceeds the supply, slavery is also very attractive. If you can assure yourself of a large enough number of laborers and any way of keeping them, where naturally rich unowned land is abundant, your profit is assured. Slavery and the principles of liberty and equality that ultimately led to its destruction grew out of the same soil.

The combination of propitious economic, political, and religious factors contributed to the development of tastes, inclinations, habits, and institutions among Americans that were strong and deeply ingrained when the Constitution was written in 1787. The relevance of the pre-existing American character, in my understanding of it, can be explained by the simple device of sometimes writing the word *constitution* with a capital *C*, to denote that I mean the frame of government, in our case set forth in a written document, and sometimes writing it with a small *c*, to denote that I mean something different, which I will now try to explain.

If we speak of the American constitution—with a small *c*—we could mean the way Americans are constituted: their character, their habits, their manners, their morals, their tastes, their countryside, their strengths, their weaknesses, their speech, their songs, their poems, their books, their sports, their machines, their arts, their heroes, their dress, their ceremonies, their homes and families, and their ways of conducting business. All of this, and more, would tell us how Americans *are constituted*. And since much of what is included in such a list would be the result of conscious effort and decision, it would also be possible to speak of how Americans *have constituted themselves*. Thus, considering how long Americans were on this continent before 1787, it is perfectly intelligible to speak of what the American constitution was before the Constitution of the United States was written, as well as to speak of the formative influence the Constitution of the United States had, subsequently, on the American constitution.

The document called the Constitution names itself in the Preamble as "this Constitution for the United States of America," but it could just as well have been called "the Articles," or "the Charter," or "the Covenant," or "the Compact," or "the Polity," or a number of other suitable words. When the Congress sent it to the original thirteen States for ratification, they gave it no caption. In most States, when it was printed for the use of the delegates of ratifying conventions and for public information, it was entitled "A Frame of Government."

The word *constitution* for this purpose grew in usage in the century from 1689 to 1789, from the Glorious Revolution to the adoption of the Constitution. Before that, the usage pointed more to the way things were ordered. According to the Oxford English Dictionary, *constitution* meant "the way in which anything is constituted or made up; the arrangement or combination of its parts or elements, as determining its nature and character. E.g., constitution of nature, of the world, of the universe, etc." The political usage indicated "the mode in which a state is constituted or organized, especially as to the location of the sovereign power, as a monarchical, oligarchical, or democratic constitution."

But *Constitution* grew out of this usage as a fitting word for a document that seeks to apply an appropriate frame of government to a people who are constituted in a discernible way. A well-designed Constitution records and proclaims how we are constituted and how we intend to be constituted for the future. Whether the Constitution is written or not, every political community has a constitution, because to be a political community it must have an accepted ordering of things and a location of the sovereign power.

Let the exception prove the rule. When we ask whether a nation ruled by a dictatorial individual or group has a Constitution, we are stretching the concept to its breaking point. For example, some nations are described as constitutional monarchies, signifying that some other monarchies are not constitutional. What we mean is that absolute monarchies have no discernible order in the ruling, that the monarch can act without restraint, without law, according to whim, not only with unlimited powers, but arbitrarily. That is why John Locke said that "absolute monarchy . . . can be no form of civil government at all."[3] And I say that any nation has a constitution, but at times there may be no Constitution and its unconstitutional rulers may not be a government.

When nations that have been ruled by tyrants overthrow them and form a new and constitutional government, it is clear that they had a constitution all along; that is, they were constituted a certain way and are now able to frame a government that is thought to suit the way they are constituted. And that "frame of government" may properly be called the Constitution. It is in this sense that we say that nations get the government they deserve.

My thesis is that the Framers considered the constitution of the American people—what they were and what they were capable of being and doing—and drew up the Constitution of the United States. They did not want to leave Americans just where they were, but, rather, starting where they were, they wanted to make them better. As was once written, long ago, by a non-American: "Lawgivers make the citizens good by training them in habits of right action—that is

[3] John Locke, *Two Treatises of Government,* Book 2, section 90.

the aim of all lawmaking, and if it fails to do this it is a failure; this is what distinguishes a good Constitution from a bad one."[4]

The Framers did not seek to remake Americans, but rather to take them as they are and lead them to habits of right action. Their task was to direct the powerful American tendency to self-interest and self-advancement so that abuses would be controlled. More, they aimed not only to control these tendencies but actually to turn them to the benefit of the people.

Other societies have tried to curb or eliminate selfish ambition and selfish interest out of a reasonable fear that when those inclinations are combined with political power, tyranny often results and the people often lose their freedom. The constitutional scheme in other societies has relied on measures such as rigorous education in the virtues of selflessness, or constant surveillance, strict discipline, and severe punishment.

The American constitutional scheme is explained briefly in *The Federalist*. Put separate parts of political power in the hands of different officials in different parts of the government—legislative, executive, and judicial—and encourage, if they need encouragement, ambition and self-interest. "Ambition must be made to counteract ambition," Publius says. "The interest of the man must be connected with the constitutional rights of the place."[5] By this means the abuses of power by one official, or several, will be opposed by others who have strong and natural incentives that need no inculcation or exhortation. In fact, if officials in one part of the government should be insufficiently moved by ambition and self-interest, a necessary balancing restraint would be lacking and the danger would increase of concentration of power in the hands of others. It seems that there is a need for very many ambitious and self-interested officials to keep our government in balance. As fundamental as separation of powers is as a principle of the Constitution, that officeholders must be ambitious and self-interested is even more fundamental.

Are these the habits of right action the Constitution aims to train us in? In part, the answer is yes. In part, however, the answer must be also that the Constitution seeks to train us in habits of restraint and moderation, because that is the only way ambitious officeholders can contend with other ambitious officeholders without falling victims to the law, or to power struggles.

---

[4] Aristotle, *Nicomachean Ethics*, Book 2, 1103b. There is, of course, no indication in the Greek text that the word *Constitution* is capitalized.

[5] *The Federalist*, No. 51.

It is a system for nonangels who nevertheless are convinced that men and women are good enough to govern themselves. What is clear is that it is a frame of government for a people so constituted that clashing with each other almost without cease is the expected daily routine.

In a discourse on the work of Isaac Newton, Thomas Simpson of St. John's College in Santa Fe made this comparison:

Our Republic was designed in the image of Isaac Newton's vision of the System of the World, set forth in the Third Book of his *Principia.* Hobbes had taught man to regard the state as an artifice to rescue himself from war and his own nature, but it was Newton who showed how exactly-counter-working forces could be composed to form a harmonious and lasting system—and this composition of forces in the system of planets about the sun was the ultimate paradigm for the authors of our Constitution as they attempted to solve the three-body problem of the legislative, the executive, and the judicial powers.

Newton, then, showed how the cosmos might be grasped by the mind as a purposeful system, an intelligent design; the authors of our Constitution showed the world in turn how man could make this insight, out of mathematical physics, serve him in the design of a balanced and rational polity.[6]

I would not dare to quarrel with Dr. Simpson about Newton, but would only accept his guidance respectfully and gratefully and do my best to understand. But the notion of the Constitution of the United States as "harmonious" is very wide of the mark. Much closer, I think, is the description of Tocqueville in capturing the character of the American constitution and political system: "No sooner do you set foot on American soil than you find yourself in a sort of tumult; a confused clamor rises on every side, and a thousand voices are heard at once, each expressing some social requirements."[7] Tumult, confused clamor, a thousand voices—not harmony—that is how America was and is constituted.[8] And the Framers wisely chose, I think, not to strive to change it, but rather to institutionalize it.

If that is the American constitution, the morality most characteristic of America, then and now, is what might be called a measured, or a restrained, or a moderated, or even a mean morality. It does not

---

[6] "Newton and the Liberal Arts," *The College,* January 1976, St. John's College, Annapolis, Md.

[7] Alexis de Tocqueville, *Democracy in America* (New York: Harper & Row, 1966), p. 223.

[8] As for Dr. Simpson's contention that the Constitution is drawn out of mathematical insight, this comment of Aristotle's should suffice: "A carpenter and a geometrician both seek after a right angle, but in different ways" (*Nicomachean Ethics,* Book 1, 1098a).

ignore or condone immorality. In fact, it holds morality very high in public esteem. As I have argued, no public policy can gain and hold the support of the American people if its moral content is not laudable and apparent to the people generally. A policy may be begun, it may be continued for a time, but if it lacks moral acceptability it cannot be sustained. But the morality that is needed must commence with the understanding that men and women are not angels.

III

Awareness that we are not angels has complex significance. It does not mean that we are evil or unrelievedly selfish. It does mean that we acknowledge that our basic motivation is self-interest and that there is a need to control the unavoidable abuses that follow from that selfishness. From somewhere, perhaps out of our selfishness—that is, out of the sense of justice that derives from the sense of injustice (which is easily come by from the natural dislike of acts of unfairness to ourselves)—but in any case in some way there comes a strong sense of morality, of fairness, or aversion to unfairness. And this strong sense of morality leads frequently to an excess of morality.

I do not agree that measure or restraint or moderation is misplaced in matters of morality. Men and women sometimes indulge themselves in excesses of morality, and such self-indulgence and such excess have the same distorting effects as do all other forms of extremism.

The morality most appropriate to the American way, to the American constitution as it was even before the Founding, and as it still is, is a morality that is moderate, that does not crusade, that accepts the fact that among human beings who are free there will be abuses, and that does not seek to eradicate all evil from the face of the earth, knowing that such moral attempts are excessive and often lead to monstrous immorality. Though we sometimes use the rhetoric, we are not true to ourselves and to our national character when we crusade, domestically or in foreign policy.

Consider the story of Carmen. When her soldier-lover hears the bugle call summoning him back to camp, she warns him that if he goes she will not meet him again. He explains that the regulations require him to report at an appointed hour, and Carmen replies with the famous line, "Gypsy love knows no law." So it is with unbounded moralism. Alluring and seductive, it, too, knows no law. The morality of our constitution is very much a bounded and law-abiding morality.

When I speak of the American character and its morality, I do not mean that we are consistent in our tendencies and reactions. Thank goodness that we are not, and that life is not so simple and dull. The truth is, and all of us know it, that as a nation we have a multiplicity of reactions, a multiplicity of individuals and groups tending to go in a multiplicity of directions; and, sometimes, a multiplicity of tendencies contend within each of us.

One of these common tendencies is for us to shrug our shoulders when we hear one more revelation of wrongdoing. It does get tiresome, after all. We develop an aversion less to the wrongdoer and more to the moralizers and wish they would do us all a favor and just shut up.

At other times we become mightily aroused; we judge quickly and harshly; we preach to others and volunteer our services as policemen to the world, ready, like Superman, to fly anywhere in the world to fight evil, at whatever cost of pain and treasure.

Sometimes, however—and at these times we are at our best, in my estimation, and most true to our real constitution—we judge and act with measured restraint, with moderation. We do not ignore the presence of evil, nor do we try to exterminate it and, perhaps, many valuable things with it. The Constitution is designed to help foster this restraint.

Practical or political morality always involves two related but separable and distinct steps. The first step, and an essential one for a moral person, is to face the fact of wrongdoing and judge it. When we fail to take that step, we slip into our worst amoral lethargy; fortunately for us as a nation that strives for decency, failure to make a moral judgment happens rarely, and when it happens it is possible for us to be roused from it, for we are not deaf to moral suasion. So the first step is to make the moral judgment, to recognize evil as evil, and not look the other way, or refuse to judge (on relativistic grounds), or shrug our shoulders and say we "don't care."

But making a moral judgment does not settle the question of policy. The second step remains: to ask ourselves, what shall we do about it? There are moral as well as practical considerations involved in the second step. The first-step moral judgment may tell us that something ought to be done, but it leaves to deliberation what that something might be.

The best example of this I know in American history is the consistent position of Abraham Lincoln on the question of slavery. The first step was easy for him, and he made it clearly and persistently in all of his public utterances, notably in his debates with Stephen Douglas. On the question of the extension of slavery into new States and territories not yet slave territory, Douglas said "I don't care" whether it is voted up or voted down. Let the local people on the spot decide for themselves—local rule, self-determination.

Lincoln said in response what must be said first: that slavery was wrong and that we cannot say "I don't care" whether this immoral institution is extended and strengthened. After all, he argued, we are the children of the Declaration of Independence, and there are principles that will not let us alone, that we cannot turn our backs on and still remain Americans. That was the first step.

As for the second step, Lincoln said he was not an abolitionist, just as he would not be a slaveholder. Abolitionists looked on the Constitution as an abomination, a compact with the Devil, and they regularly burned a copy of the Constitution at their meetings. That is an example of the unbounded moralism I spoke of before, which in its crusading striking out at evil is likely to destroy with it many good things—like the Constitution, in this case—that give us, ultimately, our best hope for persisting decency in political life. Lincoln, unlike the abolitionists, sought a way to end slavery without destroying the Union and the Constitution, the instrumentalities of our liberties.

Thus even after the Civil War had commenced, Lincoln was still trying to develop and get acceptance for a plan of gradual and compensated emancipation of the slaves. His plan could have taken as long as thirty-five years to complete emancipation of the last of the slaves, and no force would have been used. During that time there would be no spread of slavery, and the more it was diminished by purchase of the freedom of slaves from slaveholders, the weaker would become the pro-slavery forces.

Many would condemn a policy that would prolong enslavement for some for decades and pay slaveholders for slaves they had no moral right to own. But Lincoln thought that Americans, North and South, shared the blame for slavery and that the chief task was less to punish wrongdoers than to right the wrong. He thought some slavery could be tolerated so long as its increase was halted, its diminution assured, and its termination achieved without massive bloodshed, without confiscating what some people claimed under the law was property, without disrupting the Union, and without weakening or possibly destroying the Constitution.

Lincoln's plan for gradual compensated emancipation was not so much rejected as ignored. Instead, the Civil War went on; the matter was settled by unbounded moralists on both sides of the controversy; and we had, as a result, horrendous warfare, a divided nation, and deep-seated bitterness which, a full century later, has not fully abated.

In the light of all I have now said about how I think the Founders, or Publius, thought about this question and what the consequences are of the fact that men and women are not angelic, consider the brief passage that is the basis for what I have said, and judge my interpretation for yourself: "Ambition must be made to counteract ambition. The interest of the man must be connected with the constitutional rights of the place. It may be a reflection on human nature, that such devices should be necessary to control the abuses of government. But what is government itself but the greatest of all reflections on human nature? If men were angels, no government would be necessary."

Conclusion

If I am right about what kind of political morality is truly American, what kind of morality truly fits the way we have constituted ourselves as a nation, there remains still a problem of grave proportions: the question of attractiveness.

In a democratic republic such as ours, where public opinion and popular taste rule, ultimately, on everything, measures and policies must be attractive to hundreds of millions of people to gain the support that is essential to sustain them.

There is something drab and unsatisfying in moral moderation. There is a natural yearning for something higher and purer. All that aiming lower has to recommend it is that it works, but that leaves many of the best of men and women restless and dissatisfied. The search for excitement and inspiration in moderation is fruitless. For example, the only conclusion one can come to after reading the famous essay by William James, "The Moral Equivalent of War," is that there is no moral equivalent of war.

Between extremes lies a mean; it is worth pointing out that the word *mean* is, at the very least, ambiguous. One can try to dress it in finery and speak of the golden mean, but there just is no glitter in mean morality. Moderation or measure or restraint or seeking the mean in anything is not the kind of cause for which people devise banners and slogans. It is hard to compose a marching song or an inspirational poem in praise of sobriety or moderation. You cannot have neon borders flashing on and off, and brass bands parading, and cheering sections screaming at the top of their voices if the message is: "Be moderate." You can't even write such a command with an exclamation point without turning it into a joke.

Some words are suited for whispers or a soft voice: "Kiss me," or "I love you." Others can be shouted or screamed: "Hit him!" or "Kill the umpire!" or "Stop thief!" But moderation can be neither whispered nor shouted. To whisper "moderation" is insipid, and to shout it is ridiculous. Moderation is truly a mean word.

And yet unless this notion of moderation, of bounded morality, is widely accepted, it will be hard for us to think of ourselves as a truly moral nation, for that is the morality that fits us. And that conviction, that we are truly a moral nation of moral men and moral women, is essential to our survival and happiness, because of the way we are constituted. We need to believe it; and for us to believe it, it must be true. We have for a long time been the world's best hope that political decency might prevail widely. There are still, out there in the rest of the world, billions of persons longing to be free. A revitalized America, confident of its own strength and its own rectitude, is their best hope that things might ever change for the better. A sense of our own rectitude is our Samson's long hair; without it we have no strength. I think that is what enables us to say that "right makes might," which is not to say that right *is* might.

What is the chief obstacle to our reviving our confidence in our national rectitude? In large part it is our powerful sense of morality and our aversion to hypocrisy. Our strong moral sense judges and condemns our weaker moral practice. Being strongly moral, we declare ourselves immoral. The judge, out of a superabundance of morality, declares the culprit immoral, but the judge and the culprit are one and the same. Is there any solution, any way for the judge to see himself as a constant moral judge as well as an inconstant immoral culprit and—on the whole—a righteous people?

I think so, and I think Publius has shown us the way. It rests on the difference between righteousness and self-righteousness. What is that difference? If we can answer that question, we can chart a course back to the national self-confidence we need, for our own sake, for the sake of political decency, and for the sake of the hopes of oppressed men and women everywhere.

Let me attempt the distinction. Because men and women are not angels, the standard of human righteousness cannot be that one act as an angel would. The standard must be something akin to our humanity, to our nonangelic state of being. For us nonangels, a righteous person is one who strives to live and act by the light of righteous principles, which include, surely, respect for the equal rights of others to life, liberty, property, and the pursuit of happiness. Trying to follow the guidance of America's standard political principles is the first element of human-scale political righteousness, whether one always succeeds or not.

We would have to add, of course, that trying is not enough in itself; there must be a fairly high degree of success. But above all there must be a recognition that because we are not angels, and because we have freedom, there will be failures, there will be fallings off, there will be abuses, and that there must be "devices" for controlling and dealing with these failures. The devices—including ambition counteracting ambition—must be bounded, and legal, and habitual, and even institutional. If we describe a people such as that—guided by right principles, usually living in accord with them, sometimes failing to measure up, rarely in doubt about what the standards ought to be, seeking to punish abuses and prevent them but too committed to liberty to seek to root out all the possible causes of future human failings—we are describing a nonangelic, but decidedly righteous, people.

Now what about self-righteousness? Self-righteousness is rightly scorned. Self-righteousness is an excess of righteousness, a distortion and disfigurement of righteousness; it is righteousness without moderation. It is more easily recognized in the flesh than defined in words. Self-righteousness is not only boring but hateful; it has been the source of many of the most vicious and inhuman acts in the annals of history, and on a grand scale.

The self-righteous person mistakes the rectitude of his principles for his own rectitude. He confounds his beliefs and his behavior. In his mind he converts his professed righteous principles into a person, and thinks he is that person. Righteousness and "self" become as one. This confusion enables him, in the name of the highest principles of morality, to consider himself the appointed enforcer of morality, the embodiment of righteousness, as if he were the Avenging Angel, or any angel rather than a human being.

Publius is our guide in thus singling out and condemning the self-righteous moralist. In the simplest terms, the self-righteous person forgets the difference between human beings and angels. Self-righteousness in personal matters is distressing enough, but in government it is especially ludicrous, for "if men were angels, no government would be necessary."

Now I have finished. What I seek is some way to appeal—not through showmanship but through reasoning, which in most times and places has been attractive to young and other sound minds some way to appeal to the best in us and persuade us that we have and always have had what is needed to be a righteous people. Nothing that has happened since we started to constitute ourselves as one people more than three hundred years ago, and nothing that has happened since we declared our founding principles and wrote down our Constitution almost two hundred years ago, has diminished the possibilities of righteousness and morality on a national scale, so long as we do not confuse righteousness and self-righteousness.

The key to our political salvation, if such combining of the secular and the divine may be allowed, is the lesson inherent in the most basic principle of the American constitution: Men and women are not angels.

The Compromised Republic: Public Purposelessness in America

Benjamin R. Barber

THE American public has always reacted with alarm to the periodic discovery that it is without unifying national purposes. The "crisis in public purpose" reappears every so often, usually in conjunction with such related emergencies as the "leadership crisis," the "energy crisis," the "violence crisis," and the "public apathy crisis."[1] During the tepid 1950s, at the very moment public commentators like Daniel Boorstin, Louis Hartz, and Arthur Schlesinger were celebrating the unique virtues of proceduralism and purposeless consensus, *Life* and *Time* and the *Saturday Evening Post* were lamenting the absence of public goals and sponsoring an ongoing, cover-story "search for national purpose." This national purpose campaign has been revived recently as a result of the deep disaffection with American institutions that has been churned up by the backwash of Vietnam, Watergate, and economic malaise.

Those concerned with the crisis typically address it from a perspective of nostalgia, seeming to suggest that the nation has lost purposes it once had. They argue that America's postwar entanglements in a world immune to American moralism and in domestic quarrels (McCarthy, the Cold War, disarmament, racism) alien to its traditional centrism have sacrificed traditional unity to a new and dangerous spirit of faction. But the perspective of nostalgia presumes answers to what in fact is the most important question raised by the crisis in national purpose: did America ever have truly public purposes that could be lost or forfeited? Is the present crisis a new

I am grateful to my colleague Wilson Carey McWilliams, whose critical republican spirit played a part both in occasioning and motivating this essay.

[1] I have treated the leadership crisis in a different but related fashion in my "Command Performance," *Harper's Magazine*, April, 1975.

pathology, or merely the flare-up of what has long been a chronic, if essentially benign, condition?

The hypothesis offered here is that America has never had enduring public purposes and that for a long time this was properly taken to be one of the nation's fundamental strengths; that the present dilemma arises therefore not from a loss of purposes but from changes in the conditions that traditionally made public purposelessness an effective, even necessary feature of the compromises that permitted America to flourish at once as a republic and as an empire—as a constitutionally limited federal state governed by law and as an unlimited unitary state with expanding economic and territorial ambitions. Today's crisis may thus turn out to be yesterday's strength; today's vice, yesterday's virtue. Seen in this perspective, the crisis appears to be tractable: but not by the means suggested in conventional analysis—the "loss of public purpose" interpretation.

I

The American republic was founded at least in part on the political theory of classical republicanism.[2] Although its aims were plural, the motives of its founders complex, and the sources of their rationalizations manifold, the Constitution was conceived and set down in the language of republican thought—a changing but ancient idiom whose history as theory can be traced in various forms through the writings of Rousseau, Montesquieu, Harrington, Machiavelli, and Cicero back to Plato's seminal *Republic* and whose history as praxis has been visible in the living experience of Europe's commercial cities, Switzerland's mountain *Landesgemeinden*, the town republics of Renaissance Italy, as well as Rome's early republic and the *poleis* of ancient Greece. It was an idiom known and used by all of the parties to the American Founding; however little their interests coincided and however much their ideologies collided, Federalists and Anti-Federalists, aristocrats and democrats, mercantilists and agrarians all spoke this common tongue. To some degree they all shared a republican concern for a government of excellence, a citizen body of virtue, a public order defined by fundamental law (the constitution, or *po-*

2 See, for example, J. G. A. Pocock, *The Machiavellian Moment: Florentine Political Thought and the Atlantic Republican Tradition* (Princeton: Princeton University Press, 1975); Bernard Bailyn, *The Ideological Origins of the American Revolution* (Cambridge: Harvard University Press, Belknap Press, 1967); and Cecelia M. Kenyon, "Men of Little Faith: The Anti-Federalists on the Nature of Representative Government," *William and Mary Quarterly*, 3d ser. 12 (1955).

liteia) and conducive to well-being, and a community of moderation in which the governed would neither be abused nor be permitted to abuse themselves.

The traditional literature of republicanism and the historical practice in which and from which it issued did not, however, treat the republic as an ideal form that could be instituted without regard to condition; the Founders, their practical eyes fixed as much on American conditions as on European political theory, appreciated this. They understood the republican form of government to be as fragile as it was rare, and they knew it could flourish only under very special conditions. Hamilton had noted the tendency of Europe's city republics to "perpetual vibration between the extremes of tyranny and anarchy," dangers that Rousseau and Montesquieu had regarded as inevitable when republics were founded in the absence of the proper conditions.[3] These conditions, it was generally agreed, included: (1) a small-scale society limited in both population and territory; (2) social and cultural homogeneity, to insure a natural consensus on fundamental values; (3) economic self-sufficiency and (relative) autarky—usually specified in terms of a pastoral or commercial (but certainly *not* an industrial) economy; (4) frugality in life-style and manners and austerity in taste conducive to the cultivation of simple, nonmaterial public virtues; (5) rough economic and political equality of citizens; and (6) a distrust of rapid change that would be more accommodating to nature and stasis than to artifice and progress.

The classical literature argued that such conditions were prerequisite to the promotion of a strong sense of commonality, a clear public identity (the citizen as a public person holding a common moral outlook and sharing common interests), and a spirit of self-government that subordinated the private person to the public citizen no less than the private realm to the public life. Conditions conducive to a public spirit were necessarily hostile to hedonistic privatism and contentious self-interest; they thus served to insulate well-conceived republics from the high-tension privatism to which they seemed so vulnerable. Thus, for example, Rousseau insisted that the founding of a democratic republic presupposed

first, a very small state, where the people can readily be got together where each citizen can with ease know all the rest; secondly, great simplicity of manners, to prevent business from multiplying and raising thorny problems; next, a large measure of equality in rank and fortune, without which equality

[3] Alexander Hamilton, *The Federalist*, No. 9 (New York: Modern Library, n.d.), p. 47. All subsequent references are to this edition.

of rights and authority cannot long subsist; lastly, little or no luxury—for luxury either comes of riches or makes them necessary; it corrupts at once rich and poor, the rich by possession and the poor by covetousness; it sells the country to softness and vanity, and takes away from the state all its citizens, to make them slaves one to another and one and all to public opinion."[4]

The Founders of the American Republic, and perhaps even more importantly, those who had to make good on the Founders' blueprints, faced an ironic dilemma: not only were they eclectics drawing on sources other than the republican tradition, *and* ideologues with varying and contrary interests, *and* skeptics of one kind or another about the desirability, feasibility, and degree of democracy in the republican formula; they were also republican lawgivers to a people lacking almost all of the conditions deemed requisite to the founding of a republic. James Winthrop of Massachusetts wrote with incredulity: "the idea of an uncompounded republick, on an average one thousand miles in length, and eight hundred in breadth, and containing six millions of white inhabitants all reduced to the same standards of morals, of habits, and of laws, is in itself an absurdity, and contrary to the whole experience of mankind."[5] Territorially, the new country potentially embraced a continent—a prospect that the Louisiana Purchase made more than merely credible soon after the republic's founding. Patrick Henry looked at that continent and declared that to make it a republic was "a work too great for human wisdom."[6] If its territory outreached the wildest ambitions of Europe's empires, let alone Europe's traditional city-states, its people comprised as heterogeneous a lot as had ever lived under a single national roof. Could a people who barely spoke a single tongue, who answered to different mother cultures and worshipped in different churches, who knew either the hammer or the plow, the loom or the baler, but never both—could they live under a single constitution in a continental republic in what Madison, in *Federalist* No. 14, called an "extended Republic"? Surely, as critics of the Constitution insisted, it was "impossible for one code of laws to suit Georgia and Massachusetts."[7]

4 Jean Jacques Rousseau, *The Social Contract*, Book 3, chap. 4. See also the "Dedication" to the Republic of Geneva, in *The Discourse on the Origins of Inequality*.

5 *Agrippa* Letters in Paul L. Ford, *Essays on the Constitution of the United States* (Brooklyn, N.Y.: 1892), p. 65.

6 In Jonathan Elliot, *The Debates in the Several State Conventions on the Adoption of the Federal Constitution*, 2d ed., 5 vols. (Philadelphia, 1896), 3:164.

7 *Agrippa* Letters, in Ford, *Essays*, p. 64.

And even were an extended republic somehow to be founded, America's underpopulated land and endless bounty invited growth, expansion, progress, acquisition, and material prosperity—the cardinal sins of republican life against which the Constitutional Convention was repeatedly warned by men like Gouverneur Morris, but which finally seduced even the agrarian democrats and Thomas Jefferson himself (enemy of mercantilism but friend, finally, to expansionism and material growth).[8] Not only was the early American economy heterogeneous and expansionist, but it depended on the two forms least conducive to republican stability: plantation agriculture and mass (manufacturing) industrialism. Moreover, its complexity assured the proliferation of economic orders and competing factions in a fashion completely inimical to the nurturing of a common interest. Quite aside from the two subjugated populations (Black and Indian), differentials among citizens were very great. *Time on the Cross* reports that many urban white workers were poorer than rural black slaves.[9] Sectional interests not only emerged from, but were deeply implicated in, the proceedings of the Constitutional Convention.

In sum, it would be difficult to invent a set of conditions as little conducive to the founding of a democratically tinged republic as the one that described America at the time of its founding. This dilemma presented the Founders and their successors with a virtually unprecedented problem in lawgiving and nation-building: how to serve republican virtue in a land more suited to empire; how to serve empire —economic growth, progress, material well-being, and continental power—without completely surrendering the republican ideal; how, in other words, to take a country whose conditions Montesquieu would have deemed suitable only to empire and Rousseau, to corruption, and give it a constitution of moderation, freedom, and self-government. And to do all of this without falling prey to the inherent deficiencies of either factional democracies ("spectacles of turbulence and contention") or fragmentary republics ("an infinity of little, jealous, clashing, tumultuous commonwealths, the wretched nurseries of unceasing discord").[10]

---

8 Gouverneur Morris thus warned the Convention in Philadelphia: "Wealth tends to corrupt the mind and to nourish its love of power, and to stimulate it to oppression. History proves this to be the spirit of the opulent." Cited by Richard Hofstadter, *The American Political Tradition* (New York: Vintage, 1974), p. 10.

9 R. W. Fogel and S. L. Engerman, *Time on the Cross: The Economics of American Negro Slavery* (Boston: Little, Brown, 1974), 2 vols., 1, chap. 2.

10 James Madison, *The Federalist*, No. 10, p. 58; Alexander Hamilton, *The Federalist*, No. 9, pp. 49–50.

The constitutional solutions devised to treat with this dilemma were directly responsible for the national purposelessness that has characterized American public life ever since; they enable us to understand both the historical successes and the present failures of purposelessness in our national way of life. Each of these solutions was in part a response to economic and sectional interests, the fruit of a spirit of compromise that itself became integral to the spirit of the new republic; but each also aimed at using the peculiar conditions of America to reinforce in new and novel ways a republican constitution that would normally be undermined by such conditions. The constitutional solution was thus a radical and wholly untested challenge to the traditional wisdom of republican thought, one that turned the nation's early years into an unprecedented historical experiment, and one that could be met only by a people that had, in Madison's bold language, "not suffered a blind veneration for antiquity, for custom, or for names, to overrule the suggestions of their own good sense, the knowledge of their own situation, and the lessons of their own experience"—that had already managed in the Confederation to "rear ... the fabrics of governments which have no model on the face of the globe." [11] For many, many years, in many, many ways, the experiment achieved a remarkable success. Indeed it was successful enough to make its centralist features tolerable to Jeffersonian decentralists, its sectionalist propensities tolerable to Hamiltonian nationalists, and its increasingly democratic tendencies palatable to both. Only recently have its deficiencies emerged clearly; it is this that has led to what is now seen as the crisis in public purpose.

The formula designed by the Founders was anything but monolithic; it incorporated a variety of institutional innovations and procedural compromises that together created a national pluralism flexible enough to accommodate republican virtue *and* material progress *and* imperial power. The critical institutions included federalism, the representative system, presidential government, and the adversary method as the guiding principle of political procedure and political epistemology. Although they often appear as historical compromises, they were less compromises than surrogates for pristine republican institutions that could not function under America's unique conditions. Thus, for example, it might be said that private property became the surrogate for public norms, self-interest binding men to their public obligations no less surely than shared values once did; that procedural consensus became the surrogate for substantive

11 Madison, *The Federalist*, No. 14, p. 79.

consensus; that representation replaced participation, as accountability replaced self-government, and autonomy was traded for rights.

More concretely, to take the four institutions cited above, federalism was the compromise power negotiated with scale to permit the development of a national imperium that did not entirely destroy regional autonomy and local self-government. The Articles of Confederation had yielded to state sovereignty and state power a prominence "utterly irreconcilable with the idea of an aggregate sovereignty." [12] National government required a general license to operate; but powers not delegated to it had, in the words of the Tenth Amendment, "to be reserved to the States respectively, or to the people." For purposes of political participation, republican scale, autonomous self-government, and sectional autarky, America was to pass as a nation of semisovereign states. But for purposes of economic development, the security of property and debt, national defense (and imperial offense), and the public weal, it was endowed with all of the centripetal forces of the unitary nation—of, at least *in potentia*, the emerging empire.

Representation was an ingenious device with much the same utility: it used accountability to bridge the widening abyss between participatory self-government and efficient central administration. Like federalism, it permitted a form of self-government (not necessarily democratic) to survive in a land whose scale seemed to preclude self-government. To be self-governed and to be governed by representatives was, to be sure, not the same thing; but even from the skeptical vantage point of later elitist critics of representative democracy like Joseph Schumpeter, it was clear that a people who chose their masters were better off than a people who did not. If the people were to be little trusted—one of the few points upon which the Founders agreed—those who ruled in their name but not by their mandate were to be even less so; this was Jefferson's rather skeptical democratic faith. The representative, then, played two roles. He mediated the divergent interests of heterogeneous constituencies, thereby insuring the "participation" of sectional and other interests in national decision-making. [13] But he also mediated and thus moderated public

12 Madison to Randolph (1787), *The Writings of James Madison*, ed. Gaillard Hunt, 9 vols. (New York: 1900–1910), 2:336–40. The debate about the sovereignty and power of the states that divided nationalists and decentralists in the Constitutional Convention was not settled by the Constitution, as the Tenth Amendment makes clear.

13 Richard Henry Lee had thus suggested in his *Letters of a Federal Farmer* a system redolent of functional representation; e.g., "a fair representation, there-

passions; for, as Madison (sounding remarkably like Burke) had put it, the representative system could "refine and enlarge the public views by passing them through the medium of a chosen body of citizens."[14] Popular control *and* wise government, self-government *and* a national imperium, accountability *and* centripetal efficiency—these were the promises of representative government.

Presidential government was, in one sense, the crowning achievement of the representative system, the One in whom the Many could be safely united: for in the presidency was to be found the source and the symbol of the nation's collective power—the spirit of sovereign nationhood; yet in it too was preserved the right to self-government, initially of the states (through their electors), later of the people themselves—the spirit of sovereign citizenship. The President as Executive Officer and Commander-in-Chief embodied the power of the whole, of The People as a symbolic collectivity. The President as Elected Representative of the semisovereign states, as Chief Tribune, and, later, Party Leader, embodied the power of the parts, of the states and the people as self-governing entities, ruling themselves through their mandated executive representative. The dual accountability of the Presidency—to The People as Nation and to the people as citizens—has remained the source of its strength as a mediator between national power and local citizenship. It is no accident that the mythology of the common man has been more closely associated with the presidency than with any other institution; or that in 1976 Governor Brown of California and Governor Carter of Georgia, like Bryan before them, could lay claim to the presidency in the name of an alienated citizenry as if that office were wholly independent of the governmental bureaucracy against which they railed. Neater solutions to the problem of governmental leadership were to be found in parliamentary or monarchical government, but no more effective solution to the problem of accommodating republican self-government to imperial scale seem conceivable than presidential government.

The adversary method was less an institution than a procedural principle—perhaps *the* procedural principle—that governed the pro-

---

fore, should be so regulated, that every order of men in the community, according to the common course of elections, can have a fair share in it—in order to allow professional men, merchants, traders, farmers, mechanics, etc. to bring a just proportion of their best informed men respectively into the legislature" (in P. L. Ford, *Pamphlets on the Constitution of the United States* (Brooklyn, N.Y.: 1888), p. 288.

14 Madison, *The Federalist*, No. 10, p. 59.

cesses in which American institutions manifested themselves. The goal was unity (the republican ideal and the national imperative) through diversity (the democratic ideal and the sectional imperative). It seemed clear that no stubborn search for singular truths or mono-lithic standards or objective goals or agreed-upon powers could wring from the economic and social heterogeneity of America substantive consensus on anything. The adversary method in effect polarized the *pluribus* of *E pluribus unum* in order to secure a more moderate, centrist *unum*. It transformed market relations into political rela-tions, requiring of every political transaction a buyer and a seller, a purveyor and a client, a complainant and a respondent, an obligation and an interest. Only where there were two sides could there be a reasonable outcome; only where contraries were aired could unity be anticipated.

America has thus been a land of Noah where everything durable comes in twos: the two-house Congress, the two-seat-per-state Senate, the two-sided trial (by prosecutor and defense, not by judge and jury), and, in time, the two-party system and the two-authority legal system (where the Legislature *and* the Supreme Court vie in the conflicting voices of the written Constitution and a Higher Law for the right to give ultimate laws to the nation).[15] And where the system did not create polar opposites, it nonetheless generated adversaries—separat-ing and casting into opposition the major governmental powers (ex-ecutive, legislative, and judicial), institutionalizing military service rivalries, encouraging the growth of an unofficial representative sys-tem (of lobbyists, interest groups, voluntary associations) to challenge, balance, and complement the official representative system, and gen-erally nourishing an understanding of the polity as a public realm within which private forces are encouraged to seek their own advan-tage—the polity, in short, as a "pluralist pressure system." The faith has always been that from the clash of opposites, of contraries, of extremes, of poles, will come not the victory of any one but the medi-ation and accommodation of them all. The American version of truth and unity, if there was to be one, could never be forged from some ideal form. It would, as Jefferson knew, have to be hammered out on the anvil of debate.

[15] Judicial review thus challenged the positivist conception of law as a func-tion of the sovereign will advanced by the Legislature with a conception rooted in natural reason's discovery of a higher law. For a seminal discussion, see Ed-ward S. Corwin, "The Progress of Constitutional Theory between the Declaration of Independence and the Meeting of the Philadelphia Convention," *American Historical Review* 30 (1925).

The adversary method also played a secondary role as the functional equivalent of horizontal federalism: in polarizing authority it divided power; in pluralizing truth it separated powers. Making truth a function of debate, it put force at odds with itself. As Madison had argued in the Federalist Papers, "Ambition must be made to counteract ambition . . . [for] in framing a government which is to be administered by men over men . . . you must first enable the government to control the governed; and in the next place oblige it to control itself."[16]

In each of these institutions, then, central power and local control, administrative efficiency and regional autonomy, effective leadership and citizen participation, national planning and individual interest, were assiduously mediated—power (read planning, progress, efficiency, expansion, and prosperity) forever being balanced off against citizenship (read participation, excellence, fellowship, responsibility, and civic virtue). The theory of classical republicanism had been confounded: for a republic (a rather odd sort of republic, but a republic nonetheless) had been devised that would accommodate both democracy (a rather odd sort of democracy, but democracy nonetheless) and imperialism (a rather odd sort of imperialism, but imperialism nonetheless); and if the ancient conditions did not obtain, then the rules had been successfully altered to accommodate the American conditions that did obtain. American exceptionalism—the refusal to follow the historical patterns of the political culture to which America was heir—was thus built into the institutions by which the republic was fashioned; indeed, it was crucial to the initial successes of the experiment.

Despite all the Founders' quarrels, their economic differences, and their varying sympathies toward federalism and democracy, the early successes of the republic they contrived were truly extraordinary. By the time of his First Inaugural, Jefferson could thus say, "We are all republicans—we are all federalists." All of them shared, in Hofstadter's portrait, "a belief in the rights of property, the philosophy of economic individualism, the value of competition."[17] On these private and procedural purposes they constructed a public government that worked. It worked as a safeguard to republican individualism and it worked as a facilitator of imperial dominion. It satisfied the demands of unity by exploiting the energies of heterogeneity. It was short on participation but commensurately long on accountability. It

16 Madison, *The Federalist*, No. 51, pp. 335–41.
17 Hofstadter, *American Political Tradition*, p. xxxvii.

substituted contractees and clients for citizens but thereby guaranteed that private interests would play the part of absent public goals. It trusted in invisible hands to guide the pursuit of private wealth in publicly useful directions—and succeeded if only because there was so very much wealth. It protected equilibrium from the destabilizing effects of progress by leaving economic growth and prosperity in largely private hands—which, however, were permitted informally to grasp the public scepter. That is to say, its mercantilism was supervisory and paternal, only rarely direct or interventionist.

In all of this it absolutely depended on a studied obliviousness to public purposes and public interests as defined by traditional republican formulas. To insist on discovering public goods was only to generate faction and occlude those private interests that alone, pitted against each other, promised the semblance of consensus. In short, the system turned necessity into a virtue and placed public purposelessness at the very core of its value structure. This was the meaning of proceduralism, of the adversary method, of pluralism, and of the agreement to disagree. If public goals were occasionally to foist themselves on the nation—a gift of the Four Horsemen as it were—they could be gratefully accepted. But war, plague, famine, and death were sometime events, without the compelling moral power or the permanence to provide more than a temporary, reactive unity.

Purposelessness was not, then, a residual cost of implementing a republic under adverse circumstances but the guiding principle of its success. If some inspired corporate mogul was later to suggest that "what's good for General Motors is good for America," it was less a tribute to myopic self-interest than to the American ideal, which insisted quite precisely that private interests *were* the only public interests America could afford to pursue. If Jay Gould quipped, "In Republican counties I'm for the Republicans and in Democratic counties I'm for the Democrats, but everywhere I'm for the Erie Railroad,"[18] he was only saying with a grin what political scientist David Truman later said with a poker face: in the study and practice of American politics, "we do not need to account for a totally inclusive interest, because one does not exist."[19]

What began as necessity and soon turned to virtue had by the middle of this century become an awesome American ideal—the finest product of American exceptionalism. Daniel Boorstin thus suggested

18 Cited in D. W. Brogan, *Politics in America* (New York: Anchor Books, 1960), p. 222.

19 David Truman, *The Governmental Process* (New York: Knopf, 1957), p. 51.

in the 1950s that the "genius of American politics" (see his book of the same name) lay precisely in its refusal to define itself in terms of a public ideology or a politicized national interest. Louis Hartz, Arthur Schlesinger, and others wrote about the peculiarities of the American system that give to our heterogeneity and unideologized privatism the stamp of centrism and consensus.[20] An American center was possible because America lacked the usual political spectrum by which a center was measured; consensus was built around the agreement to agree on nothing substantive, to hold no exclusively public values of the kind defined by traditional republican theories or modern collectivist ideologies. In a land where the center will not hold, the new wisdom had it, it is the illusion of a public center that is most likely to loose mere anarchy upon the world. The republic worked because it never tried to contrive a center; and thus, by eliciting the assent of the citizenry to this value default, acquired a center after all—in the acquiesence of the people to purposelessness.

II

What, then, are the consequences of this historical vision for the present crisis? Traditional public purposes cannot have been lost or forfeited, for their absence turns out to have been the key to the success of America's republican experiment. But the conditions to which the experiment was addressed and on which its success depended have changed—changed radically, profoundly, irreversibly. When the Constitution was first fashioned, America stood at the threshold of a century of growth, material prosperity, and burgeoning national power. Heterogeneity provided room to operate, privatism was an invitation to speculation and growth (personal gain publicly legitimized), continental power was an unexploited promise as seductive as the frontier seemed endless, inequality appeared to be a remediable condition which, even unremediated, nurtured ambition and (upward) mobility. The threshold has long since been crossed, however, and the American people stand today at the back door of their vast mansion, all its rooms traversed, all its secret passages discovered, attic and basement alike despoiled of resources. With the land settled,

20 The most influential and important of these consensus works was Louis Hartz's *The Liberal Tradition in America* (New York: Harcourt Brace, 1955), which argued that America's exceptionalism was to be found in its uprootedness from the European feudal past and its consequent emancipation from reactive leftist ideology.

the wealth squandered, the self-sufficiency traded away for luxury, and the endless abundance quite abruptly rendered finite, the peculiar compromises between republican ideals and American conditions that have been the genius of American politics have lost their legitimacy. Open spaces, empty jobs, and unmade fortunes are the conditions that made inequality tolerable to the least advantaged in America's compromised republic; with hope gone, the compromise is itself compromised, and inequality becomes a permanent, oppressive, intolerable burden. Diversity and private interest were the necessary conditions of capitalist expansion in America; but now, in the late stages of capitalist development, in which speculation and entrepreneurship are no longer virtues and in which pointless consumption becomes more salient than expanding production, privatism nourishes alienation and despair, feeding only that scourge faction— the dark side of pluralism so dreaded by the founders. The irresistible force embodied in the endless American frontier has encountered the immovable object embodied in the limits of growth. The American nation, frozen between these awesome pressures, seems in danger of failing both as a republic and an empire—simultaneously, and, ironically, for the same reason: the failure of the institutions that once mediated federal republic and imperial nation to adapt to mutations in the conditions that made them work. Too centralized, bureaucratized, militarized, anesthesized—in a word, too imperial—to remain a republic, we are nonetheless too divided, demoralized, and privatized to flourish as an empire. The nation has become too large to accommodate the American republic at the same moment that the world and its dwindling resources have become too small to accommodate the American empire. Under these changed conditions, the very institutions that once fostered success now catalyze failure. They represent a governmental chemotherapy which, though it long sustained the nation's republican health against the twin cancers of anarchy and tyranny, is now itself imperiling the body politic.

Look, for example, at modern federalism—that once sovereign mediator of efficiency and self-government; today it stands only as a monument to unequal standards, parochialism, and factionalism (as a comparative study of state welfare systems will demonstrate). Too large and bureaucratic to enhance a sense of autonomy and self-government in the citizenry, the states are nonetheless too weak, divided, and inefficient to challenge the greater Leviathan of federal bureaucracy. No longer serving distinctive regional or sectional interests, they often impose arbitrary boundaries on what ought to be integrated areas. How many greater metropolitan regions tend today to cut across traditional state boundaries? Washington, D.C., New York, Kansas City, and Philadelphia are each cut off financially and politically from regions that benefit from their resources; most other major American cities find themselves serving extended suburban communities that have no legal or fiscal obligations to them. Thus do the antiquarian structures of federalism compound the urban crises they ought to be alleviating, serving the purposes neither of effective central government nor of regional self-government.

The representative system has undergone the same pathological metamorphosis—a benign tumor metastasized to become perilous to the body it once served. The danger was always present (which is why it can be considered a tumor, even in its benign stage): Rousseau had been certain that "the moment a people allows itself to be represented, it is no longer free; it no longer exists;" and Patrick Henry had voiced profound misgivings about representation in connection with the federal taxation issue: "I shall be told in this place, that those who are to tax us are our representatives. To this I answer, that there is no real check to prevent their ruining us. There is no actual responsibility. The only semblance of a check is the negative power of not reelecting them. This . . . is but a feeble barrier, when their personal interest, their ambition and avarice, come to be put in contrast with the happiness of the people."[21] The Founders hoped to find in representation a home for the noblesse oblige of an elite; representatives chosen by electors embodying the studied interests of property and wealth would be as much a curb on, as a vehicle of, democracy. But in modern mass democracy it is not wisdom but numbers that rule. Under the guise of mass participation, opinion becomes king and through opinion, the manipulative forces of wealth, power, and demogoguery. A representative system operating in a mass society combines the very worst features of direct democracy (the tyranny of opinion, passion, and ignorance) and of elitism (the tyranny of wealth and power)—something not even the most vociferous critics of mass democracy have fully appreciated (see J. S. Mill, Tocqueville, Ortega y Gasset, or Walter Lippmann). Sheer numbers dilute the input of individual citizens and diminish the salience of rational deliberation at the very moment that they reduce the accountability of representatives to any single citizen. At the Constitutional Convention critics worried that a 30,000 citizen constituency for a member of Congress would be too great;[22] congressional dis-

[21] Rousseau, *Social Contract*, Book 3, chap. 15; Patrick Henry, cited in Elliot, *Debates*, 3:167.
[22] See Kenyon, "Men of Little Faith."

tricts are today approaching one-half million. The inevitable consequences are everywhere visible: increased irresponsibility in the
representatives, increased apathy in the represented.

The institution of the presidency reflects these invidious changes
in the impact of representation all too well. Where once the president
embodied the powers both of people and The People (of citizens and
nation), he seems more and more frequently in recent years to embody
neither. His office has become the forum for private battles publicly
waged; his responsibilities to party, region, faction, and interest have
outweighed his loyalty to his Tribunate. In this sense Watergate
was less a perversion than a rather extravagant caricature of the presidency's current condition: not the imperial but the privatized presidency, not the stewardship of public interests but the protectorate of
private interests. Vietnam was less a matter of public than of presidential honor; it was Johnson's own face (and the faces of his foreign
policy establishment) that had to be saved, not the nation's. Nor
does Gerald Ford issue a call for renewed citizen participation in
politics when he takes the federal government out of the regulation
or the welfare business; rather, he merely acknowledges the impotence
of the public and its chief representative to deal publicly with the
nation's most pressing social and economic problems. He does not
involve people, he only exonerates himself. Thus the irony of a
presidency that is at once too powerful and too weak: too powerful,
bureaucratic, and clandestine to be representative or public-minded,
but too personal, privatized, and banal to be effective.

American proceduralism seems also to have lost much of its legitimacy. Once a device designed to reconcile Americans to their differences by offering them a way to live with them, the adversary method
seems now more often to underscore contradictions and embitter
competition. Self-sufficiency and thinking for yourself have become
self-alienation and existing by yourself. The self-interested individual
becomes the self-serving individual and then the self-consuming individual. The hand that once was to guide his private quest for
security and well-being in publicly useful directions is no longer
simply invisible: it is incorporeal, insubstantial, nonexistent. And
so, as the factionalism that drives Americans apart and tends less
and less to leave them with residual public interests intensifies, the
need for a sense of shared values in an increasingly factionalized and
anomic world grows. Adversaries who no longer find in their disagreements a basis for common norms are transformed from adversaries
into enemies. Enemies multiply, find their way into presidential as
well as private thinking; and finally that most compelling figure of

the American exceptionalist imagination—the pioneering frontiersman—turns from competitive self-sufficiency to hostile vigilantism
and in doing so goes from being an individual and a competitor to
being an outsider and an adversary; and then, in the final stage, the
outsider becomes an alien even to himself, and the modern assassin
is born: the outsider par excellence, the adversary born of adversity,
the self-serving, sharp-shooting frontiersman run amok because the
conditions that once justified his independence and satisfied his needs
are gone.

The answer, then, to the question of why America neither has nor
has been able to cultivate public purposes is simply that it was not
supposed to have them. Exceptional American conditions made the
quest for them seem both dangerous and impossible, while exceptional American institutions effected compromises that exploited
their absence to the benefit of both republic and empire. This interpretation is dismaying in that it gives to present problems historical
dimensions that make them seem intractable; but it is also encouraging: for the very failure of institutions that depended on purposelessness suggests changes in historical conditions that may be conducive
to a new, historically unprecedented public-spiritedness. Institutional
innovations as appropriate to new circumstances as federalism, representation, and the other compromises of the original Constitution
were appropriate to America's founding conditions may even reveal
that purposelessness is no longer a necessary feature of the compromised republic—that less compromising steps may finally be in order.

Certainly this kind of approach closes the door completely on solutions that are blind to new conditions or to the developments that
occasioned them. It discloses as useless, for example, the nostalgic
communitarianism that looks for hope to the retrieval of a lost sense
of purpose that, in fact, the nation never enjoyed. Those who seek in
the American compromise republic some living facsimile of republican Athens seek the absurd—and perhaps, without knowing it, the
perverse. Contemporary America remade to the specifications of ancient Athens would probably come to resemble not Athens but wartime Berlin.

Likewise, those who would rely on the revitalization of the original
compromise republic can only be disappointed; for it is the failure of
that formula to adapt to new conditions that has created the dilemmas
the revitalists wish to address. It would seem that neither constitutional atavism nor republican nostalgia can be of service in the
present crisis. What Jefferson understood when the Founding was
scarcely a generation old surely holds ten times over two centuries

later: "I am certainly not an advocate for frequent and untried changes in laws and institutions . . . but I know also, that laws and institutions must go hand in hand with the progress of the human mind. As that becomes more developed, more enlightened, as new discoveries are made, new truths disclosed, and manners and opinions change with the change of circumstances, institutions must advance also, and keep pace with the times.[23]

If new conditions doom old institutions, they also present new opportunities and invite new ways of thinking. All political thinking today is conditioned by the seeming inevitability of a limited-growth economy, by circumscribed American power, by the compulsory interdependence of an increasingly transnational world, by the emergence of national (and even international) norms as the result of a national (international) technology, economy, and communications network, and by the failure of privatism and material success to answer nonmaterial private needs or serve nonprivate life goals. Yet the result of this conditioning is that political thinking can look critically at the compromises forced on the early republic by the circumstances (now gone) of expansionism, heterogeneity, and material abundance of the founding era. Institutions responsive to the new conditions must, to be sure, still contend with problems of scale, bureaucracy, efficiency, and dominion unknown to earlier lawgivers and only conjectured by the Founders; but with the passing of unlimited growth and unchecked privatism as desiderata of the lawgiver, many innovations become possible. Some of them—although this is hardly the place to spell them out in institutional detail—challenge the current utility and perhaps even the spirit of the compromises so critical to the success of the early republic.

Federalism, for example, seems today largely irrelevant to the needs of the sectional interests it was intended to serve—at least in their contemporary manifestations. The units—greater metropolitan areas—most in need of integrated structures and autonomous self-government actually have the least. A greater New York that encompassed the suburban regions to which taxable wealth has fled might be able to solve many of its fiscal and political crisis by itself. The middle-class and corporate exodus would become academic, for a relevant regionalism would compel those who utilized the resources and services of a great city to pay for them—regardless of residence. At the same time, mass transportation could be rationalized and encouraged (imagine a city with the powers of the Port Authority of New York), while the welfare burden would be more equitably

[23] Cited by Hofstadter, *American Political Tradition*, p. 55.

distributed. Federalism remains a viable compromise: but only if it is based on periodic redistricting in accordance with crucial demographic and economic developments.

Redistricting would also give an important impetus to participatory government and thus leaven the increasingly meaningless system of representation with a degree of real political activity. But participation would also require other forms of institutional innovation. It could mean the introduction of the old communal tradition of Common Work—which requires of citizens participation not only in the deliberation and decision-making processes but also in the implementation of public policy decisions; thus, the decision to permit urban homesteading (the takeover by tenants, for a nominal sum, of landlord-abandoned inner-city housing—a policy already initiated on an experimental basis in Baltimore, New York, and elsewhere) would be decided by referendum and require the participation of the citizenry in implementing it.[24] Policies and building permits cannot remake a city; engaged, working citizens can.

The use of the referendum might also be extended, although this would probably mean, if it were to be effective, the extension of public deliberation and discussion as well as of public voting. Public-access television channels could be of use here. Indeed, technology is a potential ally of very great promise in any campaign to extend citizen participation in various phases of the public-policy process.[25] The aim would be to prevent representation from paralyzing direct participation—to transform politics from a spectator sport in which, accountability notwithstanding, the responsibility rests with the governors, into a participatory sport in which, inefficiency notwithstanding, responsibility is assumed by the governed.

These kinds of institutional innovations—and they are only suggestive in the tentative forms in which they are offered here—point toward an even more critical kind of innovation: a change in atti-

---

24 Common Work has roots in the old Germanic feudal usage of *Gemeinarbeit*. Its modern utility is suggested by its reintroduction into village life in contemporary Switzerland. For a full account see my *The Death of Communal Liberty: A History of Freedom in a Swiss Mountain Canton* (Princeton: Princeton University Press, 1974), pp. 176–79 et passim.

25 The popular discussion of the uses of television communications and electronic technology to expedite mass participation in deliberation and decision-making has been much more widespread in journalism and the media (see McLuhan), than in serious social and political thought. Modern republicans have also tended too often to be technological Luddites; but if technology can have an alienating impact on men and women, it nonetheless is a remarkable facilitator of communications, and communications are at the heart of a republican polity.

tude. Although conditions have changed, Americans still respond to
the public world in terms of the attitudes they take to be suitable to
those (now vanished) conditions of the Founding. Though they acknowledge the poverty of privatism, they think privatistically; though
they understand the insufficiency of frontiersmanship and vigilantism,
they react violently and respond vengefully; though they have learned
the risks of material ambition, they crave wealth and luxury; though
they have lost faith in the myth of self-sufficiency and the rhetoric of
independence, they distrust cooperation and regard interdependence
as a weakness. Attitudes lag behind changes in conditions, and institutions lag still further behind attitudes. Nevertheless, the successes in
the mid-seventies of politicians dedicated to public philosophies of
restraint, austerity, citizen responsibility, and (even) asceticism suggest that the public may be ready to exchange privatism for a sense
of common purpose, uncertain luxury for a stable moderation. Faced
with the prospects of unlimited growth, America once made a virtue
of necessity and modified republican institutions to meet the demands
of expansion and empire; faced with the prospect of limited growth,
perhaps eventually even zero growth, it now has the chance to make
a necessity of virtue and readapt its institutions to meet the demands
of contraction and interdependence. The new pressures of ecology,
transnationalism, and resource scarcity in combination with the
apparent bankruptcy of privatism, materialism, and economic individualism—the pathologies and the ambivalent promises of our modernity—create conditions more inviting to the generation of public
purposes and a public spirit than any America has ever known.
Abundance is the natural soil of competitive individualism; scarcity,
the soil of mutualism. Cooperation springs from a sense of common
limits, and limits of one kind or another are the key to America's new
conditions. To this extent, the problem of public purposelessness is
the product of conditions which, if understood and exploited, suggest
and nurture their own remedy.

For two centuries in this new Atlantis of America, man and nature
have been pitted in a contest that—Marxists, mercantilists, and free
marketeers all agreed—could be resolved only through the total subjugation of nature. Private men put aside public purposes to wage
a private war on economic necessity: carrying private banners, they
fought in the name of private freedom for explicitly private interests.
But the Baconian dream of emancipation through mastery was lost,
even as it was realized; nature yielded somewhat, but, as the limits of
growth suggest, less than expected. Moreover, the emancipation
wrung from nature turns out to have produced more alienation than

independence, more rootlessness than self-realization, more solitude than freedom. Genuine freedom, some contemporary Americans must begin to suspect, may possibly turn out to be an aspect of man's relationship *with* nature, of his capacity to live within its laws, of his willingness to accommodate himself to forces that cannot be subdued. The republican polity has always rested on notions of accommodation to nature and mutuality among men. If Baconian hubris has truly run its course in America, the time may finally be ripe for a burgeoning of republican ideals that until this moment have been foreign to the American enterprise in its compromised form.

Not that this will happen by itself. Our dilemma invites easier, more authoritarian solutions.[26] Fascism treats the ills of public alienation without placing burdens of choice and responsibility on the public; anarchy permits privatism to self-destruct. Visionary demagogues may find it more profitable to impose "common" values on a dispirited American people than to give them the institutional resources to discover their own. Public purposes publicly arrived at require hard work and carry with them the mixed blessing of continuous self-government; it asks much less of the people to contrive public myths, public ideologies, and public dogmas from the private interests of aspiring authoritarians; and, of course, it saves them from the burdens of self-government. Democracy in its republican form is, after all, a rare and fragile form of government.

But, history shows, America is a rare and not so fragile nation—forever exhibiting its exceptionalism in new and startling ways. It found the way in its compromised republic to reconcile republic and empire; now it must compromise the compromises and find a way to preserve the republic in a strange new world of finitude, boundaries, and interdependence. If it can again improve the formula, it may once more confound the great tradition out of which it arises by proving that a flexible, well-made, republic responsive to changing American conditions can survive the most pernicious of its modern enemies: modernity itself.

26 That the present American condition is as inviting or more inviting to fascism than to republican innovation may be seen from this remarkable passage by Fritz Stern describing the nineteenth-century German precursors of Nazism in terms alarmingly appropriate to alienated Americans circa 1976: "Theirs was a resentment of loneliness; their one desire was for a new faith, a new community of believers... they denounced every aspect of the capitalistic society, and its putative materialism. They railed against the emptiness of life in an urban, commercial civilization ... they attacked the press as corrupt, the political parties as agents of national dissension, and the new rulers as ineffectual mediocrities" (*The Politics of Cultural Despair* [New York: Doubleday, 1965]).

The Founding Fathers:
An Age of Realism

Richard Hofstadter

Wherever the real power in a government lies, there is the danger of oppression. In our Government the real power lies in the majority of the community. . . . James Madison

Power naturally grows . . . because human passions are insatiable. But that power alone can grow which already is too great; that which is unchecked; that which has no equal power to control it. John Adams

Long ago Horace White observed that the Constitution of the United States "is based upon the philosophy of Hobbes and the religion of Calvin. It assumes that the natural state of mankind is a state of war, and that the carnal mind is at enmity with God." Of course the Constitution was founded more upon experience than any such abstract theory; but it was also an event in the intellectual history of Western civilization. The men who drew up the Constitution in Philadelphia during the summer of 1787 had a vivid Calvinistic sense of human evil and damnation and believed with Hobbes that men are selfish and contentious. They were men of affairs, merchants, lawyers, planter-businessmen, speculators, investors. Having seen human nature on display in the market place, the courtroom, the legislative chamber, and in every secret path and alleyway where wealth and power are courted, they felt they knew it in all its frailty. To them a human being was an atom of self-interest. They did not believe in man, but they did believe in the power of a good political constitution to control him.

This may be an abstract notion to ascribe to practical men, but it follows the language that the Fathers themselves used. General Knox, for example, wrote in disgust to Washington after the Shays Rebellion that Americans were, after all, "men—actual men possessing all the turbulent passions belonging to that animal." Throughout the secret discussions at the Constitutional Convention it was clear that this distrust of man was first and foremost a distrust of the common man and democratic rule. As the Revolution took away the restraining hand of the British government, old colonial grievances of farmers, debtors, and squatters against merchants, investors, and large landholders had flared up anew; the lower orders took advantage of new democratic constitutions in several states, and the possessing classes were frightened. The members of the Constitutional Convention were concerned to create a government that could not only regulate commerce and pay its debts but also prevent currency inflation and state laws, and check such uprisings as the Shays Rebellion.

Cribbing and confining the popular spirit that had been at large since 1776 were essential to the purposes of the new Constitution. Edmund Randolph, saying to the Convention that the evils from which the country suffered originated in "the turbulence and follies of democracy," and that the great danger lay in "the democratic parts of our constitutions"; Elbridge Gerry, speaking of democracy as "the worst of all political evils"; Roger Sherman, hoping that "the people . . . have as little to do as may be about the government"; William Livingston, saying that "the people have ever been and ever will be unfit to retain the exercise of power in their own hands"; George Washington, the presiding officer, urging the delegates not to produce a document of which they themselves could not approve simply in order to "please the people"; Hamilton, charging that the "turbulent and changing" masses "seldom judge or determine right" and advising a permanent governmental body to "check the imprudence of democracy"; the wealthy young planter Charles Pinckney, proposing that no one be president who was not worth at least one hundred thousand dollars—all these were quite representative of the spirit in which the problems of government were treated.

Democratic ideas are most likely to take root among discontented and oppressed classes, rising middle classes, or perhaps some section of an old, alienated, and partially disinherited aristocracy, but they do not appeal to a privileged class that is still amplifying its privileges. With a half-dozen exceptions at the most, the men of the Philadelphia Convention were sons of men who had considerable position and wealth, and as a group they had advanced well beyond their fathers. Only one of them, William Few of Georgia, could be said in any sense to represent the yeoman farmer class which constituted the overwhelming majority of the free population. In the late eighteenth century "the better kind of people" found themselves set off from the mass by a hundred visible, tangible, and audible distinctions of dress, speech, manners, and education. There was a continuous lineage of upper-class contempt, from pre-Revolutionary Tories like Peggy

Hutchinson, the Governor's daughter, who wrote one day: "The dirty mob was all about me as I drove into town," to a Federalist like Hamilton, who candidly disdained the people. Mass unrest was often received in the spirit of young Gouverneur Morris: "The mob begin to think and reason. Poor reptiles! . . . They bask in the sun, and ere noon they will bite, depend upon it. The gentry begin to fear this." Nowhere in America or Europe—not even among the great liberated thinkers of the Enlightenment—did democratic ideas appear respectable to the cultivated classes. Whether the Fathers looked to the cynically illuminated intellectuals of contemporary Europe or to their own Christian heritage of the idea of original sin, they found quick confirmation of the notion that man is an unregenerate rebel who has to be controlled.

And yet there was another side to the picture. The Fathers were intellectual heirs of seventeenth-century English republicanism with its opposition to arbitrary rule and faith in popular sovereignty. If they feared the advance of democracy, they also had misgivings about turning to the extreme right. Having recently experienced a bitter revolutionary struggle with an external power beyond their control, they were in no mood to follow Hobbes to his conclusion that any kind of government must be accepted in order to avert the anarchy and terror of a state of nature. They were uneasily aware that both military dictatorship and a return to monarchy were being seriously discussed in some quarters—the former chiefly among unpaid and discontented army officers, the latter in rich and fashionable Northern circles. John Jay, familiar with sentiment among New York's mercantile aristocracy, wrote to Washington, June 27, 1786, that he feared that "the better kind of people (by which I mean the people who are orderly and industrious, who are content with their situations, and not uneasy in their circumstances) will be led, by the insecurity of property, the loss of confidence in their rulers, and the want of public faith and rectitude, to consider the charms of liberty as imaginary and delusive." Such men, he thought, might be prepared for "almost any change that may promise them quiet and security." Washington, who had already repudiated a suggestion that he become a military dictator, agreed, remarking that "we are apt to run from one extreme to the other."

Unwilling to turn their backs upon republicanism, the Fathers also wished to avoid violating the prejudices of the people. "Notwithstanding the oppression and injustice experienced among us from democracy," said George Mason, "the genius of the people is in favor of it, and the genius of the people must be consulted." Mason admitted "that we had been too democratic," but feared that "we should incautiously run into the opposite extreme." James Madison, who has quite rightfully been called the philosopher of the Constitution, told the delegates: "It seems indispensable that the mass of citizens should not be without a voice in making the laws which they are to obey, and in choosing the magistrates who are to administer them." James Wilson, the outstanding jurist of the age, later appointed to the Supreme Court by Washington, said again and again that the ultimate power of government must of necessity reside in the people. This the Fathers commonly accepted, for if government did not proceed from the people, from what other source could it legitimately come? To adopt any other premise not only would be inconsistent with everything they had said against British rule in the past but would open the gates to an extreme concentration of power in the future. Hamilton saw the sharp distinction in the Convention when he said that "the members most tenacious of republicanism were as loud as any in declaiming the vices of democracy." There was no better expression of the dilemma of a man who has no faith in the people but insists that government be based upon them than that of Jeremy Belknap, a New England clergyman, who wrote to a friend: "Let it stand as a principle that government originates from the people; but let the people be taught . . . that they are not able to govern themselves."

II

If the masses were turbulent and unregenerate, and yet if government must be founded upon their suffrage and consent, what could a Constitution maker do? One thing that the Fathers did not propose to do, because they thought it impossible, was to change the nature of man to conform with a more ideal system. They were inordinately confident that they knew what man always had been and what he always would be. The eighteenth-century mind had great faith in universals. Its method, as Carl Becker has said, was "to go up and down the field of history looking for man in general, the universal man, stripped of the accidents of time and place." Madison declared that the causes of political differences and of the formation of factions were "sown in the nature of man" and could never be eradicated. "It is universally acknowledged," David Hume had written, "that there is a great uniformity among the actions of men, in all nations and ages, and that human nature remains still the same, in its principles and operations. The same motives always produce the same actions. The same events always follow from the same causes."

Since man was an unchangeable creature of self-interest, it would not do to leave anything to his capacity for restraint. It was too much to expect that vice could be checked by virtue; the Fathers relied instead upon checking vice with vice. Madison once objected during the Convention that Gouverneur Morris was "forever inculcating the utter political depravity of men and the necessity of opposing one vice and interest to another vice and interest." And yet Madison himself in the *Federalist* number 51 later set forth an excellent statement of the same thesis:[1]

> Ambition must be made to counteract ambition. . . . It may be a reflection on human nature that such devices should be necessary to control the abuses of government. But what is government itself, but the greatest of all reflections on human nature? If men were angels, no government would be necessary. . . . In framing a government which is to be administered by men over men, the great difficulty lies in this: you must first enable the government to control the governed; and in the next place oblige it to control itself.

Political economists of the laissez-faire school were saying that private vices could be public benefits, that an economically beneficent result would be providentially or "naturally" achieved if self-interest were left free from state interference and allowed to pursue its ends. But the Fathers were not so optimistic about politics. If, in a state that lacked constitutional balance, one class or one interest gained control, they believed, it would surely plunder all other interests. The Fathers, of course, were especially fearful that the poor would plunder the rich, but most of them would probably have admitted that the rich, unrestrained, would also plunder the poor. Even Gouverneur Morris, who stood as close to the extreme aristocratic position as candor and intelligence would allow, told the Convention: "Wealth tends to corrupt the mind and to nourish its love of power, and to stimulate it to oppression. History proves this to be the spirit of the opulent."

What the Fathers wanted was known as "balanced government," an idea at least as old as Aristotle and Polybius. This ancient conception had won new sanction in the eighteenth century, which was

---

[1] Cf. the words of Hamilton to the New York ratifying convention: "Men will pursue their interests. It is as easy to change human nature as to oppose the strong current of selfish passions. A wise legislator will gently divert the channel, and direct it, if possible, to the public good."

dominated intellectually by the scientific work of Newton, and in which mechanical metaphors sprang as naturally to men's minds as did biological metaphors in the Darwinian atmosphere of the late nineteenth century. Men had found a rational order in the universe and they hoped that it could be transferred to politics, or, as John Adams put it, that governments could be "erected on the simple principles of nature." Madison spoke in the most precise Newtonian language when he said that such a "natural" government must be so constructed "that its several constituent parts may, by their mutual relations, be the means of keeping each other in their proper places." A properly designed state, the Fathers believed, would check interest with interest, class with class, faction with faction, and one branch of government with another in a harmonious system of mutual frustration.

In practical form, therefore, the quest of the Fathers reduced primarily to a search for constitutional devices that would force various interests to check and control one another. Among those who favored the federal Constitution three such devices were distinguished.

The first of these was the advantage of a federal government in maintaining order against popular uprisings or majority rule. In a single state a faction might arise and take complete control by force; but if the states were bound in a federation, the central government could step in and prevent it. Hamilton quoted Montesquieu: "Should a popular insurrection happen in one of the confederate states, the others are able to quell it." Further, as Madison argued in the *Federalist* number 10, a majority would be the most dangerous of all factions that might arise, for the majority would be the most capable of gaining complete ascendancy. If the political society were very extensive, however, and embraced a large number and variety of local interest, the citizens who shared a common majority interest "must be rendered by their number and local situation, unable to concert and carry into effect their schemes of oppression." The chief propertied interests would then be safer from "a rage for paper money, for an abolition of debts, for an equal division of property, or for any other improper or wicked project."

The second advantage of good constitutional government resided in the mechanism of representation itself. In a small direct democracy the unstable passions of the people would dominate lawmaking; but a representative government, as Madison said, would "refine and enlarge the public views by passing them through the medium of a chosen body of citizens." Representatives chosen by the people were wiser and more deliberate than the people themselves in mass assemblage. Hamilton frankly anticipated a kind of syndical paternalism in which the wealthy and dominant members of every trade or industry would represent the others in politics. Merchants, for example, were "the natural representatives" of their employees and of the mechanics and artisans they dealt with. Hamilton expected that Congress, "with too few exceptions to have any influence on the spirit of the government, will be composed of landholders, merchants, and men of the learned professions."

The third advantage of the government the Fathers were designing was pointed out most elaborately by John Adams in the first volume of his *Defence of the Constitutions of Government of the United States of America*, which reached Philadelphia while the Convention was in session and was cited with approval by several delegates.[2] Adams believed that the aristocracy and the democracy must be made to neutralize each other. Each element should be given its own house of the legislature, and over both houses there should be set a capable, strong, and impartial executive armed with the veto power. This split assembly would contain within itself an organic check and would be capable of self-control under the governance of the executive. The whole system was to be capped by an independent judiciary. The inevitable tendency of the rich and the poor to plunder each other would be kept in hand.

III

It is ironical that the Constitution, which Americans venerate so deeply, is based upon a political theory that at one crucial point stands in direct antithesis to the main stream of American democratic faith. Modern American folklore assumes that democracy and liberty are all but identical, and when democratic writers take the trouble to make the distinction, they usually assume that democracy is necessary to liberty. But the Founding Fathers thought that the liberty with which they were most concerned was menaced by democracy. In their minds liberty was linked not to democracy but to property.

What did the Fathers mean by liberty? What did Jay mean when

2 "Mr. Adams' book," wrote Benjamin Rush, often in the company of the delegates, "has diffused such excellent principles among us that there is little doubt of our adopting a vigorous and compounded Federal Legislature. Our illustrious Minister in this gift to his country has done us more service than if he had obtained alliances for us with all the nations of Europe."

he spoke of "the charms of liberty"? Or Madison when he declared that to destroy liberty in order to destroy factions would be a remedy worse than the disease? Certainly the men who met at Philadelphia were not interested in extending liberty to those classes in America, the Negro slaves and the indentured servants, who were most in need of it, for slavery was recognized in the organic structure of the Constitution and indentured servitude was no concern of the Convention. Nor was the regard of the delegates for civil liberties any too tender. It was the opponents of the Constitution who were most active in demanding such vital liberties as freedom of religion, freedom of speech and press, jury trial, due process, and protection from "unreasonable searches and seizures." These guarantees had to be incorporated in the first ten amendments because the Convention neglected to put them in the original document. Turning to economic issues, it was not freedom of trade in the modern sense that the Fathers were striving for. Although they did not believe in impeding trade unnecessarily, they felt that failure to regulate it was one of the central weaknesses of the Articles of Confederation, and they stood closer to the mercantilists than to Adam Smith. Again, liberty to them did not mean free access to the nation's unappropriated wealth. At least fourteen of them were land speculators. They did not believe in the right of the squatter to occupy unused land, but rather in the right of the absentee owner or speculator to pre-empt it.

The liberties that the constitutionalists hoped to gain were chiefly negative. They wanted freedom from fiscal uncertainty and irregularities in the currency, from trade wars among the states, from economic discrimination by more powerful foreign governments, from attacks on the creditor class or on property, from popular insurrection. They aimed to create a government that would act as an honest broker among a variety of propertied interests, giving them all protection from their common enemies and preventing any one of them from becoming too powerful. The Convention was a fraternity of types of absentee ownership. All property should be permitted to have its proportionate voice in government. Individual property interests might have to be sacrificed at times, but only for the community of propertied interests. Freedom for property would result in liberty for men—perhaps not for all men, but at least for all worthy men.[3]

---

[3] The Fathers probably would have accepted the argument of the Declaration of Independence that "all men are created equal," but only as a legal, not as a political or psychological proposition. Jefferson himself believed in the existence of "natural aristocrats," but he thought they were likely to appear in any class

Because men have different faculties and abilities, the Fathers believed, they acquire different amounts of property. To protect property is only to protect men in the exercise of their natural faculties. Among the many liberties, therefore, freedom to hold and dispose property is paramount. Democracy, unchecked rule by the masses, is sure to bring arbitrary redistribution of property, destroying the very essence of liberty.

The Fathers' conception of democracy, shaped by their practical experience with the aggressive dirt farmers in the American states and the urban mobs of the Revolutionary period, was supplemented by their reading in history and political science. Fear of what Madison called "the superior force of an interested and overbearing majority" was the dominant emotion aroused by their study of historical examples. The chief examples of republics were among the city-states of antiquity, medieval Europe, and early modern times. Now, the history of these republics—a history, as Hamilton said, "of perpetual vibration between the extremes of tyranny and anarchy"—was alarming. Further, most of the men who had overthrown the liberties of republics had "begun their career by paying an obsequious court to the people; commencing demagogues and ending tyrants."

All the constitutional devices that the Fathers praised in their writings were attempts to guarantee the future of the United States against the "turbulent" political cycles of previous republics. By "democracy," they meant a system of government which directly expressed the will of the majority of the people, usually through such an assemblage of the people as was possible in the small area of the city-state.

A cardinal tenet in the faith of the men who made the Constitution was the belief that democracy can never be more than a transitional stage in government, that it always evolves into either a tyranny (the rule of the rich demagogue who has patronized the mob) or an aristocracy (the original leaders of the democratic elements). "Remember," wrote the dogmatic John Adams in one of his letters to John Taylor

---

of society. However, for those who interpreted the natural-rights philosophy more conservatively than he, the idea that all men are equal did not mean that uneducated dirt farmers or grimy-handed ship-calkers were in any sense the equals of the Schuylers, Washingtons, or Pinckneys. It meant only that British colonials had as much natural right to self-government as Britons at home, that the average American was the legal peer of the average Briton. Among the signers of the Constitution, it is worth noting, there were only six men who had also signed the Declaration of Independence.

of Caroline, "democracy never lasts long. It soon wastes, exhausts, and murders itself. There never was a democracy yet that did not commit suicide."[4] Again:

If you give more than a share in the sovereignty to the democrats, that is, if you give them the command or preponderance in the . . . legislature, they will vote all property out of the hands of you aristocrats, and if they let you escape with your lives, it will be more humanity, consideration, and generosity than any triumphant democracy ever displayed since the creation. And what will follow? The aristocracy among the democrats will take your place, and treat their fellows as severely and sternly as you have treated them.

Government, thought the Fathers, is based on property. Men who have no property lack the necessary stake in an orderly society to make stable or reliable citizens. Dread of the propertyless masses of the towns was all but universal. George Washington, Gouverneur Morris, John Dickinson, and James Madison spoke of their anxieties about the urban working class that might arise some time in the future—"men without property and principle," as Dickinson described them—and even the democratic Jefferson shared this prejudice. Madison, stating the problem, came close to anticipating the modern threats to conservative republicanism from both communism and fascism:

In future times, a great majority of the people will not only be without landed but any other sort of property. These will either combine, under the influence of their common situation—in which case the rights of property and the public liberty will not be secure in their hands—or, what is more probable, they will become the tools of opulence and ambition, in which case there will be equal danger on another side.

What encouraged the Fathers about their own era, however, was the broad dispersion of landed property. The small landowning farmers had been troublesome in recent years, but there was a general conviction that under a properly made Constitution a *modus vivendi* could be worked out with them. The possession of moderate plots of property presumably gave them a sufficient stake in society to be safe and responsible citizens under the restraints of balanced government. Influence in government would be proportionate to property; mer-

4 Taylor labored to confute Adams, but in 1814, after many discouraging years in American politics, he conceded a great part of Adams's case: "All parties, however loyal to principles at first, degenerate into aristocracies of interest at last; and unless a nation is capable of discerning the point where integrity ends and fraud begins, popular parties are among the surest modes of introducing an aristocracy."

chants and great landholders would be dominant, but small property-owners would have an independent and far from negligible voice. It was "politic as well as just," said Madison, "that the interest and rights of every class should be duly represented and understood in the public councils," and John Adams declared that there could be "no free government without a democratical branch in the constitution."

The farming element already satisfied the property requirements for suffrage in most of the states, and the Fathers generally had no quarrel with their enfranchisement. But when they spoke of the necessity of founding government upon the consent of "the people," it was only these small property-holders that they had in mind. For example, the famous Virginia Bill of Rights, written by George Mason, explicitly defined those eligible for suffrage as all men "having sufficient evidence of permanent common interest with and attachment to the community"—which meant, in brief, sufficient property.

However, the original intention of the Fathers to admit the yeoman into an important but sharply limited partnership in affairs of state could not be perfectly realized. At the time the Constitution was made, Southern planters and Northern merchants were setting their differences aside in order to meet common dangers—from radicals within and more powerful nations without. After the Constitution was adopted, conflict between the ruling classes broke out anew, especially after powerful planters were offended by the favoritism of Hamilton's policies to Northern commercial interests. The planters turned to the farmers to form an agrarian alliance, and for more than half a century this powerful coalition embraced the bulk of the articulate interests of the country. As time went on, therefore, the main stream of American political conviction deviated more and more from the antidemocratic position of the Constitution-makers. Yet, curiously, their general satisfaction with the Constitution together with their growing nationalism made Americans deeply reverent of the founding generation, with the result that as it grew stronger, this deviation was increasingly overlooked.

There is common agreement among modern critics that the debates over the Constitution were carried on at an intellectual level that is rare in politics, and that the Constitution itself is one of the world's masterpieces of practical statecraft. On other grounds there has been controversy. At the very beginning contemporary opponents of the Constitution foresaw an apocalyptic destruction of local government and popular institutions, while conservative Europeans of the old regime thought the young American Republic was a dangerous leftist experiment. Modern critical scholarship, which reached a high point in Charles A. Beard's *An Economic Interpretation of the Constitution of the United States,* started a new turn in the debate. The antagonism, long latent, between the philosophy of the Constitution and the philosophy of American democracy again came into the open. Professor Beard's work appeared in 1913 at the peak of the Progressive era, when the muckraking fever was still high; some readers tended to conclude from his findings that the Fathers were selfish reactionaries who do not deserve their high place in American esteem. Still more recently, other writers, inverting this logic, have used Beard's facts to praise the Fathers for their opposition to "democracy" and as an argument for returning again to the idea of a "republic."

In fact, the Fathers' image of themselves as moderate republicans standing between political extremes was quite accurate. They were impelled by class motives more than pietistic writers like to admit, but they were also controlled, as Professor Beard himself has recently emphasized, by a statesmanlike sense of moderation and a scrupulously republican philosophy. Any attempt, however, to tear their ideas out of the eighteenth century context is sure to make them seem starkly reactionary. Consider, for example, the favorite maxim of John Jay: "The people who own the country ought to govern it." To the Fathers this was simply a swift axiomatic statement of the stake-in-society theory of political rights, a moderate conservative position under eighteenth-century conditions of property distribution in America. Under modern property relations this maxim demands a drastic restriction of the base of political power. A large portion of the modern middle class—and it is the strength of this class upon which balanced government depends—is propertyless; and the urban proletariat, which the Fathers so greatly feared, is almost one half the population. Further, the separation of ownership from control that has come with the corporation deprives Jay's maxim of twentieth century meaning even for many propertied people. The six hundred thousand stockholders of the American Telephone & Telegraph Company not only do not acquire political power by virtue of their stock-ownership, but they do not even acquire economic power; they cannot control their own company.

From a humanistic standpoint there is a serious dilemma in the philosophy of the Fathers, which derives from their conception of man. They thought man was a creature of rapacious self-interest, and yet they wanted him to be free—free, in essence, to contend, to engage in an umpired strife, to use property to get property. They accepted the mercantile image of life as an eternal battleground, and assumed the Hobbesian war of each against all; they did not propose to put an end to this war, but merely to stabilize it and make it less murderous. They had no hope and they offered none for any ultimate organic change in the way men conduct themselves. The result was that while they thought self-interest the most dangerous and unbrookable quality of man, they necessarily underwrote it in trying to control it. They succeeded in both respects: under the competitive capitalism of the nineteenth century America continued to be an arena for various grasping and contending interests, and the federal government continued to provide a stable and acceptable medium within which they could contend; further, it usually showed the wholesome bias on behalf of property which the Fathers expected. But no man who is as well abreast of modern science as the Fathers were of eighteenth century science believes any longer in unchanging human nature. Modern humanistic thinkers who seek for a means by which society may transcend eternal conflict and rigid adherence to property rights as its integrating principles can expect no answer in the philosophy of balanced government as it was set down by the Constitution-makers of 1787.

Ethics and Politics:
The American Way

Martin Diamond

ALL men have some notion of what we may call the universal aspect of the relationship between ethics and politics, a notion of what the relationship would be for men at their very best. The unqualified phrase in the title of this essay—"Ethics and Politics"—points to that universal aspect, to the idea of an ethics proper to man as such and to the political ordering appropriate to that ethics. But the qualification—"The American Way"—reminds that ethics and politics always and everywhere form a particular relationship, a distinctive way in which each people organizes its humanness. The whole title together indicates the intention of this essay: while taking our bearings from the universal relationship of ethics and politics, we will examine the special "American way" in which ethics and politics are related to each other here.

I

The "American way of life" is a familiar phrase that nicely captures the notion that the relationship of ethics and politics has everywhere a unique manifestation. Yet familiar as the phrase is to us, we Americans characteristically overlook that notion when we think about ethics and politics. Instead, more than most other people, we tend to consider the relationship of ethics and politics in universal terms. Perhaps this is because we have been shaped to such a great extent by the principles of the Declaration of Independence, which of course addresses itself to all mankind and conceives political life in terms of rights to which all men are by nature entitled. Our tendency to understand moral principles in universal terms may also be furthered by the lingering influence of the Biblical heritage, which

The author wishes to express his thanks to the Woodrow Wilson International Center for Scholars and to the National Humanities Institute of Yale University whose generous support he enjoyed while this essay was being written.

lays down moral principles applicable to all men in all countries. To the extent that Americans continue to be guided by the Biblical outlook, their disposition to understand the relationship between ethics and politics in universal terms is reinforced. This propensity is perhaps also furthered by a tendency of democracy described by Tocqueville. He observed that democratic people, because of their extreme love of equality, tend to abstract from human differences and thus to think of man with a capital *M*—that is to say, in generic terms—rather than in terms of the many subtle gradations of human experience. Whatever the reasons, the familiar fact is that Americans generally think about politics in terms of a universal morality and, therefore, to view the relationship of ethics and politics almost exclusively in its universal aspect.

Oddly enough, in always thinking about ethics and politics in terms applicable to all men everywhere, we have in fact narrowed the idea of ethics. Today we think of ethics, not in the broad sense in which it was understood by classical political philosophy, but rather in the much narrower sense now conveyed by the word *morality*. Our word *morality* was originally derived from Cicero's Latin rendering of the Greek word for ethics, but it gradually acquired a quite different and narrower meaning. We think of ethics or morality today primarily in the limited, negative sense of "thou shall nots," as Puritanical or Victorian "no-no's." Ethics or morality thus narrowed down to a number of prohibitions has indeed a universal status; all men *are* under the same obligation not to murder, steal, bear false witness, and the like. Since morality thus conceived applies to all men as men, all regimes are deemed as obliged to honor it; hence the relationship of ethics and politics comes to be seen only in its universal aspect. The same narrowing effect on the idea of ethics is also produced by the modern theory of natural rights. That is, in this view of civil society, the politically relevant aspect of morality or ethics is similarly reduced to negative prohibitions on what governments and men may do. And this narrowing also has the effect of making political morality universally obligatory in the same way upon all regimes.

But morality thus universally conceived hampers our understanding of the particular relationship of ethics and politics within each political order or regime. To recover this understanding and apply it to the American case, we have to recapture something of the original broad meaning of ethics as it presented itself in classic Greek political philosophy. For that purpose Aristotle's *Ethics* will suffice.

Aristotle deals of course with such universal prohibitions as those against murder, theft, and lying. However, Aristotle's understanding of ethics is not chiefly concerned with such prohibitions, but, much more importantly, with positive human excellences or virtues in the broadest sense. Notice well: excellences or virtues. Aristotle's word *arete* is usually and properly translated as *virtue*. But because the word *virtue* is now understood in the same narrow and negative sense as morality, it is important to associate with it the positive word, excellence, in order to bring out the positive implications of Aristotle's ethical teaching.

For example, the very first virtue that Aristotle discusses is courage; while late in his discussion he includes as a minor ethical virtue or excellence the quality of affability. Today we would hardly consider either courage (as Aristotle meant it, namely, the kind demanded in military combat) or affability as belonging to a discussion of virtue or morality. They might be regarded as useful or even admirable qualities, but surely not as virtuous or moral qualities; they simply do not fit our modern conception. In contrast to our narrow view, Aristotle meant by the virtues all those qualities required for the full development of humanness, that is, all those qualities that comprise the health or completion of human character. This is the key: the very word *ethics* literally meant *character* to the Greeks, and the idea of character formation is the foundation of the ancient idea of ethics. When ethics is thus understood as being concerned with the formation and perfection of human character, we may more readily understand not only why ethics and politics have a universal relationship proper to man as man, but also why a unique relationship between ethics and politics is necessarily formed within each particular political order.

This necessity is made clearer by reference to a Greek word that is still familiar to us in the English use we make of it—namely, *ethos*; indeed, this is the Greek word from which our word *ethics* derives. A given pattern of ethics forms, as it were, an *ethos*. Like the Greeks, we still mean by ethos that a group or other entity possesses certain fundamental features that form its distinctive character. Something like this is what we mean when we speak, say, of "the ethos of Chaplin's films" or "the ethos of poverty." Ethics understood in this old, broad sense, as forming an ethos, helps to make clear why there is a distinctive relationship of ethics and politics in every regime. In all political communities, humanity manifests itself in some particular way, in the formation of a distinctive character or characters.

It is the distinctive human types nurtured in each regime that manifest the ethos of that regime. This is not, of course, to say that any such community is formed of identical human types; much human variety can be found in any complex society. But still we know that something is at work that makes a certain kind of human character more likely to occur in one setting and among one people, rather than another. We would be surprised, for example, to find Cotton Mather fully formed and flourishing in the Berlin of the 1920s. We would be surprised to find a full-fledged, homegrown Oscar Wilde in old Dodge City. It is likewise most unlikely that George Babbitt would have turned up in the early Roman republic; he belongs to Zenith, the fastest growing town in the Middle West. Such distinctive human characters are the nurture of a particular *ethos*, so to speak.

How can we account for the fact that each country forms its own peculiar ethos? We know that differing physical circumstances have something to do with the matter. The character of a people permanently settled on rich agricultural land and earning its living by farming will differ from that of a tribe of desert nomads who eke out an uncertain existence from their flocks and herds as they move from oasis to oasis. Each people will tend by virtue of its circumstances to value different human qualities and to nurture them. Technological development, "modes of production," and other such factors all have similar effects in the production of modal human types. But greater than the effect of all such material factors is the effect on human development of mores and laws, that is, of the political order or the regime. The difference of human characters in the various regimes is above all the product of the distinctive relationship between ethics and politics within each regime. Each political regime is, so to speak, in the business of handicrafting distinctive human characters. Indeed, each political order is literally constituted by the kind of human character it aims at and tends to form.

We may explore the meaning of this by considering Aristotle's well-known argument regarding the way political communities come into being. The lesser forms of human association—the family, tribe, and village—do not suffice for the fulfillment of man's nature; for that purpose, Aristotle argues, the form of human association must reach to the level of the *polis*, the political community. This is because the prepolitical associations serve largely for the mere preservation of life; they correspond in some respects to the hives or herds through which other social animals, such as bees and elephants, preserve themselves. These primary and rudimentary associations are adequate for bees and elephants because mere preservation of life is all that their beings require.

But the full development of man's being requires something more. He has an ethical need, a need that follows from his possession of *logos*, his unique faculty for speaking-reasoning, the faculty that defines man and distinguishes him from all other creatures. It is this faculty that enables and impels man to ponder "the advantageous and the harmful, and therefore also the just and the unjust."[1] Man's ethical need consists precisely in his capacity to reason out a view of the "advantageous and the just" and to organize his character and his life upon that basis. Because of this inherent capacity, this need for the formation of his full human character, man is ultimately impelled toward the formation of the polis. The subpolitical associations of the family, the tribe, and the village do not form a sufficient habitat for the full development of humanness. The polis is then, above all, understood by Aristotle as an association for the formation of character. It is a partnership within which the character of citizens is formed in accordance with some shared view of "the advantageous and the harmful" for man.

From this it followed for Aristotle that the very best polis would be that one partnership which, because it was based on the true view of what is "advantageous and just," would generate the highest human character. This idea of the "best regime" in which the best human character would be formed represents the Aristotelian understanding of the universal aspect of the relationship between ethics and politics. In this Aristotle differs, of course, from the modern approach which, as we have seen, makes the universal aspect of the ethics-politics relationship that which can be demanded and actualized everywhere. In contrast, the ancient approach was paradigmatic only; the universal aspect for Aristotle consists in a model of the one best character-forming regime, a model that serves as a standard for understanding and dealing with the enormous variety of actual, imperfect character-forming regimes. As measured against that model of the best regime, all other regimes would be understood as based on varyingly imperfect views of what is advantageous and just, and all would differ accordingly in the human characters they produced. In this particular regime, courage would be nurtured to

---

[1] Aristotle, *Politics*, 1253a15 et seq. The translation here, and elsewhere in this essay, is that of Professor Lawrence Berns, who has kindly given permission to quote from a translation of the *Politics* that he is now preparing.

a fault, there piety, here the love of honor, there domination, here commercial daring, and so forth through all the shadings and combinations of the possible human qualities. This is the exact sense in which it may be said that each polis actualized human character in a particular way and hence that in each polis there is a unique relationship of ethics and politics.

On the basis of this analysis of the polis as a character-forming association, Aristotle might well have denied that most contemporary "states" are genuine political communities. In any event, he does explicitly deny the status of political community to certain aggregations of people whose arrangements sound suspiciously like our own. That is, he explicitly characterizes as subpolitical those mere alliances or contractual arrangements for the sake of commerce, and even those arrangements that, somewhat more broadly, seek to prevent fellow residents from being "unjust to one another." Societies based on such arrangements may have a thriving commerce, life in them may be secure and tranquil, and they might appear to Americans to be adequate political societies. But for Aristotle they still would lack the crucial political desideratum—namely, a "concern with what the qualities of the others are," that is, a concern for the development among fellow citizens of certain common ethical excellences and hence a common character.[2]

For Aristotle, the formation of this common character is what makes an association political, and the question of how these character-forming ethical excellences are to be developed in man is what links ethics and politics. Indeed, this is literally the link between Aristotle's two great practical works, the *Ethics* and the *Politics*.[3] At the end of the *Ethics*, when he has finished his account of the excellences that perfect the human character, Aristotle says that it will now be necessary to turn to the study of politics. This is because human nature does not find it readily pleasant to acquire and persist in the character-forming excellences. To say the least, the idea of the good is not of itself sufficiently compelling to regulate behavior. Hence men will not be perfected merely by precept and exhortation, and not even by paternal authority. Human character, Aristotle argues, can be perfected only within a comprehensive system of character-forming conditions and constraints—in short, within the political community. Only within the political community, and through what it alone can supply, namely, good laws "with teeth

2 Ibid., 1280a34 et seq.
3 Aristotle, *Ethics*, 179a33 et seq. (Loeb Classical Library ed.).

in them," can men in fact raise their characters above the merely necessitous life, or above a life of mere passional indulgence.

In the ancient view, then, politica! life had the immensely important ethical function of providing the way through which man could complete or perfect this humanness. No wonder then that the laws, by means of which human character was to be formed, had to have teeth in them. So comprehensive and elevated an end made extraordinarily strenuous demands upon the political art. The classical political teaching took its bearings from the highest potentialities of human nature. Making no egalitarian presuppositions, it did not believe that all human beings or, indeed, even most human beings, could be perfected. But it thought it right and necessary that every resource of the political art be employed to realize the highest potential of the few, while providing as just a political order as was possible for those many others whose potentialities or circumstances precluded the highest development. This helps us to understand something of the harsh demands of the classical teaching: the general sternness of the laws; the emphasis placed on rigorous and comprehensive programs of education; the strict regulation of much that we now deem "private"; the necessity of civic piety; the extremely limited size of the polis; and the severe restrictions on private economic activity. These and other stern and strenuous measures were necessitated by the height of the human excellence that the classic political teaching sought to produce. An unceasingly demanding and powerful political art was required if men were to be raised so high against the downward pulls of ease, creature comfort, and the lower pleasures.

II

In the light of all the foregoing, how might Aristotle rank America? Would he characterize it as a genuine political community, one with its own special moral foundation, or only as "an association of place and of not acting unjustly to one another and for the sake of trade"? Would he find it a place where law is only "a compact, just as Lycophron the Sophist said, a guarantor for one another of the just things, but not able to make the citizens good and just,"[4]—that is, good and just in the way their characters were formed and not merely in conformity to a compact? Or might he conclude that there

4 *Politics*, 1280b10 et seq.

is indeed an American political ethos, a unique character-forming mix of ethics and politics? In short, is there an "American way" by which this republic nurtures in its citizens certain ethical excellences upon the basis of some particular view of what is advantageous and just?

If the answer proves to be that somehow America is an authentic political community, that there is in fact an "American way" of political-ethical character formation, it will surely not be in the classical way but in a distinctively modern way. This is because America was formed on the basis of that modern political thought that waged so successful a war against the political outlook of antiquity. The classical understanding of the proper relationship between ethics and politics dominated the Western world for nearly two millennia, as did classical political philosophy generally, albeit modified by Christianity. But the great traditions of classical and Christian political philosophy came under trenchant attack during the sixteenth and seventeenth centuries by such political philosophers as Machiavelli, Bacon, Hobbes, and Locke.[5] These proponents of a "new science of politics" charged that classical and Christian political philosophy had been both misguided and ineffective, in a word, "utopian." They observed that, during some two thousand years of this elevated political and religious teaching, man's lot on this earth had remained miserable; his estate had not been relieved. Greed and vainglory ruled under the guise of virtue or piety, and the religious tyrannies and wars of the sixteenth and seventeenth centuries had but climaxed two millennia of the failure of the old, utopian political science.

Blaming classical and medieval thought for adhering to dangerous illusions regarding the way men *ought* to live, that is, for trying to shape human character by misleading and unachievable standards of perfection, the new, or modern, political philosophers purported to base their views and recommendations upon the character of man "as he actually *is*." In place of the lofty and seemingly unrealistic virtues demanded by classical and Christian political philosophy, the moderns accepted as irremediably dominant in human nature the self-interestedness and passions displayed by men everywhere. But precisely on that realistic basis, they argued, workable solutions

[5] Acknowledgment is gladly made of my indebtedness here and throughout to the late Professor Leo Strauss, whose instructive account of the "battle of the books," ancient and modern, has done so much to restore the meaning of the modern enterprise and to renew our grasp of the ancient alternative.

could at last be found to hitherto unresolved political problems. This meant, as opposed to ancient and medieval exhortation and compulsion of man to high virtue, a lowering of the aims and expectations of political life, perhaps of human life generally. As it were, the new political science gave a primacy to the efficacy of means rather than to the nobility of ends: The ends of political life were reduced to a commensurability with the human means readily and universally available. In place of the utopian end postulated by the ancients, the forced elevation of human character, the moderns substituted a lowered political end, namely, human comfort and security. This lowered end was more realistic, they argued, because it could be achieved by taking human character much as actually found everywhere, or by molding it on a less demanding model than that of the premodern understanding.

This removal of the task of character formation from its previously preeminent place on the agenda of politics had an immense consequence for the relationship of ethics and politics in modern regimes. The hallmark of the traditional ethics-politics relationship had been those harsh and comprehensive laws by means of which the ancient philosophers had sought to "high-tone" human character. But now, because character formation was no longer the direct end of politics, the new science of politics could dispense with those laws and, for the achievement of its lowered ends, could rely largely instead upon shrewd institutional arrangements of the powerful human passions and interests. Not to instruct and to transcend these passions and interests, but rather to channel and to use them became the hallmark of modern politics. Politics could now concentrate upon the "realistic" task of directing man's passions and interests toward the achievement of those solid goods this earth has to offer: self-preservation and the protection of those individual liberties which are an integral part of that preservation and which make it decent and agreeable.

One has only to call to mind the Declaration of Independence to see that such commodious self-preservation and its corollary individual liberties came to be viewed as the sole legitimate objects of government. In short, whatever the modern perspective may leave of the traditional lofty virtues for men to seek in their private capacities, it drastically reduces or limits the legitimate scope of government. Indeed, the very idea of *government*—as distinguished from the old, more encompassing idea of *polity* or *regime*—was a response to this restriction in the scope of the political. In the old, broader view, "government" was inextricably linked with "society." Since it was the task of the laws to create a way of life or to nurture among citizens certain qualities of character, then the laws necessarily had to penetrate every aspect of a community's life; there could be no separation of state or government and society, and no limitation of the former with respect to the latter. But under the new liberal doctrine, with its substantive withdrawal of the character-forming function from the domain of the political, it became natural to think of state and society as separated, and of government as limited to the protection of individual life, liberty, property, and the private pursuit of happiness. It became both possible and reasonable to depoliticize political life as previously conceived, and that is precisely what happened wherever the new view came to prevail. Perhaps above all, religion was depoliticized; belief and practice regarding the gods, which classical political philosophy had held to be centrally within the purview of the political community, was largely relegated to private discretion. Similarly depoliticized were many other traditional political matters such as education, poetry and the arts, family mores, and many of the activities we now lump under the term "economics." In the premodern understanding, these were precisely the matters that had to be regulated by "laws with teeth in them," because they were the essential means by which a regime could form human characters in its own particular mold.

With the removal or reduction from political life of what had for two thousand years been regarded as its chief function, namely, ethical character formation based on some elevated view of the "advantageous and just," what, then, became that chief function of politics in the new understanding? A striking and explicit answer to this question is to be found in James Madison's *Federalist* 10, perhaps the most remarkable single American expression of the "improved" or new science of politics. At the end of the famous paragraph in which he argues that the latent causes of faction are ineradicably sown in human nature, Madison sketches the "most common and durable" of those ineradicable causes, namely, the diversity of economic interests. He then states one of the most important conclusions of his essay: "The regulation of these various and interfering interests forms the principal task of modern legislation and involves the spirit of party and faction in the necessary and ordinary operations of government." Notice: "the principal task of *modern* legislation"; Madison is acutely aware of the modernity of his political analyses and solutions. He does not tell us what the premodern principal task was, and we may not put words in his mouth; but we will see how his principal modern task becomes intelligible precisely when contradistinguished from the principal task of the premodern political art as that has been presented in this essay. Bringing that modern task clearly to light may teach us something about the "American way" regarding the relationship of ethics and politics.

III

Madison announces his theoretical intention: "To secure the public good and private rights . . . and at the same time to preserve the spirit and form of popular government, is then the great object to which our inquiries are directed." Only by a showing that popular government can now avoid committing those injuries to the public good and private rights, which have hitherto proved its undoing, can this form of government "be rescued from the opprobrium under which it has so long labored." Taken as a whole, then, James Madison's "inquiries" provide a comprehensive statement of the way political science should address the pathology of democracy. In *Federalist* 10, Madison outlines that part of his political science upon the basis of which the gravest imperfection of popular government may be guarded against, namely, the propensity of that form of government to "the violence of faction." In examining his argument regarding the problem of faction, we want to pay particular attention to the way Madison deals with the problem of *opinion*. It is through Madison's discussion of the nature of opinion in general and its particular status in American political life, that we will learn most about what is uniquely modern in that "principal task of modern legislation."

Madison argues that all earlier democracies have "been spectacles of turbulence and contention . . . as short in their lives as they have been violent in their deaths." This was because, as he observes in *Federalist* 14, all earlier democracies had been too small in scale; they had been founded on "the error which limits republican government to a narrow district." Built on the scale of the ancient polis, these republics had been utterly unable to deal with the pathogenic element of democracy, namely, majority faction. Madison's novel but now familiar conclusion was that the hitherto fatal effects of majority factiousness could be controlled only in a republic organized on a sufficiently large scale. In the course of this general argument, Madison is obliged to analyze in detail the various causes of faction, and it is this detailed analysis that brings to the fore his treatment of the problem of opinion.

Madison's first step is to identify the nature of faction. The precise statement of the elements that constitute faction prepares the way, first, for his diagnosis of how different kinds of faction come into being and, later, for his novel solution to the problem. Here is his famous definition: "a number of citizens, whether amounting to a majority or minority of the whole, who are united and actuated by some common impulse of passion, or of interest, adverse to the rights of other citizens, or to the permanent and aggregate interests of the community." We must notice the twofold "normative" character of this definition. The generating impulse to faction is dubious or low; faction is "united and actuated" by passion or interest and not by reason. But this is not enough to denominate a group a faction. After all, not every passion or interest need impel toward policies inimical to society; although motivated by passion or interest, a group might yet seek policies that are perfectly compatible with the rights of others and the interests of the community. It is therefore further necessary that a group be following an oppressive or dangerous course of action. But this is to say in effect, as indeed becomes explicit in the very next step in the argument, that the group is possessed of an oppressive or dangerous opinion. From his definition, then, Madison's task becomes clear: to show how the conjunction of a "common impulse" of passion or interest and an "adverse" opinion in a majority may be averted or rendered unlikely.

Madison turns to the ways this may be done. "There are two methods of curing the mischiefs of faction: the one, by removing its causes; the other by controlling its effects." As to removing the causes, Madison says that there are likewise two possibilities. The first, which is to destroy the liberty essential to the existence of factions, Madison quickly rejects as a remedy worse than the disease. He then examines at length, as we must also, the remaining possible way to remove the causes of faction, which is to give to "every citizen the same opinions, the same passions, and the same interests." Opinion, passion, and interest: Madison's comprehensive theoretical statement of the causes of faction; these are the three independent generating sources of factional behavior. If all citizens have the same impulse of passion or interest, they would have no motivation to divide into oppressive or dangerous factions. And whatever the status of the passional or interested motivations, if all citizens were agreed on the same opinions, there could be no oppressive or danger-ous division of the society with respect to public policy. Unanimity of impulse and opinion would of necessity extinguish the possibility of faction.

But Madison, of course, proceeds to demonstrate that such una-nimity of opinion, passion, and interest is utterly "impracticable." He deals first with the irreducible diversity of opinion. "As long as the reason of man continues fallible, and he is at liberty to exercise it, different opinions will be formed." Notice: self-originated, self-formed opinion; opinion, so to speak, is an independent variable. That is to say, these are *not* opinions whose content is determined by underlying causes—not opinions as mere rationalization of un-derlying passion or interest, as we now typically conceive opinions to be—but rather opinions whose content is determined by the *autonomous operation of the opining faculty itself*. Thus, quite apart from the diversity or uniformity of the human passions and interests, political opinions will inevitably vary, simply as a function of man's fallible reasoning, or opining, faculty and his natural need to exercise it on political subjects. In this respect we may say that Madison is at one with Aristotle in recognizing the power and autonomy of the speaking-reasoning or opining capacity of man. But as to what should be done with that capacity, the difference be-tween them, as we shall see, is the difference between modernity and antiquity.

Having demonstrated that all men cannot be given the same opinions, Madison proceeds to demonstrate that the passions and interests of mankind likewise cannot be reduced to uniformity; like opinion, they irremovably exert a divisive factious influence upon political behavior. The details of his argument need not detain us. It suffices here simply to state the conclusion Madison reaches at this stage of his argument: The problem of faction cannot be solved by removing its causes because "the latent causes of faction are ... sown in the nature of man."

Still, this is no cause for despair because there remains the pos-sibility of "controlling the effects of faction." Madison reminds us that, while the latent causes of faction are ineradicably universal, particular factions are "brought into different degrees of activity according to the different circumstances of civil society." Which kinds of factions will be brought into a high degree of "activity" and which into a low degree all depends on the circumstances of the par-

ticular society. It is in the manipulation of these "different circumstances" that Madison's novel prescription of a "cure" is to be found.
By such circumstances Madison clearly includes the extent or scale
of the political community and the constitutional structure and
processes of government, and also apparently such things as the kind
of economy to be fostered and the beliefs citizens are encouraged to
hold. All such circumstances affect the operation of the universal
"latent causes of faction" and thereby determine what the actual
pattern of factionalism will be in any given society.

It is with precisely these circumstances that founders must deal.
Armed with the proper science of politics, a founder can choose what
kinds of factions to avoid and, since factionalism is inevitable, what
kinds to encourage. Accordingly, in order to discover how to do
the avoiding and encouraging, Madison elaborates his threefold
typology of factions. He again deals first with man's natural inclination to opining, that is, with his "zeal for different opinions concerning religion, concerning government, and many other points,
as well of speculation as of practice." These opinions, to repeat, are
not merely rationalizations of prior passion or interest, but rather
are the autonomous product of the high human need and capacity
to opine about such elevated matters as, say, what is advantageous
and just. Now, Aristotelian political science, as we noted earlier,
takes its bearing from just this high human capacity. From the
classic perspective, *the* political task is to refine and improve a regime's opinion of what is advantageous and just and to help thereby to improve the human characters formed by that regime. But
Madison instead turns away almost in horror from the human "zeal
for different opinions concerning religion, concerning government."[6] He is only too aware that such opining has rendered mankind "much more disposed to vex and oppress each other than to
co-operate for their common good." From the perspective of the
new political science, it is apparently too risky to rely on refining and
improving a society's opinions. The statesmanly task, rather, is to
mute as much as possible the force of religious and political opining
as a cause of faction. Such opinion is not so much to be improved

6 As Douglass Adair's essay on Hume and Madison has shown, further light on
Madison's view of factionalism may be sought in Hume's essay "Of Parties in
General." Hume warns against "parties from principle, especially abstract speculative principle," and warns also that "in modern times parties of religion are
more furious and enraged than the most cruel factions that ever arose from interest and ambition." Hume suggests that interest-based faction, low though
it may be, is less cruel than faction based on principle or opinion.

as tamed or devitalized. If America is to avoid the "violence of faction" that commonly destroyed earlier popular governments, "circumstances" must be so arranged that factionalism deriving from the operation of opinion must not reach to a high "degree of activity."

Madison comes to a similar conclusion regarding factions that derive directly from the human passions. These are factions caused by "an attachment to different leaders ambitiously contending for pre-eminence and power; or to persons of other descriptions whose fortunes have been interesting to the human passions." Notice that these are not the factional passions that build up around a preexisting interest or opinion; that happens commonly enough. Rather, Madison is talking here about those factions that have their genesis directly and solely in the passions themselves. He is talking about passion as an "independent variable," just as he treated opinion as such and will shortly be seen to treat "interest" in the same manner. Moreover, he is not talking about the whole range of human passions that affect political behavior. He is talking here only about that single specific passion that by itself can be the direct cause of a faction. He means that particular passion—empathy is a useful word to recall here—by force of which humans have a natural political readiness to love and hate, a kind of spiritedness that is evoked by, or reaches out to, exceptional leaders. By force of this passion, masses of men, without any reason of interest or opinion, simply are "turned on" by dazzlingly attractive leaders.

The attachments based on such loves and hates are by no means contemptible; indeed, they may well be the means by which great virtues—courage, eloquence, rectitude, wisdom—communicate their political force and charm to human beings who might otherwise never be drawn upward to such qualities of character. Nevertheless, Madison concludes that on balance such attachments are too dangerous; they generate factions that torment and destroy society and hence must somehow be avoided. What Madison is in effect saying is: no Savonarolas or Cromwells or extraordinarily "interesting" figures, thank you; what is wanted generally are men of lesser but safer political ambition and religious appeal. The thrust of the American political order must be somehow to diminish the readiness of ordinary Americans to respond to leaders who generate faction, as it were, simply out of their own "charisma."

The bold and novel requirement of Madison's political science and of the American political order, then, is to mute or attenuate the age-old kinds of political behavior that derive from two of the fundamental causes of faction. But there is also the political behavior that derives from the third fundamental cause of faction, namely, interest: "the most common and durable source of factions has been the various and unequal distribution of property." Madison is far from seeking to diminish the efficacy of this cause, as he is of the other two. On the contrary, his intention is precisely the opposite: He wishes to magnify its operation, because therein lies the new cure of the "mischiefs of faction." To anticipate the conclusion of his argument: if Americans can be made to divide themselves according to their narrow and particularized economic interests, they will avoid the fatal factionalism that opinion and passion generate. By contrast, the relatively tranquil kind of factionalism resulting from economic interests makes possible a stable and decent democracy. But this does not mean economic-based faction in general. Madison distinguishes between two kinds of economic faction, one resulting from the "unequal distribution of property" and one from its various distribution. Faction based on property inequality, like faction based on opinion and passion, also leads to the fatal factionalism that destroyed earlier popular governments— specifically, to the perennial struggle of the many poor with the few rich, fighting under the banners of grandly conflicting ideas of justice. The American polity looks to replace this struggle over the *inequality* of property by causing to flourish a new kind of economic faction derived from the *variety* of property. It is on this basis that there can arise a tranquil, modern politics of interest groups, as distinct from a politics of class struggle. This is the meaning and intention of Madison's famous "multiplicity of interests" and of democratic government based upon the "coalition[s] of a majority" that rise out of that multiplicity.

But whence derives the "multiplicity" that makes it all possible? What are the civil "circumstances" that bring the right kind of economic-based faction into a high "degree of activity"? This new, salutary multiplicity of economic factions is uniquely the product of a large modern commercial society. For millennia the mass of men had been poor in but a handful of ways, toilers little differentiated in their class-poverty by the ways they eked out their existences; the rich likewise have gained their wealth in but a handful of ways that little differentiated their common oligarchic impulses and interests. Only the modern commercial spirit flourishing in a large, complex, modern economy can supply the faction-differentiating division of labor and the great economic diversity that directs the attention of all to the moderating private pursuit of individual economic happiness.[7] "Extend the sphere" of a republic, Madison said, "and you take in a greater variety of parties and interests; you make it less probable that a majority of the whole will have a common motive to invade the rights of other citizens." But it is only in an extended *commercial* republic that men are thus moderatingly fragmented into that "greater variety" of economic activities from which alone develops the necessary variety of economic interests. In such a society men will tend to think in terms of their various immediate economic interests, that is, to think as members of an "interest group" rather than of a class or sect. They will then tend to form political opinions in defense of those interests, and then jockey frenetically, but ultimately tamely, for group and party advantage on the basis of those interests.

Madison's search for a solution to the democratic problem thus led him to envisage and help found the extended, commercial, democratic republic. Always before the politics of democracy had flowed naturally into the fatal factionalism deriving from opinion, passion, and class interest; the democratic mass of men had always turned to opinionated politics (or, as we might say now, to ideology) or to opinionated piety, or had followed some impassioning leader, or had fought the battle of the poor against the rich and had brought their democratic governments down in ruin. Employing the "new science of politics," Madison had discovered in "interest" its latent possibility, that is, a novel way of channeling the stream of politics away from these natural directions and toward that kind of factionalism with which a democracy could cope, namely, a politics of "various and interfering interests." Such is our political world— the modern world, the substratum of which consists of these narrowed, fragmented, unleashed interests—in which the "principal

7 Cf. Alexander Hamilton in *Federalist* 12 on how the "prosperity of commerce" entices and activates "human avarice and enterprise." But this leads to a result that Hamilton regards with satisfaction. "The assiduous merchant, the laborious husbandman, the active mechanic, and the industrious manufacturer— all orders of men look forward with eager expectation and growing alacrity to this pleasing reward of their toils." We will consider later a passage in Montesquieu, on a "democracy founded on commerce," which makes a similar point. And we will in that context suggest that the "avarice" of which Hamilton speaks may better be understood as "acquisitiveness."

task" does indeed become what Madison stated it to be: "The regulation of these various and interfering interests forms the principal task of modern legislation and involves the spirit of party and faction in the necessary and ordinary operations of government."

IV

The American political order was deliberately tilted to resist, so to speak, the upward gravitational pull of politics toward the grand, dramatic, character-ennobling but society-wracking opinions about justice and virtue. Opinion was now to be ballasted against its dangerous tendency toward destructive zealotry, or, to change the nautical figure, to be moored solidly in the principle of commodious self-preservation and economic self-interest. As much as possible, opinion was to be kept from reaching upward to broad considerations of the advantageous and the just by being made more nearly into a reflection of "the sentiments and views of the respective proprietors" of the various kinds of property. (Is this not precisely what came to be a distinctive aspect of opinion-formation in American political life—indeed, so much so that contemporary American political science has been beguiled, as it were, into forgetting what virile autonomous opinion is really like?) In thus seeking to tame opinion, Madison was following the general tendency of modern political thought to solve the problems of politics by reducing the scope of politics. As we saw earlier, by abstracting from politics the broad ethical function of character formation, modern political thought had begun a kind of depoliticizing of politics in general. Now Madison, as it were, depoliticized political opinion in particular.

Madison's strategy for solving the democratic problem of faction—not by trying to make opinion more disinterestedly virtuous but by reducing it to a safe reflection of diverse interests—helps to illuminate, and may be understood as part of the famous general policy of opposite and rival interests that Madison derived from the new science of politics. His general strategy for moderating democracy and thus making it commendable to the "esteem and adoption of mankind" is nowhere stated more thoughtfully, nor more chillingly, than in *Federalist* 51. He is explaining why the powers formally separated under the Constitution will remain so in practice, despite a despotizing tendency for them to become concentrated in one or another of the branches of government. "The great security against a gradual concentration of the several powers in the same department," he states, "consists in giving to those who administer each department the necessary constitutional means and personal motives to resist the encroachments of the others. Ambition must be made to counteract ambition. The interest of the man must be connected with the constitutional rights of the place." This all sounds sensible, even commonplace, to present-day Americans, who are habituated to the moral horizon of the American political system. But Madison was writing when the new science of politics was still unhackneyed, and he knew that there was something novel and shocking in his acceptance and counterpoised use of ambitious interest as the principal security for the public good; it smacked much of "private vice, public good."

He thus pauses immediately to apologize, in a way, for such a cool recommendation, admitting it to be "a reflection on human nature that such devices should be necessary," but justifying them as necessitated by the weakness of that nature. He then boldly and comprehensively states the general principle underlying such "devices": "This policy of supplying, by opposite and rival interests, the defect of better motives, might be traced through the whole system of human affairs, private as well as public." Restated very plainly, Madison is saying this: Human nature is such that there just are not enough "better motives" to go around, not enough citizens and politicians who will be animated by motives that rise above self-interestedness and the gratification of their own passions so as to get the work of government and society done. But again there is no reason for despair because we can "supply the defect," that is, make up for the insufficiency of "better motives" with "personal motives," that is, by means of a shrewdly arranged system of opposite and rival personal interests. We cannot here trace the "policy" through the whole system of the Constitution; it suffices for our purposes to return to the question of opinion and the problem of faction. As we saw in our analysis of *Federalist* 10, this "policy" was precisely the basis of the scheme whereby the "multiplicity of interests" solves the problem of faction. We may paraphrase Madison's language: the defect of better opinions is supplied by the system of "various and interfering interests."

Now, Aristotle and ancient political science had no illusions about the quantity of "better motives" available; Aristotle thought them to be in as short supply as is supposed by modern political thought. The difference between the ancients and the moderns consists in the way each addressed the problem of the "defect," and the costs of their respective solutions. For the ancients, since improving those motives—or virtues, we may say in this context—was the end of political life, there was no alternative but to try to increase or improve the stock of "better motives" or virtues. These virtues were not merely instrumental in achieving certain governmental or societal goals; they *were* the goals. Hence in the premodern perspective there was no way to conceive that the defect could be supplied by any substitute. But for modern political thought—because making the motives better, that is, forming the human excellences, was no longer the primary end of politics—a different prospect was opened. The chief political end had become commodious self-preservation, with the higher human matters left to the workings of society. It thus became possible to conceive of interested behavior as a general substitute for the too-hard-to-come-by "better motives."

With respect to the quality of opinion in particular, the answer is the same. For the ancients, since the opinions of society so decisively influence the character of citizens, the formation of which was the end of politics, there was no alternative but to arrange the polis so as to "high tone" the opinions of the citizens as much as possible in the circumstances. For the moderns, however, there is no such necessity; indeed, it is not too much to say that opinion must literally be toned down in order that democratic factionalism not rip society apart.

That raises the question of costs. The moderns say, and with some justification, that ancient and medieval political *practice* had not vindicated the high aims and claims of premodern *thought*; the cost of a political philosophy that aimed too high, we have heard them argue, was to perpetuate in practice a vast human misery. But what of the modern costs and, in particular, what of the cost of the "American way"?

In the public realm, as we saw regarding the separation of powers, Madison's policy condones and even encourages hitherto reprobated interests like self-serving political ambition. In the private realm of the "various and interfering interests," this policy not only accepts but also necessarily encourages perspectives and activities that had hitherto been ethically censored and politically constrained, namely, the aggressive private pursuit by all of immediate personal interests. The very qualities that the classical and Christian teachings had sought to subdue so that those with "better motives" could be brought to attain their full natural height, the new science of politics emancipates and actively employs. This means nothing less than to whet democratically the appetites of all, to emancipate acquisitiveness and its attendant qualities, and to create the matrix—the large commercial democratic republic—within which such appetites and acquisitive aims can be excited and sufficiently satisfied. Put bluntly, this means that in order to defuse the dangerous factional force of opinion, passion, and class interest, Madison's policy deliberately risks magnifying and multiplying in American life the selfish, the interested, the narrow, the vulgar, and the crassly economic. That is the substratum on which our political system was intended to rest and where it rests still. It is a cost of Madison's policy, the price to be paid in order to enjoy its many blessings.

From the point of view of the generality of mankind, the new policy delivered on its promises. In comparison with the premodern achievement, it raised to unprecedented heights the benefits, the freedom, and the dignity enjoyed by the great many. But the cost must be recognized, precisely in order to continue to enjoy the blessings. Again in comparison with the premodern perspective, that cost is the solid but low foundation of American political life. And *foundation* must be understood quite literally: American institutions rest upon it. Those who wish to improve American life—specifically, those who would improve the relationship between ethics and politics in America—must base such improvement upon the American foundation; and this means to come to terms with the "policy" that is an essential part of that foundation. Revolution or transformation, that is something else. But if the aim is improvement, it must be improvement that accepts the limits imposed by the "genius" of the particular political order; it must be improvement that makes America her better self, but still her own self.

Yet it is just this foundation that has baffled or immoderately repelled many contemporary students of American political life and history. This is the case with what is perhaps the most influential, and very likely the most widely read, scholarly statement on the American Founding, Richard Hofstadter's *The American Political Tradition.* Hofstadter's book is an especially revealing example of a work that cannot abide the Madisonian reliance upon, and deliberate encouragement of, the system of opposite and rival interests. By seeing that system in the light of Hofstadter's rejection of it, we will further our own effort to understand it. Perhaps we will enlarge our understanding of the American political order by seeing how it can be defended from Hofstadter's attack.

In the spirit of Charles Beard, Hofstadter admires the Founders' republican decency and "realism," but at the same time severely rebukes that realism because it antiquatedly restricts the moral possibilities of American democracy. The Founders, he claims, "did not believe in man." They had "a distrust of man [which] was first and foremost a distrust of the common man and democratic rule." Consequently, the political system they devised was aimed at "cribbing and confining the popular spirit." Notice that Hofstadter does not merely make an interpretive claim as to how the Constitution should be understood; most American disputation has been of that sort, a kind of "quarrel among the heirs" as to the precise meaning of the political heritage. Rather, Hofstadter challenges the worth of the heritage itself. He is not concerned with particular shortcomings in American institutions but with the foundation upon which the entire structure of American politics rests. In short, his criticism goes to the Founders' idea of human nature, of its possibilities and limitations with respect to human excellence. Thus Hofstadter's chapter on the Founders opens with a critical characterization of their idea of man as Calvinist in its sense of evil, and as Hobbesian in its view of man as selfish and contentious. The chapter closes with a long final paragraph that strongly condemns this idea of man and his ethical potential. It is a condemnation that is implicit in many other contemporary rejections of the American political-ethical presuppositions and rewards careful examination.

Hofstadter writes that "from a humanistic standpoint there is a serious dilemma in the philosophy of the Fathers, which derives from their conception of man." The dilemma is this: while the founders were not full-blooded Hobbesians, still they had not advanced sufficiently beyond Hobbes to be satisfactory from "a humanistic standpoint." They had at least advanced beyond Hobbes in that, while they accepted his view of man as murderously self-interested, "they were in no mood to follow Hobbes to his conclusion," namely, to the absolute Leviathan state that Hobbes deemed necessary to restrain natural, anarchic man. Rather, despite their Hobbesian view of man, the Founders nonetheless "wanted him to be free—free, in essence, to contend, to be engaged in an umpired strife." But such freedom, while an improvement on Hobbesian absolutism, is still unsatisfactory because it does not succeed in putting an end to "the Hobbesian war of each against all." Indeed, the Founders did not even have such an intention; they wanted "merely to stabilize it and make it less murderous." The crucial defect of the American Founding, then, is that the Founders "had no hope and they offered none for any ultimate organic change in the way men conduct themselves. The result was that while they thought self-interest the most dangerous and unbrookable quality of man, they necessarily underwrote it in trying to control it." And, Hofstadter continues, things have worked out exactly as the founders intended; the American political system has provided just the sort of "stable and acceptable medium" for "grasping and contending interests" that the founders had in mind.

Such a political system, and the ideas that shaped and inspirited it, cannot apparently be recommended from the "humanistic standpoint." Especially the Founders' chief idea, the idea of an unchanging human nature characterized by rapacious self-interestedness, is humanistically indefensible: "No man who is as well abreast of modern science as the Fathers were of eighteenth-century science believes any longer in unchanging human nature. Modern humanistic thinkers who seek for a means by which society may transcend eternal conflict and rigid adherence to property rights as its integrating principles can expect no answer in the philosophy of balanced government as it was set down by the Constitution-makers of 1787." The implications are unmistakably harsh: "Modern humanistic thinkers" must turn away from the American idea of man and the political system based on it; those who want society to "transcend eternal conflict" must look elsewhere if they are to achieve their humanistic goals.[8]

At first blush, one might think that Hofstadter reaches this conclusion from something akin to the Aristotelian perspective. Hofstadter says more or less accurately that, rather than expecting "that vice could be checked by virtue," the American founders "relied instead upon checking vice with vice." This might suggest that Hofstadter takes his stand with the ancients in accepting the tension in human nature between virtue and vice and that he prefers, along with them, to make the difficult effort to help virtue to prevail over

[8] To "transcend eternal conflict" means to end it, which means to solve all those human problems that have hitherto led to conflict. This is not humanism but utopianism, and it must not be permitted that humanism should thus be subsumed under the utopian perspective. Rather, it may be suggested, humanism means precisely to recognize as perennial those human sources of conflict and to face them reflectively and nobly.

vice. But Hofstadter in fact sees no intrinsic difficulty in causing virtue to triumph, and this reveals how much he differs from both the ancients and an early modern thinker like Madison.

Both Aristotle and Madison agree that political life confronts a fundamental and ineradicable difficulty: human nature is unchanging, and there is a shortage in it of virtue or the "better motives." As we have seen, they disagree over what to do about this perennial difficulty; Aristotle sees in politics the necessity to "high tone" virtue as much as possible in any given circumstances, while Madison chooses the moderating system of opposite and rival interests. But against both of them Hofstadter believes that the perennial "defect" of virtue can simply be overcome by an "organic change" in human nature, which is promised in an unspecified way by "modern science." Hofstadter's entire criticism of the American Founding rests upon his apparent certainty that it is going to be possible "to change the nature of man to conform with a more ideal system." On the basis of what can only be called this utopian expectation, Hofstadter rejects both the Aristotelian and Madisonian views. Or, rather, one might speculate that he implicitly combines them, heedless of their irreconcilabilities. He seems to take from the Aristotelian enterprise something of the elevation to which virtue is thought capable of reaching but strips it of its corollary severity and inegalitarianism; and this "high toned" expectation regarding virtue he apparently combines with the democracy and commodious well-being of Madison's enterprise, but strips it of *its* corollary, the foundation in the system of opposite and rival interests. Such complacent synthesizing or combining of irreconcilables is the hallmark of contemporary utopianism.

V

Hofstadter's characterization of the Founders' view of human nature, and of its potential for virtue, is of course not without justification. The political science of the American Founding does indeed have roots in the new political science of Hobbes, and it does seek to "check interest with interest . . . [and] faction with faction." And if that were the whole story—if Madison's "policy" were all that there is to the American political order, and all that there is to his political science—it would be difficult to defend the Founding from Hofstadter's harsh conclusions. We might still have to opt for Madison's apparently amoral "policy" against Hofstadter's utopian alternative, but it would be a most melancholy choice. Or to state this in a way that returns us to our main concerns: if this were all there is to the American political order, we might well have to conclude that, judging by Aristotelian standards, America is not a genuine political community. That is, in the light only of what we have said about the Madisonian foundation, America would seem to be little more than a clever new social arrangement, "an association of place and of not acting unjustly to one another, and for the sake of trade" among fellow residents, but not a regime that forms a common character among fellow citizens. Yet we all know in our bones that somehow there is more to the "American way" than that, that somehow we are fellow citizens within a political order, but one of a special kind. Whether what we feel in our bones is truly so is what we must now consider.

Since a regime reveals itself in the characters it forms, we must consider the American virtues or excellences, that is to say, the particular kind of human character formed among Americans. Now, the interesting thing is that however much we are not a regime in the ordinarily recognizable Aristotelian sense, we are emphatically so in one regard: We form a distinctive being, the American, as recognizably distinctive a human product as that of perhaps any regime in history. Something here turns out humanness in a peculiar American shape. What are those American virtues or excellences and how are they generated? While never forgetting its mooring in the Madisonian base, we may now consider briefly the height to which the formation of character in America reaches. This means, of course, to conclude our consideration of the particular American relationship of ethics and politics.

While the American Founders turned away from the classic enterprise regarding virtue, they did not thereby abandon the pursuit of virtue or excellence in all other possible ways. In fact, the American political order rises respectably high enough above the vulgar level of mere self-interest in the direction of virtue—if not to the highest reaches of the ancient perspective, still toward positive human decencies or excellences. Indeed, the prospect of excellences is opened up even within the very commercial interests, the unleashing of which is requisite to Madison's scheme. To see this, it is necessary to distinguish greed, or avarice, on the one hand, and acquisitiveness, on the other. The commercial society unleashes acquisitiveness; but this is by no means the same thing as to give vent to the avarice or covetousness that, traditionally, all philosophies and religious creeds have condemned. Both modern acquisitiveness and traditional avarice have perhaps the same source, namely, the desire, even an inordinate desire, for bodily things. But, as the roots of the two words suggest, in age-old avarice the emphasis is on the passion of *having*, whereas in modern acquisitiveness the emphasis is on the *getting*. Avarice is a passion centered on the things themselves, a narrow clutching to one's self of money or possessions; it has no built-in need for any limitation of itself, no need for moderation or for the cultivation of any virtues as instrumental to the satisfaction of the avaricious passion. But acquisitiveness teaches a form of moderation to the desiring passions from which it derives, because to acquire is not primarily to have and to hold but to get and to earn, and, moreover, to earn justly, at least to the extent that the acquisition must be the fruit of one's own exertions or qualities. This requires the acquisitive man to cultivate certain excellences, minimal ones perhaps from the classical perspective, but excellences nonetheless, as means to achieve his ends. He wants enlargement and increase and these require of him at least venturesomeness, and hard work, and the ability to still his immediate passions so as to allow time for the ripening of his acquisitive plans and measures. In short, acquisitive man, unlike avaricious man, is likely to have what we call the bourgeois virtues.

It is in this context that we must understand Hamilton's observation that a commercial society nurtures "the assiduous merchant, the laborious husbandman, the active mechanic, and the industrious manufacturer." Avarice, strictly understood, has no such salutary effects; acquisitiveness does. And it is not only excellences like assiduity, labor, activity, and industry that a commercial society nurtures. "Honesty is the best policy" is not acceptable prudence to the avaricious man, but it is almost natural law to the "assiduous merchant." Acquisitiveness may not be the highest motive for honesty, but if it produces something like the habit of honesty in great numbers, is not that a prodigious accomplishment? Similarly, the notion that "it takes money to make money," a maxim familiar to the acquisitive man, bears at least a relation to the ancient virtue of liberality; but the avaricious man simply cannot let loose his money to the extent that the commercial principle makes common practice. Scrooge was surely not less successful as a merchant after he acquired the liberal spirit of Christmas; indeed, the old Scrooge belonged to an older world of avarice, while the new Scrooge would perhaps be more at home in a modern commercial society. Finally, the acquisitive man is plunged by his passion into the give-and-take of society and must thus learn to accommodate himself to the interests of others. In this he is at least pointed toward something like justice. But the avaricious man is drawn by his passion wholly within the confines of his own narrow soul.

When Madison's "policy of opposite and rival interests" is understood in the light of this distinction between avarice and acquisitiveness, we can begin to see the ground for some of the excellences we all know to be characteristic of American life. We can then avoid thinking, as many have, that the vice of avarice peculiarly flourishes in America. On the contrary, we can claim that avarice here is peculiarly blunted by the supervening force of acquisitiveness and its attendant valuable qualities. No one understood this possibility more profoundly than Montesquieu, who argued that "frugality, economy, moderation, labor, prudence, tranquility, order, and rule" are virtues or excellences that are naturally generated in a "democracy founded on commerce."[9] These may be put down as merely "bourgeois virtues," but they are virtues, or human excellences, nonetheless. They reach at least to decency if not to nobility; they make life at least possible under the circumstances of modern mass society and seem more useful and attractive than ever now that they are in diminishing supply.

Tocqueville, who learned from Montesquieu, also teaches virtue in the same spirit but still more hopefully, and with him we may see a higher level to which the formation of American character reaches. The foundation, Tocqueville understands as does Montesquieu, is an acquisitive commercial order in which self-interest must be allowed to flourish; Tocqueville coolly accepts that it cannot be suppressed or transcended. Whatever might have been possible in earlier aristocratic ages, when men had perhaps been able to sacrifice self-interest for the "beauty of virtue," this is now impossible. In the modern age of equality, "private interest will more than ever become the chief if not the only driving force behind all behavior." But this is not cause for despair; if there is no hope of transcending private interest, still much depends on how "each man will interpret his private interest."[10] What is necessary is that men learn to follow

[9] Montesquieu, *The Spirit of the Laws*, Book 5, chap. 6.

[10] Alexis de Tocqueville, *Democracy in America*, trans. George Lawrence (New York: Harper & Row, 1966). Unless otherwise noted, all references are to pp. 497–99.

the "principle of self-interest properly understood." The Americans, Tocqueville says, have "universally accepted" that principle and have made it the root of all their actions: "The Americans enjoy explaining almost every act of their lives on the principle of self-interest properly understood. It gives them pleasure to point out how an enlightened self-love continually leads them to help one another and disposes them freely to give part of their time and wealth for the good of the state."

Oddly, and in a manner reminiscent of Madison in *Federalist* 51, Tocqueville interrupts his presentation at this point as if wishing to draw a veil over the harsh foundation of this "principle." But he forces himself, as it were, to a full statement of its implications.

Self-interest properly understood is not at all a sublime doctrine. . . . It does not attempt to reach great aims, but it does . . . achieve all it sets out to do. Being within the scope of everybody's understanding, everyone grasps it and has no trouble bearing it in mind. It is wonderfully agreeable to human weaknesses and so easily wins great sway. It has no difficulty in keeping its power, for it turns private interest against itself and uses the same goad which excites them to direct the passions.

The doctrine of self-interest properly understood does not inspire great sacrifices, but every day it prompts some small ones; by itself it cannot make a man virtuous, but its discipline shapes a lot of orderly, temperate, moderate, careful, and self-controlled citizens. If it does not lead the will directly to virtue, it establishes habits which unconsciously turn it that way.

One element in Tocqueville's account of these "habits," which are the common stuff of American political life, is especially worth noting. Not only does "self-interest properly understood" cause Americans to acquire certain personal excellences, and not only does it lead them regularly to help one another in their private capacities, but it also "disposes them freely to give part of their time and wealth for the good of the state." By this Tocqueville refers to the extraordinary extent to which Americans actually govern themselves; from the habit and practice of self-government, American character reaches up to the republican virtues. The imposing extent of American self-governance, and hence its character-forming significance, has been obscured in recent years because observers have brought to the question a utopian expectation that degraded the reality. But Tocqueville, by making realistic comparisons and taking his bearings from the nature of things, was able to appreciate the astonishing degree in America of self-governing and self-directing activity in all spheres of life. In fact, he warns his readers that, while they could very well conceive all other aspects of America, "the political activity prevailing in the United States is something one could never understand unless one has seen it. No sooner do you set foot on American soil than you find yourself in a sort of tumult; a confused clamor rises on every side, and a thousand voices are heard at once, each expressing some social requirements."[11] This tumult, this clamor, is the sound of men and women governing themselves. And in presupposing and summoning forth the capacity of a people to govern themselves, the American political order advances beyond mere self-interest toward that full self-governance which is the very idea of virtue.

We may very briefly note two further aspects of American life which are, in a way, at the peak of the "ascent" we are sketching. First, American democracy as understood by its Founders, whether in the Declaration of Independence or the Constitution, made only a modest claim. It never denied the unequal existence of human virtues or excellences; it only denied the ancient claim of excellence to *rule as a matter of right.* Now this denial is of immense importance because, in contrast with the ancient justification of the political claims of the few, it deeply popularizes the very foundation of political life. But the American political order nonetheless still presupposed that an inequality of virtues and abilities was rooted in human nature and that this inequality would manifest itself and flourish in the private realm of society. The original American democratic idea thus still deferred to a relatively high idea of virtue, the while denying its claim to rule *save by popular consent.* Indeed, not only was the idea of unequal excellence acknowledged and expected to flourish privately, but it was the proud claim of American democracy to be the political system in which merit, incarnated in Jefferson's "natural aristocracy," was likeliest to be rewarded with public office, in contrast with the way "artificial aristocracy" flourished corruptly in other systems. Nothing is more dangerous in modern America than those subverting conceptions of human nature or of justice that deny that there are men and women who deserve deference, or deny democracy its aspiration to be that political system which best defers to the truly deserving.

Finally, and with a brevity disproportionate to importance, one should also note gratefully that the American political order, with

11 Ibid., p. 233.

its heterogeneous and fluctuating majorities and with its principle of liberty, supplies a not inhospitable home to the love of learning. This is at a respectable distance indeed from its foundation in a "policy of opposite and rival interests."

VI

We have examined the "policy" that is the restraining or ballasting base of the "American way," and now we have some idea of what are the distinctive and respectable American virtues or excellences that rise on and above the base. In the light of those distinctive virtues, we can claim that America manifestly qualifies as an authentically political community or regime, at least with regard to the production of an ethos, or of a distinctive human character or characters. But we still have not gotten a satisfactory handle on the political side of the ethics-politics relationship here: while American character is as much our distinctive ethical nurture as is the human character formed in any other regime, it still remains a puzzle as to how that character is politically generated here.

We cannot hope to explicate the matter fully, but it will help to recur to the Aristotelian understanding of a regime. In Aristotle's view, three elements together make a community authentically political rather than merely a social arrangement that lacks a regard for "what the qualities of the others are." A community is a political regime when: (1) it forms itself upon some particular idea of what is "advantageous and just" for human beings; (2) its citizens are molded into a particular human character on the pattern of that idea; and when (3) this is done by means of vigorous, comprehensive, and penetrating laws, that is, by means of a political art that regulates—not just Madison's "various and interfering interests," but religion, education, family life, mores generally, economic behavior, and whatever helps bring into being the kind or kinds of human being contemplated by the central idea of the particular regime.

The puzzle in the American case is the discrepancy between the way we fully qualify as a regime regarding the second requirement, the forming of distinctive virtues or characters, but emphatically do not qualify regarding the last requirement, namely, the use of governmental authority to form those virtues. It is in this respect, in the absence of the censorious and sumptuary laws and institutions characteristic of ancient political science, that America is most unlike an Aristotelian regime. As we saw earlier, this removal of government from the business of directly superintending the formation of character is central to the "new science of politics," on the basis of which the American republic was largely founded. And this narrowing of the range of political authority, we also saw, resulted from a lowering of the aims of political life. This meant a lowering of the idea of the "advantageous and the just." It is likely, then, that the explanation of the puzzling American discrepancy—character formation, but not by use of the laws—will be found in the status in America of the first of Aristotle's three regime requisites, that is, in the American idea of what is advantageous and right for humans.

By the "American idea" of the advantageous and just, we mean here the idea contained in the Declaration of Independence and the Constitution, the two linked founding documents of the American republic. This is not to deny that many other elements form part of the American idea in practice—elements like the Anti-Federalist "virtuous republic" tradition, or Puritanism with its original high-pitched piety, or the high-toned Anglicanism that long persisted in this country, or vestiges of the English aristocratic tradition, or, more recently, elements derived from powerful intellectual currents in the contemporary world, or from the many other possibilities that crowd into a particular national "idea" in practice. All of these elements must be given their due weight in a full account of the American relationship of ethics and politics. But they all become most intelligible in their operation when they are seen in tension with the central American idea, the idea derived from the new science of politics, the idea decisively embodied in the "frame" of the republic, that is, in the principles, institutions, and processes of the Constitution.

The central American idea of what is advantageous and just for humans, as we have seen, is clearly less elevated than that of the classical teaching. The ethical aim of the American political order being less lofty, the kinds of human characters to be politically formed are likewise less lofty and, hence, less difficult of formation. Such human beings may be produced by softer means, subterranean in their operation and indirect, thereby rendering unnecessary the strenuous and penetrating political authority characteristic of the ancient regime. It has in fact proved possible to raise human character to the American height in this gentler, less demanding fashion.

Consider what we have called the "bourgeois virtues." As Montesquieu observed, the "spirit of commerce" of itself entices these modest excellences into being. Their formation does not require the severity and constant statesmanship of the classical political outlook; it suffices that a modern regime generate that "spirit" and then the desired virtues tend naturally to form themselves. This fundamental difference is revealed in a superficial similarity between the ancient and modern ways of generating their respectively required virtues. In one interesting respect, the modern bourgeois virtues are formed politically the same way that the ancient teaching prescribed regarding its virtues, namely, by a decision regarding the size of the political community. The decisions are, of course, exactly opposite: The classical ethical-political teaching requires the small scale of the polis; the Madisonian "policy" with its attendant "bourgeois virtues" requires the scale of a very large republic. For the ancients, the polis had to be small so as to provide a constraining environment for the appetites; for the moderns, the republic had to be large so as to excite the acquisitive appetites whence the spirit of commerce arises. But for the ancients the size of the polis of itself accomplishes little regarding the right character formation; the polis was simply the requisite setting within which a high political art could be employed to generate the appropriate virtues. But once the modern republic has been organized on a large enough scale and, of course, once its fundamental laws have established the framework for the life of commerce, government need not be used thereafter closely to superintend the formation of the bourgeois character. The appropriate ethical consequences may be expected to flow. In this respect, the relationship of ethics and politics in America is more the work of the original Founding than of a demanding statesmanship thereafter; appropriate characters are formed by force of the original political direction of the passions and interests.

We have also pointed to the American republican virtues that arise from the habit and practice of self-government. Like the bourgeois virtues, these too are formed in the milder modern way. The American republican virtues arise primarily from political arrangements that accept and seek to channel the force of human passion and interest rather than to suppress or transcend them. And these republican virtues likewise arise primarily from the original Founding and not from subsequent statesmanship shaping the character of the citizenry. The Constitution, and, thanks to federalism, the state constitutions as well, establish a basic framework of institutions that elicit ethical qualities of citizenship such as independence, initiative, a capacity for cooperation and patriotism. Tocqueville teaches us the way these qualities are formed in the American character. He shows how, by means of administrative decentralization, the jury system, voluntary associations, and the like, self-interest is "unconsciously" drawn in the direction of republican virtue. Like the bourgeois virtues, these republican decencies in the American character do not depend decisively upon constant constraint or encouragement by statesmanship but tend to flow from the operation of the political institutions as originally founded. James Madison also teaches us about the character-forming possibility of the Founding, for example, in his understanding of the Bill of Rights. Madison justified the addition of the Bill of Rights to the Constitution in part on "declaratory" grounds. "The political truths declared in that solemn manner," he said, "acquire by degrees the character of fundamental maxims of free Government, and as they become incorporated with the national sentiment, counteract the impulses of interest and passion."[12] In this sense, the Founding becomes more than an arrangement of the passions and interests; when "venerated" by the people, it can serve as an ethical admonition to the people, teaching them to subdue dangerous impulses of passion and interest. This goes far in the direction of genuine republican virtue, but it still rests on the mild and merely declaratory tutelage of the Founding, not on the sterner stuff of ancient political science.

Finally, the American Founders seem simply to have taken for granted that the full range of the higher human virtues would have suitable opportunity to flourish, so to speak, privately. They presumed that man's nature included a perhaps weak but nonetheless natural inclination to certain virtues. Although they did not rely upon these "better motives," as we have here called them, as the basis for the political order, they were apparently confident that, privately and without political tutelage in the ancient mode, these higher virtues would develop from religion, education, family upbringing, and simply out of the natural yearnings of human nature. Indeed, they even accorded to these higher excellences a quasi-public status in the expectation mentioned earlier, that American democracy would seek out and reward the "natural aristocracy" with public

12 Madison to Jefferson, Oct. 17, 1788, in *Writings of James Madison* (New York: Putnam's, 1904), 5:273. I am indebted to my wife, Ann Stuart Diamond, for calling to my attention the appositeness of this passage to my purposes. Madison's view of how the Bill of Rights can acquire "the character of fundamental maxims of free Government" should be considered in connection with his discussion of "veneration" and public opinion in *Federalist* 49.

trust. Whether these expectations of the Founders were reasonable
then or remain so now is a grave matter for inquiry, but an inquiry
beyond the scope of this essay.

We have suggested here a way through which Americans should
inquire into, and go about, the ethical enterprise of politics. We
have argued that there is a distinctive American way respecting
the relationship of ethics and politics; and hence, while taking our
bearings from the universal commands of the highest ethics, we
must as political beings seek to achieve politically only that excellence of character that, to adapt a phrase from Tocqueville, "is
proper to ourselves." That character largely remains the product
of the subtle strategy of the American Founders, the understanding
of which thus remains indispensable to us. We must accept that their
political order had its foundation in the human interests and passions; but we must appreciate also that their political order presupposes certain enduring qualities that can and should be achieved
in the American character. The preservation of that foundation
and at the same time the nurturing of the appropriate ethical excellences remains the compound political task of enlightened American
statesmen and citizens. The easy error is to deal with only one side
of that compound task. On the one hand, it is easy to be concerned
only with the foundation and to settle for a form of liberty that
consists only in the free play of raw self-interest. But this is to
ignore the subtle ethical demands of the American political order.
On the other hand, it is even easier today to make utopian demands
upon the political system for unrealizable ethical perfections. But
this is to ignore the limiting requisites of the unique American
ethos, namely, the foundation in the passions and interests upon
which it rests. Moreover, such utopianizing has the tendency inex-
cusably to ignore or depreciate the liberty and decencies which the
American political order, resting on that foundation, continues to
secure in an ever more dangerous world. In contrast to both these
one-sided approaches, it is intellectually and ethically rewarding
to grasp the compound ethical-political demands of the "American
Way" and to seek within each day's budget of troubles "to attain
that form of greatness . . . which is proper to ourselves" and even
enclaves of other greatnesses as well.[13]

13 Tocqueville, *Democracy in America*, p. 679.

The Democratization of Mind
in the American Revolution

Gordon S. Wood

T HE intellectual caliber of the leaders of the American Revolution has never been in question. Praises of their qualities of mind
have been sung so often that we are hard put to find new ways of describing them. In the last quarter of the eighteenth century, one historian has written, America "boasted a galaxy of leaders who were
quite literally incomparable." "These leading representatives of
the American Enlightenment," another historian has said, "were a
cluster of extraordinary men such as is rarely encountered in modern
history."[1] No one, it seems, can look back without being overawed
by the brilliance of their thought, the creativity of their politics, the
sheer magnitude of their achievement. They are indeed more marvel-
ous than even those they emulated—the great legislators of classical
antiquity—precisely because they are more real. They are not mythical
characters but authentic historical figures about whom there exists
a remarkable amount of historical evidence. For our knowledge of
the Founding Fathers, unlike that of many of the classical heroes, we
do not have to rely on hazy legends or poetic tales. We have not only
everything the Revolutionary leaders ever published but also an incredible amount of their private correspondence and their most intimate thoughts, now being made available with a degree of editorial
completeness and expertness rarely achieved in the long history of the
West's recovery of its documentary past.

Despite the extent and meticulousness of this historical recovery,
however, the Founding Fathers still seem larger than life, and from
our present perspective especially, seem to possess intellectual capacities well beyond our own. The awe that we feel when we look back
at them is thus mingled with an acute sense of loss. Somehow for a
brief moment ideas and power, intellectualism and politics, came

---

[1] Henry Steele Commager, "Leadership in Eighteenth-Century America and
Today," *Daedalus* 90 (1961):652; Adrienne Koch, ed., *The American Enlightenment* (New York: Braziller, 1965), p. 35.

together—indeed were one with each other—in a way never again duplicated in American history. There is no doubt that the Founding Fathers were men of ideas and thought, in fact were the leading intellectuals of their day. But they were as well the political leaders of their day, politicians who competed for power, lost and won elections, served in their colonial and state legislatures or in the Congress, became governors, judges, and even presidents. Yet of course they were neither "intellectuals" nor "politicians," for the modern meaning of these terms suggests the very separation between them that the Revolutionaries avoided. They were intellectuals without being alienated and political leaders without being obsessed with votes. They lived mutually in the world of ideas and the world of politics, shared equally in both in a happy combination that fills us with envy and wonder. We know that something happened then in American history that can never happen again.

But there is no point now, 200 years later, in continuing to wallow in nostalgia and to aggravate our deep feelings of loss and present deficiency. What we need is not more praise of the Founding Fathers but more understanding of them and their circumstances. We need to find out why the Revolutionary generation was able to combine ideas and politics so effectively and why subsequent generations in America could not do so. With the proper historical perspective on the last quarter of the eighteenth century and with a keener sense of the distinctiveness of that period will come a greater appreciation of not only what we have lost by the passing of that Revolutionary generation but, more important, what we have gained. For in the end what made subsequent duplication of the remarkable intellectual leadership of the Revolutionaries impossible in America was the growth of what we have come to value most—our egalitarian culture and our democratic society. One of the prices we had to pay for democracy was a decline in the intellectual quality of American political life and an eventual separation between ideas and power. As the common man rose to power in the decades following the Revolution, the inevitable consequence was the displacement from power of the uncommon man, the man of ideas. Yet the Revolutionary leaders were not merely victims of new circumstances; they were in fact the progenitors of these new circumstances: they helped create the changes that led eventually to their own undoing, to the breakup of the kind of political and intellectual coherence they represented. Without intending to, they eagerly destroyed the sources of their own sustenance and greatness.

There is no denying the power and significance of intellectual products of the Revolutionary era. Samuel Eliot Morison and Harold Laski both believed that no period of modern history, with the possible exception of the Civil War decades of seventeenth-century England, was so rich in political ideas and contributed so much in such a short period of time to Western political theory.[2] In the Americans' efforts to explain the difference of their experience in the New World and ultimately to justify their Revolution and their new governments, they were pressed to speak and write both originally and extensively about politics, using a wide variety of eighteenth-century instruments: newspapers, pamphlets, state papers, poetry, plays, satire, and, of course, letters. Indeed, their phenomenal reliance on personal correspondence for the communication of their thoughts made the Revolutionary years the greatest letter-writing era in American history. (Without Jefferson's letters, what would we know of his mind?) It is a remarkable body of political literature that the Revolutionaries created, and what is most remarkable about it is that this political theory was generally written by the very men responsible for putting it into effect.

Despite the intellectual creativity and productivity of the Revolutionary leaders, it is obvious that they were not professional writers. They bore no resemblance to the Grub Street scribblers hired by government officials to turn out political propaganda. Nor were they only men of letters, "intellectuals" like the eighteenth-century French philosophes or the Tory satirists of Augustan England, writers fully engaged in political criticism and using their pens to gain money and position. To be sure, there were American writers like John Trumbull and Philip Freneau who sought to make careers as litterateurs, but they were exceptions. Most of the intellectual leaders of the Revolution were amateurs at writing—clergymen, merchants, planters, and lawyers deeply involved in their separate occupations. Writing in fact was simply a byproduct of their careers and one of their many accomplishments or duties as gentlemen. Because they were gentlemen, they never wrote for money and rarely deigned to put their names on what they wrote for publication. They thought of their writing, even the belletristic sort, as a means to an end, either to make a polemical political point or to demonstrate their learning and gentlemanly status.

Yet men like James Otis, Richard Bland, Thomas Jefferson, and John Adams were not only amateur writers; in an important sense

[2] Samuel Eliot Morison, ed., "William Manning's *The Key to Liberty*," *William and Mary Quarterly*, 3d ser. 13 (1956):208.

they were amateur politicians as well. For all the time and energy
these Revolutionary leaders devoted to politics, most of them cannot
accurately be described as professional politicians, at least not in
any modern meaning of the term. Their relationship to public life
and their conception of public service were different from those of
today: their political careers did not create but rather followed from
their previously established social positions; their political leadership, like their intellectual leadership, was a consequence, not a cause,
of their social leadership. And thus they often saw their public service
—sometimes wrongly, of course, but sincerely—as unhappy burdens,
wretched responsibilities thrust upon them by the fact of their high
social rank. Few of Jefferson's letters are as revealing and filled with
emotion as his 1782 protest to Monroe over the social pressures making him engage in public service despite the miseries of office and his
longing for private repose.[3] We smile today when we hear such pro-
testations from politicians, but precisely because the eighteenth-
century leaders were not professional politicians such disavowals of
public office and such periodic withdrawals from politics as they
habitually made possessed a meaning that is difficult for us today to
recapture.

What ultimately enabled the Revolutionary leaders to be amateur
politicians and amateur writers, and to be both simultaneously, was
their status as gentlemen—the dominant social distinction of the
eighteenth century that has since lost almost all of its earlier significance. They took their gentlemanly status seriously and accepted the
privileges and responsibilities of the rank without guilt and without
false humility. Compared to the English gentry of the eighteenth
century, some of the colonial leaders may have been uncertain about
their distinctive status, but none doubted the social importance of
this distinctiveness, which was expressed in various ways—speech,
dress, demeanor, learning, tastes, and one's acquaintances and friends.
Eighteenth-century leaders took it for granted that society was a
hierarchy of finely graded ranks and degrees divided vertically into
interests and lines of personal influence, rather than as today into
horizontal cleavages of class and occupation. In such a society men
generally were acutely aware of their exact relation to those immediately above and below them but only vaguely conscious, except at the
very top, of their connections with those at their own level. It was

[3] Jefferson to Monroe, May 20, 1782, in Adrienne Koch and William Peden,
eds., *The Life and Selected Writings of Thomas Jefferson* (New York: Random
House, Modern Library, 1944), p. 56.

believed that the topmost rank, that of a gentleman—the only hori-
izontal social division that had any significance to the eighteenth
century—ought to have special sorts of men, the "better sort," men of
property no doubt, but more—men of "good character." Members of
the elite debated endlessly over what constituted the proper character
for a gentleman—John Adams and Thomas Jefferson were still going
at it in their correspondence at the end of their lives—but they never
questioned the leadership of the society by an aristocracy of some
sort. Because gentlemen saw themselves as part of an organic social
community linked through strong personal connections to those
below them, for all their feelings of superiority and elevation they
had no sense of isolation from the society, no sense of standing in an
adversary relationship to the populace. They were individuals undoubtedly, sometimes assuming a classic pose of heroic and noble pre-
eminence, but they were not individualists, men worried about their
social identities. They were civic minded by necessity: they thought
they ought to lead the society both politically and intellectually—
indeed, they could not help but lead the society—by the sheer force of
their position and character. Ordinary men would respect and follow
them precisely because the members of the elite possessed what ordinary men by definition could not have.

Because the Revolutionary leaders were gentry with special privileges and responsibilities, tied to the people through lines of personal
and social authority, the character of their intellectual activity—
what they wrote and spoke—was decisively affected. They believed
that their speeches and writings did not have to influence directly and
simultaneously all of the people but only the rational and enlightened
part, who then in turn would bring the rest of the populace with them
through the force of deferential respect. The politically minded public in eighteenth-century America may have been large compared to
contemporary England, but most of the political literature of the
period showed little evidence of a broad reading public. The Revolutionary leaders for the most part wrote as if they were dealing with
reasonable and cultivated readers like themselves. Of course, by publishing their writings, they realized they were exposing their ideas
to the vulgar, which is why they usually resorted to pseudonyms,
but yet they made very few concessions to this wider public. They still
thought of the real audience for their intellectual productions as
roughly commensurate with their social world. "When I mention the
public," wrote John Randolph in a 1774 political pamphlet, "I mean
to include only the rational part of it. The ignorant vulgar are as
unfit to judge of the modes, as they are unable to manage the reins

of government."[4] Such bluntness in public was rare and became even rarer as the Revolution approached. Although few of the Revolutionaries shared Randolph's contempt for the mass of the populace —indeed, most had little reason as yet to fear or malign the people— they vaguely held to a largely unspoken assumption that if only the educated and enlightened, if only gentlemen, could be convinced, then the rest would follow naturally.

Actually the reading public in the mid-eighteenth century may have been more limited than we have generally assumed. Certainly the prevalence of literacy is no measure of it. The price of both newspapers and pamphlets was itself restricting. Although a pamphlet cost no more than a shilling or two, even that put it beyond the reach of most. Indeed, the practice of reading some pamphlets before groups of Sons of Liberty or town meetings indicates not the general breadth but the usual limits of their circulation. Even members of the elite relied extensively on passing pamphlets from hand to hand as if they were letters.[5]

Yet there is no doubt that the intellectual climate was changing in the half century before the Revolution. In the 1720s there were fewer than a half dozen newspapers in the colonies, with a limited number of subscribers; by 1764 there were twenty-three newspapers, each with double or triple the earlier circulation. Between 1741 and 1776 men had experimented with at least ten magazines, and although none of them lasted longer than a few years, the effort was promising. Since most of the publications emphasized governmental matters, there was bound to be some raising of political consciousness, and printers were becoming more important public figures. The number of political pamphlets multiplied at an ever-increasing rate, and in some urban areas in the years before the Revolution such writings were being used with particular effectiveness in election campaigning.[6] All these

4 [John Randolph], *Considerations on the Present State of Virginia* (n.p., 1774), quoted in Merrill Jensen, "The Articles of Confederation," in Library of Congress Symposia on the American Revolution, 2d, 1973, *Fundamental Testaments of the American Revolution* (Washington, D.C.: Library of Congress, 1973), p. 56.

5 Homer L. Calkin, "Pamphlets and Public Opinion during the American Revolution," *Pennsylvania Magazine of History and Biography* 64 (1940):30, 35.

6 Frank Luther Mott, *American Journalism: A History, 1690–1960*, 3d ed. (New York: Macmillan, 1962), pp. 3–64; idem., *A History of American Magazines, 1741–1850* (New York: D. Appleton, 1930), pp. 13–67; Arthur M. Schlesinger, *Prelude to Independence: The Newspaper War on Britain, 1764–1776* (New York: Vintage, 1965), pp. 51–66, 303–4; Philip Davidson, *Propaganda and the American Revolution, 1763–1783* (Chapel Hill: University of North Carolina Press, 1941).

developments were bringing Americans to the edge of a vast transformation in the nature and size of their reading public and their
politically conscious society.

Regardless of the actual extent of the American reading public,
what is crucial is the Revolutionary leaders' consciousness of the
elitist nature of that public. We know they conceived of their readership as restricted and aristocratic, as being made up of men essentially
like themselves, simply by the style and content of what they wrote.
They saw themselves and their readers as mutual participants in an
intellectual fraternity, "the republic of letters," a view that gave them
a confidence in the homogeneity and the intelligence of their audience, which in turn decisively influenced the particular qualities of
their literary productions.[7]

First of all, a large amount of the Revolutionary literature was extraordinarily learned, filled with Latin quotations, classical allusions,
and historical citations—multitudes of references to every conceivable
figure in the heritage of Western culture from Cicero, Sallust, and Plutarch, to Montesquieu, Pufendorf, and Rousseau. They delighted in
citing authorities and in displaying their scholarship, sometimes
crowding or even smothering the texts of their pamphlets with quan-
tities of footnotes.[8] Often the newspaper essays and pamphlets were
mere extensions of the kind of speeches that political leaders might
present in legislative halls, devices by which gentlemen, in the absence
of published reports of legislative debates, might tell other gentlemen what they said, or would like to have said, within the legislative
chamber. Thus Stephen Hopkins *The Rights of Colonies Examined* was first read before the assembly of Rhode Island, which
then voted that it should appear in pamphlet form.[9] Or even more
indicative of the limited elitist conception of the audience was the
extraordinary reliance on personal correspondence for the circulation
of ideas. It is often difficult to distinguish between the private correspondence and the public writings of the Revolutionaries, so much
alike are they. Sometimes the published writings even took the form
of letters or, like John Adams's pamphlet *Thoughts on Government*,

[7] References to the republic of letters are common in the Revolutionaries'
writings. See, for example, Brooke Hindle, *The Pursuit of Science in Revolutionary America, 1735–1789* (Chapel Hill: Published for the Institute of Early American History and Culture, Williamsburg, Va., by the University of North Carolina
Press, 1956), p. 384.

[8] Bernard Bailyn, *The Ideological Origins of the American Revolution* (Cambridge: Harvard University Press, Belknap Press, 1967), p. 23.

[9] Calkin, "Pamphlets and Public Opinion," pp. 28, 35.

grew out of what were originally letters to colleagues and friends.[10]

It is not just the prevalence of scholarship and the personal form of the literature that reveal the limited and elitist nature of the audience. Even the character of the invective and polemics suggests a restricted reading public in the minds of the authors. Much of the polemics was highly personal—a succession of individual exchanges between gentlemen who were known to one another, quickly becoming unintelligible to an outsider and usually ending in bitter personal vituperation. Since such abuse was designed to destroy the gentlemanly reputation of one's enemies, no accusation was too coarse or too vulgar to be made—from drunkenness and gambling to impotence and adultery.[11] The vitriolic burlesques, like those satiric closet dramas of Mercy Otis Warren, derived much of their force from the intimate knowledge the author presumed the audience or readers had of the persons being ridiculed or satirized. Without such familiarity on the part of the audience, much of the fun of the pieces—the disguised characterizations, the obscure references, the private jokes, the numerous innuendos—is lost.[12]

Indeed, it is the prevalence of satire in the Revolutionary literature that as much as anything suggests the elite nature of the audience. For satire as a literary device depends greatly on a comprehensible and homogeneous audience with commonly understood standards of rightness and reasonableness. Since the satirist can expose to instantaneous contempt only what is readily condemned by the opinion of his readers, he must necessarily be on intimate terms with them and count on their sharing his tastes and viewpoint. If this intimacy should break down, if the satirist's audiences should become heterogeneous and the once-shared values become confused and doubtful— if the satirist has to explain what his ridicule means—then the satire is rendered ineffectual.[13] But most Revolutionary writers, at the outset at least, presumed the existence of these universal principles of right behavior and expected a uniformity of response, supposing that their audience either was, or would like to be, part of that restricted circle of men of good taste and judgment.

10 John Adams, *Diary and Autobiography*, ed. L. H. Butterfield et al., 4 vols. (Cambridge: Harvard University Press, 1961), 3:331–32.

11 Bailyn, *Ideological Origins*, pp. 4–5, 17.

12 John J. Teunissen, "Blockheadism and the Propaganda Plays of the American Revolution," *Early American Literature* 7 (1972):148–62.

13 Maynard Mack, "The Muse of Satire," in Richard C. Boys, ed., *Studies in the Literature of the Augustan Age: Essays Collected in Honor of Arthur Ellicott Case* (New York: Gordian Press, 1966).

Nearly all the literature of the Revolutionary leaders thus reflected —in its form, its erudition, its polemics, its reliance on satire—a very different intellectual world from our own, a world dominated by gentlemen who were both amateur writers and amateur politicians, essentially engaged, despite their occasional condescension toward a larger public, in either amusing men like themselves or in educating men to be or think like themselves. More than any of these characteristics, however, what decisively separates the literature of the Revolutionary generation from that of our own was its highly rhetorical character. It was in fact the Revolutionaries' obsession with rhetoric and with its requirement of effectively relating to the audience in order to make a point that in the end helped contribute to the transformation of the American mind.

Rhetoric today no longer means what it meant to the eighteenth century. To us rhetoric suggests at best elocution, or at worst some sort of disingenuous pleading, hyperbolic bombast lacking the sincerity and authenticity of self-expression that we have come to value so highly. But to the Revolutionary generation rhetoric—briefly defined as the art of persuasion—lay at the heart of an eighteenth-century liberal education and was regarded as a necessary mark of a gentleman and an indispensable skill for a statesman, especially for a statesman in a republic. Language, whether spoken or written, was to be deliberately and adroitly used for effect, and since that effect depended on the intellectual leader's conception of his audience, any perceived change in that audience could alter drastically the style and content of what was said or written.[14]

Part of the remarkable effect created by Thomas Paine's *Common Sense*, for example, resulted from its obvious deepening of the layers of audience to whom it was directed. To be sure, it was a vigorously written pamphlet, filled with colorful, vivid language and possessing a fierce, passionate tone that no other American writer could match. And it said things about monarchial government that had not been said before; it broke through the presuppositions of politics and offered new ways of conceiving of government. But some of the awe and consternation the pamphlet aroused came from its deliberate elimination of the usual elitist apparatus of persuasion and its ac-

14 On eighteenth-century rhetoric see Wilbur Samuel Howell, *Eighteenth-Century British Logic and Rhetoric* (Princeton: Princeton University Press, 1971); Peter France, *Rhetoric and Truth in France: Descartes to Diderot* (Oxford: Clarendon Press, 1972); Warren Guthrie, "The Development of Rhetorical Theory in America, 1635–1850," *Speech Monographs* 13 (1946):14–22; 14 (1947):38–54; 15 (1948):61–71.

knowledged appeal to a wider reading public. Paine's arguments are sometimes tortured, and the logic is often deficient. There are few of the traditional gentlemanly references to learned authorities and few of the subtleties of literary allusions and techniques known to the Augustans. Paine scorned "words of sound" that only "amuse the ear" and relied on a simple and direct idiom; he used concrete, even coarse and vulgar, imagery drawn from the commonplace world that could be understood even by the unlearned, and he counted on his audience being familiar with only one literary source, the Bible— all of which worked to heighten the pamphlet's potency and to broaden its readership, pointing the way toward a new kind of public literature.[15]

As the Revolutionary cause became more fervent and as the dimensions of the public that needed persuading expanded in men's minds, other kinds of changes appeared. Take, for example, the inflated emotions displayed in the annual public commemorations of the Boston Massacre that began in 1771 and continued on until 1784, when they were replaced by the equally grandiloquent orations celebrating the Fourth of July. Here is Joseph Warren speaking in 1775:

Approach we then the melancholy walk of death. Hither let me call the gay companion; here let him drop a farewell tear upon the body which so late he saw vigorous and warm with social mirth—hither let me lead the tender mother to weep over her beloved son—come widowed mourner, here satiate thy grief; behold thy murdered husband gasping on the ground, and to complete the pompous show of wretchedness, bring in each hand thy infant children to bewail their father's fate—take heed, ye orphan babes, lest, whilst your streaming eyes are fixed upon the ghastly corpse, your feet slide on the stones bespattered with your father's brains.[16]

This sort of lurid exaggeration, this kind of sensational melodrama, strikes us today as incredible, even ludicrous. Yet we must remember that such oratorical utterances were rhetorical in a way that we can no longer appreciate, designed by the speaker not as an expression of his personal emotions but as a calculated attempt to arouse the emotions of his listeners. Rhetoric was the art of relating

15 Bernard Bailyn, "Common Sense," in Library of Congress Symposia on the American Revolution, *Fundamental Testaments*, pp. 7–22; Paine, *Common Sense* (1776), in *The Complete Writings of Thomas Paine*, ed. Philip S. Foner, 2 vols. (New York: Citadel Press, 1969), 1:8; James T. Boulton, *The Language of Politics in the Age of Wilkes and Burke* (London: Routledge and Kegan Paul, 1963), chap. 7.

16 Joseph Warren, "Oration Delivered at Boston, March 6, 1775," in H. Niles, ed., *Principles and Acts of the Revolution in America . . .* (Baltimore: Printed and published for the editor by W. O. Niles, 1822), p. 20.

what was said and how it was said to the needs and requirements of the audience. Since the speaker or the writer aimed above all to make a point and sway his public, rhetoric was necessarily less concerned with the discovery of the truth than with the means of communicating a message. Not that the truth was to be falsified or perverted; everyone assumed that rhetoric was to be the servant of truth and that the good orator or writer, the good statesman, had to be a good man—which is one reason why eighteenth-century gentlemen so carefully guarded their personal reputations. But it is clear, simply from the examples of Paine and Warren, that the demands of persuading and adapting to an audience, especially when that audience was perceived as diffuse and vulgar, could break through the usual stylized rules of rhetoric and lead both to a new kind of directness and commonness of expression and to the kind of verbal excesses and emotional extravagance that increasingly came to mark much of American public utterance in the decades following the Revolution.

Such an art, such a use of rhetoric, resembling our modern notion of propaganda, seems to us dangerous because we are not as confident as the Revolutionaries were that the audience will be, in Jefferson's words, "an assembly of reasonable men." What ultimately justified the eighteenth century's use of rhetoric and kept it from becoming propaganda as we know it was the intellectual leaders' civic sense of being part of the network of society with responsibility for the welfare of that society and of having an intimate and trusted relationship with their rational audiences. Society was the only measure of man; all his writing, all his utterances, all his intellectual and artistic activity had preeminently a social, and hence rhetorical function. Even Jefferson's intense efforts to create a classical style for America's public buildings flowed from his sense of the social significance of architecture. Of all the arts architecture was the most rhetorical because, as Jefferson put it, it was "an art which shows so much." Hence all sorts of other considerations—including function and cost—could be sacrificed for the sake of the elevating effects a replica of a Roman temple would have on its viewers.[17]

In such a rehetorical world the intellectual leader had no business standing apart from the society in critical or scholarly isolation. Thus someone like Benjamin Franklin never thought the role of closet scientist, no matter how distinguished, compared in significance with that of public servant. Franklin in fact saw his whole life and career in rhetorical terms: all of his artful posing, his role-playing, his many

[17] Eleanor Davidson Berman, *Thomas Jefferson among the Arts: An Essay in Early American Esthetics* (New York: Philosophical Library, 1947), pp. 210, 130.

masks, his refusal to reveal his inner self—all these characteristics followed from Franklin's obsessive civic-consciousness and his intense awareness that he was a persona in a drama whose actions and statements would profoundly affect his audience.[18] Today we are instinctively repelled by such calculation, such insincerity, such willingness to adapt and compromise for the sake of society; yet our distaste for such behavior is only one more measure of our distance from the Revolutionary era.

That eighteenth-century rhetorical world, that neoclassical world of civic-minded philosopher-statesmen, is now clearly gone. But it was going even then, even as it expressed itself most forcefully and brilliantly. While the Revolutionary gentry were still busy creating their learned arguments to persuade reasonable men of the need for resistance or of the requirements of government, there were social processes at work that would in time undermine both their political and intellectual authority. A new democratic society was developing, becoming both a cause and a consequence of the Revolution. As egalitarian as American society was before 1776, as broad as the suffrage was in the several eighteenth-century colonies, the republican society and culture that gradually emerged after the Declaration of Independence were decidedly different from what had existed earlier. The older hierarchical and homogeneous society of the eighteenth century —a patronage world of personal influence and vertical connections whose only meaningful horizontal cleavage was that between gentlemen and common people—this old society, weaker in America and never as finely calibrated as in England, now finally fell apart, beset by forces released and accelerated by the Revolution, to be replaced over the subsequent decades with new social relationships and new ideas and attitudes, including a radical blurring of the distinction between gentlemen and the rest of society. New men, often obscure ordinary men, were now touched by the expanding promises of opportunity and wealth in post-Revolutionary America and clamored for a share in the new governments and in the economy. The "people" were now told repeatedly that they rightfully had a place in politics, and lest they should forget, there were thousands of new rising popular tribunes, men who lacked the traditional attributes of gentlemanly

[18] Franklin to Cadwallader Colden, October 11, 1750, in *The Papers of Benjamin Franklin*, vol. 4, ed. Leonard W. Labaree et al. (New Haven: Yale University Press, 1961), p. 68; Robert F. Sayre, *The Examined Self: Benjamin Franklin, Henry Adams, Henry James* (Princeton: Princeton University Press, 1964), pp. 12–43.

leaders, to remind them, cajole them, even frighten them into political and social consciousness. Under such pressures, within a generation or so after Independence the old eighteenth-century world was transformed; the gentry, at least outside the South, gradually lost its monopoly of politics and intellectualism as the audience for politicians, writers, and orators ballooned out to hitherto unimaginable proportions.

Although few of these changes actually began with the Revolution, it was during the Revolution that they became evident. Before the Revolutionary movement only a few Americans, mostly royal officials and their connections, had worried about the expanding size of America's political society. But the imperial controversy had the effect of making all Americans more conscious of the power of the people out of doors. Political leaders, in their contests with royal authority, vied with each other in demonstrating their superior sympathy with the people—and in the process considerably widened and intensified their public audience.[19] Given the Whig tradition of celebrating the people against the Crown, it was a tendency that most American leaders found difficult to resist. In 1766 the Massachusetts House of Representatives erected a public gallery for the witnessing of its debates—a momentous step in the democratization of the American mind. The Pennsylvania Assembly followed reluctantly in 1770, and eventually the other legislatures too began to reach out to a wider public, usually provoked by the desire of Whig leaders to build support among the people for opposition to Great Britain.[20] Yet old habits died hard, and it was difficult to shed the conception of assembly proceedings being in the nature of private business among gentlemen. Votes in the legislatures continued to remain unrecorded and reports of debates were rarely carried to the outside world. When in 1776 the Revolutionaries met in their conventions to discuss the forms of their new state constitutions, they felt no need either to report what they said or to extract vows of secrecy to prevent leaks of what they said to the people out of doors. As a result we know very little of what went on during those momentous closed meetings in the months surrounding the Declaration of Independence. Apparently the leaders believed that nearly everyone who counted and ought to hear what was said was within the legislative or convention halls.

19 Gary B. Nash, "The Transformation of Urban Politics, 1700–1765," *Journal of American History* 60 (1973):605-32.

20 J. R. Pole, *Political Representation in England and the Origins of the American Republic* (London: St. Martin's, 1966), pp. 69-70, 277-78.

A decade later, however, by 1787, the situation had become very different. In many of the states, particularly in Pennsylvania and Massachusetts, legislative debates had begun to be reported by a growing number of newspapers (which now included dailies), and political leaders had developed a keen, even fearful, awareness of a larger political society existing outside of the legislative chambers. Politics no longer seemed an exclusively gentlemanly business, and consequently gentlemen in public discussions increasingly found themselves forced to concede to the popular and egalitarian ideology of the Revolution, for any hint of aristocracy was now pounced upon by emerging popular spokesmen eager to discredit the established elite leaders. Under these changed circumstances the delegates to the Philadelphia Convention in 1787 felt it necessary to take extraordinary measures to keep their proceedings private: no copies of anything in the journal were allowed, nothing said in the Convention was to be released or communicated to the outside society, and sentries were even to be posted to prevent intruders—all out of a sensitivity to a public out of doors that had not existed ten years earlier.

By the late 1780s gentlemen in the Convention had become convinced not only that this public—"the too credulous and unthinking Mobility," one delegate called it—was now interested in what went on within doors but that, if allowed access to the debates through publication by "imprudent printers," this hovering presence of the people would inhibit the delegates' freedom of expression.[21] Events bore out the significance of this deliberate decision to impose secrecy. The delegates to the Philadelphia Convention showed a remarkable degree of candor and boldness in discussing what were now sensitive issues, like aristocracy and the fear of popular power, that was notably missing from the debates in the various ratifying conventions held several months later. Since the ratifying conventions were open and their proceedings widely publicized in the press, the difference in the tone and character of the respective debates is revealing of just what a broader public could mean for the intellectual life of American politics. Madison later reportedly declared that "no Constitution would ever have been adopted by the convention if the debates had been public."[22] As it was, the defenders of the proposed Constitution knew very well that "when this plan goes forth, it will be attacked by the popular leaders. Aristocracy will be the watchword; the Shibboleth

---

[21] Alexander Martin to Governor Caswell, July 27, 1787, in Max Farrand, ed., *The Records of the Federal Convention of 1787*, 4 vols. (New Haven: Yale University Press, 1911–37), 3:64.

[22] Jared Sparks: Journal, April 19, 1830, ibid., 3:479.

among its adversaries."[23] Hence the proponents of the Constitution found themselves in the subsequent public debates compelled to stress over and over the popular and "strictly republican" character of the new federal government. Men who only a few months earlier had voiced deep misgivings over popular rule now tried to outdo their opponents in expressing their enthusiasm for the people. "We, sir, idolize democracy," they said in answer to popular critics of the Constitution.[24]

Although aspects of this public exuberance by the Federalists over the democratic character of the Constitution appear disingenuous and hypocritical to us in light of their private fears of popular power, in the debates they were only doing what their liberal education in rhetoric had taught them: adapting their arguments to the nature and needs of their audience. Yet the demands of rhetoric were not supposed to lead to dishonesty and duplicity by the intellectual leader, particularly if his audience was the people. Such a gap between private and public feelings as was displayed in the debates over the Constitution only raised in a new form an issue that had been at the heart of American public discussions throughout the eighteenth century, and never more so than at the time of the Revolution.

During that entire century, and even earlier, enlightened men everywhere had been obsessed by what was often called "Machiavellian duplicity," the deliberate separation between men's hidden feelings or motives and their public face—an obsession that the rhetorical attitude only enhanced. It was taken for granted that men could and would assume roles and play falsely with their audience or public. The worst villain was the one who, like Iago, achieved his end through plots and dissembling; indeed, the enlightened eighteenth century was incapable of locating evil anywhere else but in this kind of deceiving man.

Assumptions like these lay behind the character of American political life in the eighteenth century and eventually became central to the decision to revolt in 1776. Time and time again, opposition spokesmen against royal authority in the colonies had emphasized

---

23 John Dickinson, ibid., a:a78.

24 John Marshall (Va.), in Jonathan Elliot, ed., *The Debates in the Several State Conventions on the Adoption of the Federal Constitution*, 2d ed., 5 vols. (Washington, D.C., 1836–45), 3:222; Gordon S. Wood, *The Creation of the American Republic, 1776–1787* (Chapel Hill: Published for the Institute of Early American History and Culture, Williamsburg, Va., by the University of North Carolina Press, 1969), pp. 524, 526–64.

the duplicity and flattery of courtiers who selfishly sought the favor of great men while they professed service to the public. Dissimulation, deception, design were thus accusations quickly made, and suspicion of men in power pervaded the political climate. The alternative to the courtier, opposition spokesmen said, was the true patriot, a man like themselves who did not need to dissemble and deceive because he relied solely on the people. As the conventional theory of mixed government pointed out, the people may have lacked energy and wisdom, but they made up for these deficiencies by their honesty and sincerity. Hence writers and critics, themselves gentlemen, delighted in posing as simple farmers or ploughjoggers in attacking the aristocratic pretensions and duplicity of other gentlemen who had acted condescendingly or who seemed to possess privileges and powers they had no right to have—all the while citing in support of their arguments eighteenth-century writers from Richardson to Rousseau who were increasingly celebrating the moral virtue of sincerity, or the strict correspondence of appearance and reality, action and intention.

At the beginning of the Revolution few American Whig gentlemen had any deep awareness that, in drawing these contrasts between the aristocratic guile and pretensions of the rank they belonged or aspired to and the sincerity and honest hearts of the body of common people, they were unleashing a force they could not control. In 1776 many of them, including the likes of John Adams and Thomas Jefferson, watched with equanimity and indeed enthusiasm the displacement in political office of proud and insolent grandees by new men "not so well dressed, nor so politely educated, nor so highly born. . . ." There was little to fear from such a "political metamorphosis," to use Jefferson's term, for these new men were "the People's men (and the People in general are right). They are plain and of consequence less disguised, . . . less intriguing, more sincere."[25]

Out of these kinds of changes in values, fed by the vast social transformation taking place on both sides of the Atlantic, developed a new sentimentalization of the common man and of natural and spontaneous speech. In this atmosphere the use of Greek and Latin as the

25 John Adams to Patrick Henry, June 3, 1776, in *The Works of John Adams . . .*, ed. Charles Francis Adams, 10 vols. (Boston: Little, Brown, 1850–56), 9:387–88; Thomas Jefferson to Benjamin Franklin, August 13, 1777, in *The Papers of Thomas Jefferson*, ed. Julian P. Boyd et al. (Princeton: Princeton University Press, 1950–), 2:26; Roger Atkinson to Samuel Pleasants, November 23, 1776, quoted in James Kirby Martin, *Men in Rebellion: Higher Governmental Leaders and the Coming of the American Revolution* (New Brunswick, N.J.: Rutgers University Press, 1973), p. 190.

exclusive property and ornament of gentlemen was disparaged, and the written and spoken word itself became suspect, as men, taking off from Locke's mistrust of imagery, increasingly urged that what was needed in communication was things, not words.[26] And since words, not to mention the classical languages, were associated with cultivated learning and with aristocracy, it was the common man, the simple untutored farmer or even, in the eyes of some like Jefferson, the uncorrupted Indian with his natural gift of oratory, who became consecrated. It was not long before all gentlemen, those "lawyers, and men of learning and money men, that talk so finely, and gloss over matters so smoothly," were brought into question.[27]

By the final decade of the eighteenth century the implications of what was happening were becoming clear to some American gentry. Growing apprehensions over the abuses of popular power had contributed to the movement to create the new federal government, and such fears of democracy eventually became the fixation of the Federalist party in the 1790s. Most Federalist leaders, at least those who were old enough to be politically conscious at the time of the Revolution, had not anticipated becoming afraid of the people. Like other good Whigs, they had assumed that the people, once free of English influence, would honor and elevate the country's true patriots and natural aristocracy in ways that the English Crown had not. But when in the decades following the Revolution the people seemed to succumb to the deceit and flattery of mushrooming demagogues, who were the popular counterparts of courtiers, the Federalists became bewildered and bitter. All respectability, all learning, all character— the very idea of a gentleman as a political leader—seemed to be under assault.

The Federalist writers and speakers of the 1790s responded as eighteenth-century gentlemen would—with the traditional elitist weapons of satire and invective, saturating the political climate with vituperation and venom the likes of which have never been equaled in our national history. But such verbal abuse and ridicule—against democracy, demagoguery, vulgarity—were rhetorical devices designed for a different culture than America was creating. Such calumny and invective as the Federalists expressed were supposed to be calculated

26 Meyer Reinhold, "Opponents of Classical Learning in America during the Revolutionary Period," *Proceedings of the American Philosophical Society* 112 (1968):221–34; Linda K. Kerber, *Federalists in Dissent: Imagery and Ideology in Jeffersonian America* (Ithaca, N.Y.: Cornell University Press, 1970), pp. 95–134.
27 Amos Singletary (Mass.), in Elliot, ed., *Debates*, 2:102.

and deliberately exaggerated, not a genuine expression of the satirists' inner emotions, and were justifiable because they were the result of the righteous indignation that any gentleman would feel in similar circumstances.[28] Hence, to be effective such rhetorical anger and abuse were dependent on an instantaneous uniformity of recognition by the audience of the universal principles of truth and reasonableness to which the satirist appealed. But the democratization of American society and culture that was occurring in these years was not only broadening and diversifying the public, weakening those common standards of rightness and good behavior that underlay the potency of satire; it was destroying the ability of the Federalist writers to maintain a rhetorical detachment from what was happening. The Federalists thus groped during the next decade or so to discover a rhetoric that could persuade their audience without at the same time alienating it.

The Federalists found it increasingly difficult to publicly speak the truth as they saw it and not get punished for it. Anonymity was now resorted to, less because it was unseemly for a gentleman in the eyes of other gentlemen to expose his writings to the vulgar than because it was harmful for a gentleman's public career in the eyes of the vulgar (who could vote) to be caught writing, especially if that writing contained anything unpopular.[29] "In democracies," the Federalists concluded, "writers will be more afraid *of* the people, than afraid *for* them," and thus the right principles of political science, like those that had been discovered by the Revolutionary leaders, would become "too offensive for currency or influence" and America's intellectual contributions to politics would cease.[30] Some Federalists took a stubborn pride in their growing isolation from the public, regarding scorn by the people as a badge of honor and counting on posterity to vindicate their reputations.[31] Other Federalists, however, could not

---

[28] George L. Roth, "American Theory of Satire, 1790–1820," *American Literature* 29 (1958):399–407; idem, "Verse Satire on 'Faction,' 1790–1815," *William and Mary Quarterly*, 3d ser. 17 (1960):473–85; Bruce I. Granger, *Political Satire in the American Revolution, 1763–1783* (Ithaca, N.Y.: Cornell University Press, 1960), p. 2.

[29] Robert E. Spiller et al., *Literary History of the United States*, 3d ed. (New York: Macmillan, 1963), p. 175; Benjamin Spencer, *The Quest for Nationality: An American Literary Campaign* (Syracuse, N.Y.: Syracuse University Press, 1957), p. 65.

[30] Fisher Ames, "American Literature," *Works of Fisher Ames*, ed. Seth Ames, 2 vols. (Boston: Little, Brown, 1854), 2:439–40.

[31] Richard Buel, Jr., *Securing the Revolution: Ideology in American Politics, 1789–1815* (Ithaca, N.Y.: Cornell University Press, 1972), p. 113; Gerald Stourzh,

easily abandon their role as gentlemanly leaders and sought desper-
ately to make their influence felt, some eventually concluding that
they too must begin flattering the people, saying that if they could
not achieve their ends "but by this sort of cant, we must have recourse
to it." They came to realize, in Hamilton's words, that "the first thing   ✳
in all great operations of such a government as our is to secure the
opinion of the people." But in competition with their Republican
opponents, the Federalists, said Fisher Ames, were like "flat tranquility against passion; dry leaves against the whirlwind; the weight
of gunpowder against its kindled force."[32] They could not shed fast
enough their traditional eighteenth-century rhetorical and elitist
techniques. They continued to rely on a limited audience of reasonable gentlemen like themselves who alone could respond to their
satirical blasts against democracy and vulgarity. And they preferred
private correspondence among "particular gentlemen" to dealing
with the unlettered multitude through the newly developing media
of communication, especially the newspapers.[33]

In the 1790s both the Federalists and their opponents recognized
the changing role popular media of communication were coming to
play in American public life.[34] The sale of every sort of printed
matter—books, pamphlets, handbills, periodicals, posters, broadsides
—multiplied, and through new channels of distribution these publications found their way into hands that were not used to such literature. In New York City alone the number of booksellers increased
from five in 1786 to thirty by 1800.[35] No vehicle of communication
was more significant than newspapers; in time men of all persuasions
came to believe that the press was almost singlehandedly shaping the
contours of American political life. The number of newspapers grew
from fewer than 100 in 1790 to over 230 by 1800; by 1810 Americans

Alexander Hamilton and the Idea of Republican Government (Stanford: Stanford
University Press, 1970), pp. 95–106.

32 John Rutledge, Jr., to Harrison Gray Otis, April 3, 1803, quoted in David
Hackett Fischer, *The Revolution of American Conservatism: The Federalist
Party in the Era of Jeffersonian Democracy* (New York: Harper & Row, 1969),
p. 140; Alexander Hamilton to Theodore Sedgwick, February 2, 1799, in *The
Works of Alexander Hamilton*, ed. Henry Cabot Lodge, 12 vols. (New York: Put-
nam's, 1903), 10:340; [Fisher Ames], "Laocoon. No. 1," in his *Works*, 2:113.

33 Thomas Truxtun to John Adams, December 5, 1804, quoted in Fischer,
American Conservatism, pp. 133–34.

34 Donald H. Stewart, *The Opposition Press of the Federalist Period* (Albany:
State University of New York Press, 1969), pp. 634, 638, 640.

35 Sidney I. Pomerantz, *New York: An American City, 1783–1803* (Port Washington, N.Y.: Ira J. Friedman, 1965), p. 440.

were buying over 22 million copies of 376 newspapers annually, the largest aggregate circulation of newspapers of any country in the world.[36] With this increase in readership came a change in the newspaper's style and content. Although much of the press, especially that in Federalist control, retained its eighteenth-century character, other papers began responding to the wider democratic public. Prices were reduced, new eyecatching typography was used, cartoons appeared, political information replaced advertisements on the front pages, political speeches, debates, and rumors were printed, editorials were written, and classical pseudonyms were dropped as "a friend of the people" or "one of the people" became more attractive signatures. In most public writing there was a noticeable simplification and vulgarization: the number of footnotes, the classical and literary allusions, the general display of learning, all became less common, as authors sought, in the way Paine had, to adapt to the new popular character of their readers.[37]

Not all gentlemen in the 1790s became Federalists of course, nor did all gentlemen become apprehensive over what was happening. Jefferson and the other gentlemen who came to constitute the Republican leadership retained a remarkable amount of the earlier Whig confidence in the people and in what Jefferson called the "honest heart" of the common man. Part of this faith in democracy on the part of Jefferson and his Republican colleagues in the South can be attributed to their very insulation from it, for most of the southern planters remained comparatively immune to the democratic electoral politics that were beginning to seriously disrupt northern society and to eat away the popular deference to "the better sort" that the southern gentry took for granted.[38] Moreover, because these democratic developments in the North—not only the new popular literature and the broadened public but the expanded suffrage, the new immigrants, the mobilization of new men into politics—all tended to support the Republican cause, they seemed unalarming to Republican gentlemen everywhere and only vindications of their trust in the people and fulfillments of the Revolution.

[36] Mott, *American Journalism*, p. 167; Merle Curti, *The Growth of American Thought*, 3d ed. (New York: Harper & Row, 1964), p. 209; Stewart, *Opposition Press*, pp. 15, 624.

[37] Fischer, *American Conservatism*, pp. 129–49; Stewart, *Opposition Press*, p. 19; Jere R. Daniell, *Experiment in Republicanism: New Hampshire Politics and the American Revolution, 1741–1794* (Cambridge: Harvard University Press, 1970), pp. 235–36.

[38] Buel, *Securing the Revolution*, pp. 75–90.

Nevertheless, the Republican intellectual leaders at first showed little more knowledge than the Federalists in dealing with an expanded American public. To be sure, Jefferson, in good Enlightenment manner, had always favored the full exchange of ideas and almost alone among the Founding Fathers had disliked the Philadelphia Convention delegates' "tying up the tongues of their members"—a decision, he said, which only reflected "their ignorance of the value of public discussion." And right at the outset of the 1790s Madison had urged as being favorable to liberty and republican government the development of "whatever facilitated a general intercourse of sentiments," such as roads, commerce, frequent elections, and "particularly *a circulation of newspapers through the entire body of the people.*" [39] But during the 1790s, when the popularization of American culture was proceeding rapidly, Jefferson continued to rely extensively on private correspondence for the dissemination of his views, and Madison continued to write learned pieces, like his "Helvidius" essays, for a restricted audience of educated gentlemen.

Others, however, hundreds of writers and speakers, common, ordinary obscure men, men without breeding, without learning, without character—in short, persons who were not gentlemen—were now presuming "without scruple, to undertake the high task of enlightening the public mind." By 1800, wrote the Reverend Samuel Miller in his elaborate compendium of the Enlightenment entitled *A Brief Retrospect of the Eighteenth Century*, much of the intellectual leadership of America had very recently fallen into "the hands of persons destitute at once of the urbanity of gentlemen, the information of scholars, and the principles of virtue." [40] And these intellectual upstarts were for the most part supporting the Republican party, and in their literature were exceeding even the Federalists in scurrility and vituperation and reaching out to touch an audience as obscure and ordinary as themselves.

To the Federalist this upstart nature of both authors and audience was precisely the point of their frenzied response to the literature of the 1790s. It was one thing to endure calumny and abuse from one's own social kind. That had been a constant part of Anglo-American political life for a century or more. But it was quite another thing to

39 Jefferson to John Adams, August 30, 1787, in Farrand, ed., *Records of the Federal Convention*, 3:76; Madison, "Public Opinion," *National Gazette*, December 19, 1791, in *The Writings of James Madison*, ed. Gaillard Hunt, 9 vols. (New York: Putnam's, 1900–1910), 6:70.

40 Samuel Miller, *A Brief Retrospect of the Eighteenth Century . . .* , 2 vols. (New York: Printed by T. and J. Swords, 1803), 2:254–55.

suffer such invective from social inferiors, from nongentlemen, from "un-educated printers, shop boys, and raw schoolmasters," and to have such criticism and vituperation carried down to the lowest levels of the society.[41] Like freethinking and deistic religious views, such personal abuse was socially harmless as long as it was confined to the gentlemanly ranks. But when it spread to the lower orders, as it was doing in the 1790s at the hands of Republican publications, it tended to destroy the governing gentry's personal reputation for character and the deferential respect for the rulers by the common people on which the authority of the political order was based. It was these considerations—the belief that the channels of communication between governors and governed were rapidly becoming poisoned by mushroom intellectual leadership and the fear that the stability of the entire political order was at stake—that lay behind the Federalists' desperate resort to coercion, the sedition law of 1798—an action that more than anything else has tarnished their historical reputation. The Federalists' attempt to stop up the flow of malice and falsehood from the Republican presses by the use of state power may have been desperate, but it was not irrational, as the subsequent debate over the Sedition Act showed. For at issue in the debate was not simply freedom of the press but the very nature and structure of America's intellectual life.

The debate over the Sedition Act marked the crucial turning point in the democratization of the American mind. It fundamentally altered America's understanding not only of its intellectual leadership but of its conception of public truth. The debate, which spilled over into the early years of the nineteenth century, drew out and articulated the logic of America's intellectual experience since the Revolution, and in the process it undermined the foundations of the elitist eighteenth-century classical world on which the Founding Fathers stood.

In the discussions over the sedition law the Republican libertarian theorists rejected both the old common law restrictions on the liberty of the press and the new legal recognition of the distinction between truth and falsity of opinion which the Federalists had, they thought, generously incorporated into the Sedition Act. While the Federalists clung to the eighteenth century's conception that "truths" were constant and universal and capable of being discovered by enlightened and reasonable men, the Republicans argued that opinions about

41 Fisher Ames to Jeremiah Smith, December 14, 1802, quoted in Fischer, *American Conservatism*, p. 135.

government and governors were many and diverse and their truth could not be determined simply by individual judges and juries, no matter how reasonable such men were. Hence, they concluded that all political opinions—that is, words as distinct from overt acts—even those opinions that were "false, scandalous, and malicious," ought to be allowed, as Jefferson put it, to "stand undisturbed as monuments of the safety with which error of opinion may be tolerated where reason is left free to combat it."[42]

The Federalists were incredulous. "How . . . could the rights of the people require a liberty to utter falsehood?" they asked. "How could it be right to do wrong?"[43] It was not an easy question to answer, as we are recently finding out all over again. The Republicans felt they could not deny outright the possibility of truth and falsity in political beliefs, and thus they fell back on a tenuous distinction, developed by Jefferson in his first inaugural address, between principles and opinions. Principles, it seemed, were hard and fixed, while opinions were soft and fluctuating; therefore, said Jefferson, "every difference of opinion is not a difference of principle." The implication was, as Benjamin Rush suggested, that individual opinions did not count as much as they had in the past, and for that reason such individual opinions could be permitted the freest possible expression.[44]

What ultimately made such distinctions and arguments comprehensible was the Republicans' assumption that opinions about politics were no longer the monopoly of the educated and aristocratic few. Not only were true and false opinions equally to be tolerated but everyone and anyone in the society should be equally able to express them. Sincerity and honesty, the Republicans argued, were far more important in the articulation of ultimate political truth than learning and fancy words that had often been used to deceive and dissimulate. Truth was actually the creation of many voices and many minds, no one of which was more important than another and each of which made its own separate and equally significant contribution. Solitary individual opinions may thus have counted for less,

<hr/>

[42] [George Hay], *An Essay on the Liberty of the Press* . . . (Philadelphia: Printed at the Aurora office, 1799), p. 40; Jefferson, Inaugural Address, March 4, 1801, *Writings of Jefferson*, p. 322.

[43] Samuel Dana, *Debates in Congress*, January 1801, quoted in Buel, *Securing the Revolution*, p. 252.

[44] Jefferson, Inaugural Address, March 4, 1801, *Writings of Jefferson*, p. 322; Rush to Jefferson, March 12, 1801, *Letters of Benjamin Rush*, ed. Lyman H. Butterfield, 2 vols. (Princeton: Princeton University Press, 1951), 2:831.

but in their numerous collectivity they now added up to something far more significant than had ever existed before. When mingled together they resulted in what Americans now obsessively labeled "public opinion"—a conception that soon came to dominate all of American intellectual life.[45]

Public opinion is so much a part of our politics that it is surprising that we have not incorporated it into the Constitution. We constantly use the term, seek to measure whatever it is and to influence it, and worry about who else is influencing it. Public opinion exists in any state, but in our democracy it has a special power. The Revolution in America transformed it and gave it its modern significance. By the early years of the nineteenth century, Americans had come to realize that public opinion, "that invisible guardian of honour—that eagle eyed spy on human actions—that inexorable judge of men and manners—that arbiter, whom tears cannot appease, nor ingenuity soften—and from whose terrible decisions there is no appeal," had become "the vital principle" underlying American government, society, and culture.[46] It became the resolving force not only of political truth but of all truth—from disputes among religious denominations to controversies over artistic taste. Nothing was more important in explaining and clarifying the democratization of the American mind than this conception of public opinion. In the end it became America's nineteenth-century popular substitute for the elitist intellectual leadership of the Revolutionary generation.

Although the will of the people, the vox populi, was an old idea in Western culture, it took on an enhanced significance in the latter half of the eighteenth century in response to the steady democratization of Western society. During the Revolutionary era many American leaders, echoing Hume and other enlightened thinkers, had become convinced that public opinion ought to be "the real sovereign" in any free government like theirs. Yet when Madison in 1791 referred to public opinion he was still thinking of it as the intellectual product of limited circles of gentlemen-rulers. Which is why he feared that

45 Tunis Wortman, *A Treatise Concerning Political Enquiry, and the Liberty of the Press* (New York: Printed by G. Forman for the author, 1800), pp. 118–23, 155–57.

46 William Crafts, Jr., *An Oration on the Influence of Moral Causes on National Character, Delivered Before the Phi Beta Kappa Society, on Their Anniversary, 28 August, 1817* (Cambridge, Mass.: University Press, Hilliard and Metcalf, 1817), pp. 5–6; Wortman, *Treatise*, p. 180.

the large extent of the United States made the isolated individual insignificant in his own eyes and made easier the counterfeiting of opinion by a few.[47] Other Americans, however, were coming to see in the very breadth of the country and in the very insignificance of the solitary individual the saving sources of a general opinion that could be trusted.

Because American society was not an organic hierarchy with "an intellectual unity," public opinion in America, it was now argued, could not be the consequence of the intellectual leadership of a few learned gentlemen. General opinion was simply "an aggregation of individual sentiment," the combined product of multitudes of minds thinking and reflecting independently, communicating their ideas in different ways, causing opinions to collide and blend with one another, to refine and correct themselves, leading toward "the ultimate triumph of Truth." Such a product, such a public opinion, could be trusted because it had so many sources, so many voices and minds, all interacting, that no individual or group could manipulate or dominate the whole.[48] Like the example of religious diversity in America, a comparison many now drew upon to explain their new confidence in public opinion, the separate opinions allowed to circulate freely would by their very differentness act, in Jefferson's word, as "a Censor" over each other and the society—performing the role that the ancients and Augustan Englishmen had expected heroic individuals and satiric poets to perform.[49]

The Americans' belief that this aggregation of individual sentiments, this residue of separate and diverse interacting opinions, would become the repository of ultimate truth required in the end an act of faith, a faith that was not much different from a belief in the beneficent workings of providence. In fact, this conception of public opinion as the transcendent consequence of many utterances, none of which deliberately created it, was an aspect of a larger intellectual transformation that was taking place in these years. It was related to a new appreciation of the nature of the social and historical process being developed by Western intellectuals, particularly by

[47] Madison, "Public Opinion," *National Gazette*, December 19, 1791, *Writings of Madison*, 6:70.

[48] Wortman, *Treatise*, pp. 118–19, 122–23.

[49] Jefferson to John Adams, January 11, 1816, in Lester J. Cappon, ed., *The Adams-Jefferson Letters*, 2 vols. (Chapel Hill: Published for the Institute of Early American History and Culture, Williamsburg, Va., by the University of North Carolina Press, 1959), 2:458.

that brilliant group of Scottish social scientists writing at the end of the eighteenth century. Just as numerous economic competitors, buyers and sellers in the market, were led by an invisible hand to promote an end that was no part of their intent, so too could men now conceive of numerous individual thinkers, makers and users of ideas, being led to create a result, a public opinion, that none of them anticipated or consciously brought about.

In such a world, a democratic world of progress, providence, and innumerable isolated but equal individuals, there could be little place for the kind of extraordinary intellectual leadership the Revolutionary generation had demonstrated. Because, as Americans now told themselves over and over, "public opinion will be much nearer the truth, than the reasoning and refinements of speculative or interested men," because "public opinion has, in more instances than one, triumphed over critics and connoisseurs" even in matters of artistic taste, because, as the Federalists warned, public opinion was "of all things the most destructive of personal independence & of that weight of character which a great man ought to possess," because of all these leveling and democratizing forces, it was no longer possible for individual gentlemen, in their speeches and writings, to make themselves felt in the way the Founding Fathers had.[50]

In the new egalitarian society of the early nineteenth century, where every man's opinion seemed as good as another's, either "men of genius" (they could no longer be simply educated gentlemen) became "a sort of outlaws," lacking "that *getting-along* faculty which is naturally enough the measure of a man's mind in a young country, where every one has his fortune to make"; or, in trying to emulate the civic-consciousness of the Founding Fathers, such would-be intellectual leaders ended up being "fettered by fear of popular offence or [having] wasted their energies and debased their dignity in a mawkish and vulgar courting of popular favor."[51] It was not a world many of the Founding Fathers would have liked, but they would have at least

[50] Samuel Williams, *The Natural and Civil History of Vermont*, 2d ed., 2 vols. (Burlington, Vt.: Printed by Samuel Mills, 1809), 2:394; Joseph Hopkinson, *Annual Discourse, Delivered Before the Pennsylvania Academy of the Fine Arts* ... (Philadelphia: Bradford and Inskeep, 1810), p. 29; Theodore Sedgwick to Rufus King, May 11, 1800, quoted in Richard E. Welch, Jr., *Theodore Sedgwick, Federalist: A Political Portrait* (Middletown, Conn.: Wesleyan University Press, 1965), p. 211.

[51] [Richard Henry Dana, Sr.], "Review of the Sketch Book of Geoffrey Crayon, Gent.," *North American Review* 9 (1819):327; Theron Metcalf, *An Address to the Phi Beta Kappa Society of Brown University, Delivered 5th September, 1832* (Boston: n.p., 1833), p. 6.

understood it. For it was their creation, and it was rooted in the vital force that none of them, Federalists included, ever could deny—the people. In the end nothing illustrates better the transforming democratic radicalism of the American Revolution than the way its intellectual leaders, that remarkable group of men, contributed to their own demise.

John Locke and the Preservation of Liberty: A Perennial Problem of Civic Education

Robert H. Horwitz

I N both his essay in this volume and in his much acclaimed *The Creation of the American Republic*, Professor Gordon Wood draws our attention to one of the most vexed and inadequately explored issues of the American founding.[1] The issue is this: what kind of citizenry was thought by our Founders to be requisite for the preservation and development of the American Republic, a republic which, above all, was designed to insure *liberty*. Wood reports two sharply divergent positions among those American political thinkers and statesmen who addressed themselves to the question of civic education and the preservation of liberty.

The first view, reported by Wood as having been especially significant during the revolutionary decade of the 1770s, is tellingly summarized in Samuel Adams's poignant phrase "the Christian Sparta." From the fiery crucible of revolution there was to emerge, phoenixlike, a revivified citizenry modeled after the sternest pattern of antiquity. The rationale for such a return to antiquity, so ran the argument, was that it was "the character and spirit of their people" that made the ancient republics splendid: "Frugality, industry, temperance, and simplicity—the rustic traits of the sturdy yeoman—were the stuff that made a society strong. The virile martial qualities—the scorn of ease, the contempt of danger, the love of valor—were what made a nation great."[2]

It would seem to follow from this that founders who seek to build strong republics would take every precaution to prevent the rise of commerce, as Lycurgus did in ancient times and Rousseau sought

[1] Gordon S. Wood, *The Creation of the American Republic* (Chapel Hill: University of North Carolina Press, 1969), p. 118.

[2] Ibid., p. 52.

to do in modernity. In their view, the notion of a "commercial republic" would have been a contradiction in terms, for commerce was seen to undermine the manly virtues without which a republic could not survive. It was commerce that was thought to spur the development of those petty urban crafts that weaken and demean the citizenry. Commerce opens the polis, or nation, to alien and corrupting influences. It widens the gap between the rich and the poor, degrading the latter, while producing luxuries that enervate the former.

This position was brilliantly explicated in the decade preceding the American Revolution by Rousseau in the "Dedication to the Republic of Geneva" of his famous *Discourse on the Origin of Inequality*.[3] It may have been more familiar to colonial readers through their reading of Montesquieu. Rousseau had taken great care to insure that the citizenry of a genuine republic would find it possible to realize "the general will," or, to put it in other terms, to work unfailingly and consistently for the common good. The requisite homogeneity of the populace with respect to wealth, education, and status—reinforced by the bonds of a common national religion—would give rise to the same hopes in the hearts of all the citizens, while their heads would be filled with virtually identical opinions. A salutary form of patriotism would develop and grow stronger with each generation. Under such conditions it would be difficult to distinguish between public and private concerns, and the inherent tension between them would be reduced to the minimum—despite the fact that in Rousseau's view man is not by nature "a social animal."

That the creation and preservation of such a community would require a curtailment of liberty was understood by at least some of the advocates of "a Christian Sparta." Wood tells us that "some Whigs were even willing to go so far as to advocate agrarian legislation limiting the amount of property an individual could hold" and to recommend "sumptuary laws against luxury, plays, etc. and extravagant expenses in dress, diet, and the like."[4]

The crux of this argument was that "every state in which the people participated needed a degree of virtue; but a republic which rested solely on the people absolutely required it." Indeed, "only with a public-spirited, self-sacrificing people could the authority of

[3] Note especially the seven or so criteria for a sound republic specifically set forth by Rousseau in the opening pages of this dedication.
[4] Wood, *Creation*, p. 64.

a popularly elected ruler he obeyed, but 'more by the virtue of the people, than by the terror of his power.' Because virtue was truly the lifeblood of the republic." Furthermore, "private virtue, the willingness of the people to surrender all, even their lives, for the good of the state, was primarily the consequence of men's individual private virtues." According to Charles Lee, the goal of the American polity, as shaped by this perspective, should be "a spartan egalitarian society where every man was a soldier and master of his own soul and land, the kind of society, like that of ancient Rome, where the people 'instructed from early infancy to deem themselves the property of the State . . . were ever ready to sacrifice their concerns to her interests.' "[5]

It is not easy to see how a Christian Sparta can be reconciled with inalienable natural rights, an issue with which Wood is little concerned. Perhaps this difficulty helps to explain the decline, and, more particularly, the dilution of the vision of a Christian Sparta. Its real significance is not so much as an *alternative* to a polity dedicated to the security of rights, as it is one *means* for securing them.

Whatever may have been the views of some of the "Old Republicans," it seems clear that for the Anti-Federalists—about ten years later—the *objective* was not some form of classical or Christian virtue but individual liberty. Nevertheless, most of them agreed with Sam Adams that "neither the wisest constitution nor the wisest laws will secure liberty and happiness of a people whose manners are universally corrupt." An essential and oft-reiterated concern of the Anti-Federalists was with the formation of a citizenry that would be conducive to the maintenance of a healthy, stable, and free polity. Many Anti-Federalists contended that such a citizenry could be formed only within relatively small republics (though not necessarily *poleis*) whose populace would be essentially homogeneous. Civic education could then be effectively utilized to shape the citizenry. Among the instruments of such education would be religion, and included among the goals would be sound character development and the creation of patriotism in the interests of protecting *freedom*.[6]

Many factors contributed to insuring the defeat of the Anti-

5 Ibid., pp. 68, 69, 53.

6 A. J. Beitzinger, *A History of American Political Thought* (New York: Dodd, Mead, 1972), p. 139. I am especially indebted to Herbert J. Storing for having permitted me to study the then unpublished opening volume of his epic study *The Complete Anti-Federalist* (Chicago: University of Chicago Press, 1981).

Federalists and their vision of small republics in which liberty would be fostered and guarded by the development of a virtuous citizenry. It is hardly surprising that the former colonists, having freed themselves from the bonds of an allegedly tyrannical monarchy, and an indisputably interfering parliament, were reluctant to surrender any significant part of their precious liberty to the stern demands of civic virtue.

Such unity as had been achieved within the American states during the Revolutionary War deteriorated rather rapidly. Renewed political struggle and turmoil ensued as Americans turned to their personal "pursuit of happiness." Wood reports John Adams's sad lament: " 'God forbid,' . . . that the people of Boston 'should so soon forget their own generous Feelings for the Publick and for each other as to set private Interests in Competition with that of the great Community.' "[7] That distinguished patriot Patrick Henry diagnosed the body politic as dangerously sick, as he observed the citizenry returning to the avid pursuit of personal interests. Political tensions, even violent discord of the sort illustrated by Shays's Rebellion, increased apace, with the interests of small farmers pitted against those of large farmers, advocates of soft money against those of hard money, debtors versus creditors.

The Federalists were hardly surprised by this discord. It lent weight to their argument that neither the "classical model" of republicanism, the ultimate object of which was a virtuous citizenry, nor the Anti-Federalist modification, which maintained that liberty must be safeguarded by virtue was practical. The Federalists sought a radically different solution to the political problem confronting Americans. Pushing the question of virtue largely aside, they sought to develop political arrangements and institutions that would insure " 'the existence and security of the government, *even in the absence of political virtue.'* " From this perspective, "men could now argue that '*virtue,* patriotism, or love of country, never was nor never will be till men's natures are changed, a fixed, permanent principle and support of government.' " For the first time a system of republican government was to be framed "so as to give 'fair play' to the actions of human nature, however unvirtuous." No attempt was to be made to "pervert, suppress, or ignore the evil propensities of all men."[8]

To judge from the overall character of *The Federalist*, it is evident

---

[7] Wood, *Creation*, p. 421.
[8] Ibid., pp. 429 (emphasis supplied), 610 (emphasis original), 611.

that what Madison was pointing to here was the creation of a large commercial republic, one within which the widest possible range of interests would be fostered. No attempt would be made to restrain what Machiavelli bluntly described as "man's natural desire to acquire." On the contrary, acquisitiveness would be encouraged, and the citizenry given free scope in developing the abundant resources of a new country. Every form of agricultural, manufacturing, and commercial enterprise would be encouraged. The guiding and energizing principle of the community would be the vigorous pursuit of individual self-interest.

The Federalists' position prevailed, and the Republic founded substantially on their principles has grown and prospered for nearly two centuries. This extraordinary political success does not, however, necessarily validate all of their views on government. In particular, it leaves open the question of the necessity of some form of civic virtue—an issue on which they clashed so strongly with the Anti-Federalists.

For example, how can a republic based solely on the principle of individual self-interest continue to defend itself against its external enemies if its citizenry has not an iota of patriotism, public spirit, or any element of that sense of duty that leads men to make sacrifices in defense of their country? Domestically, would not such a people be subject to such fierce factionalism as to succumb ultimately to the imposition of despotic rule by powerful individuals or groups intent on exploiting others? Would not society become ever more fragmented and men ever more estranged from one another? Tocqueville discerned this atomizing tendency in the young American republic, and he warned especially against the development of a "virtuous materialism" which could inexorably "enervate the soul and noiselessly unbend its springs of actions."

The thesis of this essay is that the dangers of which Tocqueville and others warned have progressively, perhaps inevitably, materialized, for neither the Federalists nor the Anti-Federalists provided an adequate analysis of the character and place of civic virtue in the American Republic and the need for some form of civic education. A better grasp of this issue and of a possible solution can be secured by returning to one of the most influential of the political philosophers from whom both Federalists and Anti-Federalists alike sought guidance: John Locke. In what follows, I shall sketch an interpretation of what I take to be this critically important but insufficiently understood aspect of Locke's work. I shall try to demonstrate the manner in which a republic based essentially on the pursuit of private interest could nevertheless still develop those virtues that are ultimately indispensable to the maintenance of liberty. The virtues of which Locke speaks are fully compatible with the type of polity brought into being by the Federalists. We shall see, however, that they cannot properly be understood as either Christian or classical virtues.[9]

Locke's Education for Civic Virtue

It is no longer generally remembered that shortly after publishing his *Two Treatises of Government* Locke published a seminal work on education, *Some Thoughts concerning Education*. In the discussion of the *Education* that follows, I shall pursue two major lines of argument. First, it was Locke's intention in this work to provide, among other things, an understanding of civic virtue. Locke believed that this kind of virtue was compatible with—and even indispensable for—the maintenance and well-being of legitimate republics or commonwealths. The political principles underlying such commonwealths are set forth in Locke's "Second Treatise," Locke's title for it being *An Essay concerning the True Original, Extent, and End of Civil Government*. Second, I shall argue that Locke believed that a stratum of especially bred and educated men and women was required for the preservation and well-being of civil or legitimate commonwealths in order to cope with their inherent political-educational problems to which we have drawn attention and which are inherent in them. There are two related problems that cannot be confronted here, chiefly because of a lack of data. We do not presently possess the resources to speculate meaningfully on the question of the degree to which the American Founders were directly influenced by Locke's *Education*.[10] But this we do know: some fifteen editions

[9] For some interesting and provocative reflections on this question, see Irving Kristol, "Republican Virtue vs. Servile Institutions," *The Alternative* 8, no. 5 (1975): 5–9. Kristol emphasizes that " 'republican virtue,' in the American meaning of that phrase, is a very different kind of virtue from, say, Christian virtue or classical virtue as the ancient Greeks understood it. . . . it is a political conception rather than a religious one" (p. 6).

[10] Nor for that matter do we know precisely the extent to which the Founders were influenced by Locke's work generally. On this matter see the interesting work currently being done by Charles Hyneman and Donald D. Lutz, particularly *American Political Writings during the Founding Era, 1760–1805*, ed. Hyneman

of the work appeared in English, French, and other languages between 1693 and 1779, together with many reprintings. The *Education* was included in some early editions of Locke's collected works.
It was therefore readily available and widely read.[11] Jefferson pur-
chased the *Education* for his personal library, but evidence of a
different sort is required to establish the extent of its influence.
Perhaps it had little. Unlike Locke's *Two Treatises of Government,*
it may have been widely read by our Founders, adequately understood, or both. Further, whatever the influence of Locke's *Education* on the Founders, it is a separate question whether its political-
educational principles are directly applicable to our contemporary
situation. Be this as it may, I suggest that thoughtful consideration
of Locke's educational teaching should be instructive to us in understanding the roots of pressing difficulties presently confronting
our citizenry and our country.

Locke constantly draws our attention to the inherent weaknesses
of civil societies. He observes, for example, that "the variety of
Opinions, and contrariety of Interests, which unavoidably happen in
all Collections of Men . . . would make the mighty *Leviathan* of a
shorter duration, than the feeblest Creatures; and not let it outlast
the day it was born in." What can be done to protect the "mighty
Leviathan" from this defect? If we answer this question on the basis
of Locke's strictly political teaching, the answer would have to be
nothing. Locke reinforces his observation by telling us bluntly that
"however strange it may seem, the law-maker hath nothing to do
with moral virtues and vices."[12] One infers from this that Locke
draws a sharp line between politics and morality, including (one
may reasonably suppose) any form of civic morality or civic education designed to foster morality.

---

and Lutz (Indianapolis: Liberty Press, 1983) and Lutz, "The Relative Influence
of European Writers on Late Eighteenth-Century American Political Thought,"
American Political Science Review 78, no. 1 (1984):189–97.

[11] When Mrs. Charles Carroll of Carrollton posed for her portrait by Charles
Willson Peale, that influential lady held in her hands Locke's *Education,* the
title of which Peale made clearly identifiable in the picture. Mrs. Carroll thought,
as did her husband, that Locke's work was especially appropriate for one in her
position. I am indebted to Professor Ann Diamond for bringing this fact to my
attention and to Ms. Ann Van Devanter, Guest Curator of the Baltimore Museum
of Art, for background information on both the picture and Mrs. Carroll.

[12] John Locke, *Two Treatises of Government,* ed. Peter Laslett, rev. ed. (New
York: New American Library, 1965), Book 2, pp. 376–77; J. W. Gough, *John
Locke's Political Philosophy* (Oxford: Clarendon Press, 1950), p. 190.

But before confronting this problem directly, we must be clear that this is a moral issue within the framework of Locke's thought, and we must establish it as such. One recalls from reading Locke's *Essay concerning Civil Government* that men escape from the penury and misery, yea, the overwhelming dangers of the state of nature by voluntarily contracting with others to form civil society. Men thereby vastly improve their chances for comfortable self preservation in a world that is naturally cold, hostile, and exceedingly dangerous. Mankind is said to be governed by the law of nature, but Locke quietly reveals to his readers that this law is of virtually no use in protecting men from one another.[13] It is simply ineffective, human nature being what it is, together with man's pervasive ignorance of the law of nature. It is only within civil society that man's lot may be effectively improved. It is within the genuine, social contract society, as sketched by Locke in *An Essay concerning the True Original, Extent, and End of Civil Government* that mankind can be secured in the enjoyment of liberty, be made relatively safe from the depredation of others, including the civil authorities, and accumulate virtually limitless amounts of property. Civil society makes possible the enactment and enforcement of valid legal codes based on a sound understanding of the law of nature. This understanding was to be achieved only very late in the development of mankind, and then only by one or more philosophers of the highest capacity who served as the teacher of founders, for example, the relationship of Locke's thought to the political work of Thomas Jefferson.[14]

Very good. But Locke also tells us that men are neither adequately aware of, nor sufficiently grateful for, the blessings that they enjoy, nor generally blessed with much foresight. Thus, once secured by civil society from imminent danger of loss of life, liberty, and property, they have an unfortunate propensity to cheat or chisel a bit on the social contract they have made with their fellow citizens. We are all more or less familiar with the sort of short-sighted calculation anticipated by Locke. For example, we are painfully reminded by mid-April every year that it is very important for the fiscal soundness of the country that everyone pay his full income taxes, that is, everyone

[13] For a penetrating discussion of Locke's treatment of this issue, see Richard H. Cox, *Locke on War and Peace* (Oxford: Clarendon Press, 1960), especially chap. 2.

[14] See R. Horwitz, D. Clay, and J. Clay regarding this issue in *John Locke's Questions Regarding the Law of Nature* (Charlottesville: University Press of Virginia, forthcoming).

but me. Now, unless there is some reasonably effective check on this sort of selfish calculation and the consequent action (or inaction), it is obvious that civil society cannot be maintained. Civil society makes possible civil law and provides the framework within which the moral questions that concern us as citizens must be dealt with.

But in order to understand Locke's treatment of such questions, we must identify the foundations of morality in his thought. We are assisted in this quest by an extremely interesting passage in his *Essay concerning Human Understanding* where he speaks of "the great variety of opinions concerning moral rules which are to be found among men." He relates this observation to his subsequent discussion of the bases on or by which men can be expected to keep their compacts, a condition on which the very possibility of civil society depends.

That Men should keep their Compacts, is certainly a great and undeniable Rule in Morality: But yet, if a Christian, who has the view of Happiness and Misery in another Life, be asked why a Man must keep his World, he will *give* this as a *Reason*: Because God, who has the Power of eternal Life and Death, requires it of us. But if an *Hobbist* be asked why; he will answer: Because the Publick requires it, and the *Leviathan* will punish you, if you do not. And if one of the old *Heathen* Philosophers had been asked, he would have answer'd: Because it was dishonest, below the Dignity of a Man, and opposite to Vertue, the highest Perfection of humane Nature, to do otherwise.[15]

We must afford some consideration to each of these three bases of morality for the performance of contracts. Each is understood by Locke to play some part, though rather different and unequal parts, in the preservation of civil society.

As regards the first of these foundations of morality, Locke observes that religious faith is said to be positively supported by the greatest reward available to man, namely, salvation of his soul and the assurance of its eternal felicity. Negatively, the spur to virtuous conduct based in religious faith is the awful fear of eternal damnation of the soul and the prospect of indescribable punishment. We must then briefly consider Locke's observations regarding religion as a sound and adequate foundation for virtue. Experience tells us, says he, that while "self-interest and the Conveniences of this Life, make many Men, own an *outward* Profession and Approbation" of

15 John Locke, *An Essay concerning Human Understanding*, ed. Peter H. Nidditch (Oxford: Clarendon Press, 1975), I, 3, 5, 68. For the reader's convenience, I cite book, chapter, section, and page number in the Nidditch edition.

religion, their "Actions sufficiently prove, that they very little consider the Law-giver, that prescribed these Rules; nor the Hell he has ordain'd for the Punishment of those that transgress them."[16] This observation finds support in Locke's oft repeated observation that the *actions* of men are the best "interpreters of their thoughts." Locke concludes that however fervent their professions of religious faith, most men do not have such assured "internal veneration for those rules, nor so full a persuasion of their certainty and obligation" as to make religious faith a sufficient foundation for the keeping of contracts.

Locke himself had compelling reasons for wanting to *appear* to be a devout Christian. His writings are replete with statements that he and his interpreters could advance in defense of his piety, if challenged. He went so far as to write a substantial work entitled *The Reasonableness of Christianity.*[17] One may infer that he did not want to discourage sound moral conduct based on religious belief, though we have already seen that he was far from counting decisively on the efficacy of such belief to insure good conduct, especially on the part of those people whom he intended as the subjects of his educational program. Nor should one overlook Locke's misgivings regarding misdirected religious fervor. He had long observed that fervent and misguided religious belief was a source of ferocious civil strife in England and elsewhere.

Turning to a more tangible and worldly foundation for morality, Locke speaks of the civil law. "This Law no body over-looks: the Rewards and Punishments, that enforce it, being ready at hand, and suitable to the Power that makes it: which is the force of the Commonwealth, engaged to protect the Lives, Liberties, and Possessions, of those who live according to its Laws, and has power to take away Life, Liberty, or Goods, from him, who disobeys; which is the punishment of Offences committed against this Law."[18]

No small sanctions, these, and it is surely true that hardly any

---

16 Ibid., I, 3, 6, 69 (emphasis supplied).

17 This work should be compared, however, to *A Discourse of Miracles*, which appears to undermine the possibility of establishing the dogmas of *any* religion by reason. Under the terms of his will, Locke left the question of possible posthumous publication of this *Discourse* to the discretion of certain "judicious friends," as he termed them. See Michael P. Zuckert's essay below on "Locke and the Problem of Civil Religion" for a penetrating discussion of both these works and of their relationship.

18 *Essay*, II, 28, 9, 352–53.

sane adult simply "overlooks" the civil law. Still, as Locke observes in another context, the temptation "to escape the knowledge or power of the law-maker, or the like, may make men give way to present appetite." It seems that while such men may not "overlook" the civil law, they do not therefore necessarily obey it. Overflowing prisons in all ages bear ample testimony to the fact that numerous men have thought it possible to "get away" with disobeying the civil law.

Fear of the law can, of course, be heightened in ferocious tyrannies, where powerful organizations of secret police, brutal penalties, and bestial concentration camps, as found in Hitler's Germany or in the Soviet Union, doubtless serve to deter violations of the legal code. The force of law must be taken into account, but it is by no means a sufficient foundation for morality.

We must turn finally to the most important basis for morality in Locke's thought. This basis or standard is said by Locke to have been the emphatic concern of "the old philosophers," that is, premodern philosophers. Locke terms this standard variously as "the philosophical law," the "law of opinion or reputation," or occasionally the "law of fashion." He helps us understand the character of this law in an unusually interesting passage in the *Essay*:

Virtue and Vice are Names pretended, and supposed every where to stand for actions in their own nature right and wrong: And as far as they really are so applied, they so far are co-incident with the *divine Law* above-mentioned. But yet, whatever is pretended, this is visible, that these Names, *Virtue* and *Vice*, in the particular instances of their application, through the several Nations and Societies of Men in the World, are constantly attributed only to such actions, as in each Country and Society are in reputation or discredit.[19]

This "law of opinion" is established slowly but conclusively "by a secret and tacit consent . . . in the several Societies, Tribes, and Clubs of Men in the World: whereby several actions come to find Credit or Disgrace amongst them, according to the Judgment, Maxims, or Fashions of that place."[20] Its operation depends on the desire of men for credit and reputation, or from their fear of shame and disgrace. This is nothing less than "the principal spring from which

19 Ibid., II, 28, 10, 353. In the first edition of the *Essay* Locke remarks that he terms this "the *philosophical* Law, not because Philosophers make it, but because they have most busied themselves to enquire after it, and talk about it."
20 Ibid.

the acting of men take their rise, the rule they conduct them by, and the end to which they direct them." This is the law that is decisive in determining, for example, the choice of preferred occupations among men. It "makes merchants in one country and soldiers in another. This puts men upon school divinity in one country, and physics or mathematics in another." It even "cuts out the dresses for the women, and makes the fashions for the men and makes them endure the inconvenience of all." [21]

Paradoxically, the effectiveness of this law is linked to the fact that most members of a given community accept its standards as absolutely true. At the same time, Locke reveals to us that this law of opinion is characterized by what today we would term its "relativity." We must return to this point, but first it is necessary to learn more from Locke about the effective functioning of this law and the way in which it is inculcated into a community.

Locke has told us that adherence to the law of opinion (which we may now, without being misleading, term the law of public opinion), enables men to endure inconveniences and even much more. It can persuade men to give up their most precious possessions under certain circumstances, even life itself. It enables some men silently to bear the most terrible torture: "the Hurons and other people of Canada with such constancy endure unexpressible torments." [22] The Huron Indians spoken of in this passage were warriors whose moral code, or "law of public opinion," commanded them, if captured, to die in silence, no matter how terrible their torture. One may begin to perceive in Locke's line of reasoning here a route through which a teaching about civic virtue may be understood.

Before proceeding on this path, one must ask how the "law of public opinion" could "condition" men to suffer pain voluntarily, especially since one learns elsewhere in Locke's *Essay* that the chief positive good men naturally seek in pleasure, or, put negatively, the avoidance of pain. [23]

Locke's answer is that the standards of the community, via the law

[21] James L. Axtell, ed., *The Educational Writings of John Locke* (Cambridge: Cambridge University Press, 1968), p. 153, n. 1. For the reader's convenience, subsequent citations will include Locke's section number, and page number in the Axtell edition. Axtell discovered this significant quotation in a diary entry of Locke's dated December 12, 1678. It was made while Locke was traveling in France.

[22] Ibid.

[23] *Essay*, II, 21, 43–44, 259–61.

of public opinion, can in varying degrees be inculcated into the young. Those who seek "to principle Children" can "instil into the unwary, and, as yet, unprejudiced Understanding, (for white Paper receives any Characters) those Doctrines they would have them retain and profess." These doctrines generally remain unchallenged as people grow older, for they will not be able to "find any thing more ancient there, than those Opinions, which were taught them, before their Memory began to keep a Register of their Actions." More significantly, these doctrines or opinions will seem to be "natural" to those who hold them, for virtually all members of a community will "make no scruple to *conclude, That those Propositions, of whose knowledge they can find in themselves no original, were certainly the impress of God and Nature* upon their Minds; and not taught them by any one else."[24]

It is precisely this "internalized" aspect of the law of public opinion that renders its operation most certain and its enforcement far easier, less complex, and infinitely more economical than is the case with the civil law. It is noteworthy, incidentally, that, according to Locke, the power of the conscience can be made more effective in enforcing the law of public opinion than the religious law. Locke may here be providing us with a tacit indication of the part religion *should* play in civil society. Locke has earlier observed that the actions of innumerable people testify to their belief that they can break the religious law with impunity and risk violations of the civil law, but he tells us in no uncertain terms that "no Man scapes the Punishment of their Censure and Dislike, who offends against the Fashion and Opinion of the Company he keeps, and would recommend himself to." He contends further that there is not "one of ten thousand, who is stiff and insensible enough, to bear up under the constant Dislike, and Condemnation of his own Club. He must be of a strange, and unusual Constitution, who can content himself, to live in constant Disgrace and Disrepute with his own particular Society. . . . This is a Burthen too heavy for humane Sufferance."[25]

Given the critical importance of the law of public opinion, it follows that governments, even though they are legitimately constituted by Lockian standards, will be ineffective unless they rest on a foundation of sound opinion. That in turn can be accomplished only if the content of public opinion is established through the

24 Ibid., I, 3, 22, 81 and I, 3, 23, 82 (emphasis original).
25 Ibid., II, 28, 12, 357.

proper education of those citizens on whom the proper functioning
of the commonwealth depends. This is the ultimate concern of civic
education for Locke in its most comprehensive and far-reaching
sense.

Locke's Intention in
Some Thoughts concerning Education

Our hypothesis regarding Locke's view of the relationship between
the law of public opinion and the overall character of the regimes
within which it operates is fully consistent with his statement of
intention in the Epistle Dedicatory of the *Education*. His concern
in that work supplements the sphere of the strictly political, the
specific concern of his *Two Treatises of Government*. Thus we observe that in the Preface to the *Two Treatises* he declares that he
will "make good" the ruler's "title in the consent of the people,"
while counteracting the "greatest mischief to prince and people"
that can occur, namely, "'the propagating wrong notions concerning
government." In the Epistle Dedicatory to the *Education*, Locke
tells us that "this Subject is of so great Concernment, and a right way
of Education is of so general Advantage," that "Errours in Education
should be less indulged than any."

The well Educating of their Children is so much the Duty and Concern of
Parents, and the Welfare and Prosperity of the Nation so much depends on
it, that I would have every one lay it seriously to Heart; and after having
well examined and distinguished what Fancy, Custom or Reason advises in
the Case, set his Helping Hand to promote every where that Way of training
up Youth, with regard to their several Conditions, which is the easiest,
shortest, and likeliest to produce vertuous, useful, and able Men in their
distinct Callings.[26]

Locke includes himself in the injunction that everyone, whether
parents or not, should be concerned with this educational task. He
presents himself rhetorically in this context as one who is carrying
out *his* civic duty: "for I think it every Man's indispensible Duty, to
do all the Service he can to his Country: And I see not what Differ-

[26] Epistle Dedicatory, *Educational Writings*, pp. 112–13. Unfortunately, Locke's
extremely important Epistle Dedicatory does not appear in most editions of the
Education most widely used in the United States and Britain.

ence he puts between himself and his Cattel, who lives without that Thought."[27]

We must emphasize that it is not Locke's intention in the *Education* to deal with the education of the entire citizenry, but only with that part which he regards as indispensable for the preservation of the commonwealth and of those standards requisite for the maintenance of its political legitimacy. These people provide the standards of behavior and opinion by which others are guided. It is this stratum of the populace that plays the most significant part in shaping the law of public opinion. It also carries a very significant part of the everyday political responsibilities within the commonwealth. This stratum of the populace is termed "gentlemen" by Locke. Of them he says that "if those of that Rank are by their Education once set right, they will quickly bring all the rest into Order."[28] We shall refer to these people hereafter as "the gentry."

Locke contends that a relatively small stratum of the populace of a commonwealth can, should, and must carry extraordinary responsibilities in shaping the life of the entire community. The violently antagonistic reactions that will be evoked in some by such an "elitist" doctrine may be somewhat softened by our invocation of the testimony of that eminent social scientist Max Weber, who can at least help us to understand historically the origins of the gentry. In his famous lecture "Politics as a Vocation," Weber says of these people that "the English gentry represents a stratum that the prince originally attracted in order to counter the barons. The prince placed the stratum in possession of the offices of 'self-government,' and later he himself became increasingly dependent upon them." But this was not all, for "the gentry maintained the possession of all offices of local administration by taking them over without compensation in the interest of their own social power." Weber provides us with further, helpful information about the make up of this stratum of the populace, which included "clergymen, teachers, professors, lawyers, doctors, apothecaries, prosperous farmers, manufacturers—in England the whole stratum that considered itself as belonging to the class of gentlemen." Such political organization as they had consisted at first of "occasional associations at most local political clubs."[29]

27 Ibid., p. 111.
28 Ibid., pp. 112–13. See Professor Wood's essay in this volume.
29 Hans H. Gerth and C. Wright Mills, eds., *From Max Weber: Essays in Sociology* (New York: Oxford University Press, 1946), pp. 93, and 100. In his classic

If we are to understand Locke's *Education* aright, it is imperative that we do not confuse the gentry with the titled nobility, who possessed great hereditary wealth and position. While the gentry consisted largely of families of varying degrees of wealth, within its ranks were always to be found men of modest means but of exceptional intelligence, industry, and foresight who possessed the capacity for improving their circumstances. It is important to understand that Locke did not write his *Education* as a form of apologetics for the existing gentry, to say nothing of the hereditary nobility, as is often suggested in the abysmally bad introductions to most editions of the *Education*. Quite the contrary. He berates the contemporary English gentry which, in its rural manifestations, is characterized by Locke as having the "Cup often at [its] Nose," while wasting much of its remaining time in the chase. Its urban counterpart is described as squandering its time at cards and its substance in gambling. It is in no small part Locke's concern over the widespread decay of the gentry that requires him to address himself to the problem of its re-education. "Vice . . . ripens so fast now adays, and runs up to Seed so early in young people, that it is impossible to keep a Lad from the spreading Contagion; if you will venture him abroad in the Herd." It is no exaggeration to say that Locke felt that the future of the commonwealth was threatened unless his program of educational reform was successful, for if the "Innocence, Sobriety, and Industry of those who are coming up, be not taken care of and preserved, 'twill be ridiculous to expect, that those who are to succeed next on the Stage, should abound in that Vertue, Ability, and Learning, which has hitherto made *England* considerable in the World." [30]

History, Thomas Macaulay provides us with a somewhat more detailed account of the activities of the country gentry of the seventeenth century. "He was a magistrate, and, as such, administered gratuitously to those who dwelt around him, a rude patriarchal justice, which, in spite of innumerable blunders and of occasional acts of tyranny, was yet better than no justice at all. He was an officer of the trainbands; and his military dignity, though it might move the mirth of gallants . . . raised his character in his own eyes, and in the eyes of his neighbors. . . . Thus the character of the English esquire of the seventeenth century was compounded of two elements which we are not accustomed to find united. His ignorance and uncouthness, his low tastes and gross phrases, would, in our time, be considered as indicating a nature and a breeding thoroughly plebian; yet he was essentially a patrician, and had, in large measure, both the virtues and the vices which flourish among men set from their birth in high place, and accustomed to authority, to observance, and to self-respect" (*The History of England*, 5 vols. [New York: Harper, 1849], I:300).

30 *Educational Writings*, 70, pp. 169–70 (emphasis original).

Implicit in Locke's warning is a suggestion amplified through the *Education*: the decay of the young gentry cannot be rectified by the existing English schools and universities. Why not? Because, Locke tells us, that, as for the substance of what is imparted by the existing educational institutions, he would rather not have the students' "Heads stuff'd with a deal of trash."[31] As for the pedagogical techniques by which this "trash" is implanted, Locke finds them stupid and self-defeating. They are based on a misunderstanding of the nature of children, misguided teaching techniques, and improper goals.

Given his evaluation of the existing educational institutions, it should not surprise us that Locke demands far more than mere reform. He does something far more radical. He recommends to parents that they avoid the corruption of public education altogether. He insists that parents assume full responsibility for the education of their children, a program that must be undertaken privately—far removed from the influence of state and church alike. Locke's educational program differed so radically from existing educational theory and practice that he delayed publication of his *Education* for many years. Even then he first published it anonymously, explaining that "I am not in my nature a lover of novelty, nor contradiction; but my notions in this treatise, have run me so far out of the common road and practice, that I would have been glad to have had them . . . stopped, if they had appeared impracticable, or extravagant, from going any farther."[32]

An adequate account of Locke's rich and complex educational thought cannot be presented here, so I shall address myself as much as possible to the central concern of the relationship between liberty and virtue as the problem presents itself within the *Education*. I will also attempt to provide something of an overview of the substance and technique of Locke's educational teaching. The discussion is guided by the hypothesis that a basic goal of this educational enterprise is that of developing youngsters fitted to become suitable members of a class of citizens indispensable for the creation or preservation of a Lockian civil society.

For our purposes, we may consider that the subject matter of the *Education* consists of three major categories: (1) training of the body, (2) the redirecting or rechanneling of basic human passions through

31 Ibid., 94, p. 200.
32 Ibid., p. 13, quoted from a letter dated March 28, 1693, to his friend William Molyneux of Dublin. See *The Works of John Locke*, 9 vols. (London: C. Baldwin, Printer, 1824), 3:491.

a somewhat unique process of habituation, and (3) the carefully charted activation of the mind. Before considering these aspects of Locke's educational project, we must take account of the raw materials with which the educator must work: human nature. Locke provides a thorough, though artfully presented, account of human nature in his *Two Treatises of Government*. In the *Education* he seems to suggest that we can confirm this understanding by discovering anew (at the beginning of every human life) the same essential traits that characterize human nature. Locke's accounts of the nature of infants, children, and young men and women were not simply speculative. He had spent a considerable part of his early manhood as a tutor at Oxford, and subsequently he served as a tutor (among other things) in the households of some of England's greatest statesmen. He was a physician of no mean capacity, who in the process of supervising the delivery of some of his future charges, was able to observe newborn infants at first hand. Let us listen for a moment to the observations of this kindly, old Christian philosopher, educator, and physician as he bends over the cradle to observe the tender infants within.

"I have told you" throughout the *Education*, says Locke, "that Children love *Liberty*," but "I now tell you, they love something more; and that is *Dominion*: And this is the first Original of most vicious Habits, that are ordinary and natural." This Machiavellian observation is supported by Locke's further observation that "this love of *Power* and Dominion shews it self very early." We further observe, says Locke, that "Children as soon almost as they are born . . . cry, grow peevish, sullen, and out of humour, for nothing but to have their *Wills*." They naturally want to dominate others, and, no less naturally, demand "*Propriety* and Possession" over whatever inanimate objects about them happen to catch their fancy.[33]

Nor are these the only significant natural passions that Locke observes in children. "They often *torment*, and treat very roughly young Birds, Butterflies, and such other poor Animals, which fall into their Hands, and that with a seeming kind of Pleasure." This natural cruelty is contrasted by Locke to the "unnatural Cruelty" subsequently "planted in us" through the medium of custom. Essential for Locke's understanding of human nature is his conclusion that "we are all, even from our Cradles, vain and proud Creatures."[34]

33 Ibid., 103–5, p. 207 (emphasis original).
34 Ibid., 116, pp. 225–26 (emphasis original); 119, p. 229; 131.

The significance of these natural characteristics and propensities is heightened by the fact that children "quickly learn the Trick" or art of "Dissimulation, and Falsehood, which they observe others to make Use of."

One might easily—and rightly—conclude that these newborn infants and young children described by Locke possess natures better suited for existence in either the state of nature or Hobbesian despotisms than for an education designed to prepare them for citizenship within civil society. I have stated the problem in harsh terms, for the task of the Lockian educator cannot properly be described as anything less than daunting and formidable.

In view of this understanding of the raw materials with which the Lockian educator must work, he has to make a critically important choice between two ways of proceeding. The traditional mode of education was that of imposing a harsh and very restrictive regimen on the child. Discipline of the body was guided by a simple maxim: "spare the rod and spoil the child." The child's mental "faculties" were supposedly developed by endless repetitive drill and memorization. Above all, every aspect of education was shaped by a pervasive and constant concern with the salvation of the soul. Locke enumerates a few of the materials used for this religious education, "the Horn-Book, Primer, Psalter, Testament, and Bible."[35] Schools and universities, of that age, and, indeed, of most ages in most places, rested on religious foundations, were staffed largely from the ranks of the clergy, and held their most important function to be the preparation of young men for religious orders.[36]

Locke castigates the contemporary "educational establishment," its activities, goals, and methods throughout his *Education*. He demonstrates that it is misdirected and self-defeating. Self-defeating because its victims, as Locke views those children subjected to it, call into play all of their abundant energy in order to negate the educational program imposed upon them. At best, the brutality of educators might secure an outward show of conformity on the part of students in order to minimize beatings. Then the chief objective of children, the real game of their lives, and their greatest sport, becomes that of outwitting parents and educators. While the latter believe themselves to be concerned with the child's welfare and de-

35 Ibid., 157, p. 260.

36 See Maurice Cranston, *John Locke: A Biography* (London: Longmans, Green, 1957), p. 74, for a discussion of some aspects of this point.

velopment, all that the youngsters see in these efforts of their elders is an attempt to dominate them—a cruel effort to deprive them of their cherished liberty. Such "students" long for the day when they can escape these toils and pursue their happiness.

All this is not to say that the traditional mode of education had *no* effect. Locke observes that the application of sufficient force, beatings, and heavy-handed subjugation may sometimes succeed in breaking the spirit of children. But such youngsters he regards as virtually destroyed. They would never be of use to themselves or to others. Subdued and submissive wretches are suitable subjects for despotisms but are in no way fitted for productive lives—to say nothing of active citizenship—in *civil* society.[37]

It comes as no surprise, then, to discover that Locke's approach to education is diametrically opposed in every significant respect to the contemporary approach. Instead of attempting to stifle the natural vigor of children, he contends that it must be employed positively in behalf of educational endeavor. He would harness the spontaneous vitality of children rather than oppose it. It is folly, he argues, to entomb youngsters in bleak studyhalls or dark classrooms. They will learn nothing of use, and probably nothing at all. You will only manage to enfeeble their bodies and fill them with a loathing for school. Youngsters should spend most of their time out of doors, in fair weather or foul. The initial objective of education should be to foster sound bodily growth, to toughen physiques. Locke's blunt advice to the gentry on this point is simple. They "should use their Children, as the honest Farmers and substantial Yoemen do theirs."[38] The children of the gentry should be made as little dependent as possible on the comforts by which the wealthy generally corrupt and enervate their children. Their food should be plain and simple; their meals should be somewhat irregular. They should learn to sleep on uncomfortable beds and to make-do with whatever rough expedients may be made available for the bare satisfaction of their bodily desires. Such youngsters will become ever more rugged, self-sufficient, and able to withstand not only the ever-present illnesses and perils of childhood, but also—and more significantly—their tough, robust bodies will be well-fitted to bear up under the inevitable vicissitudes of later years.

[37] *Educational Writings*, 51, p. 150. Locke castigates that severe and "slavish discipline" that may break a child's spirit and thereby produce a *"low spirited moap'd* Creature" who will prove to be a "useless thing to himself and others."

[38] Ibid., 4, pp. 115–16.

The natural passions reported by Locke as he observed the infant in his cradle should not, indeed, cannot, be suppressed or simply eliminated. What is wanted is not suppression, but *redirection*: "For where there is no Desire, there will be no Industry."[39] The powerful, relentless, and urgent drives of the passions supply the motive power by which the youngster's activities are impelled and fueled. The art of the educator is to harness this abundant power and to channel or direct it toward objectives beneficial to the child and the community. Locke furnishes us with a number of "keys" or "secrets" to this art throughout the *Education*. The first of these is familiar to contemporary Americans as the "Tom Sawyer technique." Try to force a youngster to do a task, such as whitewash a fence, and the battle is on! If the job is done at all, it will be at a snail's pace, and the child will likely manage to establish that your efforts were not worth the meager results. Locke's suggestion: keep the brushes and whitewash inaccessible, but arrange that one day the child will "happen" to see an esteemed adult whitewash a few boards with apparent relish and satisfaction. The child will be consumed with a desire to enjoy the privilege of participating in this activity of grownups. You will hardly be able to keep him from this good sport.

It is in such a fashion that Locke did in fact successfully tempt youngsters under his supervision to learn the letters of the alphabet at a very early age. He designed what we might term "alphabetical dice," which he initially made inaccessible to the children of the household.[40] The youngsters watched with wonder and envy as adults rolled the dice, identified the mysterious symbols, and composed words from them. The dice were kept under lock and key, thereby making them all the more desirable. With seeming reluctance adults granted gradually the children the privilege of participating in this grand sport, the successful pursuit of which of course required them to learn the alphabet. We all know from experience how quickly children can learn something that *they* consider of pressing importance and in which they find delight. They devote themselves wholeheartedly to such pursuits and master difficulties in short order. Locke was not unaware that the game we have described would also heighten natural competitiveness, but only under conditions of basic civility, nor would he have objected to this—as many contemporary American educators surely would do.

[39] Ibid., 126, p. 234.
[40] Ibid., 150–52, pp. 256–58.

The example of "alphabetical dice" points to the second of Locke's "keys" to sound education, for whatever activity children are engaged in presents perceptive adult spectators opportunities to bestow *praise* or *blame* on the participants. Let the child who quickly learns the alphabet or who recognizes complex words from the roll of the dice be praised for his keenness; an additional warm satisfaction is thereby added to the pleasure and rewards of the pastime that he is avidly pursuing. Well-timed, sincere, and carefully directed praise enable parents and other educators to make good use of the child's "natural pride," even as one works to socialize its effects by increasing his desire for a good reputation among those peers whom he likes and those adults whom he respects and whom he looks up to throughout his childhood.

Rechanneling Human Vices

Each of the natural vices of "the Sons of *Adam*," to use Locke's term, must be redirected into socially sound and useful channels, if it cannot be transformed. For example, Locke has told us that children are naturally possessive and quick to seize upon whatever strikes their fancy. The educator must therefore try to redirect this vice into a form of virtue, namely, "the contrary quality of a Readiness to impart to others."

This should be encouraged by great Commendation and Credit, and constantly taking care, that he loses nothing by his *Liberality*. Let all the Instances he gives of such Freeness, be always repaid, and with Interest; and let him sensibly perceive, that the Kindness he shows to others is no ill Husbandry for himself; but that it brings a Return of Kindness both from those that receive it, and those who look on. Make this a Contest among Children, who shall out-do one another this way: And by this Means, by a constant Practice, Children having made it easie to themselves to part with what they have, good Nature may be settled in them into an Habit, and they may take Pleasure, and pique themselves in being *Kind*, *Liberal* and *Civil* to others.[41]

We observe that in this illustration the child acts freely. He is not compelled to give to others, but he learns through his rewarding experiences that "generosity is the best policy." To be sure, this is a utilitarian understanding of "Liberality," but it is one that is per-

41 Ibid., 110, p. 214.

fectly compatible with a Lockian commonwealth, a political order whose legitimacy is based on the freely given consent of the governed and whose watchword is *liberty*. Locke's *Education* makes it abundantly clear to the careful reader that the goal of the educator within such a polity cannot and should not be the development of a citizenry shaped by the classical virtues as they were understood by "the old philosophers," for they left virtue "unendowed" or unrewarded. The most we can expect of the Lockian counterpart of these virtues is some reasonable facsimile thereof—but even this is by no means inconsequential for the political order.

Locke's citizenry is not likely to be significantly shaped by the Christian virtues, at least as they were understood by his religious contemporaries. We observed earlier that Locke took pains to remove his prospective students from the hands of the clergy through the simple expedient of educating them at home.[42] What kind of religious training does Locke then recommend to their parents and tutors? The answer to this question can be succinctly stated: Surprisingly little, simple, and rather curious.

Locke tells us that there ought "to be imprinted" on the child's "Mind a true Notion of *God*, as of the independent Supreme Being, Author and Maker of all Things." In the same paragraph he goes on to add that it "would be better if Men generally" accepted "such an Idea of *God*, without being too Curious in their Notions about a Being, which all must acknowledge incomprehensible." Locke would not have children, or even adults for that matter, "distract their Thoughts with curious Enquiries into his inscrutable Essence and Being." Locke firmly warns us that the "tender Mind" of the young especially must be protected "from all Impressions and Notions of *Spirits* and *Goblings*," from *"Bug-bear* Thoughts," from what we would today call "Ghost stories," such as tales of *"Raw-Head* and *Bloody Bones"*— and especially from any mention of "Evil Spirits."[43] This would surely preclude any reference whatsoever to the devil or his minions. Locke observes that such pernicious notions are all too commonly spread by uneducated and superstitious folk, especially servants, who commonly try to cow their young charges into obedience by frightening them with tales of the supernatural. Locke never tires of warning parents that they must take the greatest pains to pro-

42 Ibid.
43 Ibid., 136, pp. 241, 242; 138, pp. 242–43, 244.

tect children against this particularly pernicious source of corruption.

Still, how could such protection be afforded within a devoutly Christian household in view of the innumerable references in the New Testament to spirits, both good and evil, the devil, and endless references to the torments of hell that await the wicked, and all such things? Locke's answer is blunt and to the point. Protecting the children against superstitious servants will not suffice; they must also be protected from the Bible itself. The "Good Book" is to be kept strictly out of their hands.

As for the *Bible*, which Children are usually imploy'd in, to exercise and improve their Talent *in Reading*, I think, the promiscuous reading of it through, by Chapters, as they lye in order, is so far from being of any Advantage to Children, either for the perfecting their *Reading*, or principling their Religion, that perhaps a worse could not be found . . . what an odd jumble of Thoughts must a Child have in his Head, if he have any at all, such as he should have concerning Religion, who in his tender Age, reads all the Parts of the *Bible* indifferently as the Word of God, without any other distinction.

Locke goes on to suggest that in place of Holy Scripture the child might be provided with a brief "history of the Bible," a work designed to avoid what Locke tantalizingly terms the "inconvenient" notions of Scripture. Editors of these improved Histories of the Bible were charged with taking care to arrange that their contents were "laid down in . . . due Order of Time," with "several things omitted" from Scripture. Readers would thus be spared the "Confusion, which is usually produced by promiscuous reading of the Scripture." A good case in point, Locke suggests, is the Biblical account of *"Noah's* Flood," for he offers an alternative explanatory *"Hypothesis"* designed to take account of the "Phaenomena of the Deluge as deliver'd by *Moses*, at an easier rate than those many hard Suppositions that are made use of to explain it." Such negative suggestions aside, Locke goes on positively and reassuringly to tell us "that there are some Parts of the *Scripture*, which may be proper to be put into the Hands of a Child, to ingage him to read: such as are the Story of *Joseph*, and his Brethren, of *David* and *Goliah*, of *David* and *Jonathan*," and so on. Locke adds that there are other "Stories" that the child "should be made to read for his Instruction, as That, *What you would have others do unto you, do you the same unto them.*" It is worth observing that all of the Biblical "stories" recommended by Locke in this passage are from the Old Testament, and also that his negative statement of the "Golden Rule" follows the phraseology of Thomas Hobbes rather than Jesus Christ.[44]

There is, however, a more significant observation to be made about Locke's references to the Bible in his *Education*. Almost every time that he speaks of the possible use of the Bible for educational purposes, he refers to a strikingly different source of moral instruction, *Aesop's Fables*. The Bible, as we have seen, is to be kept strictly out of the hands of children, but *Aesop* is to be made ever so readily available to the child as soon as he has learned to read. Locke pointedly describes *Aesop* as a book that will not fill the child's head "with perfectly useless trumpery, or lay the principles of Vice and Folly. . . . I think, *Æsop's Fables* the best, which being Stories apt to delight and entertain a Child, may yet afford useful Reflections to a grown Man." Given the importance that Locke placed on Aesop, it is not surprising that he invested considerable time and effort in the preparation and publication of a unique interlinear Latin/English edition of the Fables.[45]

We must now quickly summarize Locke's overall education method. Taking human nature as it is, Locke shows how one may rechannel or redirect the natural passions and propensities of children through effective applications of "Good and Evil, *Reward* and *Punishment*," which "are the only Motives to a rational Creature." But Locke makes a radical departure from traditional educational theory and practice. The fatal mistake made by parents and other educators in the past has been in their "ill-choice" of rewards and punishments. They have foolishly connected rewards and punishments with "the Pains and Pleasures of the Body." Locke demonstrates that the infliction of pain as a punishment defeats the major goal of education. Such actions serve to "increase and strengthen those Inclinations which 'tis our Business to subdue and master."[46] The use of mere force to punish or control children can at best teach them only to fear and yield to it while they must. Nothing in this process, says Locke, leads the child to genuine acceptance of those sound standards,

44 Ibid., 158, p. 261; 191, pp. 302–3; 192, pp. 303–4; 159, p. 261. Cf. Locke's paraphrase of the Golden Rule, "What you would have others do unto you, do you the same unto them" with that of Hobbes: "whatsoever you require that others should do to you, that do ye to them" (*Leviathan*, chap. 14).

45 *Educational Writings*, 155, p. 259. For a more extended account of the content and character of Locke's edition of Aesop, see Robert H. Horwitz and Judith B. Finn, "Locke's Aesop's Fables," *Locke Newsletter*, no. 6 (Summer 1975), pp. 71–88.

46 *Educational Writings*, 54, p. 152; 55, p. 152.

the violation of which requires that he be punished. In terms of our earlier discussion, those standards, a law of public opinion with sound content, have not been "internalized." For the same reason that Locke rejects the discipline of the rod or stick, he rejects the converse, but related, practice of securing good conduct from children by offering them tempting "carrots." He would not secure good behavior from children by bribing them with the promise of bodily gratification, since this again serves only to establish an improper identification in the child's mind. In short, Locke is not training mere animals.

He is educating men, and we "must never forget that Children are to be treated as rational Creatures." The rewards and punishments utilized by Locke are the use of "*Esteem* and *Disgrace*," which are, he tells us, "of all others, the most powerful Incentives to the Mind, when once it is brought to relish them. If you can once get into Children a Love of Credit, and an Apprehension of Shame and Disgrace, you have put into them the true Principle." This, Locke proclaims, is "the great Secret of Education."[47]

The political implications of the foregoing teaching are substantial for a commonwealth based on Lockian political principles. A concern with *reputation* would be the distinguishing characteristic of children bred and educated according to the principles of Locke's educational teaching. People raised in this fashion would look with disdain on the punishments and rewards designed to ensure law-abiding conduct on the part of ordinary people. Their sense of shame would generally preclude flagrant violation of the civil law, for among other things the prospect of being seen in the prisoner's dock with common criminals would be utterly humiliating to them.

Nor would the rewards and punishments promised by religion be likely to play any significant part in insuring good conduct on the part of these people. They would conform to the established religious observances of the community, but more for appearances, for the sake of their reputations, than from deep, inner conviction. The law that would guide their lives would be the law of public opinion.

By way of concluding, let us once again state the central issue and then comment briefly on the question of whether Locke's creation of a stratum of specially educated citizens moves us in the direction of its resolution. We turned to Locke's political-educational writings

[47] Ibid., 55, pp. 152–53.

in the expectation that they might prove useful in providing a perspective from which we might best be able to evaluate the strengths and weaknesses of what we have roughly characterized as the Federalist and Anti-Federalist positions on the place and character of civic education in the American regime. Locke's *Education* makes it abundantly clear that he would not accept as adequate the position that a strong political order could be maintained *simply* on the basis of individual pursuit of self-interest narrowly understood. A healthy Lockian regime requires vigorous and solid leadership, leadership of a type that would best be furnished in his view by the development of that stratum of the population that he terms the gentry. Without the vision and vigor provided by such leadership, the rest of the populace would lack the requisite standards of a decent law of public opinion, and the political order would inevitably deteriorate.

We saw earlier that the Anti-Federalists shared a concern of this sort, as did Tocqueville and many others, and today we are faced with mounting evidence that they were not wrong. But Locke would have argued vigorously against major aspects of the Anti-Federalist prescription for curing these ills. Unlike the Anti-Federalists, he sought to provide principles applicable to the large and expansive commercial republic.

Locke provides in his *Education*, I believe, a position that incorporates some elements of both the Federalist and Anti-Federalist views on civic education, but his position transcends and transforms them. For example, Lockian commonwealths would be activated by the powerful and reliable force of individual self-interest. At the same time this pursuit of self-interest, as it was manifested by Locke's specially educated stratum of gentry, would be neither narrow nor shortsighted. This gentry would possess a form of virtue, as we have seen, but neither in the classical nor Christian forms. From this stratum would come people equipped to provide the leadership required for the vigorous development of the commonwealth in times of peace and for its defense in times of crisis.

Let us cast a final glance, then, at the character of the men and women who would be produced by Locke's program of education. These people would be physically robust, well bred, and equipped with the skills required for the conduct of business and political affairs. They would be habituated to withstand the rigor of very active lives, including the perils of travel and residence abroad. They would be characterized by an insatiable curiosity about most aspects of the world in which they live. The major thrust of their activities would be toward the acquisition of property, whether through the careful management of land or through trade, commerce, or such professions as law, medicine, or the like. Their Lockian education would have afforded them considerable scope for the application of their carefully nurtured native intelligence to the broadest possible variety of practical affairs. They would be "men of business," in the broad seventeenth-century meaning of that term.

While one might rightly say of such people that they were pursuing their self-interest properly understood, one could not simply leave it at that. The concern of these people with *reputation*, their ambition and even pride, not only within their own class, but also within the wider community, would provide the requisite motivation for engaging in public service. They would be courageous and patriotic and quite capable of performing military service, if called upon to do so. Still, they would not be tempted to such dangerous folly as dueling, even in the unlikely event that such a mode of settling personal grievances were permitted by the civil law within a Lockian community. Nor would such men be tempted by visions of becoming warlike conquerors, for they would have learned from the study of history, as Locke presents it to them, to hold conquerors in abhorrence.[48] They would have learned that the development of sound commercial relations with other countries is a far more profitable, long-lasting, and stable relationship than the despotic rule of subject people.[49]

---

48 Ibid., 199, pp. 312–13. In discussing the question of whether young men should receive instruction in fencing, Locke acknowledges that it is "a good Exercise for Health, but dangerous to the Life" (p. 312). Locke characterizes the contemporary study of history in strong terms: "All the Entertainment and talk of History is of nothing almost but Fighting and Killing: And the Honour and Renown, that is bestowed on Conquerours (who for the most part are but the great Butchers of Mankind) farther mislead growing Youth, who by this means come to think Slaughter the laudable Business of Mankind, and the most Heroick of Vertues. By these steps *unnatural Cruelty* is planted in us; and what Humanity abhors, Custom reconciles and recommends to us, by laying it in the way to Honour" (116, pp. 226–27, emphasis supplied).

49 On this score, contrast the incredible growth of Japan's gross national product in the thirty years since 1945 with her development during the half-century of military conquest, 1895–1945. Under the terms of the Potsdam Declaration the Lockian elements in the Japanese regime were greatly extended. The results of this transformation have not all been positive and point to some of the issues raised in this essay.

Such men would not generally pursue the highest political honors and offices, but they would understand that their long-term self-interest was inextricably bound up with the welfare of the commonwealth. By virtue of their education they would be fitted for service in public office, and would be ready to act in whatever capacity was demanded when they were needed. Such calls would necessarily be received from time to time. Locke tells us that they would have been prepared for public service in part by the study of "*Civil-law* and History," for these "are Studies which a Gentleman should not barely touch at, but constantly dwell upon, and never have done with." Given the broad range of public offices in which he might serve, such a man must not "be ignorant of the *Law* of his Country," for this is requisite "whatever station he is in . . . from a Justice of the Peace, to a Minister of State." [50]

We conclude with two questions: First, if Locke's teaching on education for civic virtue and its relationship to the stability of the regime is sound, then must we not ponder its implications for our quasi-Lockian political order in the United States? Second, is such an educational program possible today, and, if so, by whom would it be developed and who would be its proper recipients?

[50] *Educational Writings*, 186, p. 295; Locke distinguishes here the study of history in the sense of constitutional history from the history of bloody conquest. It is significant that his many recommendations of classic literature do not include works dealing with conquest, but rather with examples of morality and customs of ancient peoples; 187, p. 295. Cicero appears to be the classical author he most often cites and recommends.

The United States as Regime and the Sources of the American Way of Life

Joseph Cropsey

As a nation we are rather given to asking what we are, what we stand for, what our goals are. It is surprising that this should be so, for we have a national existence of two centuries during which our true being might well have become clearly manifest to us; and we have a written Constitution which was deliberately framed, extensively debated, and has been voluminously interpreted, and which is the official definition of our political essence. Our difficulties in this regard are probably not greater than those of other nations, but our experience is so long and our fundamental law so amply interpreted in civil war, jurisprudence, and scholarship that we are led to wonder not only about the meaning of our essence but about its elusiveness.

As we reflect on the peculiarities of our national self-scrutiny, we must own that our introspection is not on the whole complacent. On the contrary, much of it is darkened by self-dissatisfaction. We appear to be in the uneasiest of moods: at once unsatisfied by, and dissatisfied with, our self-knowledge. What is the meaning of our being vexed with uncertainty over what we are and with misgivings that we are what we are?

We find a clue in the recurrence of the expression "what we are." What we are as equivalent to what we stand for, what our goals are, is not necessarily the same as what we are in the sense of what kind of human beings we are in fact, and what is our way of life or mode of existence as we observe it and can experience it. To learn what we stand for as a nation and what end or ends our united existence is meant to promote, one must consult the documents of our political life. Some of those are authoritative in having the force of law; others are authoritative simply by reason of their gravity, nobility, or provenience.

Both together—the Constitution, laws, judicial opinions; and the Declaration of Independence and great public utterances of eminent men—articulate the conception that constitutes the American regime.

But the regime is what we stand for, the expression of what our goals are—freedom, equality, and rights. Why is our political essence obscure to us if it is embodied in words that can be studied and comprehended? Experience shows that the words are subject to construction and that the unchanging text of the First Amendment, for example, means different things to different judges. Apparently something, call it for the moment thought, mixes itself with the documents that embody the regime—in fact, then, mixes itself with the regime—and in so doing clarifies but also perplexes our understanding of the regime, and hence of ourselves—what we stand for and what our goals are.

This could be said no doubt of many regimes, probably of regimes as such. More characteristic of our own is its self-limitation in the name of freedom. It is obvious that regulation of religion, of art, of thought and the expression of it, of science, and of many aspects of private life is intentionally ruled out by the regime. But religion, art thought, science, private life are a large part of what we are, for they and their like hover over and penetrate our way of life and help fix us in a mode of existence. But what governs and fixes our way of life is certainly entitled to be called our regime.

It follows from this that our regime has apparently two dimensions, the one consisting of the meaning embedded in the public utterances, coercive or solemn, the other consisting of the meaning embedded in our private—though not thereby necessarily individual—psychic existences. But the meaning embedded in the great public utterances is infiltrated with thought, that is, with ongoing, changing thought; and our private psychic existence is, if the word *thought* be allowed an extended significance, largely made up of thought. These reflections expose a peculiarity of the regime. If the regime is the political fraction of what forms us and our way of life, then we must face the fact that we have an imperfect regime. It is imperfect in the sense that, as having been deliberated and as laid down, it can neither maintain itself in the direction that it selected nor can it, therefore, keep us without disruption on the course that it has set for us. It is powerfully, decisively, complemented or completed by thought. It is imperfect also in the sense that it by no means extends comprehensively over the whole of our way of life. But if the regime be conceived as not merely the political fraction of what presides over our way of life, but is taken necessarily to mean the ensemble of all decisive influences, then we must face the fact that we have an imperfect regime in another sense: while the coercive fragment of the political fraction can be thought of as under our deliberate control through suffrages and process of known law, every other element of the regime is subject to ongoing thought, which, in its political effect, if not in its origin, has so much in common with chance that we may for the moment count the two as equivalent. In recognizing that the regime includes an "ungovernable," we recognize that what governs us, the very regime, is imperfect. It is imperfect by virtue of the action within it, and upon us, and eventually upon itself, of what we vaguely call thought.

We have been pursuing the question, What is the meaning of our discomfort over the elusiveness of what we are? and we have arrived at the speculation that our discomfort is in fact over the effect produced by the imperfection of our regime, an imperfection identical with the invasion of the regime by thought. On reflection, it appears that we have also arrived at a point from which we can see the answer to the accompanying question, which was, What is the meaning of our dissatisfaction with what we are? Men become dissatisfied with themselves when, and only if, what they are does not possess them exhaustively and to the exclusion of a power to scrutinize what they are. It is tautologous but it is not useless to say that when men are dissatisfied with what they are, then what they are includes the power of self-dissatisfaction. In the case of a nation, that power is thought, still in a wide and indistinct sense. The reflexive thought that goes before and becomes indistinguishable from self-dissatisfaction does not originate in the regime as Constitution and laws, though evidently the coercive regime must enable such thought to find a place. Where the self-critical thought does originate is either outside the regime in its narrower meaning or in the ungoverned and ungovernable area of the regime in its broadest meaning. Stated somewhat differently, the regime is what teaches us to be what we are, and intrusive thought, alien to the regime but unrepressed by the regime, teaches us to be dissatsified with what we are and, incidentally, with the regime that teaches us to be what we are. Alternatively, the regime, as what truly and comprehensively teaches us to be what we are, includes both what we are dissatisfied with and what provokes us to see that we must be dissatisfied with it—with our way of life and its support in the regime. The inescapable conclusion, by either understanding of regime, is that the regime is problematic with a view to its own persistence and to the manner in which it determines the way of life of the nation; that there is an extrapolitical which is decisive for the meaning of regime and which may provisionally be called "thought"; and, as a corollary, that it is inappropriate to speak of the American regime and to imply in so doing that our way of life flows positively from authoritative politics—Constitution, laws, judicial opinions, and the speeches of public men.

If the discussion thus far has shed any light at all, it is on the question concerning the meaning of our uncertainty about ourselves, not on the question concerning the meaning of our dissatisfaction with ourselves. Perhaps we are condemned by the nature of regimes as such to be in doubt of some kind about what we are. But it is a certainty that we and our foreign observers perceive something about us that can be blamed and sometimes praised. What is it that is available to be seen, and that can be the basis for the judgments and self-judgments, especially the adverse self-judgments?

Visible in the nation are human beings and their parchment. Immediately our old problem recurs: are the human beings—their doings and relations—not merely the parchment made flesh? Why distinguish the American people from the Declaration of Independence, the Constitution, and Lincoln's Second Inaugural, for example? For one thing, because we might fail to embody our ideals, from which we must therefore be distinguished. But this is adequate only so far as it goes, for we and the world have reached a point at which the criticism directed against us, and not only from without, is not a reflection on our fidelity to our documents but rather supposes a sufficient harmony between men and their documentary or official norms. Whereas to begin with a difficulty arose over the elusiveness of the regime, and then over the mutual articulation of the official documentary regime and the people, the argument is now at a stage where those difficulties are overridden by abstracting equally from the elusiveness of the regime and from any possible disjunction between people and regime. This means simply that observers content themselves with a characterization of the American way of life and the American regime that is adequate for the purpose of passing a broad judgment on both—abstracting, to repeat, from the possible failure of the two to coincide. My purpose in what follows is not to quarrel with the easygoing ways of those who abstract so broadly in order to cut so sharply, but rather to extract what can be learned if one starts with the criticisms of us that are, indeed, especially informative as self-criticism or self-dissatisfaction.

Abstracting from the possible agreement of the human beings to their parchment regime might make the reasoning easier, but it does not do away with the fact that what one sees in looking at people is not the same as what one sees when studying the documents. Looking at people, one sees family and property. Looking at the documents, one sees life, liberty, and the pursuit of happiness. Where do

these observations lead? "Family" means the human unit that has as
its principle the generation and preservation of the young through
the closest affiliation to each other of a small number of adults whose
needs too are satisfied by it at the same time. The intimacy of the
family has made it the locus of that privacy that has been portrayed
as drawing men's loyalties away from the larger societies, political or
transpolitical. The family is the setting for the private calculations
that promote the preservation of life. It is, therewith, the setting in
which property performs its ultimate function, the support of human
life. The family means privacy, calculation, preservation. And what
do life, liberty, and the pursuit of happiness mean if not the freedom
of private calculation of the means to preservation and, to be sure,
other gratifications as well? As it appears, what one sees when looking
at the people is consistent with what one sees when one looks at the
parchment regime. And what one sees while looking at both is
protomodernity, the classic modernity of Hobbes and Locke.

How can it be maintained that the family, to say nothing of property, belongs peculiarly to classic modernity? It does so in that, by
contrast with pagan antiquity and Christian premodernity, only classic modernity is without a strong element of reservation against property and the family. In pagan antiquity this found expression in the
communism of Plato's *Republic*. In Catholic Christianity it found
expression in the celibacy and poverty of the few who lived the most
Christ-like lives. Protestant Christianity begins, in this regard, to participate in a view that bears a similarity to that of classic modernity.
It goes without saying that modernity has generated radical reservations against property and the family, but these had to arise in the
course of the development of modernity, a development that must be
considered by itself if the American "regime" is to be understood.
Before reflecting on the meaning of the development of modernity for
American existence, we may note the meaning of that development
for modernity itself: modernity has scrutinized itself with some dissatisfaction virtually from its inception, and, through thinking about
itself, has more or less continually modified itself. A mere sign of this
is the changing stance of modernity toward property and family. But
the discussion of these matters must wait until we have satisfied ourselves that we have in fact looked at America.

When one looks at America, one sees more than property and family and more than the workings of a belief in the natural rights to
life, liberty, and the pursuit of happiness. For one thing, one sees
the presence of scriptural religion. And then one sees, in all their im-
ponderable influence, natural science, socialism, existentialism, psy-

choanalysis, and their numerous derivatives in literature, art, journalism, and elsewhere. One sees, in brief, some things known and
other things wholly unknowable by the Founders of the American
regime. One sees a medley of thoughts old and modern that help to
comprise our effectual regime, if that means what presides over our
way of life. But the case is more complex than that. To consider Christianity itself for a moment, no one who is aware of the tendencies stir-
ring in schools of divinity can doubt that actual Christianity is not
free of every trace of influence coming from natural science, socialism,
existentialism, and psychoanalysis. Furthermore, it is not in their
pure forms but rather as they have sunk down into common understanding that science, socialism, existentialism, and psychoanalysis
have come to bear not only on Christianity but, through Christianity
or directly in their own names, on life itself. Thus we are surrounded
by an array of thoughts, some old and some recent, the old permeated
by the new—and doubtless vice versa—and the new already in a state
of decay. This ensemble is part of our "regime." Is there a discernible
order about it? Do the parts of the "regime" consist intelligibly with
one another?

As often happens, it is not the facts that elude us but their meaning.
The formula "life, liberty, and the pursuit of happiness" grew out of
the great act of self-emancipation on the part of European mankind
that was the opening of the modern age. Machiavelli called on men
to take their earthly existences seriously, and thus to win release for
themselves from the worst of their cares. He breathed high-heartedness on men by politicizing minds that had hitherto been fixed on
eternity. He naturalized man in the world, restoring him to nature,
so to speak, while presupposing innovations in the meaning of nature
that it would be impossible to take up here, but that entered into
Hobbes's formulations of natural rights and the state of nature. Inseparable from those formulations is Hobbes's reservation to men of
the right to preserve life, and their natural freedom to seek the means
thereto, as well as the large measure of private discretion that belongs
to men as they deliberate on the ends of their actions and seek their
satisfactions, if not their contentment, in life.

While the transition from Machiavelli to Hobbes might appear to
be a simple evolution or even a kind of repetition, it in fact includes
a development that should not be overlooked. Machiavelli can be
understood as teaching a lesson intended to harden and inspirit men.
Hobbes, teaching life, liberty, and the pursuit of happiness, prepared
what came to be known as the bourgeoisification of life, and the expansion of the private sphere of existence in all ways that did not

produce private encroachment on sovereignty. From its inception modernity has exhibited two moral meanings or tendencies, one inspiriting, reminding man of his earthbound solitude and presenting the world as an opportunity for greatness of some description, the other pointing toward survival, security, and freedom to cultivate the private and privately felt predilections. At its worst, the latter shows itself as acquisitive self-indulgence. The tension between the two dispositions present at the outset of modernity persists throughout the modern age. It concerns us immediately because it manifests itself decisively in our history, and indeed it is crucial in the definition of our "regime." It is the thesis of this paper that the parchment regime is dominated by the strand of modernity that invokes preservation and privacy—life, liberty, the pursuit of happiness—but that the United States, any more than any Europeanized nation, could not be insulated against the shocks generated within modernity as the Western mind scrutinized its heritage, scrutinized therewith itself, and could not find contentment. In brief, the currents of thought that have run through Europe have been at the same time the writhing of self-dissatisfied modernity and the source of every major nonscriptural ingredient of the American regime outside what I have called the parchment regime. The United States is an arena in which modernity is working itself out. The founding documents are the premise of a gigantic argument, subsequent propositions in which are the decayed or decaying moments of modern thought, superimposed on relics of antiquity. Knowing this helps us to consider more concretely those elements of our "regime" that surround the official or documentary regime; for we are aware that the two elements of the comprehensive regime do not simply coexist side by side but live in a condition of energetic tension.

Classic modernity, the modernity of Hobbes and Locke, provided for the preservation of life, for liberty, and for the pursuit of happiness through a doctrine that reached its practical consummation in man's passage out of the state of mere nature and into the condition of political society. Classic modernity provided for life, liberty, and the pursuit of happiness by means of politics, or it provided for them so far as the means available to essentially liberal politics will reach, perhaps only so far as any parchment regime can reach. But this provision gave rise to misgivings almost immediately. Spinoza saw the need to speak of life and liberty in terms that pointed to the happiness of a private man as such, of a philosopher on whose part an act of introspection would accomplish what citizenship could at best claim to prepare. Rousseau rejected the conception of life that attached it simply to preservation and denied that the liberty and happiness that are afforded by Hobbesian politics are worthy of the names, for they ignore the amplitude of development of a man's powers of self-sufficiency, of action, feeling, and discipline—in brief, life—without which life is reduced to drudgery and hypocrisy, thus bondage. Kant in turn brought to a very high level the reflections on liberty and happiness as they can be understood within the framework of nature perceived as modern natural science perceived it, as a theater of necessity. Of course he could not be satisfied that a doctrine of liberty that was not also a doctrine of the will could suffice; nor could he accept the simple politicization of the pursuit of happiness, which left unrecognized the problematic status of happiness itself when reduced to calculation and not distinguished from obedience to duty as a goal of life.

Roughly through the time of Kant, the modern thinkers who contemplated modernity recognized that the troublesome implications of modernity for the quality of man's life were inseparable from the ruling conception of nature, that conception which was also the ornament of modern understanding that criticism was not free to profane. With Hegel's discovery of the historical phenomenology of spirit, nature took its place among the moments of man's consciousness and, as the work of Nietzsche testifies, was in a measure replaced by history as the unassailable premise that both sustains and lowers upon human life and freedom.

The change of focus from nature to history produced no mitigation of modern man's dissatisfaction with the absence of any exaltation, vivacity, or high-heartedness from official political modernity as laid down by Hobbes and Locke and, incidentally, embodied in our parchment regime. On the contrary, it appears that the historicization of philosophy contributed to an intensification of that same dissatisfaction that broke out in Marxism and in what is now recognized as the protoexistentialism of Nietzsche. Marx expressed revulsion over the impoverishment of life that accompanied the generation of wealth under the auspices of privacy, and he denied that liberty was effectual or happiness distinguishable from gross satiety under the same auspices. Nietzsche found modern men so decayed in their spirit that by the light of his thought one may wonder whether any ennobling or inspiriting message could remind them of the very meaning of life, so possessed are they with mean impulses to stay alive, enjoy their liberty as guaranteed by liberal government, and pursue the futile gratifications that they absent-mindedly conceive to be happiness. Finally, Heidegger, in 1953, was repeating what he said in 1935 in praise of the "inner truth and greatness" of National Socialism, which consisted in "the encounter between global technology and modern man."[1] Men are alienated from their soil and their origins by a deadness to the meaning of their own being, a meaning that cannot fail to escape humans who are permeated by the calculating, planning, exploiting spirit of a technological age that thrives on using everything and that has come to the height of a long career in objectifying nature by discovering atomic energy. Gone is all tranquility in the presence of things and gone also is the authenticity of the privacy we so vaunt ourselves upon. Life is trivialized, liberty is an illusion without authentic existence, and the pursuit of happiness is the pursuit of no such thing. Heidegger finds this equally true of the Soviets as of the Americans. It is a fact of modern life in general, and modern science, far from being the remedy, is part of the disorder, for it feeds the spirit of calculation. One might say that the seed planted by Kant has grown into the curious shrub of Heidegger—the rejection of calculation enlarged to encompass the criticism of that science that Kant would not abandon.

Even if modern natural science had not spontaneously become so conspicuous in the argument, it would have forced itself to the foreground by way of a question concerning the propriety of characterizing modernity so heavily in terms of the thought of the moral philosophers and metaphysicians. Heidegger himself quotes from the lecture on the history of philosophy in which Hegel says, "Only now do we in fact arrive at the philosophy of the modern world, and we begin it with Descartes. With him, we in fact enter into an independent philosophy which knows that it is the independent product of reason, and that the consciousness of self, self-consciousness, is an essential moment of truth."[2] Hegel's remark emphasizes this fact: modern science was understood by its architects to have a human or moral meaning as well as a strictly technical power. Descartes especially brings together the moral fortitude or spiritual toughness that the way of science both demands and cultivates, and the promise that science holds out for prolonging life and emending souls, if only the spiritual physics or mechanics can be elaborated. At the fountain of scientific modernity, as at the sources of moral modernity, there is discernible the diremption of inspiriting and indulging that generates the energy that has moved through modernity ever since.

[1] Martin Heidegger, *An Introduction to Metaphysics*, trans. Ralph Manheim (New Haven: Yale University Press, 1959), p. 199.
[2] Martin Heidegger, *Hegel's Concept of Experience* (New York: Harper & Row, 1970), p. 27.

Modernity has grown by consuming itself. Under the circumstances, it is not surprising that it has not abolished itself but has simply increased in concentration. Modernity could be said to consist of its own self-criticism, held together by the relative stability of the horizon within which the self-criticism takes place. Nietzsche and Heidegger can claim to look beyond that horizon; but it is unclear whether they have transcended or only perfected the historicism that is the hallmark of the most highly concentrated modernity.

That the discussion has moved away from the regime and our ways of life is defensible if the movement has been in the direction of the sources of that regime and those ways of life. We may begin to see that it has been so by reflecting on the opinion commonly found among us that our lives are excessively competitive. This is another way of saying that we are in the grip of invidiousness, the sign of egoism and thus of asociality. We are dissatisfied with ourselves because our regime and life are marked by private striving for the satisfaction of individual goals rather than seeking to attain our individual ends through the mediation of a perfectly social act of provision. Alienated from one another, we are alienated from ourselves, for it is contrary to the nature of humanity to live in a state of even latent uncooperativeness with the others. In brief, to provide life in a way that divides a man from his fellows and within himself is to destroy life in the act of providing for it. Moreover, the liberty enjoyed by the mere egoist is illusory, for he must always be subject to his acquisitiveness and to those private men and private powers who either control or threaten to control his access to what sustains life. As for the pursuit of happiness, the term is deprived of its serious meaning by the impossibility of happiness for a being who is at odds with himself and his kind. The socialist element of our effectual regime, of which the foregoing is a simple reminder, is part of the modern world's self-criticism, selectively drawn not only from Hegel but from Rousseau, whence the moral impetus for it probably emanated.

No one can read Rousseau's moral and political writings, say especially *Emile*, and remain in doubt that Rousseau perceived a need to elevate men above the level of elementary self-interest and mere civil collaboration that Hobbes and Locke provided for. Rousseau speaks of happiness and of self-dependent fortitude, of resilience of spirit; and of course also of the tender sentiments. His strictures on invidiousness, on mean self-interest, on wealth in contradistinction to labor as the support of life, while evoking an antipathy to decadent opulence, do not point toward the social guarantees of welfare characteristic of communism but toward a moral renaissance to be embodied in the sturdy citizen-paterfamilias. The movement from Rousseau to Marxian socialism is not only a transition from righteous indignation to resentful hatred but a falling away from a doctrine of hardy self-dependence to one of socially secured preservation. Of course it is paradoxical that modern men should consider themselves to be fleeing from the preoccupation with mere life foisted on them by Hobbes and Locke when they turn to socialism.

As familiar as the socialist element in our ruling opinions is another set of beliefs that relate to authenticity, choice of one's own way, and the invalidity of the claim of reason to be the ultimate criterion of human choice and being. Through literature and many other media, we blame ourselves, by the light of those beliefs, for the decay of our individual personalities or selves. Thus we blame ourselves for a failure to experience life that rests on a failure to perceive that liberty means in fact a freedom of expression that takes in the whole range of moral and political choices—choices which, if restrained by established institutions, are replaced by routine that is incompatible with the personal pursuit of happiness. Of course, when we blame ourselves for the decay of ourselves, we blame the established institutions which fashion us to be supine and which punish transgressions against conformity. This means that we blame the "regime," that which is taken as the established, and therewith as the self-repressing manifestation of other-than-selfhood. It goes without saying that this particular self-criticism looks toward existentialism, which descends from Nietzsche and Heidegger to the level of ordinary opinion on which we have been speaking of it. While Nietzsche spoke of the will to power, the overman, and the invitation to the eternal recurrence of the nauseous, and Heidegger proclaimed the authentic separation of *Dasein* from the dominance of the mass called "Them" or "They" (*der Man*) with an intention that was compatible with his own National Socialism, it cannot be doubted that the project of authentic existentialism is to harden—perhaps into petrification—the liberalized spirit of modern man and not to license it for petulant or hedonistic self-assertions. What exists among us now, as part of the extended regime that forms us and shapes our existence, is the ominous human discipline of high existentialism, passed through the medium of the liberalistic modernity it is intended to reform, and transformed by it into willfulness, consciousness-raising, and moral latitudinarianism. It would be morally wrong to pass from the subject of the vulgarization of existentialism without referring to the Nazism to which it lent itself, as well as to the attempts to turn it to the uses of communism that have an especial prestige in Europe.

Impossible to measure and impossible to overlook is the influence of psychoanalytic theory on the ways of our life. When Freud tried to present his work to the public in compact form, he began by discussing the mysterious, but not for that reason deniable, correspondence between body and mind ("the hypothesis of a psychical apparatus, extended in space") on which he erects the well-known structure of eros and destruction, or death, part of a science that he assimilated to physics.[3] As in the world described by physics, psychic events are not causeless and there is no evaporation of energies into nothing. On the contrary, there is a minute mechanics and dynamics in which no "error" is meaningless and no circumstance in principle unanalyzable, even though there is no possibility of reaching intelligible things in themselves. From this amalgam of elements more than reminiscent of ingredients in the thought of Spinoza and Descartes, Rousseau, and Kant, Freud constructs his famous account of man's psychic life, with a primary orientation upon therapy. He formulates in blunt language a radical generalization of the scope of sexual eroticism, develops a theory of the id, the ego, and the superego as psychic members of an economy presided over by the beleaguered ego, and proclaims the scientific infeasibility of a sharp distinction between the psychologically normal and abnormal. He discovers a therapy that depends on the liberation of repressed psychic material and its return to a place in the psychic economy where it can fortify the ego in its endless contest with the internal and external forces with which it must contend.

A spectator of psychoanalysis must be impressed by the difference between the authentic article and the popular impression of it. Striking is the transformation of repression from an act performed within the psyche by the conscious on the unconscious, to an act simply performed by the superego on the whole man, or, just as simplistically, by civilization as such on mankind. Taken in the latter vulgarized senses, it points toward a license to violate the rules, especially the rules governing sexual behavior, that emanate from civilized society. Moreover, Freud's reflections on the stress produced in a human being by the pressures of civilized life apparently were not part of a thought on his part that, as between civilization and surrender to the instincts, civilization—that is, restraints—must simply yield in the interest of mental health or happiness. On the contrary, he recognized a limit to the pursuit of happiness which is enforced by an irremovable destructiveness or aggressiveness in the human psyche

[3] Sigmund Freud, *An Outline of Psychoanalysis*, trans. J. Strachey (New York: Norton, 1949).

that demands and presumably will forever demand the restraints of civilization, though according to rules he did not attempt to predict. Freud's psychoanalysis is a criticism of Hobbesian modernity as being unconcerned with the unconscious (thus of the realm of life, liberty, and happiness that politics as such is blind to); and it is a criticism of Rousseauan modernity as committed to the boundless malleability of man. Psychoanalysis shares the fate of the other strands of self-critical modernity in being received into the stream of modern life in the form of its own vulgarized hedonization. As always, the vulgarization is not without a basis in the primary thought: as existentialism might be seen as the criticism of modernity in the interest of spiritedness, (crudely, "aggressiveness"), psychoanalysis is the criticism of civilization altogether, and therewith of modernity, in the interest of eros.

To this point I have attempted to indicate, by the use of a few conspicuous examples drawn from the atmosphere that we ourselves breathe, the basis for the assertion that we would not understand ourselves as a nation if we did not conceive our "regime" in the wide sense that includes not only our great political documents but the important influences on our way of life that emanate from unofficial thought. More specifically, I have tried to mtaintain that important, indeed decisive, elements of our "extended regime" consist of derivations from critical reflections on the classic modernity that informs our official or Constitutional regime. I have maintained further that those derivations typically have the character of distortions of the serious thought from which they are derived and that the distortions have in general the quality of catering to our self-indulgence, even when the original thought had the opposite intention. Perhaps this is to be explained as the revenge that is taken implacably on all subsequent criticisms by their target—the original principle of life, liberty, and the pursuit of happiness. It follows that the United States is the microcosm of modernity, repeating in its regime, on the level of popular consciousness, the major noetic events of the modern world. Our national self-dissatisfaction is the mirror of modernity's self-criticism. In our own way, we are mankind.

Of the preceding observations it must be said that at best they suffice only so far as they go. They neglect the bearing on what we are and on what we can comprehend ourselves as standing for, of such immense moral influences as scriptural religion and natural science. These awesome forces, with their many manifestations, appear to stand toward each other in unrelieved antithesis. In fact they both presuppose a universe that is ultimately mysterious and in which the most important things can yet be known to man, especially the truth that there is a one, or absolute, the being of which dominates the whole. Scripture teaches that the absolute notices man as such while science conceives it as incapable of noticing anything. Scripture has therefore a clear moral meaning for all men: self-effacing obedience that must find expression, under the Christian dispensation, in love turned away from the body and in unshakeable conviction of faith. As one might say, eros has been immaterialized and spiritedness has been directed away from the moral goal of nobility praised by the pagans, toward the realm of truth and error, where in the worst case it appears as conscientious obstinacy. Like other great influences on humanity, it has a softening and a hardening aspect, a teaching about yielding to others and about urging one's own (even if one's own is borrowed). Natural science does not have such a clear moral meaning for all men. As can be seen from the *Discourse on Method,* it has a moral meaning for scientists: resoluteness and privacy. Resoluteness is the virtue of the man who faces the unknown by choosing, even arbitrarily, a path (or better a direction) from which he does not swerve, on the model of a man lost in the wilderness. Resoluteness includes also the hardihood to be the chief and sole maker especially of one's greatest artifacts. Privacy is the necessary condition for scientific work. It means minding one's own business, sharing perhaps but not imposing, and generally abiding by the rule of live and let live, with "help live" emerging as a by-product. Resoluteness is the tacit criticism of guilty self-doubt and its consequent wavering in action. Privacy is the tacit criticism of dogmatic obstinacy. But the inspiriting lesson of modern science is much vitiated by the intimation that the resolute choice of a direction is a choice made in a wilderness—rather arbitrarily, for there is no final cause. Morally considered, objectivity without the object is hard to distinguish from subjectivity. The subjectivism that emerges from scientific resoluteness accords excellently with the mutual tolerance that emerges from scientific dedication to privacy. If natural science in the modern age has been thought of as the antidote to the hardness and softness peculiar to Christianity, the judgment would have to be scrutinized with strong reservations, not so much because the moral value of natural science had to pass down, from the scientists to the multitude and thus undergo deformation, which it has, as because its moral value does not squarely confront the moral thrust of Christianity. Christian love, of which the present-day political equivalent is liberalism, marches in step with the beneficence of science and with that tolerant subjectivism of science that now support relativism. Moreover religion has, at least in the West, lost its dogmatic obstinacy, though it is true that science has at the same time become the source of notions that can exist in the minds of most human beings only on the strength of the authority of qualified experts. (In civilized countries they are accepted voluntarily, and there are no civil penalties for rejecting or accepting a given theory of genetics, for example.) As scriptural religion has put itself in tutelage to science, and to many another worldly doctrine as well, it has converged on science in becoming more "erotic" and less inspiriting, if one may speak so; more mollifying and less fortifying of the human spirit; and the conscience that once made obstinate martyrs and pitiless torturers now makes, to our unheroic relief, constitutionally protected militants. More generally: even or especially if modern natural science be considered part of the great critical reaction of modernity against the effeminating education spoken of by Machiavelli, the conclusion looms that the target and the weapon achieved a modus vivendi by which everything inspiriting has either been transformed into, or been made ministerial to, the mollifying or indolent.

If we return to the question, What is the status of scriptural religion and natural science as sources of our way of life or ingredients of our "regime"? we find that the answer runs in terms of a dialectic in the course of which the indulgent silently consumes the inspiriting. It would be absurd to make this a matter of reproach against troubled mankind, forever seeking to rid itself of the burdens and constraints without which it cannot live and with which it cannot be happy. Without any moralizing intent, however, one is justified in saying that not only has modernity constituted itself by criticizing and transforming itself and concentrating its own principles by a process of self-indulgent distillation downward toward everyday life; but even on the plane of modernity's confrontation with premodernity, a similar process can be observed. The self-criticism of modernity is an episode of the continuous self-criticism of western man. Our self-dissatisfaction as a nation is our experience of that enormous comprehensive phenomenon. This, I take it, is the meaning of the United States regime in its comprehensive sense, at the same time that it explains the meaning of our self-dissatisfaction.

Have we, with more pain than success, reinvented Hegel? I do not think so. Even if the whole dialectic of man's intellectual experience were precipitated only in our national existence, which I have not suggested, there is no reason to conclude either that we stand at the peak of a historic ascent or that attaining a perfection of self-consciousness—say understanding perfectly that man's life is encapsulated in us and we are therefore man's life—answers the question,

What are we? If our "regime" and we ourselves are as I have tried to set them forth, then we are only one of a number of national microcosms of man's dialectical or self-critical noetic experience. Each nation apparently modifies and vulgarizes available thought according to a principle of selection and mutation that is, or is best articulated in, its own parchment regime, its Constitution, its guiding conception of justice and right. Politics originates nothing. Only if politics became philosophy or became united with philosophy, if practice united with theory, could politics, by dissolving itself, emancipate itself from its dependence on that over which it cannot gain control.

Yet politics, if dependent, is not inert, as is shown by the fact that the various nations resonate differently to the vibrations that flow over them as the stream of thought. Perhaps the highest task of political philosophy is to understand, as the highest task of statesmanship is to govern, the relation of political life to thought. The genius of the American regime assigns this highest task of statesmanship to the people themselves, and in so doing brings the nation to the outer limit of self-government rightly understood. This means that the character of the people is called on to stand in the place of wisdom. Our prospects in our third century appear to depend on the possibility that our moral resources will incline to fortify themselves at the spirited wells of modernity.

Locke and the Problem of Civil Religion

Michael P. Zuckert

Two of the most thoughtful men of the nineteenth century who explored the question of the moral foundations of the American republic concluded that underlying the moral foundation must be a religion. The young Abraham Lincoln proclaimed America's need for a civil religion, and in the great speeches of his maturity he attempted to preach the doctrines of that civil religion.[1] The prophetic French student of American democracy Alexis de Tocqueville concluded on a similar note, that no mode of political life required a healthy moral foundation more than democracy, and that religion is an indispensable support of that moral foundation. He was quite frank in his advocacy of a civil religion: "Though it is very important for man as an individual that his religion should be true, that is not the case for society. Society has nothing to fear or hope from another life; what is most important for it is not that citizens should profess the true religion but that they should profess religion."[2] Tocqueville indeed attributed much of American democracy's success to the way in which religion and democracy mutually supported each other here, in contrast to his native France, for example, where they were generally hostile to each other.

Not every student of American political life has been persuaded, however. Civil religion, as a general religion, not connected specifically with any of the particular religions to be found in America, is

[1] Abraham Lincoln, "On the Perpetuation of Our Political Institutions," *The Collected Works of Abraham Lincoln*, ed. Roy P. Basler (New Brunswick, N.J.: Rutgers Univ. Press, 1953), I:108–15. Cf. Harry V. Jaffa, *The Crisis of the House Divided* (New York: Doubleday, 1959), ch. 9; cf. Leo Paul de Alvarez, ed. *Abraham Lincoln: The Gettysburg Address and American Constitutionalism*, (Irving, Tex.: Univ. of Dallas Press, 1976); Glen Thurow, *Abraham Lincoln and American Political Religion* (Albany: State Univ. of New York Press, 1976); William I. Wolfe, *Lincoln's Religion* (Princeton: Pilgrim Press, 1970).

[2] Alexis de Tocqueville, *Democracy in America*, trans. George Lawrence (New York: Doubleday, 1969), p. 290. Cf. Catherine H. Zuckert, "Not by Preaching: Tocqueville on the Role of Religion in American Democracy," *Review of Politics* 43 (1981):259–80.

seen by some to be too diluted, too lukewarm to hold the loyalties and help form the character of citizens. The civil religion, centering on the civic life of the nation and thereby providing both religious or divine support for its chief political institutions, and a set of standards in terms of which the political life of the nation may be judged, is held by some to be idolatrous. Religion, critics like Herbert Richardson argue, neither can nor ought to legitimate particular political orders. It must retain its stance toward transcendence, or, as Jürgen Moltmann puts it, its orientation by the cross. According to Richardson, Christianity rejects "the claim of every earthly Caesar and *civitas* to be ultimate," at the same time that it affirms that "what is higher than all earthly kings is not some heavenly king, but the suffering Christ."[3]

Opposition to the notion of civil religion comes from the civil side as well. These opponents hold to a different view of what America has been and even more of what it should be: not a nation sanctified and legitimated through religion, even "civil" religion, but a "secular city," serving secular ends, and legitimated by secular principles that generally lack and indeed do not require religious support. One need not, this view holds, adhere to any particular, or even to any, religion at all in order to be a loyal citizen of this regime. As a political society America has no religious goals and requires no religious support. They understand America to be, in a word, a "liberal regime" and often look back for authoritative support to Jefferson and Madison, and behind them, frequently, to John Locke, one of the acknowledged architects of the liberal political solution.[4]

But I intend to show in what follows that Locke, a champion of the liberal secular understanding of the state, affirms the necessity for something like a civil religion and thus can be seen as supplying an answer to the secularists which we ought to take with the seriousness that the source of the answer imposes on us. I will go further and argue that one of Locke's main intentions in his writings, especially in his *On the Reasonableness of Christianity*, was precisely

[3] The modern debate over civil religion was triggered by Robert Bellah's essay "Civil Religion in America," which is conveniently reprinted, together with many essays both for it and against it, in *American Civil Religion*, ed. Russell E. Richey and Donald G. Jones (New York: Harper and Row, 1974), pp. 21–45; Herbert W. Richardson, "What Makes a Society Political?" and Jürgen Moltmann, "The Cross and Civil Religion," in *Religion and Political Society* (New York: Harper and Row, 1974), pp. 9–49, 95–120.

[4] Cf. Walter Berns, "Religion and the Founding Principle," this volume, for a discussion of this point of view.

to show that Christianity was a proper civil religion, possessing both qualities we identified earlier—generality, and transcendent support and guidance for the political order. He thus supplies an answer of sorts both to those who object to civil religion from the perspective of "religion" (that is, of the "heavenly city") and to those who object from the perspective of the civil (of the "secular city"). Our examination of Locke, moreover, will not only bring out an important defense of civil religion but will at the same time display one of the chief sources of the civil religion that has prevailed in America.

Christianity as Civil Religion

To say that Locke finds Christianity a "civil religion" requires some initial clarification of terms. The phrase "civil religion," more accurately, "civil theology," is usually traced back to Marcus Terentius Varro, a Roman scholar whose life coincided with the final years of the Roman republic. We know Varro's writings on civil religion largely through the extended discussions of them in Augustine's *City of God*. Varro, it seems, distinguished civil theology from natural theology, the latter being the preserve of philosophers, the former the body of religious beliefs established by law in the cities. Although Varro does not admit it openly, Augustine shows rather persuasively that he gives no credence to the verity of civil religion whatever. It is "a collection of frivolous fantasies," with no claims to truth; it is, nonetheless, suited to the moral and intellectual character of the average citizen. Even though untrue, the civil religion is politically necessary, and so Varro goes out of his way to support and even defend it.[5]

The Varran perspective on civil religion thus takes its bearings by an explicit, if subdued, reference to philosophy. His doctrine rests on the twin affirmations of the untruth of the prevalent opinions about the divine, on the one hand, and the recalcitrance of political society to the truth as understood by the philosophers, on the other.

When Locke presents Christianity as a civil religion, the evidence seems to show, he does not share the Varran perspective we have just outlined. He insists, rather, on the truth of Christianity's teachings, but he attempts to show that Christianity, properly understood,

---

[5] Augustine, *City of God* VI, 4–7; IX, 30–31. Augustine brings out Varro's connections to the Old Academy at XIX, 2; cf. VIII, 5.

is not merely true, but is "civil" as well.[6] Its teachings are the same as those of reason on the requirements of civil life, and it contributes to the satisfaction of those requirements. Locke thus stands much closer to Augustine in the latter's polemic against Varro: Christianity, the truth about the divine, can also serve as the basis of society. Augustine rejects the philosophers' insistence on the closedness of society to the truth as such. With the coming of Christianity, truth need make no concessions to untruth; the way is open for the thorough routing of all superstition.[7]

Locke brings out the "civil" dimensions of his concerns in the *Reasonableness* in his later defenses of that work against the vigorous attacks of the Anglican divine John Edwards. His book, he thought, would "tend to peace and union among Christians" by leading them to "receive Christianity as it is." Heretofore, "the Christian church . . . has been so cruelly torn, about the articles of Christian faith, to the great reproach of Christian charity, and scandal of our true religion." These contests over doctrine have been "fierce" and have produced "cruel havock amongst christians," with contending parties threatening "pain of fire and faggot in this, and hellfire in the other world" against those who disagree with them. Rather than being a source of peace, harmony, and unity in society, Christianity, Locke contends, has itself been a source and object of contention "these thousand years and upwards," resulting in "schisms, separations, contentions, animosities, quarrels, blood and butchery."[8]

Locke is very certain as to the immediate cause of Christianity's heretofore uncivil character. "What else can be expected among Christians, but their tearing, and being torn in pieces, by one another; whilst every sect assumes to itself a power of declaring fundamentals, and severally thus narrow Christianity to their distinct systems?" The "peace of Christianity" has been drastically disturbed, and "the Christian religion has suffered such horrible effects . . . from the impositions of men in matters of faith."[9]

Christianity may be the one true religion, but, Locke insists, it has also been nearly unique in its infestation by "schisms . . . quarrels, blood and butchery." The special propensity of Christianity

[6] Cf. Ellis Sandoz, "The Civil Theology of Liberal Democracy: Locke and His Predecessors," *Journal of Politics* 34 (1972):2–36.

[7] Augustine, *City of God* IV, 30.

[8] John Locke, *A Second Vindication of the Reasonableness of Christianity*, 189, 169, 231, 358.

[9] Ibid., 296, 395.

to this fate derives, Locke argues, from a combination of two qualities that together distinguish it from other religions. Christianity and Judaism differ from the pagan religions in that in the latter, "no one of their Divinities pretends to be the one only true god." No one of the pagan gods attempted "to establish his worship alone, or to abolish that of the other" gods. Thus Judeo-Christian monotheism, with its insistence that there shall be no other gods, is one source of Christianity's uncivil character.

The other source distinguishes Christianity from the pagans again, and also from the Jewish tradition. Neither the pagans nor even the Jews put so much weight on "Articles of Faith . . . as necessary to be believed." [10] Christianity takes so much concern in "articles of faith" because Christianity is a doctrine of justification: "The Scripture was direct and plain, that it was faith that justified." [11] Locke, it should be noted, does not here endorse Luther's formula that it is faith *alone* that justifies, but he does note the relatively large role of faith, as opposed to deeds, ritual, or sacrament, within Christianity. Thus within Christianity the question What faith that was that justified? came naturally to the fore in a way it need not for any other religious group. It naturally prompted Christians to formulate and impose fundamental articles of faith to which all men must subscribe.

Yet unless men are very cautious in defining "the fundamentals" of the faith, they will, as fallible beings, be certain to disagree with the fundamentals discovered by others: "There is nothing more ridiculous, than for any man, or company of men, to assume the title of orthodoxy to their own set of opinions, as if infallibility were annexed to their systems, and those were to be the standing measure of truth to all the world: from whence they erect themselves a power to censure and condemn others, for differing at all from the tenets they have pitched upon. The consideration of human frailty ought to check this vanity." [12]

Rather than being moved by "consideration of human frailty," however, men are too often driven by a love of their own opinions, an attachment, as Locke puts it, "to a fondling of our own." [13] Thus, naturally and almost inevitably result the wrangling and fighting that have characterized Christianity for upwards of one thousand years.

10 Locke, *A Discourse on Miracles*, 452.
11 Locke, *Second Vindication*, 374.
12 Ibid., 376.
13 Locke, *An Essay concerning Human Understanding*, IV, xx, 16.

The imposition of creeds, or fundamental articles of faith, is identified by Locke most clearly with "popery," but the Protestant Reformation of the church, he contends, has made no real difference. All the sects, even the liberal Socinians, are "warm for their own doctrines" and ready to impose their favorite set of "fundamentals" on others. All the sects, Locke concludes, are as bad as Rome.[14] Although he hardly makes an explicit point of it, the sixteenth- and seventeenth-century history of England must have been strongly present to his mind as he wrote these words. More than a century of intense religious conflict, not only between the old Roman faith and ecclesiastical order on the one side, and the newer reformed faith and order on the other, but between various sects of reformers as well had culminated in major civil war, a regicide, a restoration, further intense theologicopolitical conflict at the times of the Exclusion Crisis, the Monmouth Rebellion, and finally the Glorious Revolution of 1688. Each shift in government was marked by a shift in the religious polity. Religious conflict was both a cause and a consequence of each shift. So, as Locke makes clear, Christianity, especially reformed Christianity, had not served as a civil religion.

Locke of course was not the first to so observe, but his concern differed from some other political philosophers of the early modern period. Machiavelli, for one, had blamed Christianity in comparison with the more "civil" pagan religions for "effeminating" men. Where the pagan religion made men strong, especially strong for warfare, Christianity made men weak.[15] Locke, however, writing with an experience of one hundred and fifty years, more or less, of European religious warfare in mind, seems to have been impressed more with the warlike fierceness Christianity could inspire than with the weakness Machiavelli contemned.

In his *Second Vindication* Locke explains the genesis of his book in the "stir over the doctrine of justification."[16] Not only was justification by faith a doctrine characteristic of Christianity in general, but it had been at the center of the Reformation, as seen in Luther's formula—justification by faith alone. That concern with faith, we have already seen, was part of Locke's diagnosis of the ancient character of Christianity, but the affirmation of "faith alone" pointed to yet another way in which Christianity tended to be "uncivil." From the very earliest discussions of the civil functions of religion, the divine

14 Locke, *Second Vindication*, 293, 295, 297.
15 Cf. Nicolò Machiavelli, *Discourses on Livy*, I, introd.
16 Locke, *Second Vindication*, 186.

had been appealed to as a sanction for the virtues necessary for moral and political life: both Zeus and Yahweh are gods particularly related to the doing of justice and the keeping of oaths.[17] Such gods perform a civil function by standing behind and lending sanction to the just works or good deeds of men. Reformation theology certainly throws into question the divine support for works. Divine reward and punishment follow, not on the quality of one's actions, but on the contents or quality of one's faith. According to the Thirty-Nine Articles of the Church of England, "we are justified by faith alone. . . . Works done before the grace of Christ . . . are not pleasant to God."[18] Or, as the Westminster Confession, drawn up during the Puritan Revolution, puts it: "The principal acts of saving truth are accepting, receiving, and resting upon Christ alone for justification, sanctification, and eternal life, by virtue of the covenant of grace."[19] While it would be a drastic mistake to hold, as many of Luther's critics did, that the reformed faith has no concern for good works, or that it encourages men to evildoing with a clear conscience, yet the connection between works and divine sanction is no longer so direct as in the more works-centered religions, and the status of works, on reflection, proves to be rather puzzling. Good works do not procure salvation but are the fruits of justifying faith. They are to be performed, not for the sake of the rewards of God, but as ways in which "believers manifest their thankfulness . . . and glorify God, whose workmanship they are."[20] The reformed doctrine severs the sanctions from the works and renders religion a much less clear support for civil society.

The issue is further complicated by admixture of the typical reform doctrines of providence and predestination. "Some men and angels are predestined unto everlasting life, and others foreordained to everlasting death."[21] The acceptance of such a belief, no matter how much it may follow necessarily from a grasp of the majesty of God, does not comport well with an attitude of looking to God as the source of sanctions for just behavior in this life.

The chief substantive doctrines of Locke are well seen as efforts by him to respond to the two ways in which Christianity historically

[17] Cf. Leo Strauss, *Natural Right and History* (Chicago: University of Chicago Press, 1954), pp. 83–85.
[18] Articles XI, XIII.
[19] *Westminster Confession*, chap. XIV.
[20] Ibid., chap. XVI.
[21] Ibid., chap. III.iii.

had failed to be a truly civil religion.[22] Locke's doctrine retains the
form of reform theology, but the content is modified: there is a "saving faith," a faith that, as Locke puts it, "makes a man a Christian,"
but that faith consists of but one article: Jesus is Messiah. And Locke
understands that article in a sufficiently broad or ill-defined manner
that any number of different sects could happily subscribe to it. As
his polemical opponent, John Edwards, points out, Locke's foundation warily leaves open the question of the divinity of Jesus and
therewith does not require acceptance of the doctrine of the trinity.
On the other hand, those who accept the trinity surely could endorse
Locke's article. Locke means to overcome the bloody sectarianism of
Christendom through bringing men to such a comprehensive formulation of the fundamental article of faith. Not only could Socinians
and Arians join together in this article, but so, if they would accept
the right of others to accept less than they did, could Puritans and
Roman Catholics. Locke's one article, together with the teaching on
toleration he presents in his *Epistola de Tolerantia*, would go very
far toward overcoming that thousand-year history of which he speaks.

The second part of his doctrine in the *Reasonableness* insists that
faith alone is not sufficient for salvation: everywhere and always
Jesus preached "Repent." According to Locke, "Repentance is as
absolute a condition of the covenenant of grace as faith, and as
necessary to be performed as that." Repentance is "not only a sor-
row for sins past, but is a turning from them into a new and contrary life." It is "a sincere resolution and endeavor, to the utmost of
our power, to conform all our actions to the law of God" or to "the
law of Christ." Locke restates the demand for repentance very simply
as "a good life," and puts it as "an indispensable condition . . . to
be performed by all who would obtain eternal life."[23] Thus Locke
affirms a very clear connection between the divine sanctions and the
deeds of men in this life, much more straightforward than the connection drawn in most reformed theology.

According to Locke the "law of God" that men must obey in
order to obtain eternal life is nothing other than "the law of reason,
or, as it is called, of nature." These laws of nature, these "just measures of right and wrong," are "the bonds of society, and of common
life, and laudable practices."[24] Thus, the "works" which God rewards
and punishes in the hereafter are precisely those that support or

22 Cf. Sandoz, "Civil Theology," pp. 3, 29.
23 Locke, *Reasonableness*, para. 167, 171, 172.
24 Ibid., paras. 14, 243; cf. paras. 180, 182, 228, 229–35.

undermine the requirements of civil life. Just what works those are can be gleaned from the New Testament preaching of Jesus, or from reason itself. In the *Reasonableness* Locke does not go very far toward specifying in any detail how to work out the connections between the laws of reason, or of nature, and the needs of civil society, but, I think we can safely presume, that is a task he carries further in his *Two Treaties of Government*.[25] The *Reasonableness* does not, for example, attempt to show what kinds of political regimes the principles of the law of nature would support, nor does it attempt to settle the political questions with which Locke and his contemporaries were concerned, such as whether subjects possessed a right of resisting the secular authorities under any conditions. In the *Treatises* Locke turns to such questions.

Thus far I have shown that Locke presents Christianity as a civil religion in that it meets the criteria discussed above, of being broad or comprehensive enough to be able to hold the allegiance of many who disagree over other specific items of faith (and thus not itself constitute a source of contention), and of providing a religious or divine support and guidance for the moral and political ordering of a society.

The Reasonableness of Christianity

The brunt of Locke's work is to show that Christianity, "civilized," as described above, is not only compatible with the requirements of civil life but is also the authentic and true Christianity. Locke maintains that his version of Christianity conforms better with authentic scriptural teaching than the versions of Christianity presented by the system builders, creedmakers, and theologians. He also wants to show that Christianity understood in his manner conforms to the teachings of reason, that is, that it is "reasonable."

His book is addressed to a twofold audience. On the one hand he wishes to show the theologians that what Scripture teaches is necessary for a man to be a Christian; on the other, he wishes to show deists that reason does not support them in their view that Christ and Christianity are dispensable in favor of a pure "religion of nature."[26] He addesses also those who, for one reason or another, could not ac-

---

[25] Locke, *Two Treatises of Government* II, 135.

[26] Cf. Locke, *A Vindication*, 188–89; cf. I ECHU iii; cf. Eldon Eisenach, *Two Worlds of Liberalism* (Chicago: University of Chicago Press, 1981), p. 84.

cept certain doctrines which they thought were necessary to be Christians. He hopes to persuade these men that to be a Christian does not require accepting teachings that their reason has difficulty understanding or affirming, or conversely, that reason adds its voice to revelation in urging men to Christ.[27]

Thus Locke establishes two criteria that his construct of Christianity as a civil religion must satisfy: it must be adequate according to Scripture, and it must be adequate according to reason. Paradoxically, perhaps, Locke suggests that a vigorously literalist approach to Scripture will most clearly bring out its "reasonable" character. The sectarian, system-building impulse produces the alleged deformities and unreasonable teachings that men have claimed to extract from the text. In any case, Locke proclaims his method in language directly conformable to the main thrust of Protestantism. He decided to "betake himself to the sole reading of the Scriptures . . . for the understanding of the Christian religion."[28]

Not all of Locke's contemporaries were persuaded by his rendition of Christianity. As he says more than once in his *Vindications* of the *Reasonableness*, his little book met with "a great outcry." John Edwards went so far as to claim that Locke's position not only was Socinian but amounted to atheism. He even identified the doctrine of the *Reasonableness* with the "Great Master and Lawgiver" of the atheists—Thomas Hobbes, an identification other controversialists also made, provoking Locke to deny, not very plausibly, that he ever had read the "justly decried" Mr. Hobbes.[29]

In the face of that disagreement and of the over one-thousand years of controversy over Christianity, it would be presumptuous, even foolish of me to attempt to assess the adequacy of Locke's scriptural account of the fundamentals of Christian faith. But one set of comments seems appropriate at this time. While many, if not all, of Locke's contemporaries were surprised at his "stripped down" version of Christianity, there is something incredibly powerful about his method and its conclusions. Edwards, for example, complained that Locke omitted many material and fundamental doctrines from his rendition of Christian faith; Edwards cited not only postbiblical traditions, creeds, and confessions but several very clear New Testament texts in which doctrines like the trinity were affirmed as evi-

27 Locke, *Second Vindication*, 188.
28 Locke, *Reasonableness*, preface.
29 Locke, *Second Vindication*, 184–85, 420–21; John Edwards, *Some Thoughts concerning the several Causes and Occasions of Atheism* (London, 1695), p. 129.

dence for the claim that more than Locke's one article is necessary to be believed. For example, Edwards says in one place that Locke "forgot, or rather wilfully omitted a plain and obvious passage in one of the Evangelists, 'Go teach all nations, baptizing them in the name of the Father, and of the Son, and of the Holy Ghost.' "[30] From that passage Edwards infers "consequently more is required to be believed by Christian men . . . than that 'Jesus is the Messiah.' " Belief in the trinity, Edwards holds, is made "absolutely necessary." Edwards focuses attention on the doctrine of the trinity, but finds many other omissions in Locke.[31]

Locke concedes Edwards's point: "In other places they taught other things." But that in itself does not make those "other things . . . articles of faith, absolutely required to make a man a Christian." No matter what is said on different occasions, Locke is certain that only his one article is "absolutely necessary," because, as he showed, there were numerous times when men were admitted into the church by no less authorities than Jesus and his apostles on affirming one article alone.[32] Any other doctrines that were sometimes preached may be part of Christianity in some sense, but they cannot be necessary to make a man a Christian and to secure him the benefits of Jesus' coming because Jesus and the apostles at least sometimes pronounced men to be Christians and to have even "eternal life" merely for believing "Jesus is the Messiah." Locke's nearly three-hundred pages of rebuttal to Edwards consist largely of seemingly endless variations on this basic theme. While Edwards on the whole does not appear through his polemical writings as a likable man, yet one can sympathize with him when he finds Locke "tedious" in going on at such length with this one argument. Indeed, it is noteworthy that Hobbes made his very similar argument in a rather short chapter.[33]

On the basis of Protestant commitments to *sola scriptura*, Locke's argument, no matter how different its conclusions from more standard Christian orthodoxies, has great power. When to its inherent power one adds the practical appeals he makes for Christian unity, it is no wonder that he becomes influential among the more liberal-spirited of his fellow Christians.[34]

30 Matthew 28:19.
31 Edwards, *Some Thoughts*, pp. 105, 106, 110–15.
32 Locke, *Second Vindication*, 227; cf. *Reasonableness*, paras. 26–163.
33 Thomas Hobbes, *Leviathan*, chap. 43.
34 Hunt, 187:I, 183–88; cf. Matthew Spinka, *Christian Thought from Erasmus*

Yet for all its power Locke's position has on its face at least one difficulty. Salvation within Christianity requires, we must recall, both faith in the one article and works, which Locke derives from the constant scriptural preaching of repentance. But the argument Locke deployed against other articles of faith applies equally well against his own scriptural derivation of works from the preaching of repentance. For example, in paras. 37–42 Locke adduces the preaching of the apostles Philip and Paul (in Acts 8–17) as evidence for his position on the necessary article of faith: in none of these passages, however, did the apostles conjoin the call to repentance with the preaching of Jesus as Messiah.

But the one needful article of faith and the duty to works do not stand on the same footing: "The law of faith, being a covenant of grace, and not of natural right, or debt, nothing can be absolutely necessary to be believed, but what, by this new law of faith, God of his good pleasure hath made so."[35] The law of faith is, in effect, a positive law. Its articles cannot be derived from the nature of things but only gathered from the will of the lawmaker as evidenced in Scripture. But the law of works is different. Whether Scripture explicitly mentions the law of works or not, it binds.

It is impossible that he should justify those who had no regard to justice at all, whatever they believed. This would have been to encourage iniquity, contrary to the purity of his nature, and to have condemned that eternal law of right, which is holy, just, and good, of which no one precept or rule is abrogated or repealed, nor indeed can be while God is a holy, just and righteous God, and man a rational creature. The dictates of that law, arising from the constitution of his very nature, are of eternal obligation; nor can it be taken away or dispensed without changing the nature of things; overturning the measures of right and wrong, and thereby introducing and authorizing irregularity, confusion, and disorder in the world.[36]

When Locke speaks of the "reasonableness" of Christianity, therefore, he points to its incorporation of the law of nature in the law of works which it retains.

But that is not all that Locke means when he calls Christianity "reasonable": (1) it is reasonable to believe in Christianity; (2) Chris-

to *Berdyaev* (Englewood Cliffs, N.J.: Prentice Hall, 1962), p. 52; H. McLachlan, *The Religious Opinions of Milton, Locke and Newton* (Manchester: Manchester Univ. Press, 1941), chap. 3.

[35] Locke, *Second Vindication*, 234–35.

[36] Locke, *Reasonableness*, para. 180.

tianity is reasonable in content; and (3) it is reasonable that there was a revelation of Christianity, even though its truths are rational and hence available as truths of reason.

"The evidence of our Savior's mission from heaven is so great, in the multitude of miracles he did before all sorts of people, that what he delivered cannot but be received as the oracles of God and unquestionable veracity." God ordinarily acts through the course of nature, but relies on miracles "in cases that require them for the evidencing of some revelation or mission to be from him." The miracles of Jesus and of his apostles "were done in all parts so frequently, and before so many witnesses of all sorts in broad daylight, that . . . the enemies of Christianity have never dared to deny them—no, not Julian himself." The miracles testify that Jesus "was sent by God"; the undeniable fact the miracles occurred means that "the truth of our Savior's doctrine and mission unavoidably follows."[37]

The undeniable testimony of Christian miracles establishes the reasonableness of accepting the Christian revelation, but the content of that revelation is, according to Locke, reasonable as well. He attempts to show "the reasonableness, or rather necessity," of the two "indispensable conditions of the new covenant," faith in Jesus as the Messiah and a good life, both "to be performed by all those who would obtain eternal life." He does this through showing Christianity to be a "doctrine of redemption" that in no way contradicts what reasonable men hold to be just or suited to a beneficent, righteous, and powerful God. Locke is especially concerned to clear Christianity from a variety of objections based on doctrines which seem unjust or which make Christ seem superfluous.[38] Locke is writing, one might say, a prose *Paradise Lost*.

So rational is the Christian scheme of redemption that, according to Locke, men are able to understand it and to win redemption quite apart from the positive revelation of the Bible and the coming of Jesus. The Christian scheme of redemption examples God's "mercy to mankind," or "his peculiar care of mankind." He expresses that care most generally in His promises, in particular, in His promises of forgiveness, where He "shows his bounty and goodness." But one can know of God's "mercy and good-will" and can "rest assured of his rewarding those who rely on him . . . either by the light of nature or by particular promises." The faith which justifies was "nothing

[37] Ibid., paras. 237, 243, 240, 242; cf. *Discourse on Miracles*, 451–58.
[38] Locke, *Reasonableness*, para. 172, 1.

but a steadfast reliance on the goodness and faithfulness of God, for those good things, which either the light of nature, or particular promises, had given them grounds to hope for." Thus peoples who have never received a revelation of Jesus can know, "by the light of reason," that God "is good and merciful," just as all men can know by the light of reason that they are subject to the law of nature, and deserving of punishment for falling short in obedience to that law. In a key passage Locke explains the natural law equivalent to the Christian dispensation, as follows: "The same spark of the divine nature and knowledge in man which, making him a man, showed him the law he was under, as a man, showed him also the way of atoning the merciful, kind, compassionate Author and Father of him and his being, when he transgressed that law. He that made use of this candle of the Lord, so far as to find what was his duty, could not miss to find also the way to reconciliation and forgiveness, when he failed of his duty."[39]

Locke only sketches lightly, however, his explanation of how men arrive at this knowledge through reason. Part of the law of nature, Locke says, affirms "that a man should forgive, not only his children, but his enemies, upon their repentance, asking pardon, and amendment." Generalizing from reason's teaching with respect to their own children, and even their enemies, men can or do conclude that a good and merciful God "would forgive his frail offspring, if they acknowledged their faults . . . and resolved in earnest, for the future, to conform their actions to this rule." While this derivation sounds more like a psychological explanation than a logical deduction of the proposition in question, and no doubt Locke intends it just that way, nonetheless, the availability to reason of an entire and adequate doctrine of redemption clears Christianity, and the Christian God, from some of the charges of unreasonableness and injustice that Locke takes most seriously. Were it not for this natural scheme, men to whom God had not revealed himself would, first, be condemned for violating a law they never knew, and, then, those who knew not of Jesus would be arbitrarily and unjustly shut out from the possibility of redeeming their lapses.[40] Christianity, therefore, is reasonable for Locke in a very powerful sense: the doctrine of redemption it teaches is more or less identical to knowledge accessible entirely to reason. Moreover, Christianity meets the demands of rea-

39 Ibid., paras. 19, 21, 178, 228, 229. 231.
40 Ibid., paras. 232, 19, 228, 230.

son and justice, just so far as reason is able to supply all men knowledge of the creating and caring God, of the law to which that God obliges man, and of the way to atone for lapses in obedience to that law.

So independent of positive revelation and Jesus does Locke find the divine scheme of redemption, that he is forced to raise two questions: What need is there of a Savior? What advantage have we by Jesus Christ?[41] In attempting to answer these questions, Locke completes his teaching on the reasonableness of Christianity by showing that it is reasonable that Jesus came, reasonable that the positive revelation of Jesus was added to the conclusions at which reason could arrive.

Christianity is thus not superfluous; indeed, "the great and many advantages" of it "show that it was not without need that [Jesus] was sent into the world." While Locke identifies at least five such "advantages," we can conveniently focus attention on two, where the "need" for Jesus seems most clear. In the first place, says Locke, "though the works of nature in every part of them sufficiently evidence a Deity, yet the world made so little use of their reason that they saw him not when, even by the impression of himself, he was easy to be found." Reason failed in a double sense. Most men proved unable to infer "the one only true God" from nature, because of "fearful apprehension." The miniscule "rational and thinking part of mankind," on the other hand, did find "the one supreme invisible God." This did no good, however, for two reasons. The philosophers were unable to convince the people; indeed, the example of Socrates shows how violently resistant the people, immersed as they were in superstition and dominated by self-serving priests, were to the heterodox views held and sometimes taught by the philosophers. More importantly, however, the "one supreme invisible god" which the philosophers discovered in nature through the use of their reason was not one that was necessarily to be "acknowledged and worshipped." That is, the "God of the philosophers" is not in fact the God of the Bible. Thus, contrary to what Locke suggests throughout the book, "natural theology" does not lead to the same God recognized by believers in the revealed religions.[42]

The Christian revelation was also needed in order to provide most men with "a clear knowledge of their duty." The pre-Christian

41 Ibid., para. 234.
42 Ibid., 236, 238.

philosophers arrived, it is true, at systems of morality, which contain many, if not all, of the precepts to be found in the law-of-nature preaching of Jesus. Nonetheless, Locke concludes, "human reason unassisted failed men in its great and proper business of morality." The pursuit of the law of nature via the use of the natural reason failed, and necessarily failed in at least two different ways. The philosophers failed, in the first place, to arrive at knowledge of the law of nature. "Such a body of ethics, proved to be the law of nature from the principles of reason, and teaching all the duties of life, I think nobody will say the world had before our Saviour's time." The philosophers discovered much that was conformable to "the right," but they fell short of having "the right" as the law of nature. They were unable to "make out its obligation from the true principles and foundations of morality."[43]

The philosophers fell short of presenting the "obligation" of the law of nature as understood in the Christian tradition in that they, "who spoke from reason, made not much attention of the Deity in their ethics. They depended on reason and her oracles, which contain nothing but truth." The truth vouchsafed to philosophers through reason apparently does not include knowledge of a God who legislates morality in the mode of the law of nature, a conclusion that corresponds exactly to our earlier observation about the difference between the "God of the philosophers" and the God of believers. A related failing of the philosophers was their failure to understand the role of the afterlife in ethics: "the philosophers seldom set their rules or men's minds and practices by consideration of another life." Indeed, "before our Savior's time, the doctrine of a future state, though it was not wholly hid, yet it was not clearly known in the world."[44]

In the second place, reason failed in that it could not persuade men of the ethical principles it had discovered. The philosophers were not only unable to "build their doctrines upon principles of reason, self-evident in themselves," from which they could "deduce all the parts . . . , by clear and evident demonstration," but even if they could do so, it would not be good enough to establish morality among men. "Philosophy seemed to have spent its strength and done its utmost, or if it should have gone farther, as we see it did not, and from undeniable principles given us ethics in a science like mathematics, in every part demonstrable—this yet would not have been as

43 Ibid., paras. 241, 242; cf. the titles of the *Two Treatises.*
44 Locke, *Reasonableness,* paras. 243, 245.

effectual to man in this imperfect state, nor proper for the cure."[45]

Men, for the most part, lack the time and the ability to follow demonstrations. "You may as soon hope to have all the day-laborers and tradesmen, the spinsters and dairymaids, perfect mathematicians, as to have them perfect in ethics this way." Since "the greatest part cannot *know* . . . they must *believe*." The only effective form of popular ethics, therefore, is in the form of an authoritative ethics. Even if Locke or some other philosopher of the future could remedy reason's failings heretofore in discovering the full law of nature, morality necessarily must continue to be taught to the people in the form and with the support of religion; not merely the people's want of time, ability, and interest in reasoning, but the direction of their passions makes them unlikely to be able to understand the principles of morality in any other way. Most men are moved by "fearful apprehensions" of "superior unknown beings." One can teach most men only by relating explicitly and directly to those fears and corresponding hopes. "He, that anyone would pretend to set up . . . and have his rules pass for authentic directions, must show . . . his commission from heaven, that he comes with authority from God to deliver his will and commands to the world."[46]

Thus, it is reasonable and even necessary that Christianity came into the world, because reason both failed to discover the God of Christianity and to put morality onto the footing which it has within Christianity. But Locke has thus shown that it was reasonable for there to have been Christianity only by denying altogether the chief claims according to which he had pronounced Christianity reasonable in content. What we have treated here as the second and the third senses in which Locke pronounces Christianity reasonable, turn out to be simply contradictory of each other. More than that: Christianity was presumed just and true on the basis of its conformity to the teachings of reason. But, Locke shows by the end of the *Reasonableness*, Christianity does not at all conform to the dictates of reason in its content.

Is Locke's considered judgment, then, that Christianity remains "reasonable" in only the first and third senses, that is, that it is reasonable to accept Christianity on the basis of the miracles which attest to its source and authority, on the one hand, and reasonable in the further sense that it was needed to make up the failings of reason?

45 Ibid., paras. 242–43.
46 Ibid., paras. 238, 242, 243, 245; cf. Eisenach, *Two Worlds*, pp. 85–89.

His argument for the rationality of believing in the Christian revelation depends on some very strong affirmations he makes about the power of the miracles of Jesus and the apostles to substantiate the source and truth of the message they preached. Since reason cannot vouch for the authenticity of the Christian doctrine, miracles must do so. His argument proceeds in two stages. The miracles, he holds, were so numerous and so public, that "they never were, or could be, denied by any of the enemies or opposers of Christianity." Universally accepted as miracles, they "cannot but be received as the oracles of God and of unquestionable verity."[47] Locke focuses the issue by citing the example of the emperor Julian; even he "never dared to deny" the miracles. Locke continues, however, in a most curious way that entirely undercuts the argument for miracles: "He dared not deny so plain a matter of fact, which, being granted, the truth of our Savior's doctrine and mission *unavoidably* follows." Apart from the fact that Locke strongly overinterprets Julian's comments on the miracles of the Christians as implying an acceptance of their character as authentic miracles, the instance of Julian himself contradicts Locke's point in a way Locke must have meant to convey.[48] Given the fact that Julian was "an enemy of Christianity," and that there were other enemies too, it must be that men could and did in fact deny either "the matter of fact" of the miracles or the "unavoidable" truth of Jesus' doctrine and mission. That is, Locke sets up the standard that establishes the miracles as a validator of Christianity in such a strong form that, he shows, they cannot meet the criteria he establishes. Locke expands a bit on the reasons for the lack of decisiveness of the miracles when he points out that the Pharisees interpreted Jesus' miracles of casting out devils as deriving from "Beelzebub." That is, from the mere existence of the miracles, it does not follow "unavoidably" that Jesus was sent by God and that his preaching was true. The Old Testament itself warns of false prophets and their ability to perform miracles; these miracles do not prove the authority of the performer, even from the point of view of the Bible, a point Locke reaffirms strongly in his posthumously published *Discourse of Miracles*.[49]

Indeed, Locke goes out of his way to emphasize the sort of men

[47] Locke, *Reasonableness*, para. 237.
[48] Julian, *Against the Galileans*, 230A.
[49] Locke, *Reasonableness*, paras. 90, 137; cf. Deut. 18:20; *Discourse on Miracles*, 454–55.

with whom miracles have special force: "poor, ignorant, illiterate men, mere children"—the apostles and men like them, "the bulk of mankind"—were "convinced by the miracles they saw him do."[50] In summary, the Christian miracles do not, according to Locke, have the evident force and necessity that compels a reasonable man to accept them as validators of the truth of Christianity.

Locke and the Problem of Civil Religion

It appears, then, to have been Locke's considered judgment that Christianity was reasonable in the third sense alone. Contrary to first impressions, Locke very much shares the Varran perspective. He affirms Christianity as a civil religion in Varro's sense, as well as attempting to reinterpret it so as to be more civil, as we have seen. The core of his position is based on the proposition that since "the greatest part cannot *know*, . . . they must *believe*."[51]

Yet Locke's position differs importantly from Varro's as well. The philosophers took "the chief of their arguments . . . from the excellency of virtue, and the highest they generally went was the exalting of human nature, whose perfection lay in virtue." They "indeed showed the beauty of virtue; they set her off so, as to draw men's eyes and approbation of her; but leaving her unendowed, very few were willing to espouse her." The philosophers, Locke suggests, showed the beauty of virtue, but not her truth. Failing to capture "the effective truth" of things, they left virtue "unendowed." Rather than the excellence or beauty of virtue, the "true foundations" of "the just measures of right and wrong" are "the bonds of society, and conveniences of common life, and laudable practices." But neither "the rational and thinking part of mankind" nor the other parts are content to have morality rest on these "true foundations." The few aim at something higher or more noble; the many are attracted to superstition and dominated by "fearful apprehensions."[52]

The beautiful ethics of the philosophers "satisfied not many with such airy commendations." Philosophical ethics do not align men's "interests" to their moral prescriptions. "Mankind," Locke insists, "must be allowed to pursue their happiness,—nay, cannt be hin-

---

50 Locke, *Reasonableness*, para. 141.
51 Ibid., para 243.
52 Ibid., paras. 233, 243, 245.

dered" from doing so. As Locke makes clear in *Essay concerning Human Understanding*, the pursuit of happiness means taking one's bearings by pleasures and pains.[53]

Christianity as civil religion does better than the moral teachings of the philosophers, because it appeals to the overriding comment to "the pursuit of happiness." "The view of heaven and hell will cast a slight upon the short pleasures and pains of this present state, and give attractions and encouragements to virtue, which reason and interest and the care of ourselves cannot but allow and prefer. Upon this foundation, and upon this only, morality stands firm and will defy all competition. This makes it more than a name—a substantial good, worth all our aims and endeavors."[54]

Yet from Locke's point of view, Christian ethics, however much they may seem better than the philosophers' systems, face similar shortcomings. The morality developed by the "followers of Jesus" had "no tang of prepossession or fancy, no footsteps of pride or vanity, no touch of ostentation or ambition." "It is," says Locke, "all sincere. It is such a rule of life . . . that all men would be happy, if all would practice it." But is this last claim equivalent to the claim that each man who practices it would be happy? We suspect not, because Locke observes that "the good are most of them ill-treated here," a fact which, he says, might well lead some men to posit another world in which the good receive their just rewards. "The portion of the righteous has been in all times taken notice to be pretty scanty in this world. Virtue and prosperity do not often accompany one another, and therefore virtue seldom had many followers." Christian morality, just as much as the morality of the philosophers, takes insufficient account of the "frailty of our minds and weakness of our constitutions." Since all do not practice it, it leads the good to suffering, not happiness. Man's passions always tempt and often prevail against "the strict rules of his duty," a fact which Locke believes is visible to anyone who "looks abroad into any stage of the world."[55] "Any stage of the world" includes the Christian stage as well; the promise of divine rewards and penalties leaves morality hardly any better endowed than it was by the philosophers. Locke seeks a better endowed, or more effective, morality, which means a morality on friendlier terms with the passions than either philosophic or Christian morality is.

[53] Ibid., 245; II ECHU xxi.
[54] Locke, *Reasonableness*, para, 245.
[55] Ibid., paras. 243, 245, 246.

By this point the core dilemma of Locke's moral and political philosophy has come rather clearly into focus. For reasons we have sketched above, human society requires civil religion, which, in Locke's historical situation, means the endorsement of Christianity. Locke thus accepts Christianity and attempts to present his own teaching in its terms, not only in the *Reasonableness* but in the *Treatises* and elsewhere.[56] At the same time, however, Christianity is sufficiently far from the truth, not only the truth that Locke, like the ancient philosophers, accepts for himself, but the truth that he believes ought to prevail in society, that he is driven to sometimes radical reinterpretations of Christian doctrine, and even to radical undermining of the entire biblical tradition.

More broadly put, Locke attempts to reinterpret Christianity so as to use it to overcome the attitudes characteristic of the biblical orientation. In his *First Treatise* Locke identifies those attitudes essentially as gratitude and guilt.[57] Men feel gratitude for the "provided world" in which they find themselves; they feel guilt for falling short of what the good and provident God requires of them. Both the gratitude and the guilt rest on the affirmation of the primacy of the good.

Locke, by contrast, holds that neither gratitude nor guilt is the proper attitude. As he says in the *Second Treatise,* nature, and therefore "nature's God," provides only the almost worthless raw materials. What is valuable is provided by men, by human labor, broadly conceived. Men will benefit themselves fully and rationally only when they are freed from the attitudes of gratitude and guilt, which, different as they are, conjoin to induce men to accept the world as it is, either as gift or as punishment, or as both together.

Locke's reinterpretation of Christianity contributes in two ways to his larger project of unleashing human labor to transform the world and society for the sake of making life more "convenient" for man. He reinterprets Christianity so as to deny guilt. Neither mortality nor scarcity results from any fault of man's. They have no normative claims on mankind. In the nature of the case, Locke could not altogether dispense with the notion of God's goodness, but, following a hint within Christianity itself, Locke transfers the locus of that goodness from the provided existence to the redemp-

56 Cf. Locke, II Tr. 4.

57 Cf. Michael P. Zuckert, "An Introduction to Locke's First Treatise," *Interpretation* 8 (1979);58–74.

tion God offers men when, as Locke emphasizes, existence is not so well provided.[58]

But Locke's reinterpretation is both too little and too much from the point of view of his own project. It is too little because he cannot entirely rid Christianity of its rooting in an attiude very different from the one he wishes to promote. There are limits to how much new wine one can put in old wineskins. As we have seen, the "pure" ethics of the Sermon on the Mount remain as distant from Locke's moral redefinition as the beautiful but unendowed ethics of the ancient philosophers.

On the other hand, Locke's reinterpretation is too much: based on an understanding very different indeed from that expressed in the biblical tradition, an understanding that Locke wished to see transform human consciousness, to some extent at least, his reinterpretation contains much that runs counter to and undermines religion in any form, whether the original scriptural understanding or the version he presents. Locke is in the difficult position of both affirming the necessity of a civil religion, and thus the continued dominance of a "religious attitude," no matter how transformed or reinterpreted, and of purveying ideas that undermine the possibility of the religious attitude, and thus of civil religion.

The undermining side of Locke's thought, carefully balanced in his own works by efforts to shore up a transformed religious attitude, came out sooner in some circles, later in others, but the history of Western thought since his time shows the relatively steady encroachment and spread of ideas spawned by or related to Locke which have helped make the civil religion he tried to develop a fragile, even failed enterprise indeed. The spread of those ideas has produced what one commentator calls a "crisis of the civil religion," rooted, he believes, in a broader "crisis in theology."[59] Almost immediately after Locke wrote, men who claimed to be followers of his—Toland, Tindall, Collins—produced critiques of Christianity that definitely show the marks of Locke's influence, but, far more explicitly and openly than he, brought out the critical and undermining implications of Locke's thought. Embarrassedly but somewhat disingenuously, Locke disowned them all. He did so with some justice, it is true, because they forgot an important part of

[58] Locke, *Reasonableness*, paras. 1–11; cf. Hegel, *History of Philosophy* Pt. II, introd.

[59] Robert Bellah, "Epilogue," Richey and Jones, *American Civil Religion*, pp. 255–72.

what he had argued; but, on the other hand, they not only brought out arguments implicit in Locke's work but attempted to carry out more thoroughly a part of his public project—the overcoming of the biblical orientation for the sake of the liberation of men. Soon, other and more famous students of Locke, like David Hume, did the same. They brought out the radical implications of Locke's philosophical position, implications he had gone to pains both to develop and to hide.

Locke's doctrine of civil religion, to repeat, brings out the core dilemma in his entire philosophical project. He shares with the ancients, as he understands them, the conviction that society can never rest on a strictly philosophical foundation, for most men cannot philosophize. "The greatest part cannot know, . . . they must believe." At the same time, however, he sees the desirability of transforming the dominant understanding held by men of the human situation in the world for the sake of improving that situation physically, politically, and morally. His doctrine of civil religion represents his attempt to make that combination work, but the way his philosophy undermined the conditions for the persistence of the civil religion indicates the central unresolved conundrum in his thought. Locke thus both made a powerful case for the necessity of civil religion on the basis of modern philosophic principles and at the same time contributed to creating a climate of opinion in which civil religion, even in support of the regime he attempted to bring into being, is most difficult if not impossible to maintain.[60] Locke thus does not so much unequivocally support either the partisans or the antagonists of civil religion, but he reveals with great clarity what the problem of civil religion, and thus of civil society, is, within the context of modern political philosophy.

[60] Cf. Michael P. Zuckert, "Fools and Knaves: Locke's Doctrine of Philosophic Discourse," *Review of Politics* 36 (1974):544–64.

Religion and the Founding Principle

Walter Berns

JEFFERSON'S Bill for Establishing Religious Freedom in Virginia was, in his opinion, one of the three most notable achievements of his long and distinguished public life, the two others being the Declaration of Independence and the founding of the University of Virginia. In his preamble to the bill he wrote a statement that has been quoted many times by civil libertarians and misunderstood—or misused—by them almost as often. The statement reads as follows:

> ... that to suffer the civil magistrate to intrude his powers into the field of opinion and to restrain the profession or propagation of principles on sup-position of their ill tendency is a dangerous falacy [sic], which at once destroys all religious liberty, because he being of course judge of that tendency will make his opinions the rule of judgment, and approve or condemn the sentiments of others only as they shall square with or differ from his own.[1]

Despite the fact that the statement occurs in the context of the (successful) effort to establish religious liberty in Virginia and despite the explicit reference only to "religious liberty," there is a tendency among civil libertarians to misunderstand the principle of it to apply to political as well as to religious opinion. Zechariah Chafee, Jr., for example, in his celebrated study *Free Speech in the United States* flatly asserts that Jefferson's "words about religious liberty hold good of political and speculative freedom, and the portrayal of human life in every form of art."[2] Leonard Levy says: "This statement does refer to 'the field of opinion' generally, although in context only freedom of religion is provided for and explicitly named. Yet the principles of the statement could, theoretically, apply with equal vigor to speech and press which are related and linked together with freedom of religion in the First Amendment."[3] Theoretically, he says, what goes for religious speech or opinion goes for political speech or opinion,

---

[1] *The Papers of Thomas Jefferson*, ed. Julian P. Boyd et al. (Princeton: Princeton University Press, 1950), 2:546.
[2] *Free Speech in the United States* (New York: Atheneum ed., 1969), p. 28.
[3] Leonard W. Levy, *Legacy of Suppression: Freedom of Speech and Press in*

and, after all, they are linked as predicates in the same sentence of the First Amendment. And Dumas Malone, Jefferson's principal biographer, insists that since "freedom of thought was an absolute" for Jefferson, "*it may be assumed* that he applied not merely to religious opinion but to all opinion this maxim: 'Reason and free enquiry are the only effectual agents against error.'"[4]

There is, as we shall show, a good deal of evidence that Jefferson thought that religious and political opinion were to be governed by different principles; and there is even more evidence that he differentiated them in practice. Levy acknowledges the differentiation in practice and criticizes him on that score. "Between his words and deeds on religious liberty there was an almost perfect congruence, but it was not a congruence that was characteristic."[5] There is, we are told, "the darker side" of Jefferson's record on civil liberties, the side characterized by his alleged failure in certain political disputes to adhere to the principles he elaborated in the Declaration of Independence. Oscar Handlin, in his Foreword to Levy's book on this subject, makes this charge explicitly: "Jefferson, after all, was the author of the brilliant phrases of the Declaration of Independence; and he has for generations been venerated as the apostle of American liberty. Yet a confrontation with the facts leads to the conclusion that he did not directly apply to practical political problems a libertarian creed to which he adhered consistently."[6] But this charge of inconsistency rests on a misunderstanding of the Declaration of Independence and on a failure to see the distinction between religious and political opinion, a distinction that Jefferson regarded as fundamental. It is not by accident that Dumas Malone has to *assume* that the principle of the absolute freedom of religious opinion applied as well to other forms of opinion; he is driven to make the assumption because, as Harry V. Jaffa has argued, evidence for this proposition does not exist, and it does not exist "because Jefferson did not say what he did not believe."[7] And, contrary to what is usually under-

---

Early American History (Cambridge: Harvard University Press, Belknap Press, 1960), p. 189.

[4] Dumas Malone, *Jefferson and the Ordeal of Liberty* (Boston: Little, Brown, 1962), p. 393 (italics supplied).

[5] Leonard W. Levy, *Jefferson and Civil Liberties: The Darker Side* (Cambridge: Harvard University Press, Belknap Press, 1963), p. 15.

[6] Ibid., p. viii.

[7] Harry V. Jaffa, *Equality and Liberty: Theory and Practice in American Politics* (New York: Oxford University Press, 1965), p. 186.

stood by libertarians today, in maintaining the distinction between religious and other forms of opinion, Jefferson was not violating the principles of free government as these appear in the Declaration of Independence and are expounded in the thought of the political philosophers who first discovered them. On the contrary, these principles require the distinction. As Madison put it in a latter-day letter to Jefferson, although it is as difficult to frame a "political creed" as it is to frame a religious creed, "the public right [is] very different in the two cases."[8] The failure to note the distinction may be traced to—or, at least, can be said to reflect—the failure to appreciate the role played by the religious question in the beginning of free government. No question was then more important, none played so prominent a role in the thought of the pertinent theorists—Hobbes, Locke, Spinoza, Bayle, and, to a lesser but still significant extent, even Montesquieu—and even if it could be said that they solved it, or answered it, in principle, it was left to the American Founders to be the first to solve it, or to try to solve it, in practice.

The Separation of Religion and State

The Constitution as it was sent by the Philadelphia convention to the people of the states for their ratification contained a single provision dealing with religion, the proscription in Article VI of religious tests for office. This did not satisfy the six states (or five states plus the minority in Pennsylvania) that included a demand for a guarantee of the rights of conscience in their general call for a bill of rights. The typical demand made by these states was for an amendment protecting freedom of conscience, but no one, ratifier or nonratifier— or, as the nonratifier Elbridge Gerry inelegantly put it, "rats or antirats"[9]—expressed an opinion opposed to freedom of conscience. There was simply no debate on the subject, or even a recorded difference of opinion, and this is not unrelated to the fact that freedom of conscience has not been an issue in the subsequent history of the country. More strikingly, especially to anyone with a memory of British and even American history during the seventeenth and eighteenth centuries, the fact that freedom of conscience was not an issue shows the great extent to which the religious question had already

[8] Madison to Jefferson, Feb. 8, 1825, in Gaillard Hunt, ed., *The Writings of James Madison* (New York: 1900–1910), 9:220.

[9] *The Debates and Proceedings in the Congress of the United States*, 1:756 (August 15, 1789) (cited hereafter as *Annals of Congress*).

been solved in America at the time the Constitution was being written. There was a debate as to whether an amendment was necessary to protect it, but that posed no serious problem. There was considerable controversy on the question of whether the House should take time from the consideration of the pressing necessity to establish the offices of government in order to honor a pledge, which some of them did not regard as a pledge, to add a bill of rights to the Constitution; but that too proved tractable. The real difference was not discussed at all, although it can be glimpsed in the variety of formulations given the amendment; this was a difference that divided the participants among themselves and divided the more profound of them within themselves. In one sense they were opposed to religion, to the organized religions of the day; in another sense they recognized the role religion could play—and perhaps would have to play—in free government. Unlike freedom of conscience, this difference, the ambiguity on this aspect of the religious question, gave rise to an issue that has played a role in the subsequent history of the country, and it underlies the disagreement concerning the meaning of the First Amendment.

In 1947, for example, the Supreme Court said of the establishment clause that it means at least that neither a state nor the federal government may set up a church or pass laws aiding one religion or all religions or prefer one religion over another.[10] This is a view widely held among constitutional scholars, but it is by no means the only view. It was not the view held by Edward S. Corwin or by Mark DeWolfe Howe, or by others still living and writing.[11] It was not the view of the Court when it upheld the statute granting tax exemptions to churches for properties used for worshipping purposes.[12] Presumably, it was not the view of Mr. Justice Douglas when, in the second "released-time" case, he wrote that Americans "are a religious people whose institutions presuppose a Supreme Being," although it was his view a few years later, when he wrote that the purpose of the religious clauses was "to keep governmental neutral, not only between sects, but between believers and nonbelievers."[13] Of course the federal govern-

---

[10] *Everson* v. *Board of Education*, 330 U.S. 1, 15 (1947).

[11] Edward S. Corwin, "The Supreme Court as National School," *Law and Contemporary Problems* 14 (Winter 1949); Mark DeWolfe Howe, *The Garden and the Wilderness: Religion and Government in American Constitutional History* (Chicago: University of Chicago Press, 1965).

[12] *Walz* v. *Tax Commission*, 397 U.S. 664 (1970).

[13] *Zorach* v. *Clauson*, 343 U.S. 306, 313 (1952); *Walz* v. *Tax Commission*, U.S. 397 U.S. 664, 716, Dissenting opinion.

ment may not "set up a church"; there has never been any argument about that. But may it aid religion, provided it does so on a non-discriminatory basis? May the states? It turns out that in its debates on the religious clauses of the First Amendment, the First Congress was also divided on these questions.

In the Virginia ratifying convention Patrick Henry had complained that under the proposed Constitution the states would lose their sovereignty and thereby make insecure the rights of conscience protected under the state constitutions and specifically under the Virginia Constitution. In response to Henry, and to others who in other states had expressed similar apprehensions, Madison opened the debates in the First Congress by proposing an amendment forbidding the establishment of "any national religion" or the infringement of "the full and equal rights of conscience." The issue here had to do with the relation of nation and states; but it was not much of an issue. The states had sought some reassurance and the Founders had no objection to providing it. The House Select Committee formulated Madison's proposal as follows: "no religion shall be established by law, nor shall the equal rights of conscience be infringed," which led Benjamin Huntington of Connecticut to express the fear that this language could be read—not by him but by others—to forbid state laws requiring contributions in support of ministers of religion and places of worship. In addition, although he favored the free exercise of religion, he was anxious, he said, to avoid any language that might "patronize those who professed no religion at all."[14] The same concern for the right of the states to foster religion was expressed in both the House and the Senate, and was embodied in a variety of formulations of what we know as the Establishment Clause. The Senate, for example, accepted an amendment to the House version that would have forbidden Congress merely to make any law "establishing one religious sect or society in preference to others," and the version it finally adopted and sent back to the House would certainly have permitted not only the states but the Congress to assist religious sects in a variety of ways but on a nondiscriminatory basis. It read as follows: "Congress shall make no law establishing articles of faith, or a mode of worship, or prohibiting the free exercise of religion." The language as we know it came out of a conference committee on which Madison served, which led his principal biographer to claim that it embodied fully Madison's views respecting an "absolute separation of church and state and total exclusion of government aid to re-

14 *Annals of Congress*, 1:451 (June 8, 1789), and pp. 757, 758 (August 15, 1789).

ligion."[15] But this cannot be accepted. This same Congress, with Madison's approval, readopted the Northwest Ordinance of 1787, the third article of which reads as follows: "Religion, morality, and knowledge, being necessary to good government and the happiness of mankind, schools and the means of learning shall forever be encouraged."[16] It is not easy to see how Congress, or a territorial government acting under the authority of Congress, could promote religious and moral education under a Constitution that promoted "the absolute separation of church and state" and forbade all forms of assistance to religion. Whatever his own views, Madison was in no position to ignore the concern so widely expressed in the congressional debates that nothing be done to prevent aid to religion. Thus, as merely one further example, when Peter Sylvester of New York objected to the provision, in one version of the Establishment Clause, that "no religion shall be established by law," because "it might be thought to have a tendency to abolish religion altogether," Madison replied that he understood the language to mean merely that "Congress should not establish *a* religion, and enforce the legal observation of it by law."[17]

By the addition of the article, Madison seems to have expressed a willingness to accommodate those who wanted to permit nondiscriminatory assistance to religion. This can probably be said of the phrase "respecting an establishment of religion," the language that was finally adopted by the Congress and ratified by the states. There were those who insisted on room for such assistance, and the language permits it. What is beyond question is that both the states and the federal government have traditionally acted as if the language permitted it. Thus, when Justice Douglas insists that the First Amendment was intended "to keep government neutral, not only between sects, but also between believers and nonbelievers,"[18] he is required to look elsewhere for supporting authority—to Madison's "Memorial and Remonstrance," for example. Written in opposition to the Virginia Bill "for establishing a provision for teachers of the Christian religion," this famous statement of Madison's own views calls for the separation not only of church and state but of religion and state.

[15] Irving Brant, *James Madison: Father of the Constitution, 1787–1800* (Indianapolis: Bobbs-Merrill, 1950), pp. 271, 272.

[16] Act of August 7, 1789; I *Statues at Large* 50. The actual form of the action taken by the First Congress was a law to "adapt" the Ordinance to the new "Constitution of the United States."

[17] *Annals of Congress*, 1:757 (August 15, 1789) (italics supplied).

[18] *Walz* v. *Tax Commission*, 397 U.S. 664, 716 (1970). Dissenting opinion.

But it is clear that more than Madison's own views went into the First Amendment.

In the past, and especially in that recent English-speaking past well known to Founders, religion had been the most divisive of political issues, the cause of civil strife and wars, of test oaths and recusancy, of revolutions and regicides, of political problems that threatened to defy solution, of, as Madison put it in the "Memorial and Remonstrance," "torrents of blood" spilled in the vain attempt to "extinguish Religious discord."[19] What is noteworthy in the debates leading to the adoption of the First Amendment is the absence of that kind of religious problem. It is not the differences among the participants in that debate but rather the extent of their agreement that is worthy of being remarked. What divided them were differences on what can only, in the light of that history, be called secondary issues: whether government depended in some way on religion and, therefore, whether it should be permitted, in some way, to foster religion, and whether this should be done at the federal as well as at the state level. On these questions Madison especially differed from Samuel Livermore and his friends; but even Madison made no attempt in the First Amendment debates to have Congress adopt the policy he favored so eloquently and effectively in his "Memorial and Remonstrance." Compared to these differences, the agreement among them was massive. There was no dispute about freedom of conscience or the free exercise of religion; the adoption of the clause protecting free exercise was an altogether perfunctory matter, giving rise to no difference whatsoever. There was no dispute with respect to the principles on which the Constitution was built; stated in its most radical form, they all agreed that our institutions do *not* presuppose a providential Supreme Being. This is a fact of considerable significance, and, as I shall argue, it makes it possible to understand why the Founders distinguished between religious and political opinion and why they could accord absolute freedom to the one and not to the other.

One of the striking facts about the original, unamended Constitution, then, is the absence of any statement invoking the name of God or providing for the public worship of God or according special privileges or places to churchmen or stating it to be the duty of Congress to promote Christian education as part of a design to promote good citizenship. There is nothing in it similar to the provision in the Massachusetts Constitution of 1780 declaring it to be not only the right but the duty of the "towns, parishes, precincts and other

19 Madison, *Writings* (Hunt ed.), 2:189.

bodies politic" to support, and to provide moneys for the support of, "the public worship of God."[20] Instead, the Constitution merely makes it possible for legislative majorities to enact—or not to enact— laws of this sort; but what is regarded as primary or essential is not left to the discretion of legislative majorities or to chance. We have grown so accustomed to what we today call the secular state that we tend to ignore the significance of the absence of such provisions in the federal Constitution. If the Founders had intended to establish a Christian commonwealth (and, under the circumstances, it could not have been any other variety of religious commonwealth), it was remiss of them—indeed, sinful of them—not to have said so and to have acted accordingly. If they thought that all government is derived from God, they would have been remiss in not establishing constitutional institutions calculated to cause Americans, or to assist them, to live according to his laws. Instead, the first of Madison's amendments, proposed in response to the demands of the states for a bill of rights, was a declaration insisting, not that all power derives from God, but "that all power is originally vested in, and consequently derives from, the people."[21] Instead of speaking of men's duties to God and to each other, they spoke—and again in this first of the proposed amendments—of men's indubitable, unalienable and indefeasible rights, including the right freely to acquire and use property.

All this is not to say that Americans were not, in some sense—in most cases, some subordinate sense—"a religious people." In the debates on the First Amendment there were indeed people who spoke on behalf of religion, but even their cause was a far cry from the causes defended by religious enthusiasts of the past. Massachusetts did indeed require in its 1780 constitution that men had a duty publicly to worship God—but this was significantly qualified by the concession that each man do this according to "the dictates of his own conscience." What is more, this duty was imposed for a political reason. The towns "and other bodies politic" were to provide support for "the public worship of God" *because* "the happiness of a people, and the good order and preservation of civil government, essentially

20 Francis Newton Thorpe, *The Federal and State Constitutions* (Washington, D.C.: U.S. Government Printing Office, 1909), 3:1888.

21 *Annals of Congress*, 1:451 (June 8, 1789). This was dropped only because it was thought to be unnecessary: the Preamble to the Constitution already acknowledged the source of power to be in the people, and this acknowledgment was affirmed when the words "or to the people" were added to what we now know as the Tenth Amendment (ibid., p. 790).

depend upon piety, religion, and morality."[22] This position was better stated in the Massachusetts ratifying convention when John
Turner said that "without the prevalence of Christian piety and
morals, the best republican constitution can never save us from
slavery and ruin."[23] On the basis of such statements it might even
be said that whereas our institutions do not presuppose a Supreme
Being, their preservation does. This is a venerable opinion. Tocqueville goes so far as to say that it was the opinion of all Americans:

Indeed, it is in this same point of view that the inhabitants of the United
States themselves look upon religious belief. I do not know whether all
Americans have a sincere faith in their religion—for who can search the
human heart?—but I am certain that they hold it to be indispensable to the
maintenance of republican institutions. This opinion is not peculiar to a
class of citizens or to a party, but it belongs to the whole nation and to
every rank of society.[24]

To some extent Americans were taught this political lesson by the
Founders.

In his First Inaugural, Washington paid homage "to the Great
Author of every public and private good," and suggested that Americans above all peoples must "acknowledge and adore the invisible
Hand which conducts the affairs of men." Statements similar to
these can be collected in the hundreds—and have been[25]—to the end
of supporting the proposition that the United States is, or was intended to be, a Christian, or less specifically, a religious, commonwealth—at any rate, the sort of commonwealth whose institutions
"presuppose a Supreme Being." There must have been present at the
beginning Americans who truly believed this, and believed it in an
altogether unsophisticated way; but this cannot be said of the men
whom we call the Founders. It cannot be said of Washington, who,
rather than God, to say nothing of Jesus of Nazareth, invoked the
name of "that Almighty Being," and "the Great Author," and "the
Invisible Hand," and "the benign Parent of the Human Race." There
were others who made specific references to the God of the Scriptures,
but Washington here sounds more like the Freemason he was than

22 Thorpe, *Federal and State Constitutions*, 3:1888.
23 Bernard Schwartz, *The Bill of Rights: A Documentary History* (New York:
Chelsea House, 1971), 2:709.
24 Alexis de Tocqueville, *Democracy in America* (New York: Vintage Books,
1945), 1:316.
25 See, for example, Russell Kirk, *The Roots of American Order* (La Salle, Ill.:
Open Court, 1974).

ng_effortiew of ">Religion and the Founding Principle

a pious Christian in an orthodox sense. His reasons for acknowledging divine assistance in the constituting of the United States and for doing it in this manner are both suggested in the following statement in his Farewell Address:

Of all the dispositions and habits which lead to political prosperity, religion and morality are indispensable supports. In vain would that man claim the tribute of patriotism who should labor to subvert these great pillars of human happiness, these firmest props of the duties of men and citizens. The mere politician, equally with the pious man, ought to respect and to cherish them. A volume could not trace all their connections with private and public felicity. Let it simply be asked where is the security for property, for reputation, for life, if the sense of religious obligation *desert* the oaths, which are the instruments of investigation in courts of justice? And let us with caution indulge the supposition that morality can be maintained without religion. Whatever may be conceded to the influence of refined education on minds of peculiar structure, reason and experience both forbid us to expect that national morality can prevail in exclusion of religious principle.

In the light of this statement, we are permitted to say that Washington too looked at religion from the point of view of the political, and from this perspective saw reason to doubt that a civil society founded on the rights of man could sustain itself in the absence of the extraneous support provided by religious belief. Even more significantly, considering his reputation, Jefferson too was persuaded of the necessity of some sort of religious conviction—not for himself or Washington and others with "minds of peculiar structure" and "refined education," but for the great body of Americans. "And can the liberties of a nation be thought secure when we have removed their only firm basis, a conviction in the minds of the people that these liberties are of the gift of God?" Jefferson asks this question in his discussion not of religion—he had apparently disposed of that subject in the previous query (or chapter)—but of slavery, and in that context its appearance is especially striking. Slavery exists in Virginia, but it is contrary to the rights of man and natural justice. Not only is it contrary to natural justice; in its effects it is deleterious to master and slave alike. It must be abolished, but Jefferson has no illusions about the strength of the passions that stand in the way of that just conclusion. Greed and, especially in a warm climate, sloth stand in the way: "For in a warm climate, no man will labor for himself who can make another labor for him."[26] Thus, natural rights are opposed by

[26] *Notes on the State of Virginia, The Works of Thomas Jefferson,* ed. Paul Leicester Ford (New York: Putnam's, 1904-5) (Federal ed.), 4:83.

these passions, liberty by economic interest; and liberty can win in this contest only if it gains the support of religious conviction, specifically, the conviction in the minds of the people that it is the gift of God. It must be the policy of the government to promote this conviction, which it can do by supporting religion in the form of a "multiplicity of sects" while favoring no particular one of them. Pennsylvania and New York, he had pointed out in the previous query, had shown the way for Virginia (and the United States as a whole). They had "long subsisted without any establishments," but religion was well supported there—"of various kinds indeed, but all good enough" from his political point of view, "all sufficient to preserve peace and order [and] morals."[27] Harvey C. Mansfield, Jr., has stated the conclusion to be drawn from this: "For the sake of liberty, government must support religion in general, but no particular religion."[28] That this was Washington's opinion we know from the Farewell Address, and it explains the style of his First Inaugural. Government cannot afford to be neutral "between believers and nonbelievers"; good government depends on the existence of a certain kind of believer because there is, or was thought to be, a connection between religious belief and the moral character required to restrain the passions inimical to liberty. If religion "does not impart a taste for freedom," Tocqueville was to observe a few years later, "it facilitates the use of it."[29] As we might expect from a man whose thought was strongly influenced by a tradition derived from Rousseau, Tocqueville's opinion was that liberty cannot govern "without faith [and] is more needed in democratic republics than in any others."[30]

But the Constitution was ordained and established to secure liberty and its blessings, not to promote faith in God. Officially, religion was subordinate to liberty and was to be fostered—by public assistance, for example, and by exemplary admonitions on state occasions—only with a view to securing liberty. Moreover, before religion could be publicly fostered, it had to be reformed and rendered harmless. While this "reformation" had largely taken place before the constituting of the United States, Jefferson, quietly, and Tom Paine, openly and blatantly, addressed themselves to that task.

[27] Ibid., p. 80.
[28] Harvey C. Mansfield, Jr., "Thomas Jefferson," in Morton J. Frisch and Richard G. Stevens, eds., *American Political Thought: The Philosophic Dimensions of American Statesmanship* (New York: Scribner's, 1971), p. 38.
[29] Tocqueville, *Democracy in America*, 1:316.
[30] Ibid., p. 318. And see Rousseau, *The Social Contract*, Book 4, chap. 8, "Civil Religion."

The Religious Problem

Instead of establishing religion, the Founders *established* religious freedom, and the principle of religious freedom derives from a non-religious source. Rather than presupposing a Supreme Being, the institutions they established presuppose the rights of man, which were discovered by Hobbes and Locke to exist prior to all government—in the state of nature to be precise. To secure these rights, men must leave the state of nature, which they do by giving their consent to civil government. Nevertheless, the rights presuppose the state of nature, and the idea of the state of nature is incompatible with Christian doctrine. According to Christian doctrine, "the first and great commandment" is to love God, and the second, which is like unto it, is to love one's neighbor as oneself. In the state of nature, however, man is not obliged to love anyone, but merely to preserve himself and, what is more to the point, "to preserve the rest of mankind [only] when his own preservation comes not in competition."[31]

Just as they spoke frequently of natural rights and of founding government in order to secure these rights, and of compacts being "the vital principle of free government as contradistinguished from governments not free," the Founders spoke of and took seriously the state of nature.[32] This was not a "verbal construct" for them, or a hypothetical condition useful as an element in "theory construction"; to them it was the situation in which man found himself originally and into which he would lapse under certain conditions. One of the first debates to take place in the First Congress turned on the question of whether Americans, upon declaring their independence of Great Britain, had "reverted" to a state of nature. The question was posed when a petition was introduced calling upon the House of Representatives to declare William Smith of South Carolina ineligible to take his seat in the House because he did not meet the constitutional requirement of seven years citizenship. As a young boy of twelve in 1770, Smith had gone to England to be educated; he had lost both his parents during his absence from America, had endeavored to return during the Revolutionary War, but had suffered a series of misadventures and difficulties, including a shipwreck. He finally managed to reach Charleston, South Carolina, in November 1783. After serving in the state legislature, he was duly elected to the House

31 John Locke, *Two Treatises of Government*, Book 2, section 6.
32 Madison to Webster, March 15, 1833, in Madison, *Works* (Congressional ed., 1865), 4:294.

of Representatives and appeared to take his seat in the First Congress, only to be met, in May 1789, with the challenge that he was not—or had not for the necessary seven years been—a citizen of the United States. It was said against him that he had not been a citizen at his birth in 1758—indeed, he, like most if not all of the others in Congress, was born a British subject—had not, unlike the others, acquired it by fighting in the Revolution, or by taking an oath to one of the states, or by tacit consent, or, finally, by adoption. Madison, who supported him, replied that Smith was a citizen "on the Declaration of Independence," by which he apparently meant, on the occasion of, or because of the occasion of, the Declaration of Independence, and that he continued to possess citizenship unless he had somehow forfeited it. The Declaration of Independence had absolved his "secondary allegiance" to George III but not his allegiance to the society of which, even as a child, he had been a member. "This reasoning will hold good," Madison said, "unless it is supposed that the separation which took place between these States and Great Britain, not only dissolved the union between these countries, but dissolved the union among the citizens themselves: that the original compact, which made them altogether one society, being dissolved, they could not fall into pieces, each part making an independent society; but must individually revert into a state of nature." Madison did not "conceive that this was, of necessity, to be the case." Such a revolution did not, he believed, "absolutely take place." The colonies remained "as a political society, detached from their former connexion with another society, without dissolving into a state of nature; but capable of substituting a new form of Government in the place of the old one, which they had, for special considerations, abolished."[33] The difficulty of the question is one that must be acknowledged by any reader of the last chapter of Locke's *Second Treatise* ("Of the Dissolution of Government"), and Madison spoke without his customary assurance. Not so James Jackson of Georgia. His reading of the situation was that there had been only one allegiance to Great Britain and, that being dissolved, they had all, Smith included, experienced "a total reversion to a state of nature amongst individuals." After this, "every man made his election for an original compact, or tie, which, by his own act, or that of his father for him, he became bound to submit to."[34] This Smith had not done, or had done only on his return in 1783, a mere six years earlier, and, therefore, he was not eligible to take his seat in the House. Fortunately for Smith, the House voted overwhelmingly

33 *Annals of Congress*, 1:421–22.
34 Ibid., p. 423.

in his favor, which is to say, overwhelmingly in favor of Madison's reading of Locke and of the events of 1776. They were deciding a question of right, not of expediency, Madison insisted; but what is of primary interest here is the source of the guidance they sought on such questions, or the source of the principles on which they acted politically: so far as the Constitution of the United States is concerned, in the beginning was not the word ("and the word was with God, and the word was God"); in the beginning was the state of nature, and the word was with the philosophers of natural rights. It was from them that the Founders learned the new "science of politics," and with it the principles of free government.[35]

These principles require the establishment of religious freedom, the right of men to hold whatever opinions they choose respecting God or gods. That men *must* have this choice is not itself a matter of choice or indifference. Jefferson insisted on this, and Jefferson is acknowledged to be the authoritative American spokesman on this subject. In his *Notes on the State of Virginia*, the only book he ever wrote and containing probably his deepest reflections on political questions, he said that because their institutions are not built on a religious truth, Americans are not entitled to regard it as an injury— or an injury for which the law will provide a remedy—for their neighbors to say there are twenty gods or no God. Such religious opinions neither pick their pockets nor break their legs, as he put it in his famous formulation;[36] and because such religious opinions do not injure them or the commonwealth, their neighbors are entitled to an absolute right to hold them. Any denial of this would, of necessity, be based on a particular religious doctrine. For example, a law forbidding the opinion that there are twenty gods would arise out of the opinion that there is one God, or no God, or some other number of gods; and to legislate on such a basis would be to transform what in the eyes of the Constitution is merely an opinion, and, officially at least, must remain so, into an official truth, and this would be incompatible with the Constitution and the political philosophy underlying it. Furthermore, religious freedom must be established because "difference of opinion is advantageous in religion," not advantageous to religion (although that may be true incidentally), but politically advantageous. That is to say, it is politically advantageous to have religious differences in the country, to have present a variety of religious sects, because the "several sects perform the office of a

35 *The Federalist*, No. 9.
36 Jefferson, *Works* (Federal ed.), 4:78.

Censor morum over each other."[37] The rights of man are protected by a "multiplicity of sects," as Jefferson's friend and colleague, Madison, said in *Federalist* 51, and what matters is the rights of man (and not a particular religious doctrine concerning eternal salvation or anything else). Thus, the establishment of religious freedom rests on the proposition that there can be no officially recognized creed or doctrine—that officially, all religious doctrines are equal—and Jefferson and Madison did their best to establish this principle not only in federal public law, but in the public law of Virginia as well. The state religious establishments might have to be accommodated in practice, but they were, nevertheless, incompatible with the principle on which the country was founded.

While the United States recognizes no religious truth, it is founded on the "self-evident" philosophical truths respecting the natural freedom and equality of all men. Being naturally free, men contract one with another to form civil society—"all power is originally vested in, and consequently derives from, the people." This contract represents their agreement to be governed—their consent to be governed—and this agreement or consent, which is the beginning of all legitimate government, is required by the fact of their natural freedom and equality. Being free and equal with respect to natural right, and however unequal they may be according to any religious doctrine or in any other respect, no man may justly rule another without his consent, although before the formation of the United States this right was not recognized or acknowledged in practice. Kings, in the course of time and from place to place, may have been required to make laws only with the consent of the lords spiritual and temporal and the commons in parliaments assembled, but they claimed to hold their crowns by the grace of God, independent of the consent of those they governed. In this fundamental political respect, men were held to be unequal.

Discovery of the rights of man changed that. "All eyes are opened, or opening, to the rights of man," Jefferson said. "The general spread of the light of science has already laid open to every view the palpable truth, that the mass of mankind has not been born with saddles on their backs, nor a favored few booted and spurred, ready to ride them legitimately, by the grace of God."[38] This "palpable truth" is a scientific truth, not a religious truth or opinion, a truth discovered by the new political science, and the United States was the first country

---

[37] Ibid., p. 80.

[38] Jefferson to Roger C. Weightman, June 24, 1826, in Jefferson, *Works* (Federal ed.), 12:477.

to organize itself on it. It was the first country to recognize the self-evident truths of the natural freedom and equality of all men and, therefore, that legitimate government can arise only out of consent. It was, as the motto on its Great Seal proclaims, a *novus ordo seclorum*, a new order of the ages. In this decisive respect it was the first "new nation," and its newness consisted in large part in the nonreligious character of its founding principle. The uniqueness of this fact is emphasized in the thought of John Locke, the Englishman frequently called "America's philosopher," and whom Jefferson, referring to him as one of the three greatest men ever to live, accepted as one of his teachers. In the first of his *Two Treatises of Government*, Locke goes to what today are regarded as extraordinary lengths to show what we would regard as self-evident, namely, that kings do not rule by virtue of any donation from God to Adam and his heirs. This having been shown, he says at the outset of the *Second Treatise*, it is necessary "to find out another rise of government, another original of political power," [39] and by saying this he suggests that the only alternative to government based on the religious doctrine of divine donation is, as it turns out, government based on the nonreligious doctrine of the rights of man and the contract men make with each other. To secure these rights governments are instituted among men.

Such a government was not established with the settling of the American colonies, and although its principles were well known to Jefferson and his colleagues, it had not been fully established in Virginia even by the end of 1781, when Jefferson wrote his *Notes on the State of Virginia*. As he saw it, the people of Virginia had not yet been sufficiently instructed in these principles, even after they had declared their independence. "The convention of May 1776, in their declaration of rights, declared it to be a truth, and a natural right, that the exercise of religion should be free; but when they proceeded to form on that declaration the ordinance of government, instead of taking up every principle declared in the bill of rights, and guarding it by legislative sanction, they passed over that which asserted our religious rights, leaving them as they found them." [40] Heresy was, in principle, still punishable under the laws of Virginia; a Christian could deny the doctrine of the Trinity only at the price of his right to hold "any office or employment ecclesiastical, civil, or military," and, if he should persist in his denial, at the price of his liberty, his right to sue, to inherit property, and even of his "right to the custody of his

---

[39] Locke, *Treatises*, Book 2, chap. 1.
[40] Jefferson, *Works* (Federal ed.), 4:76.

own children." This, Jefferson explained, "is a summary view of that religious slavery under which a people have been willing to remain, who have lavished their lives and fortunes for the establishment of their civil freedom." Men are endowed with natural rights, and rulers have no authority over these rights except as men, in the compact forming civil society, have submitted to them. But it was Jefferson's view, and he was sustained in this by the existence of the Virginia law as well as by the strength of the opposition he and Madison had to overcome in order to establish religious freedom in the state, that too many Virginians persisted in the error of regarding it as proper for the rights of conscience to be submitted to government.

This Virginia law and the religious establishments that continued to exist in some other states were vestiges of the orthodox Christianity that had come under attack in the seventeenth century from the new political science. It had to be attacked or somehow displaced because, as Professor Mansfield has said, any revealed religion is incompatible with modern natural right. A revealed religion is revealed only to the godly and the godly are only too likely "to take advantage of the favor of revelation to demand political power for themselves or their allies."[41] In a limited way—limited when compared with the claims staked out by the priests and princes against whom Hobbes, Spinoza, and Locke had to contend—this is what the nominally pious Virginians were doing. To destroy the political power of revealed religion it was first necessary to destroy or displace the authority of revealed religion, which, in America as in the Europe of the seventeenth century, meant the authority of Scripture, and especially of the New Testament wherein the proof of Jesus' authority is supplied by "the multitude of miracles he did before all sorts of people." This is necessary because "where the miracle is admitted, the doctrine cannot be rejected." Thus Hobbes wrote a critique of "miracles, and their use,"[42] and Locke a *Discourse of Miracles*, from which the passage quoted above is taken,[43] and Spinoza attempted to demonstrate that "God cannot be known from miracles."[44] Christianity had to be made reasonable, which is why Locke, in addition to writing *Some Considerations of the Consequences of the Lowering of Interest and*

41 Mansfield, "Thomas Jefferson," p. 28.

42 Thomas Hobbes, *Leviathan*, Book 3, chap. 37.

43 *The Works of John Locke* (1812 ed.), 9:259. The nature of Locke's critique of miracles is suggested in the fact that he specified that it should not be published until after his death.

44 *Theologico-Political Treatise*, chap. 6 in *The Chief Works of Spinoza*, trans. R. H. Elwes, 2 vols. (New York: Dover), I:87.

Raising the Value of Money, found it necessary to write, *The Reasonableness of Christianity*.

Jefferson, of course, was a statesman, not a philosopher, but his statesmanship was informed by what he had learned from the natural rights philosophers who preceded him. From them he had learned that Christianity had to be made reasonable, and he was willing, albeit in words that he was careful to keep from the public, to commit his thoughts to paper. He denied the divinity of Christ. He nevertheless described himself as a Christian, not the sort of Christian that any of the Christian churches could have recognized, but a Christian "in the only sense [Jesus] wished anyone to be." He was perfectly willing to attribute to Jesus "every *human* excellence," which, he insisted against the churches, was all Jesus ever claimed for himself.[45] The so-called Christians think otherwise because they had been corrupted, taught to believe in the Bible and that the Bible is a record of God's revealing himself to man. This doctrine, wholly false in his judgment, Jefferson traces to the fact that Jesus, like Socrates, "wrote nothing himself," thereby making it possible for "the most unlettered and ignorant men [writing] from memory and not till long after the transactions had passed [to commit] to writing his life and doctrines."[46] Hence, the doctrines "he really delivered . . . have come to us mutilated, misstated, and often unintelligible," and they were further "disfigured by the corruptions of schismatising followers, who have found an interest in sophisticating and perverting the simple doctrines he taught by engrafting on them the mysticisms of a Grecian sophist, frittering them into subtleties, and obscuring them with jargon, until they have caused good men to reject the whole in disgust, and to view Jesus himself as an imposter."[47] His moral doctrines, Jefferson goes on, are in fact "pure and perfect" and inculcate a "universal philanthropy, not only to kindred and friends, to neighbors and countrymen, gathering all into one family, under the bonds of love, charity, peace, common wants and common aids."[48]

To say that Jefferson advocated religious freedom and the separation of church and state, and to leave it at that, is to miss what was then the truly radical character of his views on religion. Americans, he suggests, no more than the immediate addressees of Locke's writ-

[45] Jefferson to Benjamin Rush, April 21, 1803, in Jefferson, *Works* (Federal ed.), 9:457 (italics original).

[46] "Syllabus of an Estimate of the Merit of the Doctrine of Jesus Compared with Those of Others," ibid., p. 461.

[47] Ibid., p. 462.

[48] Ibid., pp. 462–63.

ings, are not going to accept a policy of freedom and separation, or of toleration (and Jefferson made copious notes and significant use of Locke's *Letter concerning Toleration*),[49] until they can be persuaded to accept the ground of this toleration, and the ground of this toleration is the opinion that traditional Christian doctrine is false. When it is shown to be false, and when the truth of this falseness is, "by the light of science," spread among the mass of mankind, it will be possible for men to attach themselves more firmly to the god of the Declaration of Independence—"Nature's God"—and the religious problem will be solved and free government secured.[50] But Jefferson circulated these opinions only among a few of his correspondents.

No book is needed to read the will of "Nature's God"; at least none is needed by men with "minds of peculiar structure" capable of being influenced by a "refined education," to use again Washington's words from the Farewell Address. The others, initially, at least, would need some help, and the American who set out most vigorously and openly to provide this help was Tom Paine. Unlike Jefferson, and much more openly than the equally radical, but nevertheless far more subtle, critiques written by his more learned seventeenth-century predecessors, Paine does mount an attack on miracles, and prophecy, and mystery. Also unlike Jefferson, who concealed his most radical religious views from the eyes of the public, Paine, dedicating his book to his "fellow citizens of the United States of America," informs them that Christianity is the most "absurd," "repugnant," "derogatory," "unedifying" and "inconsistent" religion ever "invented."[51] The Bible, he says, is a book of fables, not the revealed word of God. God has revealed himself in his works, as first cause of these works. God can be discovered only by studying his created world, and the Bible and the churches are positively detrimental to this project: they have traditionally stood as obstacles in the path of science and will continue to do so as long as they hold power over the minds of men.

Paine does his best to destroy that power in page after page of argument, ridicule, anger, and unconcealed contempt for the enemies of

49 See S. Gerald Sandler, "Lockean Ideas in Thomas Jefferson's *Bill for Establishing Religious Freedom*," *Journal of the History of Ideas* 21 (1960):110–16. In three parallel columns Sandler cites five ideas concerning toleration as they appear first in Locke's *Letter*, secondly in the notes Jefferson made on Locke's *Letter*, and thirdly in the *Bill for Establishing Religious Freedom*. The similarity is remarkable. As Sandler says, "There can be little doubt of [Jefferson's] indebtedness to Locke for his ideas on religious toleration."

50 In the event, the problem was solved in the manner suggested to Americans by Montesquieu.

51 Thomas Paine, *Age of Reason* (New York: Willey Book Co., n.d.), p. 248.

what he regards as scientific truth. This truth does not need the 'crutch" of fable[52]—or, as Jefferson put it, "truth can stand by itself."[53] God, "the Almighty Lecturer," speaks to man not indirectly through the Bible, but directly in his display of "the principles of science in the structure of the universe [and] has invited man to study and to imitation."[54]

Jefferson never deigned publicly to speak so boldly, but there is nothing in the *Age of Reason* that does not find a place in the thoughts Jefferson committed to letters and other such papers. If we are no longer shocked by them as Paine's contemporaries were for a while shocked by them, that merely shows the extent of the change that has occurred in our opinions. Despite the extravagance of his presentation, Paine was a representative spokesman of his age, the age of reason. It is not by chance that he wrote another book, entitled *Rights of Man*, or that he thought it appropriate to dedicate it to George Washington.

Under the reign of the doctrine of the rights of man, the day might come, and Paine and Jefferson in their different ways worked to hasten its coming, when the typical Anglican priest of Virginia will have long since ceased his agitation for the presumed benefits of establishment and will be less concerned with what separates the various religions than with what they have in common. He might come in time to speak of the "Judeo-Christian tradition," for example. Whatever might be said of this from the point of view of orthodox Anglo-Catholicism and orthodox Judaism (which, Jefferson said, was also in need of "reformation" and to "an eminent degree"),[55] it will bespeak (and, of course, does bespeak) a situation that allows both Anglo-Catholic and Jew, as well as others, to enjoy the rights to which they are entitled as men: to live in liberty and to worship as they please, because neither will be inclined to prevent the other from doing so, or to think it important or even legitimate to do so.

The origin of free government in the modern sense coincides and can *only* coincide with the solution of the religious problem, and the solution of the religious problem consists in the subordination of religion. Before that time it was thought to matter whether a nation believed in twenty gods or one God or no God, or whether the one God was this God or that God. That is why the question of religion

[52] Ibid., p. 88.

[53] *Notes on the State of Virginia*, Jefferson, *Works* (Federal ed.), 4:79.

[54] Paine, *Age of Reason*, p. 52.

[55] Jefferson, "Syllabus of an Estimate of the Merit of the Doctrines of Jesus, Compared with Those of Others," *Works* (Federal ed.), 9:461.

used to figure so prominently in the works of the political philosophers. Then it was a political question, now it is not. One can say that the natural rights philosophers spent so much time on the religious question in order to make it possible for the politicians who followed them to ignore it.

That this lesson was learned by Americans (and not by the besieged residents of Northern Ireland, for example) was obvious even in Tocqueville's time;[56] but it is not at all obvious that it was learned directly from Paine's teaching. It is more likely that Americans—whose strong attachment to material comforts led Jefferson in 1781 to predict that, on the successful conclusion of the Revolutionary War, they would be concerned solely with making money—were led by this attachment to accept an "understanding of Christianity which [was] not in conflict with it."[57] And the Constitution certainly did nothing to discourage a life devoted to the acquisition of material comforts.

The Founders did not establish religion, but they did establish commerce and the commercial republic, and by so doing, facilitated the acquisition of the material comforts it would provide. In a statement whose significance cannot be overemphasized, Madison, in the most famous of the *Federalist Papers*, says that the "protection of different and unequal faculties of acquiring property . . . is the first object of government."[58] Previous generations would have regarded such a statement as outrageous, and even today there are Americans who refuse to concede that Madison meant what he said. It is too blunt for us, too shocking to our sensibilities, too seemingly lacking in a concern for the less well-endowed or less fortunate, those who do not fare well in the competition. But that was not an ill-considered statement tossed off in the press of meeting a journalistic deadline;

56 Tocqueville, *Democracy in America*, 1:45.

57 Thomas I. Pangle, *Montesquieu's Philosophy of Liberalism* (Chicago: University of Chicago Press, 1973), p. 257. In Montesquieu's words, the way "to attack a religion is by favor, by the commodities of life, by the hope of wealth; not by what drives away, but by what makes one forget; not by what brings indignation, but by what makes men lukewarm, when other passions act on our souls, and those which religion inspires are silent. *Régle générale*: with regard to change in religion, invitations are stronger than penalties" (Montesquieu, *The Spirit of the Laws*, Book 25, chap. 12, trans. Pangle). Professor Pangle's comment on this makes the point even clearer, and more clearly relevant to America: "Christianity will be overcome by making men 'forget' everything which is at a tension with securing 'the commodities of life.' All that is required on the part of 'political writers' like Montesquieu is to show the way to an understanding of Christianity which is not in conflict with devotion to commerce and comfort; the inherent attractions of these things will do the rest" (pp. 256–57).

58 *The Federalist*, No. 10.

he had said essentially the same thing on the floor of the constitutional convention.[59] Commerce and the material comforts it promises will entice men away from their austere religions and, in addition, will provide the needed substitute for the moral habits religion inculcated. This was Locke's, and later and in more precise detail, Adam Smith's teaching,[60] but it was left to Madison to apply it to an actual political situation. This he did in *Federalist* 10.

The argument goes as follows: The United States, a nation founded on the principle of self-interest ("to secure these [individual] rights, governments are instituted among men"), faces the severe problem of somehow moderating self-interest. The problem will manifest itself, and in 1788 has already manifested itself in the various states, as the problem of faction, defined as "a number of citizens . . . united and actuated by some common impulse of passion, or of interest, adverse to the rights of other citizens, or to the permanent and aggregate interests of the community." The "mischief" can be cured by removing its causes—but only at the price of liberty—or, the old religious way, by giving everyone the "same opinions, the same passions, and the same interests": making everyone an Anglo-Catholic, for example, as Britain and more recently even Virginia had tried to do. Madison, speaking for the United States, rejects that "cure." Besides, the states were demonstrating that it was, in fact, a cure no longer available in America. "From the conclusion of this war," said Jefferson at the end of his discussion of religion, "we shall be going down hill [and] the people will forget themselves, but in the sole faculty of making money."[61] The states, despite their affirmations, were not succeeding in restraining this passion. Massachusetts may have required public support of public worship—because the preservation of civil government was thought, or said, to depend "upon piety, religion and morality"—but Massachusetts was the scene of Shays's Rebellion, and in the Founders' minds no event better illustrated the extent to which a democratic people could trample on the rights of man. There was, Madison argued on the floor of the Constitutional Convention, no security in the states for private rights and the steady dispensation of justice. "Interference with these were evils which had more perhaps than anything else, produced this convention." In a republic the majority rules, and, when the majority is united by a common in-

[59] Max Farrand, ed., *The Records of the Federal Convention of 1787*, 4 vols. (New Haven: Yale University Press, 1911–37), 1:134–36.

[60] Locke, *Treatises*, Book 2, especially chap. 5; Adam Smith, *The Wealth of Nations* (New York: Modern Library), esp. pp. 753–55.

[61] *Notes on the State of Virginia*, Jefferson, *Works* (Federal ed.), 4:81–82.

terest or passion, the rights of the minority are in danger. What, he asked, will restrain it? Not a "prudent regard to the maxim that honesty is the best policy"; not a "respect for character"; not "conscience"; not religion. Indeed, "religion itself may become a motive to persecution and oppression." [62] The states called for morality, but they had not succeeded in providing it. The states praised sumptuary laws, John Adams noted, but such laws were more often praised than enacted.[63] That was why an entirely different approach, an approach embodying a substitute for morality, had to be found.[64]

Fortunately, a substitute was available. The "mischief" could be cured by controlling the effects of faction: instead of attempting to make men moral by preaching to them to love their neighbors as themselves, which will not work in the United States ("we well know that neither moral nor religious motives can be relied on as an adequate control"), instead of trying to control the passions, and especially acquisitiveness or greed, the passions of men will be directed to the pursuit of material goods, and it is in this context that Madison says that the "protection of different and unequal faculties of acquiring property . . . is the first object of government." Instead of the rule of an unrestrained majority operating within each state and riding roughshod over the rights of others, the large commercial republic delineated in *Federalist* 10 will make the formation of such a majority extremely difficult. And instead of civil strife and wars caused by disputes between Catholics and Protestants, Christians and Jews, or high church or low church, men can live in peace and liberty if permitted to pursue their passion for material well-being and succeed (and they will succeed—and they have succeeded) in the large commercial republic dedicated to promoting "different degrees and kinds of property." [65] In short, instead of pursuing eternal salvation and fighting over how to achieve it, if men seek material gratification

[62] Farrand, ed., *Records of the Federal Convention*, 1:134–35, and see also *The Federalist*, No. 15.

[63] *The Works of John Adams, with a Life of the Author*, ed. Charles Francis Adams, 10 vols. (Boston: Little, Brown, 1850–1856), 4:199 and 7:53–54. As cited by John Agresto, "The Debate over the Nature of Republican Government in the American Founding Period: The Problem of Republican Virtue," Diss. Cornell 1974, pp. 59–60.

[64] This issue of the republic founded on public spirit and virtuous citizens or the republic founded on self-interest and the commercial spirit was the issue debated in the ratification struggle, with the Anti-Federalists contending for the former and the Federalists for the latter. The Anti-Federalists, of course, lost the debate, which proved to be decisive for the subsequent history of the country.

[65] Unless otherwise noted, all the quotations in the three preceding paragraphs are taken from *The Federalist*, No. 10.

and win it, republican government will be possible. We know the result under the name of capitalism. Capitalism, understood as the right of unlimited acquisition, will promote "The Wealth of Nations" and, by so doing, secure the rights of man. This is what it means to say that acquisition is the substitute for morality.

The Constitution protects property and its acquisition—this was, after all, "the first object of government"—and does nothing for morality except to allow for religious freedom and, in the establishment clause of the First Amendment, for the support, on a nondiscriminatory basis, of the institutions, primarily the churches, whose job it is to provide a degree of moral education. There is room for Sunday Schools—indeed, there is a need of them as the source of those good habits that ought to guide the business life—provided it is understood that they are subordinate to the "regular schools." This order of priority follows from the Founders' awareness both of the principles underlying free government and of the character of their fellow countrymen, whose acquisitiveness even then was apparent to some observers. The unsurpassed material prosperity of the United States (as well as some conspicuous characteristics of the American people) is a reflection of this original priority.

Imbued, however, with the happy conviction that one can dedicate oneself to material prosperity and the relief of one's estate on this earth without thereby jeopardizing his chances to succeed in another world, the American has made his obeisances, even if he has not committed his soul, to the generous God who is said to sanction this. In the First Amendment the Constitution permits him to be worshipped, and the laws have traditionally made it relatively painless financially for Americans to support the places of this worship. Justice Douglas was right when he complained—even if he was wrong *to* complain—that our "system at the federal and state levels is presently honeycombed with such financing."[66] In God (reasonably defined) we do indeed collectively trust, and there is even room for those who trust in him first and foremost (a matter of no small significance) provided their piety stays within the bounds required for "peace and order." Until those bounds are violated, Jefferson said, it is unnecessary for "the State to be troubled with [them]."[67]

Americans have, as Tocqueville observed, succeeded in combining the spirit of religion and the spirit of liberty, but they have done so by subordinating the former to the latter. In this, he suggested, they were wise:

[66] *Engel* v. *Vitale*, 370 U.S. 421, 437 (1962). Concurring opinion.
[67] *Notes on the State of Virginia*, Jefferson, *Works* (Federal ed.), 4:81.

It may be believed that a religion which should undertake to destroy so deep-seated a passion [as "the love of well-being"] would in the end be destroyed by it; and if it attempted to wean men entirely from the contemplation of the good things of this world in order to devote their faculties exclusively to the thought of another, it may be foreseen that the minds of men would at length escape its grasp, to plunge into the exclusive enjoyment of present and material pleasures.

The chief concern of religion is to purify, to regulate, and to restrain the excessive and exclusive taste for well-being that men feel in periods of equality; but it would be an error to attempt to overcome it completely or to eradicate it. Men cannot be cured of the love of riches, but they may be persuaded to enrich themselves by none but honest means.[68]

Conclusion

It is sufficiently clear from the debates leading to the adoption of the First Amendment, principally from what was not at issue as well as from the ease with which the secondary issues were resolved, that the religious problem was well on the way to being solved at the time the Constitution was written. It is also clear, however, that the Founders knew it had to be solved—knew that Americans would have to agree with them that religion must play only a subordinate, even if necessary, role in their lives—before free government could be successfully established in the United States. It is this official subordination of religion that underlies the principle of the absolute freedom of religious opinion. Because the country was not founded on a religious truth, it could—and indeed must—permit a variety of religious opinions. Instead of founding itself on what was claimed to be a religious truth, the country was founded on political truths respecting man and his natural rights, truths held to be "self-evident." It follows from this that whereas the extent of the freedom accorded religious opinion could and must be absolute, the extent of the freedom accorded political opinion could not and must not be absolute. Political opinion must be compatible with the self-evident truths regarding man and government on which the country was founded. The health of the country was held to depend on an attachment on the part of its citizens to these political truths, and it was understood that those who governed it could not afford to be indifferent to the existence of this attachment. That is why even Jefferson called for a "conviction in the minds of the people that these liberties are of the gift of God."

[68] Tocqueville, *Democracy in America,* 2:27.

That is why Jefferson also counseled against the admission of immigrants—at a time when additional population was sorely needed—who were attached to contrary political principles, to monarchy or anarchy ("an unbounded licentiousness"), for example. Such immigrants and their children would share in lawmaking and thereby "infuse into it their spirit, warp and bias its directions, and render it a heterogeneous, incoherent, distracted mass." [69] That is why Jefferson could also say that difference of opinion is advantageous in religion and harmless in physics and geometry, and *not* say it regarding the fundamental principles of government. [70]

Toleration of different religious opinion rests, and can only rest, on this political truth. Men are endowed with rights to life, liberty, and the pursuit of happiness, and they consent to government in order to secure these rights, not to improve their souls. If this were merely an opinion, it would be necessary to accept as legitimate the claim of a Charles I to suppress religious freedom and replace it with an established church. Or, as Professor Mansfield put it, if this "truth were but an opinion, it could not protect free inquiry into other opinions." [71] Thus, the Founders drew a distinction between the liberty of religious and political opinion: the former was absolute while the latter, of necessity, was not. The idea that they are to be treated indistinguishably, as if entitled to equal protection, as it were, was given official sanction only in 1940, in the case of *Cantwell* v. *Connecticut*. [72] It is an idea that is now widely, if not generally, held. It derives from the gradual acceptance of the view, first expressed on the Court by Holmes in his *Gitlow* dissent, [73] that the Constitution rests on nothing at all, or, on no principle immune from the whims of transient majorities. The association of the religious and the speech and press provisions in the same amendment may have made it easier for the Court to accept the view that they are to be treated alike, but once having jettisoned or forgotten the reason for the distinction, it was probable that the distinction itself should suffer the same fate.

[69] *Notes on the State of Virginia*, Jefferson, *Works* (Federal ed.), 3:488.

[70] Jefferson, *Works* (Federal ed.), 4:79–80: *Papers* (Boyd ed.), 2:545–56 ("A Bill for Establishing Religious Freedom").

[71] Mansfield, "Thomas Jefferson," p. 37.

[72] 310 U.S. 296 (1940). This point is made by Mark DeWolfe Howe in *The Gardens and the Wilderness*, p. 108.

[73] *Gitlow* v. *New York*, 268 U.S. 652 (1925). Holmes said that if "in the long run the beliefs expressed in proletarian dictatorship are destined to be accepted by the dominant forces of the community, the only meaning of free speech is that they should be given their chance and have their way" (ibid., p. 673).

On Removing Certain Impediments to Democracy in the United States

Robert A. Dahl

W HAT this nation can become will be influenced, though not fully determined, by the ways in which we think about ourselves as a people. With a people as with a person, it is a sign of wisdom and maturity to understand and accept limits that are imposed by nature's laws and the scarcity of resources, whether physical, human, or political. In this sense we Americans may at last be entering into our maturity. But to accept as real, limits that are imposed only by our own minds, is not wisdom but self-inflicted blindness.

Out of our past we have inherited ways of thinking about ourselves that condemn us to try too much and accomplish too little. We fail not so much because our aspirations are too high but because they conflict; and within ourselves, too, we are conflicted in ways we do not fully recognize. In this sense our consciousness, both individual and collective, distorts our understanding of ourselves and our possibilities.

An important part of this distortion comes out of a series of historical commitments this country has made. It might free up our consciousness for greater political creativity if we were to see those commitments more clearly, to understand better how they conflict with one another, and to choose self-consciously rather than blindly among our possible futures.

The expression "historical commitment" may carry misleading connotations. An historical commitment in the context of this article is nothing neat, tidy, wholly self-conscious, broadly understood, much less agreed to by all, nor a well-shaped historical drama with a clear beginning, a middle, and an end. Rather, it pertains to periods in our history in which some alternative possibilities seemed open to the principal historical actors, who, however, were in conflict over the relative desirability of the alternatives they perceived. The conflict among them became overt, bitter, sometimes prolonged, and in one way or another finally came to involve a substantial number of citizens. In time, however, one set of advocates won out. Thereafter the issues so fiercely contested ceased to be salient in American political life. What had recently been a sharply contested possibility thus came to be accepted as pretty much an undebatable aspect of the status quo by the major parties, political leaders, writers and publicists, and (so far as these things can be discerned) the voters themselves. If dissenters continued to fight rearguard actions, they were few in number and on the margins of American politics, public attention, and political acceptability. Thus the historic commitments soon came to possess all the extraordinary advantages of things as they are and, after a generation or so, as they seem always to have been. This article will focus on five historical commitments this country has made to goals that are in some respects incompatible and will condemn us to a confused sense of national purpose unless and until we recognize these conflicts and decide on our priorities.

Five American Commitments

The first commitment was the one this country made to a liberal political and constitutional order that gave primacy to the protection of certain political and civil rights among its citizens. Although the whole colonial period was crucial to the development of sentiment favoring that commitment, the most active stage might be conveniently if rather arbitrarily placed somewhere between 1776 and 1800 or thereabouts. Sometime not long after 1800, conflict over the validity of the existing constitution pretty much recedes and soon hardly an American voice is heard in opposition to it. So profound is its acceptance, in fact, that the great constitutional quarrels to follow were not so much over the validity of the Constitution as over its meaning, assuming its unquestioned validity.

The second historical commitment, consolidated somewhere between 1800 and 1836 or thereabouts, was to the belief that the only proper constitutional and political system for Americans is a democracy. Although democracy mainly meant adhering to democratic procedures in the operation of the government, is also carried with it notions of a larger society within which social and economic conditions would favor the high degree of political, social, and economic equality necessary to democracy. By extraordinary luck, such a social order already existed in the United States. This was an agrarian society where, in an economy predominantly of family farms, the adult white male citizens lived with fewer social, economic, and political inequalities than any larger number of persons in history had existed up to that time, and very likely since. Tocqueville was not the first observer nor would he be the last, though he may have been the most gifted, to see how marvelously the agrarian society fostered a condition of equality among the citizens, or rather among the white males.

Yet that agrarian order was not only an historical rarity, but it had no future. During the harsh struggles over the new socioeconomic order that was to replace it, Americans who wished to retain the old order were the most numerous, persistent, and politically successful opponents of the new. But even with the whole weight of tradition on their side, they and their occasional allies were unable to prevent the displacement of the old agrarian order by a new order based on commercial and industrial capitalism, in which the ideal engine of economic production and growth was no longer to be the privately owned family farm but the privately owned commercial, financial, or industrial corporation. The contest that eventuated in the triumph of the new order over the old dominated American political life through the last three decades of the nineteenth century. During this time a number of alternatives to the new order—agrarianism, anarchism, socialism, individually owned consumers' and producers' cooperatives, selective government ownership and operation, economic regulation, limits on corporate size, monetary schemes, enforced competition, and many others—were thrust forward, debated, and finally pretty much defeated. The election of 1896 might be taken as the turning point in the victory of the new order over its rivals. Thereafter, the national commitment to the socio-economic order of corporate capitalism swelled into a current so powerful that opponents could make no headway against it and were swept out of the mainstream of American life. Even socialists, who in Britain and Europe gained greater support as industrial capitalism expanded, remained a small and largely uninfluential minority in the United States.

If by 1900 or so this country was committed to corporate capitalism, aspects of the new order nonetheless remained at issue. Widespread hardships were engendered by an economy with as little public control as the dominant political coalition demanded. These hardships were real enough to ensure a following for a politician who advocated reform—at any rate so long as he did not attack the basic commitment to private ownership, whereupon his following would shrink into futilities of minor party politics. Thus if socialism was unpopular, reform was not. As a result, from time to time regulatory laws won out in particular states and occasionally, as with Wilson's New Freedom, even in the federal government. But the country's commitment to only a modest interference by government in the conduct of corporate capitalism was more accurately reflected by the administrations of McKinley, Taft, Harding, Coolidge, and Hoover and by Theodore Roosevelt's bombastic style and ineffectual policies—speak loudly but carry a small stick—than by the brief interlude of reform during Wilson's first term. As we all know, it took the trauma of the Great Depression finally to convert a hitherto oppositional minority into a majority coalition. The product of this coalition was the fourth historic commitment which was, of course, to the idea and institutions of a welfare state. The prior commitment to private ownership and control of economic enterprises, and thus to corporate capitalism, was mainly upheld. Yet some of the most acute hardships and injustices generated in the socioeconomic order were to be removed or alleviated by government actions—mainly by the federal government. Orthodox as this commitment now seems, one who did not live through that period may find it difficult to recapture how intense, bitter, and at times violent was the conflict over the inauguration of a welfare state by Franklin Roosevelt and the New Deal. However, as with the preceding commitments, the main elements of this one soon gained such wide acceptability that opposition to the commitment itself, as distinguished from criticism of specific means, came to be an exercise in political futility.

Even before the main battles of the New Deal were finished, conflict had begun over what was to be the fifth historic commitment. This was the commitment to play an international role as a world power. Again, it may be hard to recapture how bitterly divided Americans were over this issue in the late 1930s. Yet the advocates of an American role as an active world power were riding an overpowering current of events that swept along most of their opponents and swamped the rest or left the few survivors stranded far behind the main body of American opinion.

All five of these historic commitments remain strong. Even after the shame and disaster of Vietnam, there is not really much likelihood of our renouncing our position as a world power, though the way we use our position and power cannot possibly be to everyone's liking or, alas, to everyone's benefit, and could easily be as harmful to ourselves and others once again as it has been in the recent past. Within limits, the strength of each of the five commitments seems to wax and wane; one is eroded here and another grows firmer there.

But the commitments still dominate the way we think about ourselves and our future. And that is a source of difficulty, for the commitments are in some ways incompatible.

Impediments to Democracy

In particular, certain impediments to the realization of democracy in the United States have resulted from the other historic commitments. We can begin with the Constitution itself, the political system it helped to form, and the political ideas and beliefs embedded in and strengthened by the constitutional and political system. As we have seen, this country's commitment to democracy came after and not before the formation and adoption of the Constitution. Even as late as the Constitutional Convention, the desirability of a representative democracy was a debatable issue. Consequently, the framers could not and did not agree to establish a representative democracy. They could and did agree to establish a representative republic with a framework of government that would, as they believed, rest on popular consent and yet ensure as best they knew how the preservation of certain basic rights to life, liberty, and property that they held to be morally inalienable. In this sense, the framers were liberals and republicans though they were not democrats; they intended to establish a liberal framework of government, though it could be, and later was, democratized to a degree that, for a time, would astonish the world.

The political system the framers helped bring into existence was in at least two major respects defective by democratic criteria. First, in spite of the eloquent universality of the language used in the Declaration of Independence and common at the time, in actuality the framers gave much narrower scope to the principles of consent and political equality. Without seriously qualifying, much less abandoning their universal norms, they nonetheless created a government that would demand obedience to its laws from a majority of adults —women, non-whites, and some white males—who were excluded from active participation in making those laws, whether directly or through their elected representatives. The majority of adults were thus provided with as little opportunity to give their active consent to the laws which they were bound to obey as their colonial predecessors had enjoyed under laws enacted by the English Parliament.

Second, in order to achieve their goal of preserving a set of inalienable rights superior to the majority principle—a goal many of us would surely share—the framers deliberately created a framework of government that was carefully designed to impede and even prevent the operation of majority rule. Thus when the country committed itself to their framework of government, two different arguments became confounded in the national consciousness, and they remain confounded to this day. There is the liberal argument that certain rights are so fundamental to the attainment of human goals, needs, interests, and fulfillment that governments must never be allowed to derogate from them. But in addition there is the American constitutional argument that the highly specific, indeed unique, set of political arrangements embodied in our constitutional and political practices is necessary to preserve these rights. While the writer accepts the liberal argument, the American constitutional argument seems seriously defective.

Now the matter of what ought to constitute inalienable rights beyond the reach of any government, and the proper relationship between such rights and democratic procedures, are questions far too complex to examine here. Certainly the solutions are not easy to come by, either theoretically or practically. Moreover, we might agree on the need to preserve fundamental rights against government without necessarily agreeing on what these rights should be. The point is, however, that the elaborate system of checks and balances, separation of powers, constitutional federalism, and other institutional arrangements influenced by these structures and the constitutional views they reflect are both adverse to the majority principle, and in that sense to democracy, and yet arbitrary and unfair in the protection they give to rights. However laudable their ends, in their means the framers were guilty of overkill. As only one example, the presidential veto has generally been used, and quite recently, for purposes no loftier than simply to prevent the adoption of policies disliked by the president and the political coalition whose interests he seeks to advance. It is not as if a president uses the veto only when a majority coalition threatens the inalienable rights of a minority. What is typically at stake is purely a disagreement about policy. Insofar as all policies have costs and gains and thus influence the distribution of advantages and disadvantages, the policies of a majority (like those of a minority) are likely to be adverse to the interests of some persons; but we can hardly say—nor can the framers have intended to say—that every privilege that happens to exist does so by inalienable right.

Yet there is this strong bias against majorities in the political system the framers helped to create. Because they succeeded in designing a system that makes it easier for privileged minorities to prevent changes they dislike than for majorities to bring about the changes they want, it is strongly tilted in favor of the status quo and against reform. In their effort to protect basic rights, what the framers did in effect was to hand out extra chips in the game of politics to people who are already advantaged, while they handicapped the disadvantaged who would like to change the status quo. From a moral perspective, the consequences seem arbitrary and quite lacking in a principled justification.

We ought to be able to design a way of preserving fundamental rights that is not so biased in favor of existing privilege and against reform. A number of other countries that place fewer barriers in the way of majority rule than exist under our political system manage to preserve at least as high a standard of political liberty, with less procedural unfairness. But of course to bring about such changes meets precisely the obstacle to change just mentioned, the antimajoritarian bias of the constitutional and political system.

This brings us to another consequence of the framers' antimajoritarian design that is unsatisfactory both as a protection for morally inalienable rights and as a device for procedural democracy. It may not be going too far to say that although the framers were unable to prevent the democratization of the constitutional system, they created a potentially lethal instrument for that democratization in the presidency. When the democratic commitment referred to earlier was undertaken, the antimajoritarian constitutional design was not merely preserved but identified with democratic government itself, a confusion that remains all but universal among Americans, as visitors from other democratic countries and teachers of political science to American undergraduates repeatedly discover. However, democratizing the Constitution required a transformation that some of the framers had feared and had sought to prevent. The claim was now made that the president was the sole authentic spokesman for and representative of national majorities. Indeed, the constitutional framework hardly provided any other possibility. Given the nature of the Senate and even of the House, the claim on behalf of the presidency was plausible, and one that the defenders of Congress found hard to rebut. In the long run, as we know, Congress failed to uphold its claim and the claims made on behalf of the presidency pretty much won out. Endowed with legitimacy deriving both from constitutional interpretation and democratic ideology, the presidency became the institutional center from which a majority coalition, if there was to be one at all, would be mobilized, organized, and given voice. Thus one consequence of the framers' institutional design was to channel the process of democratizing the Constitution into transforming the presidency, a process that was not to end, if it has yet ended, before that office became what lately has been variously called an elective monarchy, an imperial presidency, a plebiscitary chief executive, and other epithets still harsher.

The irony is, then, that the first and second historic commitments taken in their entirety endow us with a political system in which any majority coalition supporting changes adverse to existing privileges is likely to succeed only if the presidency has access to a concentration of political resources great enough to make the office a standing danger to majority rule and procedural democracy itself. Thus the justifiable effort to strengthen the majority principle in a constitutional system that was designed to impede it has led not to democratization of the Constitution but rather to the pseudo-democratization of the presidency.

Under the agrarian economic order, the pseudo-democratization of the presidency did not matter very much nor would it have gone very far. The white males who comprised the demos enjoyed an astounding degree of autonomy in relation to one another and to all governments. Their political resources, and the opportunities and incentives for using them should the need arise, were vast in comparison with the weak coercive means available to any of the American governments. Hence, the potentiality of widespread governmental coercion of the demos or any substantial part of it was perhaps as minimal as it had ever been anywhere among a numerous body of people. As for the members of the excluded majority, their very exclusion from political rights meant that they could not successfully appeal to the government to prevent private or public coercion, unless they happened to have the support of a majority of white males, and not necessarily even then if a substantial minority in the demos opposed the change sought by or in behalf of the disfranchised. In practice, then, the excluded groups had little protection against oppression.

The third historic commitment was to change the distribution of resources so favorable to the demos. An agrarian order that historically speaking was extraordinarily congenial to democracy was now displaced by a new socioeconomic order of corporate capitalism that was much less compatible. The basis of the new order was a fundamentally different kind of economic enterprise. The small family owned and operated farm that was modal if not universal in the agrarian order was now displaced by one of the most radical innovations that mankind has ever invented for economic organization, control, and growth. This was the privately owned and operated business corporation. Through a highly successful case of ideological transfer, the Lockean defense of private property, which in the agrarian order made good sense morally and politically, was shifted over intact to corporate enterprise. This ideological triumph successfully warded off attacks not only from nascent socialist movements opposed to private property in the means of production but also from the historical rear guard defending the old agrarian order, which had at hand no convincing way of distinguishing private ownership and control of one kind of enterprise, the farm, from private ownership and control of a radically different kind, the business corporation. Thus by an extraordinary ideological sleight of hand, the corporation took on the legitimacy of the farmer's home, tools, and land, and what he produced out of his land, labor, ingenuity, anguish, planning, forbearance, sacrifice, risk, and hope. The upshot was that the quite exceptional degree of autonomy the farmer members of the demos had enjoyed under the old order, an autonomy vis-à-vis both government and one another, was now granted to the corporation.

Two consequences of this new order were particularly adverse to democracy. First, the new order generated much greater differences than the old in political resources, skills, and incentives within the demos itself. The degree of social and economic differentiation that had already been foreshadowed in the cities of the eastern seaboard was no longer marginal, as it had been when the socioeconomic order was overwhelmingly agrarian, but central to the new order. Great differences in wealth, income, social esteem, education, occupational skills, and ethnic status now differentiated wage earners and pieceworkers in industry, ship, mine, and forest—a rising proportion of whom were immigrants—from the middling strata of white-collar and professional people, who for some time to come were predominantly Anglo-American in origins, and these in turn from the opulent few. Because differences like these are readily convertible into political resources, the wide, if by no means perfectly equal dispersion of political resources among the demos in the agrarian order was now considerably more concentrated. Inequalities in political resources added further to the handicaps of any majority coalition that sought changes in the allocation of privileges and disadvantages.

Second, because the internal government of the corporation was not itself democratic but hierarchical and often despotic, the rapid expansion of this revolutionary form of economic enterprise meant that an increasing proportion of the demos would live out their working lives, and most of their daily existence, not within a democratic system but instead within a hierarchical structure of subordination. To this extent, democracy was necessarily marginal to the actual political system in which the members of the demos lived their daily lives. Thus the transfer of the Lockean view to the corporation was a double triumph. By making ownership the only, or at least primary, source of legitimate control over corporate decisions, the new order not only excluded democratic controls in the internal government of the enterprise but placed powerful ideological barriers against the imposition of external controls by a government which, for all its deficiencies, was much more democratic than were the government of business firms.

The fourth and fifth commitments extended the domain of hierarchy even further. To be sure, from the New Deal onward the commitment to a welfare state helped to reduce the autonomy of economic enterprises. By protecting the rights of workers to join unions and bargain collectively with employers, the New Deal helped to democratize some aspect of some enterprises for some employees. By regulatory devices of various kinds it also reduced the autonomy and thus the arbitrary and sometimes despotic power of the rulers of economic enterprises. However, if the commitment to a welfare state has altered it has not profoundly reduced the two adverse consequences of the corporate capitalist order mentioned a moment ago. The evidence seems to show that what appear to be great changes in levels of taxation and transfer payments have not much reduced the inequalities in the distribution of wealth and income and thus the relative political advantage or disadvantage associated, at least loosely, with access to these resources. And except for the limited effects of trade unions among a minority segment of the labor force, the American commitment to a welfare state has not done much to alter the hierarchical structures of corporate government under which so many Americans live.

In fact, the commitment to a welfare state has added even more burdens to democracy. For one thing, the reforms undertaken in behalf of the commitment could not be carried through without the leadership of an energetic president, who could increase, organize, and exploit all the political resources of the office. If we want to find the recent rather than the Jacksonian origins of the imperial presidency, as good a place as anywhere to begin is the presidency of Franklin Roosevelt. Among other things, what his presidency did was to disarm most intellectuals and academics, not least political scientists, who, being mostly in favor of reform, enthusiastically came forward with whatever was needed in the way of a justification for enhanced presidential power. Moreover, in order to achieve its gains, the welfare state needed extensive governmental bureaucracies. Even if these are never fully controlled by official hierarchies, or for that matter, by anyone else, they do provide an ambitious president with very considerable political resources—far beyond anything the framers ever dreamed of—for persuasion, inducement, manipulation, and coercion. By now this proposition needs no documentation beyond what Watergate has furnished us. Finally, like the governments of corporate enterprise, the bureaucracies in the government of the state are also hierarchical in structure. Far from diminishing hierarchy, therefore, even in the course of regulating economic enterprise the welfare state has multiplied the number, domain, and scope of hierarchies in American life.

The fifth commitment, of course, compounded these consequences adverse to democracy. As an active world power, the country had need—at first quite suddenly—of a large military establishment, thus still another hierarchy, even more rigidly hierarchical than the rest, one perhaps even more difficult to control, yet available to the president for executing foreign and military policies that could be, as events were to show, the arbitrary and personal expressions of a chief executive whose decisions on these matters were for all practical purposes beyond the control of Congress, the courts, or the demos. In a further irony, constitutional language and interpretation had left a substantial gap in the framers' imposing array of checks and balances. Successive presidents plunged through and widened this gap. By action and inaction, the Congress, the courts, and the demos—cheered on, it has to be said, by political scientists, historians, lawyers, and other intellectual spokesmen who should have known better—all gave their blessing to the emerging imperial presidency. It took national shame, disaster, scandal, and prolonged investigation to make us realize what sort of an institution the presidency had become.

To understand these changes in the presidency it is important to keep in mind that for the better part of two generations this country was involved in war, near-war, war crisis, or cold war. Three decades of war would be enough, one might think, to undermine a weaker republic. Perhaps we should consider ourselves lucky that our first two commitments held as well as they did. Even so, as a world power things were done and widely thought to be justified that surely would have been condemned as unjustifiable in less paranoidal circumstances. An obsession with national security and loyalty fostered secrecy in government, the enormous expansion of domestic spying, the harassment of radicals, and other excrescences. And even if some important reforms were carried out, mainly with respect to civil rights, these decades were on the whole unfavorable to reform, and certainly to any changes that might seem to question the validity of our historic commitments.

The Doctrine of Procedural Democracy

If we were now to search for a perspective on our potentialities as a people that would not be distorted either by self-glorification or self-hatred, that recognized our capacities for great evil, great good, and plain mediocrity, and discerned in the conflicting commitments of our past that weigh heavily on our present some criteria of excellence against which to measure our achievements in the future, where would we begin?

We might begin near the beginning, with our first two commitments. Ignoring for a moment the contradictions described earlier, these may be interpreted as an aspiration toward a society with a political system in which liberty, equality, and justice would jointly prosper, a society therefore requiring also a socio-economic system that would foster these ends by supporting the kind of policy necessary to them. Thus interpreted, these two commitments would give priority to political ends over economic ends, to liberty, equality, and justice over efficiency, prosperity and growth, a priority that the commitment to corporate capitalism reversed both in ideology and in practice, and which has remained reversed down to our own day.

The guiding criteria against which to measure political performance implied by this interpretation are, in the author's view, the criteria of procedural democracy, which, together with their most crucial assumptions, constitute what one might call the doctrine of procedural democracy. What follows is a very brief and incomplete account of that doctrine.

To become fully operative with respect to any association, the doctrine of procedural democracy presupposes a judgment that at least two conditions exist among some set of persons who constitute or intend to constitute an association.

First, there is a *need for collective decisions* binding on the members of the association. That is, this set of persons is confronted by a matter which they think it would be disadvantageous to leave entirely to individual action or to choices made exclusively through a market, and comparatively advantageous to make collectively and enforce on the members.

Second, among the persons obligated to abide by collective decisions on this matter, there is a subset, the *demos*, whose members are *roughly equally qualified, taken all around.* That is, no member of this qualified subset, or demos, believes that any other member of the association or any subset of persons different from the demos is significantly more qualified than the demos to arrive at a correct choice with respect to matters requiring collective decisions. Under the *maximal* interpretation, the members believe that the demos includes all qualified members of the association and all members of the demos are in all relevant characteristics equally qualified with respect to matters requiring collective decisions. Under the *minimal* interpretation, no members of the association are in any relevant characteristic so clearly more qualified as to justify their making the decision for all the others on the matter at hand.

A government of any association in which these conditions are judged to exist is, on these matters, a *putatively democratic government in relation to its demos.* Thus a judgment that these conditions exist implies a rejection of claims that might be advanced on behalf of a government over the demos on these matters by a putative aristocracy, meritocracy, or governing elite.

The doctrine of procedural democracy holds that for any putatively democratic government, collective decision making by the demos should satisfy at least three criteria:

1. The criterion of *political equality.* The decision rule for determining outcomes must equally take into account the preferences of each member of the demos as to the outcome. To reject this criterion is to deny the condition of roughly equal qualification, taken all around. This criterion implies that the procedures and performance of any putatively democratic government ought to be evaluated according to the extent to which the preferences of every member of the demos are given weight in collective decisions, particularly on matters members think are important to them.

2. The criterion of *effective participation.* In order for the preferences of each member of the demos to be equally taken into account, every member must have equal opportunities for expressing preferences, and the grounds for them, throughout the process of collective decision making. This criterion implies, then, that any putatively democratic government ought to be evaluated according to the op-

portunities it provides for, or the costs it imposes on, expression and participation by the demos.

3. The criterion of *enlightened understanding*. In order to express preferences accurately, each member of the demos ought to have adequate and equal opportunities for discovering and validating, in the time available, what his or her preferences are on the matter to be decided. This criterion thus implies that any putatively demo cratic government ought to be evaluated according to the opportunities it furnishes for the acquisition of knowledge of ends and means, of oneself and other selves, by the demos.

Any government that satisfies these criteria, and only such a government, is *procedurally democratic in relation to its demos*.

As the doctrine is interpreted here, the demos defines itself. This is one of the most tricky and difficult aspects of democratic theory and practice. Because the demos defines itself, it need not include all the members of the association who are obliged to obey its rules. Whenever this is so, some members of the association, who are excluded from the demos, will also be excluded from the rights, opportunities, and protections of procedural democracy. Probably no association that has ever attempted to constitute a government for a state has admitted children into the demos. Now if children are excluded from the demos because they are judged to be unqualified, and yet are subject to the laws, then of course they are governed without their consent. Yet few of us would argue that the interest of children, inadequately as they are often protected, would be served better if they were made full voting members of the demos. To protect the rights, needs, and interests of children, we must rely not on procedural democracy but on the strength of adult feelings toward children of love, nurturance, pity, joy, compassion, and hope, and on laws and practices that these feelings may foster.

It is a very different matter with adults, among whom these feelings are ordinarily much too weak to ensure adequate protection for those who may be excluded from the demos. Consequently, we need to make explicit in the doctrine a proposition that has often been omitted or obscured. To do so requires a fourth criterion, that of *inclusiveness*. The demos includes all adults who are obliged to obey the rules of the association. Because the demos is inclusive, the criteria of procedural democracy apply to all the adults. Any government that satisfies all four criteria might be called a *full procedural democracy*.

One further point: probably no one who believes that full procedural democracy is a relevant aspiration thinks that it must hold for all matters, including judgments on highly technical, judicial, and administrative matters of every kind. Rhetorical assertions that seem to make procedural democracy the only proper method of making decisions have again and again been shown to be illusory and self-defeating. Yet as with the problem of inclusion, there is an exceptionally tricky problem here, one that can be dealt with only summarily in this article by stipulating a fifth criterion, that of *final control by the demos* ("popular sovereignty"). That is, the scope, domain, and procedures for making decisions other than by full procedural democracy are subject to decisions made by full procedural democracy. An association that satisfies all five criteria might thus be called a *fully democratic association in the procedural sense.*

Before turning to the implications of this doctrine for the United States, let us consider several objections. It is often said that procedural justice, and thus procedural democracy, does not guarantee substantive justice. This is true. It is said further, however, that as a consequence substantive justice should take priority over procedural justice and therefore over procedural democracy. This is partly right but mainly wrong. It is partly right because procedures should be judged by the ends they serve. Procedures that do not tend toward good ends cannot be judged good procedures. But the criticism is mainly wrong in implying that other solutions, particularly solutions that accept the claims of a putative governing elite, are more likely to lead to substantive justice. This is rarely a better short-run solution and practically always worse in the longer run. Finally, it is said that procedural democracy is in any case too anemic in its standards to compel us toward the robust aspirations of our nobler selves, for it speaks only to process and thus says nothing about the content of a good society. This criticism is only partly right in its premise and thoroughly wrong in its conclusion. It is obvious that all societies, including our own, fall very far short of satisfying the criteria of procedural democracy. If we in this country are to reduce the gap between criteria and performance in a large way, we shall have to make changes of great moment. What is more, these changes will have the effect of satisfying many of the claims for substantive justice as well. Such claims as could remain would constitute the very essence of healthy controversy—controversies that are properly adjudicated by means of procedural democracy and not by yielding to the claims of a putative governing elite or allowing a minority to impose its views on a majority.

Needs and Prospects

Suppose we were to interpret our first two historic commitments, taken together and after eliminating the inconsistencies, as a commitment to procedural democracy. Suppose further that we were to test our commitments against the requirements of this doctrine. Suppose, finally, that we resolved to move toward procedural democracy by reducing obstacles to it, at any rate up to some limit at which the trade-offs in other values became excessive. Given these suppositions, what changes would we make? Of course, not everyone accepts these suppositions; and even if they did, we might disagree about the answers. We might disagree both because the location of the limit at which trade-offs become excessive cannot be satisfactorily described in a precise way, and also because different persons will evaluate the trade-offs differently and thus reach different judgments about the location of the limit.

Nonetheless, it is possible to specify some directions in which changes are needed. At the outset these require changes in the way we think about ourselves and our institutions.

Consider the liberal thrust of the first historic commitment, to the preservation of morally inalienable rights. Such rights are assumed to be beyond the reach of government, and superior to any claims to other rights that conflict with them. But it has never been clear what rights are to be understood as inalienable or primary, and what rights are secondary and alienable, and hence must yield when they conflict with primary rights. The difficulty is that the grounds are not at all clear on which the distinction between primary and secondary, or inalienable and alienable rights, is to be made and justified.

Yet the conditions and criteria contained in the doctrine of procedural democracy are very rich in their implications for rights. For example, any judgment that the conditions for a putatively democratic government exist among some set of persons asserts a right to a government that satisfies the criteria of procedural democracy. Obviously, an assertion never establishes the validity of a claim. As with other rights, there is no automatic, self-enforcing determination of the validity of a claim. Judgments have to be made, and among a large number of people such judgments will rarely be unanimous. Claims may be rejected, justly or unjustly. Rights asserted usually have to be fought for.

Consider claims advanced on behalf of adults excluded from the demos that they are qualified to participate in American political life. The whole burden of American experience demonstrates not only that any group of adults excluded from the demos will be lethally weakened in its own defense, but also that those who govern will fail to protect the rights, needs, and interests of the excluded group. There is no convincing evidence in American history for the existence of one group of adults qualified to rule over adults who are excluded from full citizenship in the demos.

Yet for 200 years after the lovely universalistic phrases of the Declaration, the wellsprings of American national life were poisoned by the denial of claims to full citizenship, and by the injustice and oppression this denial entailed. To reject these claims, as American policy and practice did, was in effect to deny that full procedural democracy ought to exist in the United States. If we are now on, or past the threshold at which these claims are finally accepted as valid, then we are also obliged to accept the criteria of procedural democracy as valid measures of our national performance.

These criteria imply the existence of a body of primary rights, the rights necessary, though not sufficient, if a people is to govern itself. It could be readily shown that this body of primary rights must include most, though not all, of the rights and liberties the Supreme Court has held to be protected by the Constitution. As long as the primary rights necessary to procedural democracy exist, then all the political rights exist that are necessary if a people is to govern itself. Surely no narrower definition of inalienable rights ought to be acceptable to us. At the same time, however, any broader definition that includes rights inconsistent with these primary rights ought not to be acceptable to us. For to claim a right inconsistent with the primary rights necessary to procedural democracy is to deny the validity of procedural democracy and thus the capacity and right of a people to govern itself. If doctrine and practice were to treat these primary rights as inalienable, then all claims to rights inconsistent with these primary rights would be subject to final determination by the ordinary processes of collective decision making, and thus by voters, representatives, and legislators. To hold otherwise would be to deny that, taken all around, citizens are roughly equally qualified to make judgments on matters involving secondary rights. But since practically any public policy will infringe upon someone's existing privileges and thus give rise to a claim that a right has been diminished, if citizens are held to be incompetent on all matters involving secondary rights, what matters are they qualified to decide?

Viewed in this light, the commitment to corporate capitalism needs to be reconsidered. Earlier, when the framers had discussed their fears about majorities that might invade the rights of minorities, more often than not they mentioned rights to property. Their reasoned justification of a right to property, if they held one, would no doubt have been Lockean. Yet the Lockean justification of property makes no sense, it was suggested earlier, when it is applied to the large modern business corporation. It is absurd to regard as inalienable one's right to buy and thereafter own shares in ITT, and it approaches the ridiculous to argue that because one owns shares in ITT one possesses an inalienable and exclusive, if in practice quite useless, right to choose the directors of the firm, and that the primary legal obligation of the directors and management is, by a legal extension of the original doctrine, to protect the interests of owners above those of any other claimants.

If we abandon the absurdities in extending Locke on private property to ownership or control of the modern business corporation, then the rights of owners must be seen as secondary in relation to the primary rights that are necessary to self-government.

If ownership and control of corporate enterprise are matters of secondary not primary right, then the mere assertion of a right to private property does not provide a rational justification for private ownership of a large economic enterprise. If privately owned enterprise can be justified at all, it must be on the grounds of comparative social effectiveness: that is, of all the possible alternatives, this form provides the greatest social advantage with least social disadvantage. The only question we need to ask, then, is whether a privately owned corporation is more effective in achieving our social purposes, including procedural democracy, than all the possible alternatives to it.

In this perspective, any large economic enterprise is in principle a public enterprise. It exists not by private right but only to meet social goals. Questions about these social goals, and the comparative advantages and disadvantages of different forms, are properly in the public domain, matters for public discussion, choice, and decision, to be determined collectively by processes that satisfy the criteria of procedural democracy.

To be sure, none of this implies a direct answer to the question of how a large enterprise should be organized, controlled, or owned. To arrive at a correct answer depends as much on technical as on philosophical or ideological judgments, and perhaps a good deal more. Although this assertion contradicts a nearly universal dogma held on all sides, it is readily demonstrable by even the briefest consideration of the range of alternatives. If we were to take into account only the most obvious possibilities with respect to the internal government of enterprises, external controls, markets, prices, and the locus of ownership together with the rights and obligations of owners, we would quickly arrive at a very large array of theoretically possible combinations. Few of these can be dismissed a priori as unsuitable. Probably none can be shown to be superior to all the others in all circumstances. Consequently what has already become standard practice in advanced countries in this century will, one hopes, be taken for granted by citizens in advanced societies in the twenty-first century: a complex society cannot protect the rights, needs, and interests of its people with one single, prevailing form of economic organization but requires instead a network of enterprises organized in many different combinations of internal government, external controls, and ownership.

However, in choosing among the large number of possible combinations available in any particular instance, citizens of a country committed to procedural democracy would obviously want to avoid consequences adverse to procedural democracy. Earlier it was suggested that this country's commitment to corporate capitalism resulted in at least two such adverse consequences. As to those resulting from the unequal distribution of political resources, a country committed to procedural democracy must either place effective limits on the extent to which economic resources can be converted into political resources, or else ensure that economic resources are much more equally distributed than they are in the United States at present. So far we have tried only the first; that approach has largely failed. Perhaps it may prove possible by regulation to reduce the direct and indirect impact on political equality, effective participation, and political understanding of vast differences in income and wealth, but the record so far is dispiriting. It is time—long past time—to consider the other approach. Moreover, considerations of substantive distributive justice would seem to require a considerable reduction in inequalities in wealth and incomes. At the very least, the question of distribution of wealth and income ought to be high on the agenda of national politics.

As to the second of the adverse consequences of corporate capitalism, the enormous expansion of hierarchical systems of control, we need to be open to new ideas about governing economic enterprises and to a rapidly growing body of experience and experiments in this country and abroad. The author believes that the requisites of procedural democracy hold among the people who work for economic enterprises, and that the criteria of procedural democracy ought therefore to be applied to the government of firms. But a reasonable claim can be made for each of many other possibilities. Moreover, it seems obvious, though often ignored, that forms of control are not fully determined by forms of ownership. Government ownership is as consistent as private ownership with despotic control of enterprises. The form of control should be treated as a problem that is prior to the question of the form of ownership. What is a desirable form of ownership ought to be viewed, at least in part, as subordinate to and dependent on a judgment as to what is a desirable form of control. In any case, the range of alternatives this country ought to consider and experiment with is really quite broad and needs a great deal of systematic study.

Let us now turn back to the fourth and fifth historic commitments of the United States mentioned earlier. It is not an excessively harsh judgment to say that over three decades the presidency was transformed into a kind of plebiscitary principate with despotic tendencies toward arbitrary, ruthless, and self-aggrandizing exploitation of power. What is more, the other major political actors, including the Congress, the Supreme Court, the parties, the electorate, and the most active and attentive political strata all collaborated in that transformation. Only with the utmost reluctance and in the final hour was the Congress compelled to rediscover in the impeachment process a constitutional means for firing a president guilty of criminal acts. Now that impeachment has been used successfully and shown to be effective and salubrious, it is not too much to hope that the machinery will be kept oiled and ready for use. No president should ever again forget that he or she is anything other than the chief executive officer of a democratic republic.

If one part of the Constitution has proved to be workable, the fact that there was a need for impeachment proved how badly the constitutional system had been working. Yet nothing has changed in the fundamental institutional structure itself to reduce the pressures toward the pseudo-democratization of the presidency. For it still remains true that without a strong concentration of political resources in the presidential office, the policies preferred by a majority of citizens and their elected representatives stand a good chance of defeat by a well-entrenched opposition. Not only is this arrangement inconsistent with procedural democracy but it is arbitrary and unfair in its substantive results. Moreover, taken over any considerable period of time the evidence does not show that these minority vetoes constitute a defense of primary rights; rather, they tend to ensure the triumph of secondary rights or privileges over primary rights.

Taking all these problems into account, political scientists need to begin a serious and systematic reexamination of the constitutional system much beyond anything done up to now. They need to give serious and systematic attention to possibilities that may initially seem unrealistic, such as abolishing the presidential veto; creating a collegial chief executive; institutionalizing adversary processes in policy decisions; establishing an office of advocacy to represent interests not otherwise adequately represented in or before Congress and the administrative agencies, including future generations; creating randomly selected citizens assemblies parallel with the major standing committees of the Congress to analyze policy and make recommendations; creating a unicameral Congress; inaugurating proportional representation and a multiparty system in congressional elections; and many other possibilities. Unfortunately, designing a constitution is very far from an exact science. It is questionable whether the best political scientists, or for that matter citizens drawn from any source, have the knowledge and skills to excel the performance of the framers. Probably we do not even know how best to proceed toward the cultivation of the knowledge and skills of constitution making that we or our successors may one day be expected to provide.

The difficulty of arriving at knowledge of this kind points directly to the most challenging of the criteria of procedural democracy, the criterion of enlightened understanding. The criteria of political equality and effective participation are intended to ensure that citizens have a final say as to the goals that effectively determine the ends of public policy, and whenever they wish, a final say as to the means as well. But if a people were to meet these criteria perfectly and yet meet the criterion of enlightened understanding badly, the democratic process would be irrelevant to their preferences, needs, and interests. For if people regularly choose means that impede rather than facilitate attaining their goals, or if they invariably choose goals that damage their deeper needs, then of how much value is the process?

The criterion of enlightened understanding is not only the most difficult to meet but the most resistant to precise statement. Every key word in the criterion as it was presented earlier is ambiguous, and the concepts the words are intended to signify are difficult and complex. However, even if it might well be impossible to define the criterion so rigorously as to specify quite precisely what we would regard as a condition of satisfactory fulfillment, it is a much less difficult task to judge when the criterion is *not* satisfactorily met and what some of the obstacles are. Surely it is far from being satisfactorily attained in this country and elsewhere.

In a loose and general way, it is obvious that if people are to know their preferences, they need knowledge both of means and ends. Adequate knowledge of means and ends requires an understanding not only of the external world but also of the inner world of the self.

It seems obvious too that if citizens are to understand the external world, they must have access to experts. It may have been realistic for Rousseau or Jefferson or the framers but it would be profoundly unrealistic today to expect citizens, even highly educated ones, to have enough technical knowledge. Think of the complexities of current policy decisions; breeder reactor, B-1, Trident, Middle East, catalytic converter, inflation-unemployment trade-offs, rate of increase in the money supply, costs and administrative problems of alternative health care arrangement, SST, Amtrak, limitations on artificial losses, outer continental shelf. . . . Most of the time all of us ordinary citizens without a great deal of technical knowledge about matters like these. Consequently, whatever may have been the situation in previous centuries, in our own and surely in the next, it is foolish to think that the demos can achieve its purposes without experts.

Yet even in the best of circumstances experts are hard to control. Decisions as to means can also determine ends. Democracy only for general ends and meritocracy for means will soon become meritocracy for both means *and* ends. Thus if the demos is to retain final control over ends, citizens will also need responsible and responsive intermediaries—quasi-experts—to help them hold experts accountable, and to gain an adequate understanding of their own basic rights, needs, and interests, and of the policies best designed to satisfy these needs. Even if all our elected officials were to perform this intermediary role well—and many do not—they would not be enough. We need quasi-expert intermediaries spread among the whole body of citizens, so that every citizen has ready access to technical understanding. While it is surely asking too much to expect that most citizens can be experts on many of the issues of national politics, it is not foolish to hope that one day almost every citizen might be sufficiently informed about some of the issues so that a less informed citizen could readily turn to a more informed fellow citizen, a quasi-expert, for a responsible clarification of the matter at hand.

When we turn toward the inner self and ask what we need in order to understand the needs and interests of the self, including those crucial aspects of oneself that are inextricably bound up with and require a sympathetic understanding of other selves, we confront a question to which the answer is inescapably open-ended. The answer must be open-ended because at any given moment human consciousness is necessarily limited by itself, that is, by its own condition. It seems not wildly unrealistic to hope that in the epoch ahead, human consciousness will change profoundly, and that what we might now consider as enlightened understanding, and the best ways to reach it, will be seen by our successors in a vastly different perspective. If mankind is spared as much time as separates us from Socrates, or even as brief an interval as separates us from the historical situation that necessarily limited the understanding of Mill, Lincoln, Freud, and Marx, we cannot say what vast transformations human consciousness may undergo. The criterion of enlightened understanding beckons us forward but it cannot tell us what we shall discover.

It goes without saying, of course, that the world is full of the most acute dangers to human progress and even to human survival. More perhaps than at any time in some millions of years, the prospects of humankind depend on the outcome of a perilous race in which the growth of an enlightened understanding of ourselves and our universe is pitted against the consequences of actions taken out of ignorance or misunderstanding of our most fundamental needs and interests.

No matter what it does, this country alone cannot ensure a successful outcome to that race, though we can by our own unaided mistakes cause a fatal outcome. Some Americans may be tempted to conclude that in a world so hazardous, our salvation and that of the world require us to bring the rest of humanity rapidly around to our way of thinking. But experience suggests that when Americans, or anyone else for that matter, begin to talk about a national mission to save the world, it is time for everyone to run for cover. Instead, one might propose a very different approach. If we want to move a bit closer toward the best standards to which we are already committed by our national experience, a good way to start is not so much by trying to change others as by changing ourselves.

In Defense of Republican Constitutionalism: A Reply to Dahl

James W. Ceaser

Robert Dahl's "On Removing Certain Impediments to Democracy in the United States" is an essay of unusual scope and interest. Written by one of America's most well-known and highly acclaimed political scientists, it addresses two of the most fundamental questions of American political life: (1) What are the merits of the regime under which we live? (2) Should that regime be retained, or should it be replaced by a new system? In answering these questions, Dahl provides a direct and succinct statement of his mature views on the subject of this volume: the moral foundations of the American republic.

The structure of Dahl's essay consists of three main arguments. First, Dahl contends that the historical choices Americans make are largely the result of our national "consciousness," meaning the "inherited ways [we have] of thinking about ourselves." Thus, contrary to the view of Marxist interpreters of American history, Dahl holds that the movement of history is *not* predetermined by objective material conditions (at least not in the present historical moment), but depends mainly on subjective human factors such as beliefs, ideas, and values.

The elements that make up our national consciousness, according to Dahl, have been shaped by five basic historical "commitments" that "still dominate the way we think about ourselves and our future." These commitments are: (1) constitutional liberalism (deriving from the period of 1776–1800), (2) democracy (from 1800–1836), (3) corporate capitalism (from the latter part of the nineteenth century), (4) the welfare state (from the 1930s), and (5) status as an active world power (from the 1940s).

This statement of historical causality is followed by Dahl's second argument, in which he offers a diagnostic method for examining the health of our consciousness. Our failure to realize our greatest potential—to "free up our consciousness for greater political creativity" —results from the existence of contradictions or conflicts among the elements that form our consciousness and from our lack of awareness of these contradictions. Human choice may govern history, but Americans have not always made their choices rationally: "We fail not so much because our aspirations are too high but because they conflict. . . . our consciousness, both individual and collective, distorts our understanding of ourselves and our possibilities."

The reasons why "we fail" suggest the formal properties of a cure. If we can become aware of our submerged conflicts and analyze them, we will be in a much better position to resolve our historical contradictions and "choose self-consciously rather than blindly among our political futures." Up to now, one might say, we have been unable to achieve full self-understanding. But with the therapeutic assistance of Professor Dahl's analysis, which brings to the surface the contradictions of our national (sub)consciousness, we may "at last be entering into our maturity." We have the chance to leave the realm of contradictions and to enter the realm of freedom.

In his third argument, Dahl goes beyond this formal diagnostic approach and prescribes the general content of a remedy. He thus breaks with the dominant school of political science in the United States which, as it were, offers no guidance to its patients about ultimate standards or ends. For Dahl, there is a simple standard of health: *democracy*. Proposing changes of "great moment" in our society and politics, Dahl calls for nothing less than the substitution for the current order of a new regime he calls "procedural democracy." This new regime will replace the Constitution and its moral foundations. Whereas James Madison, the Father of the Constitution, beheld "a republican remedy for the diseases most incident to republican government," Robert Dahl, as would-be progenitor of our new constitution, beholds a democratic remedy for the diseases most incident to democratic government.[1] Or, to put the same point into contemporary language, Dahl's new founding will follow the maxim that "the cure for the evils of democracy is more democracy."[2]

---

[1] James Madison, Federalist No. 10, in Alexander Hamilton, James Madison, and John Jay, *The Federalist Papers*, Intro. Clinton Rossiter (New York: Mentor Books, 1961), p. 84.

[2] This is the contemporary version of the maxim first popularized by the well-known American philosopher and educator John Dewey. In the original version, "ailments" stood in place of "evils." See John Dewey, *The Public and Its Problems* (Chicago: Gateway Books, 1946), p. 146.

I

While logic demands an analysis in sequence of the three parts of the argument, curiosity bids us to steal a brief initial glance at Dahl's new regime. His choice of the name "procedural democracy" would almost appear misleading, for the changes he has in mind have as much to do with what most would consider substance as with procedure. Dahl calls not only for a transformation of our political institutions to promote more formal control by popular majorities but also for a major restructuring of society to redistribute economic power and resources in a more egalitarian way. Procedure and substance in Dahl's view, are in this case perfectly complementary. Considerations of democratic procedure require that each citizen's preferences be "equally taken into account," which means that government may need to equalize those resources, like wealth, that bear on the capacity of citizens to promote their preferences. At the same time, Dahl holds that redistributing economic resources promotes "substantive distributive justice," that is, what is just in itself, apart from considerations of effect on the distribution of political power.

The direction in which "procedural democracy" would take us is not especially original, nor does Dahl claim it to be. In fact, the core of Dahl's program is the ordinary staple of the left wing of most European socialist parties (especially when those parties are out of power). The elements of that program consist of (1) an assertion in principle of the public character (and hence the public's right to possess and control) of what are now considered private corporations; (2) a substantial redistribution of wealth and income to obtain greater equality; and (3) *autogestion*, or industrial democracy, meaning the control of the decision-making process of business firms by a democratic procedure involving all of a firm's workers.

To supplement this standard European socialist diet, Dahl blends in a few ingredients from the American Left of the 1960s and 1970s. These include: (1) a strong hostility to executive power as it is manifested in America's "imperial presidency" (to deal with this problem, Dahl suggests we consider a parliamentary arrangement consisting of a single house with a multiparty system and proportional representation); (2) a participatory ethic with undercurrents of suspicion for formal representative institutions (Dahl urges consideration of citizen assemblies chosen by lot to advise congressional committees); (3) a centralist view of democracy in the political sphere (Dahl attacks "constitutional federalism" as a device contrary to "the majority principle"); and (4) a not-so-veiled indictment of America's role as a major power in world affairs for being "paranoidal," militaristic, and jingoistic (Dahl seems to lend his support to a kind of neo-isolationist foreign policy in order to help us to protect the world from our own excesses).

In view of the radical break Dahl seeks from the existing regime, one might think that he would present himself as a severe critic of the fundamental principles of the American political tradition. This is in fact the position of most other intellectual critics of the American regime who propose some kind of socialist or democratic alternative. For these critics, the fundamental values of the American tradition—referred to variously as "bourgeois capitalism," "outmoded Lockean liberalism," and "purposelessness and privatism"— are the cause of our problems, not the source of a solution.[3] If America is to be saved, according to these critics, we must look to anchor our regime in moral foundations that come from *outside* the American tradition.

On this issue Dahl refuses to follow any party line. The values that underlie his regime of procedural democracy, he claims, come from *within* the American tradition and represent the "best standards to which we are already committed by our national experience." While Dahl can be as unstinting as his fellow critics in attacking the current regime, it is not because he rejects our tradition but rather because he sees the present regime as a *negation* of our own best standards. These standards derive from the commitments of the Jeffersonian-Jacksonian era (1800–1836) and, to a much lesser degree, the founding era. In Dahl's view, these commitments

may be interpreted as an aspiration toward a society with a political system in which liberty, equality, and justice would jointly prosper, a society therefore requiring also a socio-economic system that would foster these ends by supporting the kind of policy necessary to them. Thus interpreted, these two commitments would give priority to political ends over economic ends, to liberty, equality, and justice over efficiency, prosperity and growth,

---

[3] "Bourgeois capitalism" is the usual Marxist epithet used to describe the American regime; Walter Dean Burnham, one of the political science profession's most well-known electoral analysts, uses the term "Lockean Liberalism," first coined by Louis Hartz; and Benjamin Barber uses the words "purposelessness" and "privatism" in his essay in this volume, "The Compromised Republic." Both Burnham and Barber can fairly be described as leftist critics of the American regime.

a priority that the commitment to corporate capitalism reversed both in ideology and in practice, and which has remained reversed down to our own day.

It is in this reading of the American tradition, rather than in the familiar content of Dahl's socialist-type program, that we find the originality of the essay. Few have gone so far in arguing that a mixing of the principles of the Founding and the Jeffersonian-Jacksonian eras yields support for a socialist program created by a powerful central authority unconstrained by any element of federalism. Dahl's striking interpretation seems to contradict what both friends and critics have recognized as fundamental to those commitments. We know, for example, that the Founders specifically rejected an equalization of property, arguing that "an inequality in property would exist as long as liberty existed, and that it would unavoidably result from that very liberty itself."[4] And we know that Jackson was an ardent foe of too vigorous a central government and a strong supporter of states' rights, as exemplified in his famous veto of the National Bank bill on the grounds that it threatened powers "scrupulously reserved to the states."[5]

How has Dahl managed to transform or transcend these traditional interpretations? Or has he? It must be understood that Dahl's objective in the essay is to extract the "aspiration" from each commitment, a purpose that presumably frees him from being bound to the particular form which an aspiration assumed under its original circumstances. Even so, there is only so much poetic license that such an approach can afford. The looseness of Dahl's language ("may be interpreted as an aspiration") may tempt one to think that he has abandoned genuine historical interpretation in favor of a project of creative myth-making in which standards from outside the American tradition are smuggled in and elevated to the highest status.

While such speculations would be unworthy to pursue, it is worthwhile to observe that Dahl's interpretation of American history—leaving aside for the moment any consideration of its veracity —offers a distinct rhetorical advantage over the interpretations of

---

[4] Alexander Hamilton, from his speech of June 26 at the Constitutional Convention, in James Madison's *Notes of Debates in the Federal Convention* ed. Adrienne Koch (New York: Norton, 1966), p. 196. Madison makes the same point in his famous speech earlier the same day.

[5] Andrew Jackson, "Veto of the Bank Bill, 10 July 1832," in Alpheus Mason, *Free Government in the Making*, 3d ed. (New York: Oxford University Press, 1965), p. 451.

most of his fellow critics of the regime. In a nation that has enjoyed at least the modest success of the United States, a good many people, including even some intellectuals, feel a strong attachment to their tradition and an almost instinctive desire to stand up in its defense. Those who choose to attack the tradition at its core may risk provoking a spirited response. But Dahl's interpretation, by praising the aspirations of the oldest parts of the tradition, seems to offer a way of disarming this reaction. Whereas Dahl's fellow critics inveigh against the American tradition, Dahl wraps himself, selectively to be sure, in its mantle. In the United States, it is clearly preferable— if you can do it—to run with James Madison and Andrew Jackson than with Karl Marx and Herbert Marcuse.

Dahl's general argument is similar in its structure and potential appeal to the argument made earlier in this century by the influential historian Charles Beard.[6] Both use one part of the American tradition to call into question another, and both conjure up a Golden Age within American history said to embody pure democratic values. For Beard, the Golden Age was the period from the Revolution until the oligarchic reaction of the Constitution, while for Dahl it is the Jeffersonian-Jacksonian era. Both view the history of America since their respective golden ages as one of reversal or decline. In Dahl's case this reversal includes not just the oligarchic excesses of the corporate capitalist era—which undoubtedly were foremost in the minds of many readers of Beard in 1913—but also the subsequent liberal reforms of the welfare state era, many of which Beard's followers helped to enact. For Dahl, these liberal reforms have been no more than sops that stabilize a system that at its core mocks our earlier commitments to liberty, equality, and justice. American history since the 1830s has thus been one of objective decline, although fortunately the progress in understanding made by a few enlightened intellectuals keeps alive the possibility of leading us to our true potentialities.

II

Dahl's interpretation of the American tradition may allow some critics of the system to "feel good" about our heritage, even while

---

[6] Charles Beard's thesis was developed in his well-known work *An Economic Interpretation of the Constitution of the United States* (New York: Macmillan, 1954, originally published in 1913).

they continue their efforts to destroy the present regime. But will Dahl be able to inspire a similar sense of euphoria among serious students of American history, or even satisfy them that he has not impoverished the very idea of a tradition?

Studying a tradition, if it is a great one, should be an experience that deepens and enriches one's understanding by presenting perspectives that challenge the axioms of contemporary conventional wisdom. This does not mean that one must accept the tenets of the tradition, but it does mean taking them seriously and remaining open to the possibility of learning from them. It is this possibility which makes a genuine encounter with a great tradition so rewarding and which, in the case of the American tradition, has drawn so many students to a study of our past thinkers and statesmen.

Yet it is hardly in this spirit that Dahl approaches our tradition. Rather than making an effort to determine the worth of different values, Dahl begins, a priori, with the supreme value of democracy, announcing that he will explore "certain impediments to the realization of democracy in the United States [that] have resulted from the other historic commitments." To label as "impediments" the consequences of certain commitments clearly assumes, of course, that these consequences (and to some degree the commitments) are bad and should, as the title of Dahl's essay recommends, be "removed." But what if the very commitments that "impede" democracy (in Dahl's sense) are necessary for promoting things that are more worthwhile than democracy (in Dahl's sense)? In that case, would we not be wiser on balance not to remove these impediments? Indeed, if we were to find that by adopting Dahl's standard we should destroy things we consider more desirable, then might it not be appropriate to regard expanding democracy as an "impediment" to maintaining a healthy regime?

Dahl's exploration of the American tradition is not so much false as it is unenlightening. To be sure, some might charge Dahl with belaboring and exaggerating the undemocratic aspects of American history while neglecting or belittling major democratic achievements. It is curious, for example, that an essay on American democracy never calls attention to the fact that the United States is becoming, in the words of the Mexican philosopher Octavio Paz, "the first multiracial democracy in human history."[7] But such objections,

7 Octavio Paz, *Tiempo Nublado* (Barcelona: Seix Barral, 1983), p. 47. This theme is explored in the essay in this volume by Herbert Storing, "Slavery and the Moral Foundations of the American Republic."

even if valid, do not controvert Dahl's main contention that some of our major commitments were not intended to maximize procedural democracy. If, after all, you begin by claiming democracy to be the supreme value and then define it to encompass a large measure of egalitarianism, it is hardly surprising to learn that many American commitments stand as "impediments" to democracy. Some commitments were clearly never meant to promote Dahl's version of democracy, but to promote values other than democracy or to promote democracy in a quite different sense.

To determine whether we prefer Dahl's democracy to his impediments or the impediments to his democracy, we can look at the same commitments Dahl identifies and "remove" those elements that create the impediment. Readers can then decide whether on balance they prefer the impediments—with all that these entail—to the circumstance that would obtain (or would have obtained) in their absence. We shall consider the commitments in reverse order, moving from the most recent to the earliest.

World power status. This commitment impedes democracy, Dahl argues, because it produces a concentration of power in "hierarchical" institutions, notably the president and the military (an establishment "more rigidly hierarchical than the rest"). The same objections, it may be observed, were voiced during the debate over the ratification of the Constitution. The opponents of the Constitution (known as the Anti-Federalists) charged that the new government would endanger democracy by allowing for the establishment of a standing army and a strong executive. The Founders' response was clear: while the United States might enjoy a more democratic form of government without the hierarchies of a strong president or a professional military, the government would be unable to defend itself or protect its interests. Since providing for the common defense is one of the principal moral foundations of the republic, without which other moral attributes cannot be easily enjoyed, some degree of democracy must regrettably give way to the necessity of national defense.

The Anti-Federalists, according to the Founders, were unable to make a hard choice. At one moment they conceded in principle the necessity for defense in a world in which the United States could not control the actions of other nations or regulate the nature of the threats to our security. The next moment, however, they proposed measures in the name of promoting democracy, such as limiting the standing army to 3,000 persons, that would cripple the capacity of the nation to defend its interests. The Anti-Federalists, the Founders charged, refused to *think constitutionally*—to realize that certain objectives, perhaps desirable in the abstract, could not be attained without producing other, more undesirable consequences; or that certain desirable objectives could not be achieved in full without sacrificing other, more desirable ends.

America's military establishment has clearly become much larger than anyone in the 1780s could have imagined. The growth dates from the 1930s, when the size of the army, smaller than that of Portugal's, did nothing to help deter Hitler's aggressive designs. Yet the expansion of the American military in the past half century, far from being explicable as the simple consequence of a sentiment for militarism, reflects in large part an adaptation to changed circumstances and new threats. Until this century the United States was a secondary power, protected by the oceans and the British navy. The foreign powers with whom we dealt were not bent on total world domination. All this changed during World War II with the decline in the relative power of the European democracies and the emergence of new kinds of foes, exemplified by Nazi Germany and the Soviet Union, claiming a right or mission to rule the world in the name of unquestionable ideologies.

There is no disputing Dahl's claim that our role as a major world power has placed tremendous strains on our system of government and created certain impediments to democracy. But this observation, while reminding us of a problem, does not instruct us about how to deal with it. Either we can attempt to cope with the challenge, working to maintain a republican form of government in the face of these new difficulties, or we can seek to remove the impediments by weakening the presidency and disarming the military establishment. Say all that one will about a national paranoia and an "obsession with national security," it may not be so clear that we should prefer more procedural democracy to our continued safety and existence as a free nation. In urging a reassessment of our latest historical commitment, Dahl tells us that "experience suggests that when Americans, or anyone else for that matter, begin to talk about a national mission to save the world, it is time for everyone to run for cover." By reminding us, albeit in passing, that others besides ourselves may have designs for world domination, Dahl may inadvertently have offered the very reason for maintaining our military establishment, which in today's world may afford slightly more protection than running for cover.

There are, moreover, other values in addition to protecting our own security that are implicit in our role as a world power. First, the American military hierarchy has done a great deal to defend the cause of democracy around the world. Two of the world's leading democracies—West Germany and Japan—were forged under United States military occupation, and the American military remains the principal defensive shield for most democratic nations in the world. While the presence of American troops has not always promoted democracy, it is clear that where American armies have been driven back in defeat—as in Southeast Asia and North Korea—there is neither democracy nor the prospect of democracy. Second, being a world power imposes on us the responsibility for decisions that affect the fate of the world. This responsibility brings with it a sense of vitality that is known mainly in nations powerful enough to influence the unfolding of world history; it also imparts a seriousness to our national political life that helps check against a politics focused solely on physical or psychic gratification. Finally, while the military is in one sense an undemocratic hierarchy—soldiers do not practice *autogestion* when deciding to attack or withdraw—there is another sense in which it has had a respectable democratic record since World War II. If by *democratic* one includes the idea of a fair or equal chance to advance in society without regard to irrelevant criteria, the military, while being far from perfect, has served as one of the leading institutions in our society in opening up opportunities to minorities who have suffered continual discrimination from other institutions.

Welfare state capitalism. Let us turn next to a consideration of the commitments to corporate capitalism and to the welfare state. These may be treated together, for Dahl presents them as two phases of the national response to the development of the economic system beyond the simple agrarian-based order of the early nineteenth century. Dahl's objection to these commitments echoes the one he makes against our becoming a world power: they create hierarchies that stand as impediments to democracy. In the case of corporate capitalism, the hierarchy is the business enterprise itself. In the case of the welfare state, it is both the business enterprise, which the welfare state regulated but did not fundamentally alter, and the federal bureaucracy, which has accumulated vast new powers. "Far from diminishing hierarchies," Dahl writes, "the welfare state has multiplied the number, domain, and scope of hierarchies in American life."

Again, there is no disputing Dahl's premise that modern economic organization and its regulation have created certain impediments to democracy. But it is essential to ask whether we prefer the conditions that accompany the impediments to the situation that would obtain if we sought to remove them. The most direct approach to obtaining the last objective, analogous to the plan to disarm, would be to destroy our industrial base (or, viewing the matter historically, never to have developed it in the first place). We could be a nation of farmers and shepherds, with corn growing in New Haven and sheep grazing in Palo Alto. Yet in exchange for this condition of pastoral bliss, what would we have to sacrifice?

First, development beyond agrarianism is an essential component of economic and military power. America's edge in the world has long been tied to its technology and its conquest of nature. It is doubtful whether an agrarian nation could manage to defend itself, even assuming that our farmers would be the virtuous citizen-soldiers that agrarian theorists imagined. This was a lesson Jefferson himself learned in the aftermath of his ill-fated embargo policy, when he conceded that a nation of free and independent husbandmen could not be a free and independent nation. Hierarchies had to be accepted as the price of national independence.

Second, the process of economic development in America has been one of the major democratic events in modern history, and it remains so today. If by *democracy* one includes the notion of the chance to rise in life without regard to previous status, then the American system has served as a vehicle of democracy for millions of the world's poor and oppressed, offering either to them or to their children a way up in life. (Meanwhile, many of the more socialist-minded states in Europe are requiring their immigrant workers to accept departure funds to go back to their countries of origin.) This democratic achievement could not have been attained in an agrarian society for the simple reason that there is insufficient land to support so large a population. It is for this reason that the Anti-Federalists and agrarians, solicitous about equality, often opposed immigration, while those favoring industrial development, like Hamilton, sought to encourage "an increase of the . . . acquisitions to the population, arts, and industry of the country."[8] That economic development produced "hierarchies" and inequalities—indeed, outright exploitation—is a matter of historical record; but that this development has been a clear loss for democracy, as Dahl implies, may be disputed. The American ideal of democracy and equality has traditionally placed a greater emphasis on creating and opening up new opportunities than on redistributing the existing stock of resources. Whoever does not see this side of the story of development misses an essential element of the American experience.

Finally, economic development is the direct source of a certain quality of life. In choosing or permitting economic development, America has allowed for a way of life quite different from the peace and bliss of quiet rural existence—what Karl Marx labeled the "idiocy of village life." Those who urged development did so not just because they wanted to advance material wealth but also because they believed that the differentiation characteristic of a complex economy provided an opportunity to satisfy the desires and talents of different individuals. A complex economy, in Alexander Hamilton's words, would "furnish greater scope for the diversity of talents and dispositions which discriminate men from each other."[9] It would promote human development, not always in ways that foster egalitarian results, but in ways that lead to pluralism, diversity, and a striving for success and excellence.

Listing the benefits of economic development may seem slightly off target, for Dahl never directly calls for the elimination of America's advanced economic infrastructure. Although he uses the supposed equality of America's agrarian era as his base for criticizing the subsequent undemocratic consequences of development, in the end he apparently accepts the inevitability, if not the desirability, of modern economic development. Yet by doing so, he would appear also to have to accept certain hierarchies of society in its present phase of development, for many of these, such as differences in skills and education, are a product of the nature of the tasks to be performed in a modern economy. The real alternative against which Dahl must measure welfare state capitalism, therefore, is not agrarianism but some other arrangement broadly consistent with advanced economic

[8] Alexander Hamilton's "Report on Manufactures, 1791," in *The Works of Alexander Hamilton*, ed. Henry Cabot Lodge, vol. 4 (New York: Putnam's, 1904) pp. 70–198.
   [9] Ibid.

development. This could be: the Soviet system (which is generally conceded to be more hierarchic than our own); some existing system with a great socialist component (none of which is more than marginally different from our own in terms of private hierarchies but most of which have larger nonmilitary government bureaucracies); or a system that does not yet exist (which is the option Dahl selects).

It is in this connection that one must consider Dahl's attack on the welfare state component of the economic system. Liberals, who worked so hard to eliminate or mitigate the excesses of an unfettered capitalist system, will no doubt be dismayed by Dahl's criticisms. They are likely to discover, however, that part of Dahl's critique bypasses their own concerns and that part of it is misleading. The first criticism Dahl makes of the welfare state—that it has "not much reduced the inequalities in the distribution of wealth and income"—creates a standard that, at least until recently, was not central to its purposes. Rather, the chief end of the welfare state was to provide certain rights for workers, place a floor beneath people in society, and protect people against the vagaries of the business cycle.

Even if it were true, as Dahl asserts, that income inequalities have not "much" been reduced since the advent of the welfare state, it would surely *not* follow that "relative political advantages and disadvantages" have been unaffected. When employers can no longer exclude workers from all security benefits or deprive them of livelihood in their old age, the power in the relationship between capital and labor has been fundamentally altered, regardless of whether the ratio of inequality in earnings remains the same. Furthermore, "relative political advantages and disadvantages" that can be linked to the use of money as a political resource do not depend solely on the ratio of inequality in earning power, but to some extent on *absolute* levels of income. Workers living in poverty will have no disposable income to use for politics, whereas those who have achieved a measure of prosperity can become contributors in the political arena.

Liberals are apt to find Dahl's other criticism of the welfare state—that it has led to the growth of "extensive government bureaucracies"—even more unfair, for these bureaucracies, in the absence of some other kind of solution, seem to be necessary to promote many of the ends Dahl espouses. Indeed, if one wants to observe "extensive government bureaucracies" in the world today, they can be found to exist to a much greater degree in socialist societies than in our own welfare state system. For the most part, public bureaucratic hierarchies have grown to provide social services that Dahl never suggests eliminating, such as providing welfare and health care. Moreover, in contrast to socialist states with large public enterprises, only a very small part of the public bureaucratic structure in America's welfare system is involved in running or policing business activities. It is therefore difficult to see how Dahl's plan for revamping the economic system, under which "any large economic enterprise is in principle a public enterprise," would help in any way to shrink the public bureaucratic hierarchies that he deplores.

Liberals and democratic reformers probably cannot help feeling frustration at being dismissed by one who speaks in the name of equality and democracy. Yet by now, perhaps, they have begun to realize that many of today's theoretical proponents of democracy will have nothing to do with their reforms, but will always be found leaping ahead to a position beyond any option under practical consideration. From this haven, these critics can easily disassociate themselves from the problems of failures of liberal reforms by denying that such reforms are "genuinely" democratic.

Oddly enough, Dahl seems to borrow many of his criticisms of these reforms from conservatives. Has the welfare state developed meddlesome bureaucracies, particularly as it has moved more and more to engineer an equality of results? For many years conservatives have said yes, and Dahl agrees—only for Dahl it is not because of the movement to democratic egalitarianism, but because the welfare state is not egalitarian enough. Has the presidency demonstrated certain problems associated with its "democratic" character? For many years republican theorists said yes, and Dahl agrees—only for Dahl it is not because such changes were really democratic but because they were "pseudo-democratic." Whereas conservatives have been literal-minded enough to accept the liberals' claim that their reforms are democratic (and to point out that this is the source of some of the problems), Dahl hurdles the whole dispute, disclaiming any connection between his democratic principles and those mundane democratic reforms that have fallen short of realizing their initial expectations.

The obvious problem that liberals and ordinary reformers face in dealing with this kind of criticism is that no matter how far they go, it can never be far enough to be truly democratic. There will always be a true democratic position beyond any in the real world from which all real world positions can be dismissed as paltry or "pseudo." Earlier it was said that Dahl accepted the maxim that the cure for the evils of democracy is more democracy. That statement was inadequate. For Dahl the cure for the evils of democracy can only be his purest form of procedural democracy. Nothing less will do.

Despite Dahl's claim that welfare state capitalism has moved us further away than ever before from the ideal of pure democracy, he is nonetheless confident that we can reverse our decline. This confidence, we said earlier, rests on the premise that consciousness determines history and that America's consciousness is on the verge of a great leap forward. But Dahl's discussion of the origin of corporate capitalism, in which he acknowledges the inevitability of economic development, suggests that objective material conditions play a much larger role in his understanding of what moves history than he formally allows. If this is so, we may wonder what he considers to be the objective material conditions today that support the emergence of the "new" consciousness in favor of true procedural democracy. The answer at which Dahl hints near the beginning of his essay, and which has now become a pervasive element in the thought of many critics of the American regime, is that we have entered an era of "limits" in which we can anticipate an end of economic growth and development.

The espousal of the idea of an "era of limits" by so many critics of the American regime is one of the most interesting developments in modern social thought. Students of Marx will recall that he celebrated economic growth and never doubted that it must be continued until nature was fully conquered; indeed, Marx proclaimed the necessity (or superiority) of communism in part on the grounds that capitalism would be unable to continue to promote economic development. This Marxist theme was present in the thought of both communists and socialists at least up though the 1950s. Until that time, socialists, in addition to proclaiming the superior justice of their system, also held that capitalism was inefficient and that socialist planning was a superior method for assuring development. But in light of the performance of capitalist welfare economies in the thirty prosperous years from the end of World War II to the mid 1970s, this claim began to ring hollow.

In reaction to this success, many on the left in the 1960s began to shift ground. No longer did they praise economic growth and the conquest of nature but turned instead to a celebration of more "humane" and pastoral values. Conceding that capitalist welfare systems might indeed be efficient engines of economic growth, they now charged that economic growth was itself undesirable. To use the popular expressions of the day, economic development in capitalist societies was "alienating" and "dehumanizing." Yet as long as growth continued, this New Left, while having a certain appeal to over-indulged and dissatisfied youth, could be dismissed by most as no more than a plaintive romantic reaction to the problems of modernity.

In the 1970s, the Left attempted to break out of this romantic mold. The occasion was a slowdown in economic growth in Western societies and the predictions by many analysts that we had reached, in Dahl's words, the "limits that are imposed by nature's laws and the scarcity of resources." The Left seized on this theme of "limits" with obvious delight, for it could be used to argue that capitalist systems, whatever their past achievements, had lost their economic reason for existence and that it was therefore time to move beyond capitalism to a new and more just system. Moral progress became a genuine historical possibility in light of the paradoxical opportunity presented by the end of material progress.

Once again the Left could claim to be on the cutting edge of history, only history was now said to cut in a different way from what Marx and the previous generation of socialists had predicted. On this point, Benjamin Barber, another writer in this volume, speaks with more directness than Dahl:

Faced with the prospects of unlimited growth, America once made a virtue of necessity and modified republican institutions to meet the demands of expansion and empire; faced with the prospect of limited growth, perhaps eventually even zero growth, it now has the chance to make a necessity of virtue and readapt its institutions to meet the demands of contraction and interdependence. The new pressures of ecology, transnationalism, and resource scarcity in combination with the apparent bankruptcy of privatism, materialism, and economic individualism—the pathologies and the ambivalent promises of our modernity—create conditions more inviting to the generation of public purposes and a public spirit than any American has ever known.

This criticism of welfare capitalist systems raised an important intellectual challenge. Defenders of the welfare capitalist system have in fact long celebrated as *one* of its virtues its capacity to stimulate growth. Does it follow, therefore, that the rationale for this system depends solely on its capacity to promote growth, and that if growth should cease, the grounds for maintaining this system would come tumbling down with it? Posing this question has forced defenders of the American system to seek a clear statement of their position on terms that ground its moral foundations in principles more fundamental than economic growth.

Yet to say that the deepest moral foundation for the American system does not consist in constant economic growth, and to admit that steady growth along the lines experienced from 1946 to 1976 is not inevitable, is *not* to say that economic growth is bad or should be avoided. On the contrary, while material progress cannot be equated with moral progress, growth has brought more wealth for the average person, has eased the tensions among social classes, and has helped stem pressures for redistribution. Capitalist welfare states therefore do have a stake in promoting growth, and if we should be entering a new period of growth based on advanced technologies—as some now predict—the defender of the American economic system, unlike Benjamin Barber, will be able to accept this news without disappointment.

What is clear is that the Left's "realism," expressed in its constant evocation of limits, is not realistic at all. Its motive has not been to assess the actual possibilities of economic growth but rather to use a period of limited growth as an excuse to refashion the political system. If a new era of growth should occur—a fact we cannot know with certainty—we may expect that many thinkers will shed their tough rhetoric of realism and crawl back into the warmer cocoon of a romantic version of socialism.

Agrarian democracy. Dahl's Golden Age of American history came in the Jeffersonian-Jacksonian era, when the nation made its commitment to democracy. Although an act of human choice must have been involved in making this commitment, Dahl gives little weight in this instance to the independent role of thought or ideas, emphasizing instead the influence of the objective socio-economic order, which "fostered a condition of equality among the citizens." Under the circumstances of this agrarian order, "white male citizens lived with fewer social, economic, and political inequalities than any larger number of persons in history had existed up to that time, and very likely since."

It may seem strange that Dahl uses the equality in this era as standard, given its dependence on an economic circumstance acknowledged to have been "an historical rarity" that "had no future." If the conditions required to support procedural democracy are so particular, the effort to reproduce equality under totally different circumstances could prove as difficult as reinstituting paradise in a fallen world.

Of greater interest, however, is the question of whether Dahl has correctly characterized the commitment of this era. That it was democratic is clear; but there are different senses of democracy from the one Dahl has in mind. The era's most prominent democratic figure, Andrew Jackson, straightforwardly declared in his famous Bank veto message that "equality . . . of wealth cannot be produced by human institutions." What each person was entitled to, Jackson went on, is "the full enjoyment of the fruits of superior industry, economy, and virtue." The equality Jackson sought was an end to acts of government that accorded artificial advantages. It was the rich, he argued, who were taking advantage of these artificial privileges.[10]

Dahl might cite changes in circumstances as a way of explaining away such apparent differences as his own endorsement of the principle of public ownership of corporations and Jackson's opposition to public assistance for the National Bank; his dismissal of federalism and Jackson's defense of state prerogatives; and his acceptance of a vast extension of public authority over societal activities and Jackson's defense of the private market. But it is more difficult to see how Dahl might account for what seem to be very different underlying philosophies. Dahl's socialist vision of democracy is predicated on an equalization of results, Jackson's on an end to artificial privilege. Dahl's emphasis is on sharing equally the product, Jackson's on expanding opportunities. Are these aspirations really similar?

The Founding. Let us now turn to Dahl's analysis of the Founding and the Constitution. Dahl gives the Founders a mixed review, praising them for establishing liberty but criticizing them for not committing us to democracy. Their undemocratic legacy, according to Dahl, is found in the very form of our government, which, through such devices as federalism, separation of powers, and bicameralism, impedes simple majority rule.

Dahl proposes to remove this impediment to democracy by doing away with these "anti-majoritarian" devices—in short, by doing away with the Constitution—and by replacing it with a multiparty, unicameral parliamentary system. While one might argue over whether this system would work quite as democratically as Dahl

10 Jackson, "Veto of the Bank Bill, 10 July 1832."

supposes (real majority sentiment can sometimes get lost in the bargaining process among parliamentary parties), it seems reasonable to assume that, by his own standard of democracy, his system would be more democratic than the Constitution.

But as in the case of our other commitments, the pertinent question is whether we prefer the impediments, with the values connected to them, to Dahl's form of democracy. In this instance—and this instance alone—Dahl attempts to answer the question by presenting an account of the different values that the Framers weighed when they constructed the Constitution. What we discover is that the founders did have a "laudable" value in mind: the protection of fundamental rights. But, Dahl goes on, we now know that the antimajoritarian elements of the Constitution were not really necessary for that purpose and that the Framers "were guilty of overkill." The existence of these antimajoritarian devices serves—and perhaps even was partly intended to serve—the very different purpose of aiding the privileged in society: "Because they [the Founders] succeeded in designing a system that makes it easier for privileged minorities to prevent changes they dislike than for majorities to bring about the changes they want, it is strongly tilted in favor of the status quo and against reform."

What is striking about this account of the Constitution is its reduction of the possible aims of government to protecting individual rights and promoting mass national democracy. This interpretation, however, fails to take into account many of the objectives of our complex governmental structure and the reasons for its antimajoritarian devices. If by *democracy* one takes Dahl's standard of a unitary national government under the rule of a unicameral parliament, there are other important objectives, besides protecting individual rights, that would explain the Founders' dislike for this form of government. Dahl seems to have shown his respect for the Framers by not exposing their other antimajoritarian heresies. Here we shall have no such scruples.

Why, for example, does the Constitution support the antimajoritarian device of federalism? Not only to protect individual rights, the Founders tells us, but to assure a sphere of partial autonomy for governments below the national level. By including this device, the Framers were thus guilty of the antimajoritarian goal of allowing people to participate in state and local governments and of permitting local majorities to make certain decisions that differ from those of national majorities.

Why did the Framers provide for a separation of the executive from the legislature? Again, it was not only to protect individual rights but to promote the goal of a "vigorous executive" whose performance of the *essential* executive tasks would not be immediately dependent on the shifting majorities in the legislature. An independent executive, according to Alexander Hamilton, was necessary for "the protection of the community against foreign attacks . . . and [for] the security of liberty against the enterprises and assaults of ambition, of faction, and of anarchy."[11]

This language may sound archaic and no longer relevant, especially in light of the widespread belief among so many political scientists about the supposed superiority of the parliamentary system. Yet parliamentary systems succeed in solving the problem of energy in the executive only where the governing party has a majority or a near majority in the parliament. Where, as Dahl prefers, there is a multi-party system, and where no party approaches a majority, we sometimes find dangerously weak governments, as in Israel and Italy today or in France during the Fourth Republic (1946–58). The last example, in fact, offers an instructive case for assessing schemes to improve our system of government by adopting a parliamentary model. In 1958, the French parliament could not form an effective government in the face of the Algerian crisis and the imminent threat of a military coup. While parliament fiddled, Paris nearly burned. To remedy this flaw, the founders of the Fifth Republic, drawing in part on the American model, instituted an independent executive designed to ensure that there would always be a force to act for the state, even in the absence of a majority in the legislature.

Why, finally, do we have bicameralism and checks and balances? Again, not just to protect individual rights but to reduce the likelihood of unwise choices by democratic majorities. The Founders were not afraid to state openly that democratic majorities, pandered to by flatterers or encouraged by demagogues, could produce unstable policies or make unwise decisions. Requiring concurrence by more than one body represented an effort by the Founders to find an institutional arrangement to help cope with this problem. If this system sometimes blocks or retards policies sought by a majority that are not unwise or mistaken—as it surely has—this does not by itself discredit the arrangement, for there is almost no institutional solution that does not entail some costs in producing a benefit.

[11] Alexander Hamilton, Federalist No. 70, *Federalist Papers*, p. 423.

The foregoing discussion presupposes an acceptance of at least the possibilities that majorities may not always know what is best and that there may be a decision-making process able to improve on majority opinion. The Framers called their version of this improved system "representative" or "republican" government, distinguishing it from "democracy." Early in his article, when attacking the system of checks and balances and the presidential veto, Dahl comes close to denying the existence of any standard, except for the protection of individual rights, by which it might be claimed that majorities can err. Yet when it comes time to sketch the character of his own regime, Dahl concedes that democracies can fail in making the correct choices if citizens do not meet the "criterion of enlightened understanding." But instead of relying like the Framers on institutions of government to help deal with this problem, Dahl puts his faith in an ambitious program of adult education. He would make available "quasi-expert intermediaries spread among the whole body of citizens," who could help the less-informed citizens "to gain an adequate understanding of their own basic rights, needs, and interests, and of the policies best designed to satisfy these needs." Although this proposal to put a policy analyst in every shopping mall would surely resolve the employment problem for doctoral candidates in the social sciences, it remains an open question how many citizens would avail themselves of this opportunity to be patronized and, more important, how many would actually leave with their options having been made measurably more enlightened.

When encountering the criticisms of someone who argues that the present-day regime in the United States is not democratic, defenders of the regime may feel tempted to deny the charge and congratulate themselves on how democratic it is. The denial is by and large in order, but the congratulations should be made with care. Despite the minor deviations noted above, the American regime today is quite democratic in its procedures. Of all the world's democracies, or at least of those of considerable size, it is, all things considered, quite possibly the most democratic, although such comparisons are admittedly difficult and often meaningless. The American separation-of-powers system is practically the only one that gives extensive powers on a day-to-day basis to a popular legislature; midterm legislative elections provide an occasion for popular input at intervals more regular than that found in any other democratic system; and candidates for party nominations are selected for the most part in popular primaries (a unique arrangement). If there is one reason to hesitate in proclaiming the democratic character of the American regime, it surely has to do with the role played by the federal judiciary, which has ventured deeply into the policymaking process, in ways never intended by the Framers, to make many policies that have often been opposed by local or national majorities. Curiously, however, while Dahl decries time and again the "pseudo-democratic imperial presidency," he never once criticizes the policymaking authority of the judiciary, even though it would seem to present a formidable "impediment" to procedural democracy. Perhaps Dahl's hands-off treatment of the judiciary owes something to the Supreme Court's egalitarian views of "substantive justice" in the decade preceding the writing of his essay.

The fact that the American regime is so democratic, however, is not necessarily a cause for rejoicing. Dahl readily concedes that "pseudo-democratic" developments do not always produce good government; perhaps the same could be said sometimes of real democratic developments. While there are clearly elements of the American regime that have been improved by democratization and might be further improved by still more democratization, there may be facets of the regime for which the opposite is true. Is it clear, for example, that we have improved our system by every cause in recent decades that has marched under the banner of democratic reform? Even to begin to make such judgments, of course, requires abandoning the modern prejudice that equates the good exclusively with the democratic. It requires instead a search for the principles of good government itself. Not a bad place to begin would be a genuine encounter with the American tradition, and in particular with the Founders.

III

What would it be like to live in Dahl's regime? Let us put aside further discussion of governmental institutions and turn to the principles that animate his society. Although the picture Dahl paints is sometimes fuzzy, his regime is intended to combine the aspirations of liberty and democracy (or equality). As between the two, however, the principles governing Dahl's society would seem to promote, in Tocqueville's words, "a more enduring love for equality than for liberty"—so much so that when the two conflict, as surely they must, preference would be given to equality. Dahl's more enduring love for equality than liberty can be seen most clearly in his treatment of property.

The attack on the principle of liberty in property is introduced indirectly. Procedural democracy, Dahl tells us, requires giving equal weight to each citizen's preferences. The unequal distribution of wealth and income threatens this equality, since money is a political resource and since those who have more of it begin with an advantage. Although this advantage might conceivably be negated by placing limits on the *use* of money in politics, this approach has not worked adequately. Dahl therefore recommends the "other approach" of going to the root of the problem and attacking inequalities in wealth and income. To eliminate one of the sources of inequality in promoting preferences, Dahl proposes sacrificing the principle of economic liberty and private property.[12]

This "back door" attack on economic liberty and property may leave one wondering about Dahl's final standard of judgment. There are clearly other resources besides money, such as positions within organizations and access to media, that are as important in influencing the capacity of individuals to promote their preferences in the political arena. Yet Dahl never suggests employing the "other approach" in these instances and attacking the political inequalities by sacrificing other rights. Dahl's chief objection is perhaps therefore to the existence of differences in wealth and property, and his reason for singling these out may finally have to do with his goal of enforcing his own standard of "substantive justice." The

[12] In speaking of the principle of private property as a right in modern society, nothing so simplistic is intended as an absolute natural right to whatever anyone may happen to claim as property. Indeed, except perhaps in the case of the possession of simple physical objects, a natural right to property is impossible in any precise sense in modern society, for property in a significant form requires positive law to define and create it. For example, the corporation and the limited partnership are forms of business organization that do not exist except by legal construction. (By contrast, positive law as such is not needed to create speech or religious belief.) What the principle of private property as a right refers to, then, is the presumption that government must recognize and protect what Madison calls in Federalist 10 "the different and unequal faculties of acquiring property" or the ability to produce wealth. The protection of a right to property, embodied inevitably in property law in all its diverse forms, is founded on a respect for this natural capacity. Theorists of liberalism have also been mindful of the social utilities that derive from the protection of property rights. These include promoting economic growth and limiting the scope of direct government control of a large area of social activity, thereby helping to maintain the vital distinction in liberal regimes between the state and civil society.

accumulation of wealth in unequal amounts by different skills or effort is not, evidently, considered the stuff of which even a presumptive right is made.

Actually, Dahl's view seems to be that property *once* had a claim to being a right, but has one no longer. In the Golden Age of agrarianism, wealth was produced by the farmers' "labor, ingenuity, anguish, planning, forbearance, sacrifice, risk, and hope." The implication is that in a modern capitalist economy, the qualities referred to in this formidable string of adjectives no longer systematically apply to the activity of generating wealth. Wealth, it would seem, is seen as emerging from collective social factors, with differentials in individual activity related to any worthwhile character attributes accounting for very little. Under this view, individual private property has no moral claim to protection; since the economic product of society is collectively generated, it follows that it belongs to all and that the majority should be authorized to distribute it according to the tenets of "substantive justice." The implications of this general doctrine for the extension of public authority are fascinating for any socialist to consider. Even more exciting for today's limits-minded socialist is the prospect that under this new economic system, we may never have to fear economic growth.

Many today who are not directly involved in producing wealth have little understanding of, let alone respect for, the activity of economic enterprise. The view that this activity might be necessary for the well-being of society and worthy of protection as a right is not an idea that is highly regarded in certain circles, where rights are more apt to be associated with matters of expression, privacy, or refusal to register for the draft. Yet what most sophisticated consumers of society's wealth may in fact be able to appreciate are the second-order consequences for liberty that might flow from the elimination of private property.

Liberty is valued in society in part for its "fruits"—for its diversity, for the treasures of civilization it helps preserve, and for the opportunities it provides to add to or embellish the store of human culture and knowledge. These fruits of liberty, though they cannot be bought, depend in some measure on the provision of physical resources, that is, money. Money can be supplied by private sources, by public sources, or not at all. Money coming from private sources is linked to private property and to an inequality in wealth, as certain forms of patronage for culture are supplied chiefly by the better-off. If this private source of support were eliminated or diminished, part of the loss might well be made up by increased public spending. Yet quite apart from the new bureaucratic hierarchies this would create, there are certain institutions and activities that democratic governments might find difficult to support. One thinks, for example, of certain private elite universities in this nation in which the resources lavished on a small number of students and faculty might strike some as excessive. Indeed, in a regime committed to an egalitarian standard of distributive justice, it is difficult to see why the crucial resource of intellectual talent should not be redistributed on a more equal basis throughout the entire system. Whatever the problems attached to the unequal distribution of wealth, and these differ from one society to another, those who love liberty and appreciate its fruits will think twice before adopting a regime principle that endorses the justice of economic equality.

Almost as important for liberty as the protection of a right to individual private property is some notion of private property for business corporations, a concept Dahl not only opposes but ridicules. But the ridiculous here may have a touch of the sublime, even if one readily concedes that a right of property for business corporations has a partly analogical and fictive character. Whoever speaks of liberty should speak in the same breath of the practical instruments in society that protect and maintain it; these are its guardians and fences. To define liberty in terms of rights and wave that definition around like a talisman is not enough, for abstract principles are not self-executing. Nor is it sufficient to rely exclusively on the courts, for a judiciary powerful enough on its own to be the guardian of liberty is also powerful enough to pose a threat to it. It is far better if the overall conditions in society provide a balance of power that renders liberty more secure. Those things that serve to protect liberties, even where they may create certain dubious privileges or entail certain regrettable costs, may be justifiable.

Liberty may be threatened, as we know, by the failure of the state to use its power against private sources in society that would deprive individuals of their rights. As these private sources become larger and more powerful, the authority of the state may need to be expanded to supply the necessary check. This was part of the rationale for curbing corporate power under the welfare state and modifying certain absolute or excessive claims made on behalf of corporate private property. Yet the threat to liberty that comes from private entities, however dangerous it may be, is limited by the fact that these entities lack plenary power and full moral authority.

Far different is the threat to liberty posed by the state, which, because of its power and its moral authority, possesses the potential for much greater evil. Whatever tends, therefore, to check or balance the power of active sovereignty of the state in ordinary times works, all other things being equal, to support liberty. Those today who devise doctrines that help to join the power of society's most formidable private entities—the business corporations—to the power of government are no friends of liberty; they are the modern counterparts of those in the middle ages who sought to fuse the power of church and state. By contrast, those who have helped to devise a presumption of at least a partial right of property in the business corporation have been among the benefactors of liberty in modern times. And let it be added, to avoid any simplistic identification of this position with every injustice associated with economic development, that the principle of private property in the corporation does not preclude state protection of the worker's welfare. Neither does it prevent a variety of modes of ownership, among which is included the possession by employees of their own firms, or experimentation with different systems of industrial relations, such as worker participation or codetermination of production decisions.

Dahl has no end of poking fun at "the absurdities in extending Locke on private property to . . . the business corporation." Yet Dahl's interpretation of Locke as a mild-mannered, avuncular defender of a simple agrarian order is not without interest of its own. The Locke that Adam Smith and Karl Marx read provided the philosophic tools that undergirded modern economic development. Dahl's transformation of Locke is reminiscent of his transformation of "the best" in the American tradition. In his sanitized interpretations, both have been made to serve his peculiar vision of democracy. Here is an instance, however, where the naked truth of the unexpurgated version may prove not only more exciting but more enlightening as well.

IV

The central point of Dahl's essay is his call to overturn the existing regime in the United States and to begin again with a new arrangement of government and society. By discussing so bold a proposition without precondition, we have so far indulged in a kind of abstract theorizing about political life in which the question of choosing regimes has been treated in much the same terms as one might treat an ordinary policy decision: you decide by a nice, abstract intellectual discussion which policy (or regime) is best and then you set about to implement it. But reasoning in these terms has something of the air about it of children at play or madmen at work.

In the real world, where lives, fortunes, and beliefs are at stake, a change in regimes can never be considered so lightly, for the slate is never clean and there are usually "sunk investments" of great magnitude. These investments in the United States today include a Constitution that has endured for two hundred years, a people that accepts the basic principles and framework of its current government, and a large number of nations around the world that depend on the stability of the United States for their defense against totalitarian domination. The sheer weight of such real-world interests makes a mockery of the pretensions of seductive intellectual appeals to wipe the slate clean; it demands a form of theorizing about politics that incorporates a prudential account of the circumstances under which it might make sense to pull down an existing regime and elevate the "science" of political science to the awesome task of building a new one.

Such an enterprise, it would appear, might be reasonable if the existing regime was precarious or destined soon to fall, for in that case nothing is really being risked. Alternatively, such an enterprise would make sense if the existing regime was fundamentally flawed, for in that case, even if the change fell far short of what you hoped for, it might in all likelihood lead to an improvement. In other circumstances, advocating total change becomes a much more problematic venture. It requires an assessment of what a science of politics can reasonably expect to teach us, of the likelihood that the counsels of that science would in fact be followed, and of the risks and costs of change itself, including the possibility of catastrophe.

If Dahl engaged in this or any other explicit process of prudential theorizing about the circumstances for advocating total change, it is certainly not evident in "On Removing Certain Impediments to Democracy in the United States." If one were to attempt, however, to piece together his answer, it might be the following. It is clear to begin with that Dahl does not think that the Constitution is destined soon to fall, for he marvels at its resiliency in surviving three decades of war and an imperial presidency. Next—and this comes as no great surprise—Dahl does not foresee, or at any rate does not mention, any of the potential costs or risks involved in his project of throwing out the Constitution and refounding the regime. But Dahl goes on to provide a mild surprise when he warns against inflated expectations regarding the technical prowess of modern political science to match the correct means to the desired ends. In fact, he tells us, we have no grounds for supposing that we possess "the knowledge and skills to excel the performance of the framers." Since the Framers, in Dahl's view, mistakenly constructed a government that produced very harmful consequences, it is likely that we, too, in our attempt to establish procedural democracy, will commit mistakes of a similar magnitude.

What, then, can justify the call for a change of regimes, even when we know of the likelihood of our committing serious blunders? The answer, which helps explain Dahl's insistence on a progressive degeneration in the moral quality of the regime, is that our regime today is so fundamentally flawed that we can have no reasonable grounds for fearing that a change could work out for the worse. As long as we know that we are committed to a superior standard of political health—and this we know—the superior result of a new effort at constitution making cannot be much in doubt.

This leads us back to our point of departure: Dahl's standard of political health. For Dahl, political health is marked by the progressive growth in consciousness to the point at which we can transcend conflict by embracing the warmer unity of a more egalitarian order. More even than his love of equality, it is Dahl's desire for an end to our being "conflicted" which characterizes the goal of his political science and which seems to distinguish it from the political science of the Founders. What the Founders teach us is that the good things in politics themselves often conflict and that the object must be, in James Madison's words, "mingling them in their due proportions."[13] Designing and maintaining a constitution is not an exercise in avoiding conflict but an effort at discovering the institutional forms that achieve the best possible "mingling" of the goods of political life.

Despite having presentiments of nuclear annihilation, Dahl in the final analysis trusts in a special kind of progress according to which we can look forward to a time when we transcend our psychological conflicts, collective and individual. Near the end of his essay, Dahl beckons us forward: "When we turn toward the inner self and

[13] James Madison, Federalist No. 37, *The Federalist Papers*, p. 227.

ask what we need in order to understand the needs and interests of the self, including those crucial aspects of oneself that are inextricably bound up with and require a sympathetic understanding of other selves, we confront a question to which the answer is inescapably open-ended. . . . The criterion of enlightened understanding beckons us forward but it cannot tell us what we shall discover."

These words appear to be central to Dahl's new liberation psychology, which serves as the foundation for his new liberation political science. The new democratic "self," characterized by "sympathetic understanding" as well as "love, nurturance, pity, joy, compassion and hope," is the model for both Dahl's new world order, in which, with the elimination of America's will to dominate, peace will be more likely, and for Dahl's new American regime, in which a benevolent state ensures a happy egalitarian society. This vision of the future, however benign it may appear, represents a flight from the realism of the greatest parts of our tradition and a rejection of the sterner qualities of the human spirit that have helped to build and sustain our republic.

On Equality as the Moral
Foundation for Community

Wilson Carey McWilliams

> The gradual development of the equality of conditions . . .
> possesses all the characteristics of a Divine decree: it is uni-
> versal, it is durable, it constantly eludes all human inter-
> ference, and all events as well as all men contribute to its
> progress. Tocqueville, *Democracy in America*

EQUALITY is apparently the conquering dogma of the age. Its
march is increasingly aggressive; the gradual advance which
Tocqueville detected in history has changed into a headlong rush.
Hereditary political privilege, long in retreat, has been reduced to a
few enclaves. Racism, the most stubborn manifestation of hereditarian
thought, gives ground slowly and deviously, but has few avowed partisans. Institutions, like property and empire, once the symbols of
security and glory, have lost their moral aura and are pressed, even
where they survive. The social distinction between the sexes, once
unquestioned and considered part of the nature of things, is under
confident attack. All cultures, evidently, dash as rapidly as they
are able into the embrace of industrialism. As physical space shrinks
under the impact of technology, it is not hard to imagine a future in
which humanity rubs shoulders in the indistinction of Whitman's en
masse.

It takes considerable temerity, given all this, to argue that contemporary humanity is at best ambivalent about equality, or to
maintain that the cry for equality is too often only the rhetorical disguise for values much closer to the modern heart, but that is what I
mean to contend. And I will also argue that both the roots of our
confusion about equality and the wisdom to resolve it may be found
in our political inheritance.

I

Equality is a matter of qualities. The statement "You and I are
equal" means that we share in some essential quality: we are qualita-

tively the same in some significant respect. Equality does not exclude differences or imply identity. (The belief in human equality, Chesterton wrote, is not "some crude fairy tale about all men being equally tall or equally tricky.")[1] Quite the contrary: personal identity, a knowledge of what I am, logically demands a knowledge of what I am not, and of those wholes in which I am *included* but with which I am not *identical.* If human beings are equal, it is because all are included in the whole, humanity, and, depending on it for their equality, retain their identities as parts of the whole. If I *identify* with you, I am not regarding the two of us as equals (although I may fool a superficial observer); I am denying either your separate identity or my own. Any such maneuver, however, rejects equality: equality is the middle term in an equation which must have at least two other parts, and human equality presumes a relationship between at least two equal but separate selves.[2]

The proposition that "human beings are equal," moreover, asserts that this equality is *intrinsic.* Adding modifiers—for example, stating that "human beings are equal in rank" or "equal in rights"—tends to make equality extrinsic, part of some condition external to humanity itself. Grammatically, a proposition like "human beings ought to be equal in treatment" transforms equality from a noun into an adverb; more properly stated, it would read, "human beings ought to be treated equally." And such an extrinsic usage, obviously, does not necessarily involve the belief that human beings *are* equal at all.

A claim to equality of treatment, for example, may be no more than a tactical demand reflecting the utilitarian calculation that equal treatment is the best that I can hope for, but aiming at the maximum feasible personal advantage, not equality. A belief in equality of treatment or condition has no necessary relation to a belief in equality as a characteristic of human nature or as something to be valued in itself.

Tocqueville described two very distinct varieties of "the passion for equality." The first, which he thought "manly and lawful," perceived citizens as equal in fact, and gave equality a relatively autonomous status as a value. It was a fundamentally political sentiment, public-spirited and patriotic and rooted in participation and political community. Those moved by it rejected superiority *for themselves* as well as resenting pretensions to it in others. Their desire for civic

---

[1] G. K. Chesterton, *What I Saw in America* (New York: Dodd Mead, 1922), p. 17.

[2] Aristotle, *Nicomachean Ethics*, trans. H. Rackham (London: Penguin, 1956), pp. 145–47; see also Rudolf Ekstein, "Psychoanalysis and Education for the Facilitation of Positive Human Qualities," *Journal of Social Issues* 28 (1972):80

equality entailed the insistence that their fellow citizens share the burdens and responsibilities in governing. Demanding an equal share in ruling, such partisans of civic equality also claimed an equal right to be ruled.

The second "passion for equality," which Tocqueville considered a "depraved taste," did not believe in the reality of equality and valued it only as a second-rate alternative, at best useful and more often only a concession to necessity. It was a demand for equal *treatment* founded in a combination of individualism, self-concern, and felt weakness which, resenting being ruled, despaired of command. In public the "depraved taste" insisted that "you are no better than I am," retaining the right to declare, privately, that "I am better than you." Supremacy was its real goal, and its "taste" for equality derived from a sense of failure and from resentment of more excellent or apparently more successful others. "Aye, he would be a democrat to all above," Starbuck mused about Ahab, "look how he lords it over all below."[3]

This distinction between a civic, or communitarian, equality, based on a sense of equal worth, and individualistic demands for equal treatment is paralleled by Erik Allardt's contrast between societies that aim at similarity and likeness and those whose institutions are based on exchange relationships.[4] The first aim at common values and interpersonal bonds; the second encourage differentiation and cannot afford high degrees of solidarity or common valuation. In societies that aim at likeness, dignity derives from the quality of one's devotion to the common values; and, since commonality is one of those values, personal dignity entails a desire that others be equally devoted and equally dignified. In such societies differences based on the division of labor, while useful and necessary, are neither encouraged nor valued; hence, it is relatively easy to acknowledge another's superior *ability* without associating that skill with superior *quality*. Where command is perceived largely as an instrumental value only, equality may make few demands for equal treatment. It will, instead, insist on the common good as defined by common values.

In exchange societies, however, dignity is a function of one's rela-

3 Alexis de Tocqueville, *Democracy in America*, trans. H. Reeve (New York: Schocken, 1961), 1:61–65, 292–94. (For an excellent contemporary treatment, see Benjamin R. Barber, "Command Performance," *Harper's Magazine*, April 1975, pp. 51–56.) Herman Melville, *Moby Dick* (New York: Modern Library, n.d.), p. 244.
4 Erik Allardt, "A Theory of Solidarity and Legitimacy Conflicts," in *The Dynamics of Modern Society*, ed. W. J. Goode (New York: Atherton, 1966), pp. 169–78.

tive power in exchange. Society encourages me to demand, at least, the external validation of equal treatment as a proof of my equal worth. ("The *Value*, or WORTH of a man," Hobbes wrote, "is as of all things, his Price; that is to say, so much as would be given for the use of his Power: and therefore is not absolute, but a thing dependent on the need and judgment of another.")[5] Exchange societies value power; a "good trade" is one which is to my advantage, and I accept equality, a "fair trade," only from calculations of utility. But even if equality in exchange power is somehow imposed, we will not feel "the same": the principle of exchange is *difference*. I will have what you lack, and vice versa, and I will feel a need to control those who command what I need and cannot have. Even under conditions of equal treatment, power over others—not equality with them—remains the highest social value.

Modern polities, obviously, more closely resemble Allardt's model of exchange society, and it is to be expected that our ideas of equality should be similar to the "depraved taste" which Tocqueville detected. There is, in fact, considerable evidence to support that suspicion.

In the first place, despite all the apparent triumphs of equality in our times, there are ways in which human equality is decreasing. The technology which has brought us closer in space has made us more distant in time; the "generation gap," still real and possibly widening despite the return of relative calm, is only one example. Science and technology have also tended to divide us into "two cultures"; Newton's knowledge, John Schaar observes, was far more accessible to the ordinary citizen of his day than is Einstein's in our own.[6] In the *Meno*, Socrates evoked geometry from a slave, but if we repeated the experiment with today's higher mathematics, we would at least require much more time—and by the time we reached our goal, mathematics, like Zeno's tortoise, would have reached a new, more abstruse, point. Moreover, great political and social organizations, abetted by technology, increase the difference of power between rulers and ruled to an extent unhoped for by the tyrants of simpler times.

It is more to the point that the common symbol and slogan of radical movements in recent decades has been "liberation" and not "equality." The great themes of political passion and thought, "independence" and "autonomy," like Tocqueville's "depraved taste," strain toward mastery, supremacy, and rejection of the other. It may

[5] Thomas Hobbes, *Leviathan*, ed. C. B. Macpherson (Baltimore: Penguin, 1968), pp. 151-52.
[6] John H. Schaar, "Equality of Opportunity and Beyond," in *Equality*, ed. J. Roland Pennock and John W. Chapman (New York: Atherton, 1967), p. 232.

be argued that what is sought is "equal independence," but that does not change matters much. "Equal independence" implies an equal freedom from claims, obligations, and dependence. The goal, even if granted to all claimants, is liberation from the *shared* dependence and *mutual* claims of civic equality.

Nor has contemporary militancy often respected the "equal independence" of others when it conflicts with one's own will and desire. Advocates of abortion are largely unconcerned with their spouses; "doing one's thing" shows no great respect for those who may find that thing repulsive; insistence on a volunteer army reflects at least the willingness to accept radically inegalitarian policies if they support one's own "freedom"; nationalists discount international comity and terrorists hold human beings as pawns in their political chess games.

Tocqueville's reflection on his own times is apposite in ours: "the sympathy which it has always been acknowledged between the feelings and the ideas of mankind appears to be dissolved, and all the laws of moral analogy to be abolished."[7] Sympathy and moral analogy are the essence of any sense of likeness and equality, and where they are lacking, we must suspect that equality is little felt and not greatly valued.

That supposition finds considerable confirmation in the writings of contemporary philosophers. The case for equal *treatment* is explored in depth; arguments for human equality of *worth* are few and perfunctory. It can be argued that this neglect only reflects equality's status as an unchallengeable dogma, but it is doubly unfortunate, whatever the cause. In the first place, it is precisely in relation to "worth" that equality is most at odds with common sense, which is offended by the suggestion that Hitler was as worthy as Martin Luther King or that Einstein was no more valuable than an imbecile. Second, without a belief in equal worth, even equality of treatment rests on the shifting and uncertain ground of utility and is reduced to something not very different (at best) from Tocqueville's "depraved taste."

Contemporary arguments normally begin with the proposition that human beings constitute a class or species and, consequently, should be treated alike unless good reasons are evinced. But any class or category is alike in that common quality which defines it. "All blonds are equal" in being blond, but in order to justify the unequal treatment of blonds, we do not require that "good reasons" be very numerous or very powerful. The equality of a class is morally and politically

[7] Tocqueville, *Democracy in America*, 1:lxxvii.

important only to the extent to which we assign value to the category which defines the class.[8] Certainly, we have been confronted often enough with arguments which assert implicitly that "all human beings are equal in respect of their humanity, but humanity is not worth very much." Unless it is worth a great deal, however, exceptions to equal treatment will be justified readily if, in fact, they do not become the rule.

The importance of our common humanity, unfortunately, is only weakly defended in contemporary political philosophy. William Frankena argues, for example, that human beings are equal in possessing desires and emotions, the ability to think, and the capability of "enjoying a good life in a sense which other animals [cannot]." Similarly, Bernard Williams speaks of the human capacity to feel pain and affection for others and to desire self-respect in relation to one's own purposes.[9]

Arguments of this sort, however, are both unusually abstract and radically nonqualitative. It is doubtful, John Schaar remarks, that human beings are "equal" in any of these respects—some individuals seem, at least, to have stronger desires, affections, capabilities for thought and anguish or concern for self-respect and the good life than do others—and it is certain that the quality of these feelings, reflections, and strivings differs radically from one human to another.[10] Frankena's argument seems to prove only that humans are more like one another than they are like "other animals," but while the distinction between men and beasts may establish that I am more like Socrates than either of us is like a dog, it does not mean that I am very much like Socrates. If granted, it proves that we should treat animals differently, not that we should treat humans alike; it argues that animals are not our equals, not that our common humanity makes us equally worthy. (Like many arguments for inequality, it is also dangerous; we should beware of slighting our common animality, a point to which I will return.)

The strongest elements in contemporary arguments point to human potentialities and aspirations—"the striving to make himself something worthy of his own respect"—as the basis for equal worth,

[8] Sigmund Freud, *Works*, Standard Edition (London: Hogarth, 1971), 18:108.

[9] William Frankena, "The Concept of Social Justice," in *Social Justice*, ed. R. Brandt (Englewood Cliffs, N.J.: Prentice-Hall, 1962), p. 19; Bernard Williams, "The Idea of Equality," in *Philosophy, Politics, and Society*, ed. Peter Laslett and W. G. Runciman (Oxford: Blackwell, 1962), pp. 112, 114.

[10] John H. Schaar, "Some Ways of Thinking about Equality," *Journal of Politics* 26 (1964): 881.

not what human beings are at present. Evidently, it is the striving, and not its end, that is thought important. Hitler sought to make himself "worthy of his own respect," but the "something" for which he struggled was hardly equal in worth to that sought by Martin Luther King. Nor would it be hard to argue that Hitler's moral respect was not worth having. The fact that such arguments are made, however, suggests that contemporary philosophers are led toward teleological arguments regarding the natural end of humanity, even though their presumptions and training compel them to stop short of that teaching.

This is not surprising. The belief in human equality is necessarily at odds with empiricism or positivism. It demands a radical deprecation of appearances and insists on a distinction between humanity's essential equality and its differing accidental manifestations. As Schaar comments, the doctrine of human equality "was meant to deny precisely what observation confirmed."[11]

The most virulent inequalities in American life have been at least accentuated by the tendency of our dominant institutions and philosophies to glorify appearance. The protagonist in Ellison's *Invisible Man* was unseen because a "blindness of the inner eye" prevented white Americans from discerning (or valuing) his humanity. Those who verbally insisted on his equality were "half blind," either denying the existence of a separate black experience or proclaiming that blacks were *only* their experience. Both the blind and the half-blind were unable to see that essential humanity which is affected and educated by society but which naturally seeks self-knowledge and the good life.[12]

The idea of an equally valuable "natural end," a good life that human beings naturally seek, makes it possible to resolve the most difficult problems posed by apparent inequality. Those who feel or act basely, or who strive for base ends, do not do so because they are inferior; rather, the argument contends, they do so because they have been deprived or misled by rearing, experience, or teaching.

This argument is conventional in social science and social policy, but it is at odds with the prescription of formally equal treatment. A case for unequal treatment, in fact, follows logically from the notion of equality as an *end*. If we regard Hitler's pathology or King's virtue as due in large measure to rearing, education, and experience, then

11 Ibid., p. 876.
12 Ralph Ellison, *The Invisible Man* (New York: New American Library, 1952); see also Ellison's "The World and the Jug," in *Shadow and Act* (New York: New American Library, 1964), pp. 115–47.

clearly we need to encourage one set of family patterns, teachings, and institutions and to discourage others. The mere fact of *having* values, including the value of equality, guarantees that some qualities, institutions, and behaviors will be rewarded and others discouraged, and creates some sort of hierarchy.[13]

We may even require authority in the interest of the end equality. If it is true, for example, the Nazism and similar doctrines reflect the absence of authority—a "longing for the father"—as well as a rebellion against brutal, rigid, or indifferent authority, it would seem to follow that a humane or nurturant authority is needed to develop both equalitarian convictions and the naturally equal worth of the individual.[14]

Those who are devoted to equality as an end must reject the idea that "equal treatment" is a mechanical standard. In fact, equal treatment requires *analogous* treatment. That is, it commands that each be treated as every other would be in the same situation, but it recognizes that the "situation" includes social circumstances, abilities, education, "moral development," and the like. (The punishment of juvenile offenders is a matter of controversy, but very few of us would insist that an eight-year-old be punished by the same standard as an adult who had committed a like offense.) Against this thesis, Hugh Bedau urges that a principle of difference, like the Marxian maxim "from each according to his abilities, to each according to his need," though possibly *just*, is not equality.[15] In insisting that "equality" means formally equal treatment, however, Bedau ignores the fact that a defender of the maxim would regard abilities and needs as accidents and equality as the essence (and the natural end) of human nature.

It was precisely because they agreed that justice was in some sense equality that the classics insisted that distributive justice was a kind of equality. If we are equal in worth by nature, then we are due equality by the law of that nature. But we are evidently not equal in abilities, needs, or the attainment of wisdom and virtue. To treat us alike would violate equality as an end: it would demand too little of

13 Leo Strauss, *Natural Right and History* (Chicago: University of Chicago Press, 1952), p. 137; Schaar, "Equality of Opportunity and Beyond," pp. 230–31.

14 Rudolf Ekstein, "Reflections on and Translation of Federn's *The Fatherless Society*," *Bulletin of the Reiss-Davis Clinic* 8 (1971): 2–33; John H. Schaar, *Escape from Authority* (New York: Basic Books, 1961).

15 Hugh Bedau, "Equalitarianism and the Idea of Equality," in Pennock and Chapman, eds., *Equality*, pp. 11, 12.

the advantaged and too much of the disadvantaged. That, after all, is the basis of the graduated income tax, as well as the more complex argument that we have a right, however unlikely we are to realize it, to demand that philosophers be kings.

I will be arguing that the "liberal tradition" erred in relation to equality, partly because it attempted to make equality an empirical proposition dependent on an inaccurate and irrelevant "science," but more importantly because liberalism reduced equality to a *means*, making it ultimately dependent on assessments of its utility. So considered, equality is reduced to the rule of equal treatment, not a divine decree, but a human device and contrivance and the servant of other ends. This lowering of the status of equality is a crucial part of the real meaning of much of the teaching of our times.

The contemporary argument discussed earlier regarding the relation between human beings and beasts makes a distinction not only more extreme than is warranted by natural science but one more radical than that developed by traditional philosophy and theology. Socrates compared men to a variety of beasts, suggesting that there was at least some likeness in their virtues.[16] Genesis declares that God made man master over the beasts, but it insists that both are creatures. Indeed, man's first sin is the effort to transcend that creaturehood. Traditional thought contended that man was *more* than a beast, but it did not deny the commonality of men and beasts in some aspects of their natures.

Rejecting the notion of a nature that includes and governs humankind, modern thought has also drawn a radical distinction between humans and beasts. Following the new routes opened up by the subtle Machiavelli, which were then clearly charted for all to see by such thinkers as Hobbes and Bacon, modern thought has directed man to master nature itself. Denying the distinction between God and man, it derives equality from the distinction between human and nature. We are all equal because we are all destined to be masters, but it is mastery and not equality that constitutes the goal.

This, however, greatly anticipates the argument. For the moment, it is enough that there are evidently problems and ambiguities in the modern theory and practice of equality. Robert Frost acknowledged our doubts and confusions when he mused on Jefferson's understanding of equality:

16 For example, Plato, *Republic*, 375d; *Laches*, 196e; heavily ironic, Socrates' comments also have a serious side.

> That's a hard mystery of Jefferson's.
> What did he mean? Of course the easy way
> Is to decide it simply isn't true.
> It may not be. I heard a fellow say so.
> But never mind, the Welshman got it planted
> Where it will trouble us a thousand years.[17]

So it does, and if we would understand our present concerns, we must retrace the path of the idea of equality as it came down to those who proclaimed its self-evidence to a somewhat astonished world.

II

It is evident that Plato and Aristotle, and most classical philosophers with them, were not believers in equality as we understand it. They considered that some men were naturally more fit to rule, that it was unjust to treat unequal things alike, and that it would be unjust to give the excellent only an equal share.[18] Aristotle, as we are often reminded, defended a form of slavery, and many other examples could be offered to the same purpose.

But Plato and Aristotle also held that equality rightly understood was an end for any true polity. "A *polis* aims at being," Aristotle declared, "as far as it can be, a society of equals and peers." [19] Similarly, the Athenian stranger in *The Laws* asserted that the only truly just regime, or *politeia*, was none other than the one created in speech in *The Republic* (the Greek title of which is *Politeia*). Then and always, he contended, "*polis* and *politeia* come first, and those laws are best, where there is observed as carefully as possible throughout the whole polity the old saying 'friends have all things in common.' " For a number of reasons (to which we will recur), the Athenian Stranger noted that such a regime can never be brought into being. Still, he reemphasized the point that "one should not look elsewhere for a model constitution [*politeia*], but hold fast to this one, and with all one's power seek the constitution [*politeia*] that is as like to it as possible."[20]

Equality in the classical view was not merely formal or material; it involved an internal sense of equality, a concern for the good of the

<hr>

17 From "The Black Cottage," in *The Poetry of Robert Frost*, ed. Edward Connery Lathem (New York: Holt, Rinehart, 1930).
18 Aristotle, *Politics*, 1284a, 1301b; *Ethics*, 1131b, 1158b.
19 *Politics*, 1295b.
20 Plato, *Laws*, V, 739b6–c2, 739d9–e3.

whole, a perception of the common political life all citizens share as being more important than private goods. Criticizing Phaleas of Chalcedon, Aristotle remarked, "It is more necessary to equalize men's desires than their properties, and that is a result which cannot be achieved unless men are adequately trained by the influence of the laws."[21] Material equality, Aristotle argued, is superficial and unstable if men remain covetous, for their inegalitarian spirits will resent equality and will find means to circumvent it.

By contrast, if citizens have an inward sense of equality and commonality, of mutuality and reciprocal duty, they will not resent outward inequalities that serve the common good, nor will those who command misuse their position as a basis for contempt, arrogance, or oppression. (In fact, distributive justice, "due measure according to nature," given the goal of equality, demands more from the powerful for the good of the weak.) Recognizing that "what is equally right is what is for the benefit of the whole *polis* and for the common good of all its citizens," the citizenry will restrain the tendency of equality to level down, neither excluding the excellent nor being resented by them.[22]

Mere formal equality, on the other hand, may even teach inequality. It is possible, Aristotle observed, for citizens to receive the same education and yet be more greedy and ambitious than others. Democratic institutions may be governed, in practice, by the belief that the members of the minority are not equal and need not be considered because the majority is the stronger. That "the many" is a numerous, collective tyrant does not change the fact. In such a case it shares with individual tyrants the belief that supremacy is good and that the victor is entitled to superiority over the vanquished.[23] In such a polity, each citizen will be taught implicitly that possession of Gyges' ring is the touchstone of happiness.

Athenians praised equality, but they meant an "equality of opportunity" that let each man make the most out of his private liberty. Equal freedom, in other words, gave all citizens a chance to become unequal and made "each man zealous to achieve for himself." Athenian law liberated and stimulated competitiveness, as Pericles detected, and thereby produced citizens who were at their best when they saw in others an excellence they could hope to equal. But, when confronted with a greatness they despaired of emulating, Athenians

---

21 *Politics*, 1266b, 1257b.
22 *Politics*, 1283b, *Laws*, VI, 757a–c.
23 *Politics*, 1267b, 1292a.

became envious and sought to discredit or destroy what was beyond their grasp.[24] There was little love of equality; Athens taught a hatred of superiors, dependence, and limitation. Her collective bond lay in Athenian power and in the sense of superiority over others; Athens needed the inferiority of outsiders to preserve equality at home. She valued unlikeness, individuality, and supremacy; equality was lauded in speeches but was hated in the heart.

Creating an inward sense of equality and commonality is obviously no easy task. Property in things and in persons (such as slaves, wives, and children), the Athenian remarks in *The Laws*, is merely "called" private by convention. The senses, however, are private by nature and can be trained to act in common—so that all citizens, "so far as possible, are unanimous in the praise and blame they bestow, rejoicing and grieving together and honoring the laws that made the *polis* unified with all their hearts"—only by contrivance of the laws and education. (Yet even with the best laws and teaching, some private self-centeredness would remain.)[25]

Sparta, which exemplified equality to the Greeks even more than Athens, understood the privacy of the senses. But Sparta did not believe that the emotions could be educated to support *isokratia*. The passions in the Spartan view, could only be conquered by an education that taught men to resist pain, an austerity that limited pleasure and forced the practice of self-denial, and a rigid obedience to law supplemented by the constant watchfulness of fellow citizens. "Nor ought we to believe that there is much difference between man and man," Archidamus said (according to Thucydides), "but the superiority lies with him who is trained in the severest school."[26]

Sparta, the Athenian remarks in *The Laws*, made "each man his own enemy."[27] She did not create in her citizens a love of equality; she made them fear the consequences of their desires for private gratification and supremacy. But her citizens could not eradicate their desires, and the passions were powerful, ever-present enemies of the law. Sparta was haunted by fear; she saw her equality as artificial, fragile, and embattled and sought to shut out all influences of the foreign world that might undermine it, distrusting the unknown yet fearing the knowledge that might make it familiar. Spartan equality,

[24] Thucydides, *The Peloponnesian War*, trans. J. Finley (New York: Modern Library, 1951), pp. 103–4.

[25] *Laws*, V, 739c2–d4.

[26] *The Peloponnesian War*, pp. 48–49; see also A. G. Woodhead, *Thucydides on the Nature of Power* (Cambridge: Harvard University Press, 1970), p. 33.

[27] *Laws*, I, 626d, 633d, 644b.

like Spartan courage, was a surface phenomenon. Outside the control of public opinion and the laws, Spartans were notoriously avaricious and prone to ambition, submitting to those inegalitarian passions they had been taught they could not control alone.

As the Athenian suggested in *The Laws*, Sparta made citizens familiar with pain but not with pleasure, and left them unable to resist its temptations. True education, as some great philosophers saw it, sought to educate the pleasures, leading men to see the connection between joy and community, and between friendship, equality, and shared dependence, winning the support of the emotions, as far as possible, for equality and the common good. At this point, however, philosophy encountered a paradox, for much which is necessary for human political education and which contributes to the formation of philosophic character conflicts with the insights of philosophy itself.

In an important sense, philosophy must define equality, for it develops the idea of the universal, of a *cosmos* governed by a single law. All human beings are subject to that law; all are parts of the whole. Moreover, knowledge of the whole can never be complete or certain. Philosophy requires a "knowledge of ignorance," the recognition that human beings do not know adequately and cannot even be certain that they are in error. Human reasoning begins with opinion and ends with speculation; the most that can be hoped for is progress toward knowledge.

This is a paradoxical doctrine that cannot be "taught" in any simple sense because its meaning can be understood only by those already schooled in humility and equality. The paradox inherent in the statement "I know that we do not know" can be resolved, after all, if the "I" is not included in the "we," and that is how many, if not most, students hear the teaching. Knowledge of ignorance is understood as a weapon for discrediting conventional opinion, an excuse for shamelessness, and a justification for rejecting restraint. It is turned against philosophy itself, as an argument for regarding its discipline as pointless and for evading the obligation to seek painful knowledge or discommoding virtue. Cynicism, a vehicle for envy, may wear an egalitarian mask. It pretends to debunk the pretensions of elites, but whatever its guise, its understanding opposes equality.

Very different results follow from the humbling awareness that self-knowledge is radically incomplete and defective and that we reject and fear our mortal limitations, hoping for immortality and omnipotence. Living under the spell of illusions about the self, we despise the real self and the limited and mortal things that might otherwise bring us joy. Aware of our imperfections at some level of the mind, we seek to disguise them. Seeking perfection in others, we fear—while in the grip of our self-induced enchantment—that they will discover and desert us, and, when disillusioned regarding their "perfection," we scorn what we once admired. The tyrant dreams of love, but can never trust it; like him, humans who lack self-knowledge hope for omnipotence and are convinced of unworthiness. They are locked in a psychic dialectic between supremacy and servility that has no understanding of the value of equality.

Those who "know" the self, who have emotional as well as intellectual awareness of human nature, are, in a sense, "elevated" man. But what elevates them is a knowledge of equality in the nature and condition of humanity: "No man is an island entire of itself. . . ." But any such knowledge of ignorance and of equality depends on a prior education of the emotions in security, dependence, and the proper occasions for joy and pain.

It is now possible to return to the basic point, that what is necessary for political education, and hence required for the best politics and the broadest development of philosophic character, conflicts with philosophy, and especially with the philosophic understanding of equality.

Philosophy discerns the universal, but Plato and Aristotle agreed that the good polis, or political association, must be small. The universal state cannot be just because it cannot know individuals or their due. Moreover, it dwarfs the individual, making him feel insignificant; emotionally, it teaches withdrawal rather than equality. Speaking of religious institutions, Plato's Athenian in *The Laws* asserted the need for a polis small enough that "the people may fraternize with one another at the sacrifices and gain knowledge and intimacy, since nothing is of more benefit to the polis than this mutual acquaintance; for wherever men conceal their ways from one another . . . no man will ever rightly gain his due office or honor or the justice that is befitting."[28] Still, the polis involves a kind of injustice peculiar to itself.

Love for one's country and one's fellow citizens tends to slight the broader likeness that is humanity. The sense that "we are alike" in a given city or country leads easily to the perception of a categorical difference between "us" and "them," like the conventional Hellenic distinction between Greeks and barbarians.[29] If philosophy teaches that country may be artificial and accidental, however, it endangers

28 *Laws*, V, 738e.
29 Plato, *Statesman*, 262d; see also *Laches*, 186d.

the very patriotism that is so valuable in leading the emotions out of the fortress of the self. Patriotism is natural in general, though conventional in detail, but that logical distinction does not solve the practical problem, for most human beings are prone to identify the "conventional" with something *contrary* to nature.[30]

In a similar sense, reverence for age is useful in human education, if for no other reason than it teaches the passions to see life as an ascent, not a rise to maturity followed by a decline. But we all know wise youths and foolish dotards; age is no proof of venerability. Also, as the earlier argument suggests, in some respects men are like the beasts and the line between them is an uncertain one. But *for that reason* we do not wish to legitimate beastliness, and we may find it educationally useful to treat the distinction as categorical.

There are, moreover, quite unnatural institutions that may be necessary in a given political context. Aristotle defended a form of slavery, but he approved Alcidamas' saying "nature makes no man a slave" as an example of natural law. Plato refrained from attacking slavery, though he held no brief whatever for its naturalness.[31] Given the economy of the time, both thought slavery was necessary for excellence. In our own time, the division of labor is thought equally necessary, but it would not be hard to argue that extreme specialization is artificial and that it creates lives not essentially different from what slavery meant among the Hellenes.

In all these areas classical philosophy thought it wisest to limit discussion of these propositions to the old, whose character is already formed (or, to be more exact, to those old men whose character is not corrupt) and who can be presumed to understand the limitations of necessity. Some conventions that violate equality, however, even though partly necessary, are both unnatural and educationally corruptive. Plato certainly believed that rigid distinctions between men and women fell in this category, teaching men to despise dependence and women to seek to live vicariously and avengingly through their sons. In such cases philosophy is permitted and obligated to discuss equality with the young, while prudence may dicate silence with the old, who might be shocked without learning any better lesson.[32]

The philosophic perception of human equality, then, was a kind of mystery, an ideal and a truth safe only for adequately prepared initiates. Plato quarreled with the tragedies because some spoke ignorant-

30 Plato, *Protagoras*, 337d–e.
31 Aristotle, *Rhetoric*, 1373b18; on Plato's views, the *Meno* is a case in itself; see also *Laches*, 186b.
32 *Republic*, 451a–457b.

ly, but also because greater tragedians spoke promiscuously, without regard for the limits in human life and education. Socrates presented himself in humbler mask of comedy, but his life was high tragedy, and to its initiates philosophy offered a knowledge of equality which fulfilled the tragic aim: "Now the slave emerges as the freeman, and all the rigid, hostile walls which necessity has erected between men are shattered."[33]

III

These classical views in their various interpretations and modifications (some of which stemmed from Christian doctrine) held sway in the Western world for nearly two millenia. Conventional educators in the eighteenth century continued to emphasize the study of classical languages and literature. Yet even as the eighteenth-century student acquired some familiarity with the classics, they no longer held him enthralled. Their spell had been broken by those modern philosophers who had, as it seemed, successfully attacked both classical and Christian thought. The most influential of the American Founders must be included among those bold statesmen who rejected, by and large, both the classical and Christian philosophic and theological traditions. It was "the new science of politics," one based on a new understanding of human nature, that served as their guide. Machiavelli, Hobbes, Locke, Montesquieu, and others had successfully laid new philosophic foundations, and the architects of the American Republic were acutely aware of the radically new shape of the political order they were building on them. Their political doctrine and their philosophic vocabulary were drawn from modern sources, especially from the English tradition of contractarian theory, the common philosophic currency of reflective statesmen and men of affairs in the British Empire of that era.

Hobbes, as the founder of that tradition, confronted the issue of equality with his customary directness, but in his argument the claims of equality are less extensive than they may seem. In a rough sense, human beings are equally able to kill each other and, given time, to acquire equal prudence. Science, however, is *not* naturally equal; it is something that "few have" and each has it in only "few things."[34] The argument is qualified but deceptive, for Hobbes regarded science

[33] Friedrich Nietzsche, *The Birth of Tragedy*, in *The Birth of Tragedy and the Genealogy of Morals*, trans. F. Golffing (Garden City, N.Y.: Doubleday, 1956), p. 23.
[34] *Leviathan*, pp. 183–84.

as supremely important and vital to the right ordering of human affairs. Logically, Hobbes's argument might seem to lead to the conclusion that scientists—or, at least, political scientists—are natural sovereigns over other human beings.

Hobbes would have replied that such a conclusion is irrelevant, whatever the logic. Those who have science are few, men will not believe that many are as wise as themselves, and the many have both the force and the freedom to make their "conceit" effective. As the term is ordinarily used in civil society, men are by nature unequal in worth, but this inequality is ineffective in the "state of nature," in which equal freedom and roughly equal power produce a state of war. Self-concern and relatively equal force require that human beings be treated *as if* they were equal, for otherwise they will not consent to be governed at all. In practice, then, equality is a premise without which it is impossible to *create* civil order. Once created, civil order affords a security and freedom from anxiety which the state of nature inhibits. It does not matter whether equality is true or not; it is an indispensable means to civil society and to those human goods unrealizable in a condition of war.

In fact, Hobbes feared the teaching of an inner equality of worth because it was associated with the idea of a sovereign "conscience," and hence with the sectarian disorder of his times. It justified men in a stubborn insistence on that desire for mastery which was natural to them. Men could not truly escape the state of nature without *some* recognition of equality, but so powerful was the natural desire for independence that men could only be driven to acknowledge equality by a desperate, violent confrontation—a kind of drawn battle in which both contestants abandon the hope of victory.[35]

Hobbes's argument is radically different from the classical notion that the passions can be gently seduced into a recognition of equality. In the first place, the classical theorists presumed that the natural place of man was in the polis and that political education, consequently, was also natural to human beings; Hobbes saw civil order and the rearing associated with it as the products of convention, artifice, and contract. The classics considered that civic equality and genuine community were the end in view by which all political inequality must be justified; Hobbes justified the premise of equality as a means to civil order, which was itself justified by the fact that it permitted the development of the unequal faculties of private life.[36]

35 See Leo Strauss, *The Political Philosophy of Hobbes* (Chicago: University of Chicago Press, 1962).

36 *Leviathan*, pp. 186, 201–17.

Locke's teaching, rhetorically more beguiling than that of Hobbes, was not fundamentally different. In the state of nature, men's "perfect equality" is, in fact, a perfect freedom, an equality of "power and jurisdiction" and not of worth. Indeed, the "fall" from the *apparent* gentleness of Locke's state of nature into the state of war cannot be explained unless *some* human beings are naturally more prone than others to violate the law of nature, thereby proving morally inferior to those they attack.[37]

Locke did not in fact regard human beings as equal in virtue, potentiality, or in "excellency of parts." Each mind might begin as a tabula rasa, but there was an inequality of ability—a considerable one—among men of equal education. Locke argued, however, that there was no inconsistency between the inequality of worth he discerned in human nature and the equality of the state of nature: "I there spoke as proper to the business at hand, being that equal right that every man hath to his natural freedom."[38]

Thus, for Locke as for Hobbes, man's natural freedom and equality of force made it necessary to regard human beings as equals, despite their inequality of worth, in order to make civil government possible. Locke, however, carried the argument a step further. While unanimous consent was necessary to create civil society, it could hardly ever be realized afterwards. The rule of the majority corrected that defect by relying on the only equality that counted in politics, the equality of force and freedom: "it is necessary the body should move whither the greatest force carries it, which is the consent of the majority, or else it is impossible it should act or continue one body, one community."[39]

For both Locke and Hobbes equality was a concession to political necessity, a recognition of the rights inherent in the individual and the basis for orderliness, not a reflection of equal worth. The classics had recognized the utility of equal treatment as a protection against disorder but had regarded that consideration as prudential, not as a first principle.[40] Hobbes and Locke reduced equality to a means that

[37] In a seeming concession to religious sentiment, Locke noted that the "Lord and Master of them all" may by "manifest declaration of his will' confer "undoubted dominion and sovereignty" on someone in the State of Nature (*Two Treatises of Government*, Book 2, section 4), and there are many indications that Locke regarded such natural preeminence of force as having been the actual spur to civilization.

[38] Ibid., section 54; Sanford Lakoff, *Equality in Political Philosophy* (Cambridge: Harvard University Press, 1964), pp. 98–99.

[39] Ibid., section 96.

[40] *Politics*, 1301b, 1317b; *Laws*, VI, 757e.

permitted the establishment of inequalities. Indeed, Locke's effort to limit government to a relatively narrow sphere in part reflected his conviction that government, a creation of artifice and convention, was necessarily based on the principles of equality of rights that could not properly be extended beyond the political realm. The broader area, "society," separated from the state, was reserved for those inequalities in the interest of which human beings—and especially, human beings of the better sort—were constrained to accept government, and with it legal equality. The "Lockean tradition," in this sense, ranked equality with constables and prisons as part of the price required for civil peace and order.

The leaders of the early Republic, however, did not restrict their reading to Locke and his epigones. The "celebrated Montesquieu," for example, had a great vogue, and Montesquieu's theories expressed a somewhat different tradition of modern theorizing.

In Montesquieu's state of nature, human beings were governed by fear and felt weakness, but those feelings led them to avoid one another; isolation and not war was the rule of nature. Men were equal in being independent, but that equality had little hold on their loyalties since, almost unaware of each other, men were unaware of equality and, for that matter, were unable to make those comparisons that might have suggested inequality of ability or worth. When society begins, equality ceases. Relations of need and dependence develop, and those inequalities hidden by the state of nature become visible. From that state of unequal ability and mutual dependence, conflict and war result, and political society, in its turn, develops as a necessary response to war.[41]

As should be evident, this argument is quite similar to Locke's. Natural equality has no moral significance, and exists under conditions of grinding necessity that keep men at a level with the beasts. When humanity escapes that subhuman condition, it enters a state of nature akin to Locke's and passes from thence into a condition of war.

Montesquieu, however, lauded democracy as a political order that required, demanded, and encouraged virtue. Civil equality was a noble ideal, especially when contrasted with the privatism, self-concern, and greed of corrupt polities. Democracy, Montesquieu argued, requires *love of country* and the allied passion of *love for equality*, the latter an inward sentiment, like that praised by traditional thought, which involves a devotion to the good of the whole

41 Montesquieu, *The Spirit of the Laws*, trans. T. Nugent (New York: Hafner, 1949), pp. 3–5.

such that all "serve with alacrity" even though they cannot serve equally. What matters is not difference of talent but equal devotion to the common good. Extreme equality corrupts democracy, for such a leveling spirit destroys reverence and distinctions of ability, leading to faction, dissension, and, eventually, to despotism. "As different as heaven is from earth," the true spirit of democratic equality accepts leaders but demands that they be "none but equals."[42]

Despite this praise, we must not forget that the two "loves," patriotism and equality, are both unnatural. They are creations of custom and law alone, since for Montesquieu, no less than for Hobbes and Locke, the political order is conventional and not natural for human beings.

Moreover, democracy requires a *love of frugality*, because the state must be small and hostile to the acquisitive passions that make for successful commerce. Frugality, however, is decidedly something which, in Montesquieu's view, human beings do not naturally *love*, and even laws and customs can persuade them to be frugal only when allied with necessity and external limitation. Success in mastering the environment makes citizens realize that more is possible and that self-denial is forced on them by the laws; resentment and the decay of democracy follow in train.[43] In Montesquieu's theory, democracy is admirable, but its virtuous equality is unnatural and is too severe for human beings to long endure.

Commercial republics, by contrast, face the corrupting impact of private fortune, individualism, and the sense that one's own estate may be independent of (or even at odds with) the public good. They are, however, more comfortable with human nature, allowing greater well-being and permitting some scope for self-concern, while submitting it to the discipline of work and the market. So long as excessive wealth is prevented, commercial republics may acquire riches without utterly corrupting morals, and competition helps achieve that limitation. Commerce is a kind of mean, corrupting but curing prejudice and parochiality, rejecting both robbery and suspicion of private interest. In the long term, commercial republics serve the material interests of human progress.[44]

All republics, however, must be small, and all are threatened by war and by the rise of great powers. The development of large states is a by-product of historical necessity. The dynamics of international

42 Ibid., pp. 20–22, 40–42, 109, 111.
43 Ibid., pp. 41–42, 112.
44 Ibid., pp. 46, 96, 316, 317.

politics drive out small states, and republics can survive only in confederation.[45]

American statesmen read Montequieu with an eye to the separation of powers he saw in England, but that specific analysis was an example of a concern with the equilibrium of power that is fundamental to his doctrine. To summarize his argument: equality is associated with virtue, but it is stern and unnatural, unstable at best and possible only when the polity is environed by strait natural necessity. External political threats demand that a state expand to meet the threat or perish. Commercial republics and confederated commercial republics are not only more practical; they satisfy the truly fundamental human desires for survival and mastery over nature. Such republics can, moreover, preserve some of the virtue associated with equality by substituting *equilibrium* for equality, the external balance of interests for an internal concern for the public good. Equality becomes a functional attribute of a *system* of exchange relations, not of human beings and their immediate relationships. Feeling the call of the small state, Montesquieu gave self-preservation and historical necessity higher status as political principles. Although he accorded more moral stature to equality than many theorists of the "new science," Montesquieu also deserted that communitarian ideal of equality as an end, accepting in its stead an equality that was only a means, useful to the extent that it served the more "natural" ends of naturally private men.

IV

The American Heritage was then compounded of rather different and conflicting strains of thought that were often in conflict and sometimes poles apart. If the Declaration of Independence had evoked "harmonising sentiments," as Jefferson wrote in 1825 (by which time he had conveniently forgotten the numerous Loyalists), it is in part a tribute to ingenious political rhetoric that concealed the ambiguity of its terms and avoided other areas of conflict in the public mind.[46] Jefferson's draft, for example, referred to humanity "created equal and independent," and went on, "from that creation they derive rights, inherent and inalienable." Franklin, always prudent in mat-

[45] Ibid., pp. 126, 127, 133–48.

[46] Robert Ginsberg, "The Declaration as Rhetoric," in *A Casebook on the Declaration of Independence*, ed. Robert Ginsberg (New York: Crowell, 1967), pp. 219–44.

ters of religion, apparently suggested substituting "endowed by their Creator" for Jefferson's more scientistic "from that equal creation"; the elimination of the reference to original independence also avoided conflict with those who held that humanity was naturally social and political. Similarly, the phrase "governments are instituted among men" avoided the term "social contract," using instead a phrase familiar in Calvinist rhetoric. These persuasive turns of phrase reflect more than the guile of the Declaration's authors; they reveal how much public considerations affected the Declaration as it finally appeared, decisively affecting it as a document for the education of future generations. In American democratic political thought, one must never forget the people.

Nevertheless, there is a minimal political theory incorporated in the Declaration. What it does proclaim is that men have an original, natural liberty and equality of rights. In the state of nature those rights, as we have seen, may not be utterly ineffective, but they are not secure. Hence, governments are "instituted" to protect them. Popular consent is needed to establish government, and this, along with equal rights, requires equality as a public norm, but not because equality is especially desirable in itself. As Robert Ginsberg points out, "Deprivation of equality does not figure in the extended list of grievances against Britain, nor does equality reappear in the Declaration's portrait of civil society except as holding between distinct societies." In fact, Ginsberg comments, the Declaration "builds a case against equality in society."[47] Like Locke, and like Montesquieu's commercial republic, the Founders limited equality to a necessary public norm and presumed inequality in the social, private sphere.

The Declaration's sketchy but typical version of contract theory reflected a broad consensus, as Jefferson asserted. *The Federalist,* more "realistic" in rhetoric, says very little about equality, but its authors make it clear that they are devoted to republican government and that they accept the principles of the Declaration.[48] It was generally agreed that in the state of nature men were equal in possessing equal rights; all, that is, had a "natural liberty" in being free from obligation or authority.[49]

47 Robert Ginsberg, "Equality and Justice in the Declaration of Independence," *Journal of Social Philosophy* 6, no. 1 (1975): 8.

48 Martin Diamond, "Democracy and *The Federalist*: A Reconsideration of the Framers' Intent," *American Political Science Review* 53 (1957): 52–68.

49 James Wilson, *Works,* ed. R. G. McCloskey (Cambridge: Harvard University Press, 1967), 1:241–42; Thomas Paine, *Common Sense and Other Political Writings,* ed. Nelson Adkins (New York: Liberal Arts, 1953), pp. 5, 82, 163.

Paine was more direct than many, but most would have agreed with his arguments that the distinction between rich and poor could be "accounted for," while "Male and female are the distinctions of nature, good and bad the distinctions of heaven." Nature creates physical distinctions and the passions by which men are naturally impelled; convention and reason create institutions like property; moral distinctions beyond this are supernatural or simply unnatural. In the state of nature, then, morality as conventionally understood did not exist, and this equal lack of moral obligations is critical, for human beings in the state of nature are equal in little else. Even power is only approximately equal; society, Paine argued, was created by the weak out of a desire to equalize their relations with the strong.[50]

The dominant desire of human beings, the first law of nature, is self-preservation, and that natural egotism places man at war with nature and, derivatively, with other human beings who may frustrate or endanger him. Natural egotism and power-seeking, however, although they define the individual's "interest," are only part of his desires. The "affections," gentler and more social passions, bind human beings together in "civil society." Sympathy and the moral passions, James Wilson wrote, exert the "force of confederating charm."[51]

In civil society, however, inequalities emerge, and ties of dependence and obligation limit men.

In nature or in simple society, affection is either allied to self-preservation and interest or yields to it. Abundance or greater security, reducing the pressure of necessity on self-preserving men, leads to a division between the social bonds (affection) and ambition (interest), and hence to social decay and conflict. It was in that spirit that the authors of *The Federalist* criticized the excessively democratic state constitutions, documents that had proved workable at all, Publius contended, only because of the unity imposed by war, which could no longer be relied on.[52] "Unaided virtue" cannot govern except under conditions of dire necessity, and governments are necessary to protect both the "equality of rights" found in nature and the inequality of talent and property characteristic of society.[53]

[50] Paine, *Common Sense*, pp. 10, 83, 169.
[51] Wilson, *Works*, 1:234; Paine, *Common Sense*, pp. 4–5.
[52] *The Federalist*, No. 49; Paine, *Common Sense*, p. 5.
[53] Paine noted, for example, that property would always be unequal; he only argued for the primacy of the person, regarding property as a social and not a natural right (*Common Sense*, p. 166).

Government did not exist, however, to strengthen the hold of the affections and moral feelings. The affections were parochial, short-sighted, and concerned with comfort and immediate relationships. They restricted the fulfillment of human interests, limiting human effectiveness in the war against nature. (Even in America, Paine commented, where the absence of customary barriers and the size of the land drew men toward broader visions and humanitarian sentiments, few were able to see the effects of others' misfortunes on themselves.)[54] Liberty and interest were primary in nature, and affection should only follow and assist.

In *Federalist* 10 Madison contended that it was not only impossible to give citizens the same feelings, interests, and beliefs, but that it was undesirable. Public spirit and the inward conviction of equality are rejected as ideals in favor of more reliable, "scientific," and mechanical institutions which avoid dependence on virtue and which permit liberty and progress. Equality is limited to the uniform rules of the public sphere.[55]

Political prudence and scientific legislation, in fact, aimed at fragmenting those smaller communities and loyalties where affection is powerful and individual liberty is restricted, and hence the logic of that overlapping "division of powers" that allows both federal and state governments to appeal directly to the individual (contrary to Montesquieu's prescription for confederacies), and the argument that many factions render any one group too weak to hope for success or to make total claims on the individual.

The small polis, the model of classical theory, was thus rejected by the Federalists because it was too weak to serve human interests and because it demanded an austerity that people cannot naturally and *ought* not to endure. The polis has shown itself to be a "wretched nursery of faction" and had encouraged discord by opening the way to factions that were too large in relation to the whole. In consequence, it had often been too oppressive in the attempt to repress these factions in the interest of unity. Paine admired both public spirit and simple democracy, but he questioned the feasibility of simple democracy because it could not effectively govern an extensive state. He preferred representative government because it was "the greatest scale upon which human government can be instituted."[56]

[54] Ibid., pp. 21, 25.

[55] *The Federalist*, No. 10; Schaar, "Some Ways of Thinking about Equality," pp. 886–87.

[56] *The Federalist*, No. 9; Paine, *Common Sense*, pp. 128–30, 170; Bernard

Progress was a central goal, even though it was assumed that progress, arising from initiatives in the unequal private sphere, would result in greater inequality. In the debates in the Constitutional Convention, Pinckney argued that an upper house was superfluous given the equality of condition in America. Madison responded that Pinckney should remember "the changes which the ages will produce. An increase of population will of necessity increase the proportion of those who will labor under the hardships of life and secretly yearn for a more equal distribution of its blessings."[57] But Madison did not argue that change should be resisted; he proposed to guard against its effects, for change was essential to liberty. In the event, Madison's fears of "agrarian attempts" helped Jefferson to the acquisition of Louisiana, hoping to check the "leveling spirit" by satisfying it.

As Schaar observes, *The Federalist*'s constitutionalism designed a public realm fundamentally limited to utilitarian concerns, the acquisition of power, and the maintenance of order. Political life was only indirectly creative, and such moral purpose as it could claim derived from the hope that success in the war against nature would gradually allow the emergence of humanitarian sympathy and a diffuse sentiment of fraternity. Right was fundamentally a private matter; as Arendt comments, the Framers aimed at a government sufficiently controlled to enable individuals to devote their attention to private life.[58] Yet private life and society were reserved for inequality, not only in social teaching but in the attitudes of individuals "freed" from ties of loyalty to community, pursuing their interests and kept in order by the personal weaknesses each felt amid the multitude.

It is ironic that this privatistic vision should have been formulated by men whose vocations were so public and who so delighted in political life. Hamilton could not abide a private destiny, nor could Jefferson. Adams contented himself with the reflection that he was enabling his descendants to be private men (though one of them, Henry, did not thank his ancestor for the favor). It was, nevertheless, a theory from which very few of the Framers ever departed. Furthermore, it may well have contributed significantly to the rapid changes

---

Bailyn, *The Ideological Origins of the American Revolution* (Cambridge: Harvard University Press, Belknap Press, 1967), pp. 288–301.

[57] James Madison, *Notes on Debates in the Federal Convention of 1787* (Athens: Ohio University Press, 1966), p. 194.

[58] Hannah Arendt, *On Revolution* (New York: Viking, 1963), pp. 132–33; Schaar, "Some Ways of Thinking about Equality," pp. 88–91.

in the character of the American regime, as Professor Wood suggests in his discussion of "the Democratization of Mind in the American Revolution."[59]

The "conservative" statesmen among them were, like Adams, men who had become alarmed at the implications of their principles. The French Revolution only strengthened Adams's fear that the idea of equality might lead to attacks on property or on the law itself. Still, while that anxiety led Adams to insist that men were not equal by nature and that there must always be an unequal distribution of property and rank, he never ceased to believe in, and hope for, a recognition of equal treatment to the extent of "equal rights and duties" and the human claim to "equal laws." His argument shifted its emphasis from a concern for public equality to a zeal to defend social and private inequality, stressing the need for "equilibrium or counterpoise," but no departure from the characteristic principles of his contemporaries.[60]

Similarly, Hamilton never doubted the need for that "equal opportunity to obtain inequalities" that formed the core of the general creed. Hamilton, however, had less faith than some of his colleagues that the "self-regulating" mechanisms of government could eliminate the need for statesmen and public men. He feared that wealth, commerce, and power would produce public decay (if only from lower class resentment) and felt that governmental control was required for the common good. Distrusting the wealthy, he hoped that they would have education enough to take a broader view of their interests, and wealth enough to be tempted by honor (a more credible hope when wealth meant either landed property or a cosmopolitan commercialism that demanded considerable political knowledge).[61] But Hamilton hoped that those statesmen would devote themselves to protecting equal freedom and opportunity, and had his hopes been realized, his ruling class would have allowed competition, specialization, and privatization—emotional and evaluative, as well as social, inequality. Hamilton, like his fellows, never doubted that we should follow that "course of nature" that he discerned in history.

Jefferson, his great opponent, undeniably theorized in the same

[59] See above, pp. 102–28.

[60] *The Works of John Adams, with a Life of the Author*, ed. Charles Francis Adams, 10 vols. (Boston: Little, Brown, 1850–56), 7:462, 9:569–71; *The Diary and Autobiography of John Adams*, ed. L. Butterfield (Cambridge: Harvard University Press, 1962), 3:326–27, 333, 359.

[61] John Livingston, "Alexander Hamilton and the American Tradition," *Midwest Journal of Political Science* 1 (1957): 174, 175.

modern and "enlightened" terms then fashionable. He believed devoutly in natural rights, in the doctrine that self-preservation is the first law of nature, and in the notion that reason teaches utilitarian self-interest. He preferred large states because of the greater stability arising from the ability to play factions off against each other, and he believed passionately in the "new science."[62]

Indeed, as Daniel Boorstin observed, Jefferson's scientistic beliefs led him to seek evidences of equality in the "similarity of men's bodies," in empirical and sensory "proofs" emphasizing the biological unity of the species rather than the inward likeness of souls. Even on its own terms, however, Jefferson's quest for evidence indicates a desire to *prove* an equality of which he was already deeply convinced despite the evidence of his senses.[63] Jefferson's egalitarianism led him to the conviction that apparent inequalities would subsequently be proved to result from environmental or related influences and, in fact, spurred him on to a teaching that avoided appearances almost entirely.

Reason taught self-interest, but morality (and hence moral worth) was an affair of the "heart," a "moral sense" that provided an instinctive knowledge of right and wrong. Akin to the qualities his contemporaries attributed to affection, the "moral sense" certainly made stronger claims on man and on political legislation. The creed that men were equal in "heart" allowed Jefferson, despite his belief in the intellectual inferiority of blacks, to insist that Negroes were equal. The "moral sense" allowed Jefferson, too, to trust and value a variety of minds and a freedom of opinion, confident that this would result in neither social conflict nor moral relativism. Moral notions with which Jefferson disagreed he tended to classify as the result of some "infirmity"—a dangerous teaching, which foreshadowed later abuses in the name of "mental health," but one that shows how little Jefferson's moral convictions were affected by his nominal "first principles."[64]

Jefferson was too sophisticated, moreover, not to realize that the "moral sense," like the other senses, was originally private and required nurture and education. That knowledge led him to the belief (rare among his contemporaries) in the value of political com-

[62] *The Life and Selected Writings of Thomas Jefferson*, ed. Adrienne Koch and William Peden (New York: Modern Library, 1944), pp. 531–32, 682, 685.

[63] Arendt, *On Revolution*, p. 195; Daniel Boorstin, *The Lost World of Thomas Jefferson* (Boston: Beacon, 1960), pp. 59–60, 62, 71.

[64] Boorstin, *Lost World of Jefferson*, pp. 81–98; Jefferson, *Selected Writings*, pp. 508, 140–41, 310, 395–407, 430–31, 638–39.

munity for moral education and especially for education in the perception of equality.

Men in "barbaric" societies, Jefferson asserted, had affections which, like our own, responded to the appeals of benevolence, gradually receding in intensity as they extended away from the self. Because barbaric societies were small, political obligation coincided with intense affection, and little formal government or coercion was required.[65] But material deprivations aside, barbaric society was morally inferior, restricting sympathy too narrowly—most perceptibly in its brutal treatment of women and its penchant for cruelty toward outsiders.

"Civilization" advanced the material lot of man and broadened his sympathies, but, associated with large states, it eventually reached the point where sympathy became too weak to override vice, avarice, and self-concern. European states, with cities filled by a resentful and brutalized "*canaille*" and "higher orders" lost to arrogance and vice, had accentuated the faults of civilization by bad government, but also reflected the general rule of civilized society.

Jefferson hoped that America could establish a mean between civilization and barbarism. Some of the worst excesses of civilization could be checked by economic austerity, but Jefferson knew his Americans too well to rely on the durability of that condition. He did, however, prescribe policies to avoid excessive wealth by subdividing property and graduated taxation. Economic equality of a limited sort —and Jefferson never meant it to be more than that—would still, however, be a thing of surfaces.[66]

The small community was the natural limit of democracy, small enough to foster strong affections and to insure that political duty could be closely allied through daily participation and friendship. The sense of commonality and inward equality of these "ward republics," as Jefferson came to envisage them, would make it easy for citizens to identify and trust their "natural aristocracy," men characterized as much by greater benevolence and sympathy as by greater talent. These local natural aristocrats meeting in a representative "ward republic" of their own, could select others, until an ascending chain connected small communities to the republic while trusted leaders, returning to their communities, could educate their fellows in the requirements of broader prudence and sympathy. It was this sort

[65] Jefferson, *Selected Writings*, p. 412.
[66] Ibid., pp. 389–90, 630.

of idea that made Jefferson incline toward indirect election of the House of Representatives as more likely to produce truly able legislators, though he was easily persuaded that the benefits of immediate popular election outweighed that advantage.[67]

Jefferson's vital interest in civic education was part of his hope for a republic that could develop moral faculties, identify natural leaders, and evoke an inward sense of equality. That his educational vision was limited, by our standards, is a relatively slight criticism; the very "utilitarianism" which Boorstin finds fault with is an indication of his desire to extend education to include classes for which it had been thought irrelevant.[68]

Nevertheless, Jefferson was committed to modern theory with a loyalty that threatened many of his other aspirations. Progress entranced him, and his zeal for change included a desire not to impose on future generations. Jefferson departed from the rule of equal human rights in one vital respect. In his theory, the dead have no rights and are excluded from the human community; future generations have at least the right to be considered.[69] Jefferson knew the values of veneration and stability, but they found small support in his teaching. When the dead are excluded from the embrace of equality, the living are reminded that they are destined for a similar rejection and are trapped in a present without continuity, driven to a fever to achieve or enjoy that endangers equality and community alike. "Thus," Tocqueville wrote, "not only does democracy make every man forget his ancestors, but it hides his descendants, and separates his contemporaries from him; it throws him back upon himself alone, and threatens in the end to confine him entirely within the solitude of his own heart."[70]

V

It will be no surprise that in my view the classics were right in believing that humans are beings meant to live in the *polis,* and their high objective of civic equality associated with the *polis* should not be neglected. Of course, we cannot realize that goal in our great in-

[67] Ibid., pp. 437, 632–33, 660–62, 670, 676.

[68] Ibid., pp. 263, 265, 440, 604; Boorstin, *Lost World of Jefferson,* p. 224.

[69] Boorstin, *Lost World of Jefferson,* pp. 201–2; Jefferson, *Selected Writings,* p. 724.

[70] Tocqueville, *Democracy in America,* 2:120.

dustrial states; size alone prevents it, and those who have attempted
to impose civic equality on such states have only created monstrosi-
ties. We may, however, hope to revitalize our political life as far as
circumstances permit, but that requires that we recognize the nature
of truly political life and that we find a place to begin.

Ours is a polity dominated by exchange relations and shaped in
the image of those modern theories that informed the Framers. But
in value and desire, to say nothing of institutions, America has never
completely accepted "the liberal tradition." Our political history has
involved a conflict between modern, dominantly liberal ideas and
those derived from religion and traditional philosophies and cultures, and that "check" to exchange relations and modern ideas has
been the source of much of our political resilience. If America feels
disoriented today, it is because the resistance of the "private order"
seems finally to have been overcome.

Jefferson's thought was most distinctive in his sense of the potential
of the small community as a school for public virtue and equality
alike. Only infrequently did that idea ever coincide with our formal
legislation, but it did find reflection in that private order that the
Framers saw simply as an arena for inequality. Localities, churches,
and ethnic communities, to name only the obvious examples, provided Americans over the years with "homes," communities of orientation that conveyed traditional and substantive values and, at their
best, the foundations of knowledge about genuine equality and therefore true community.

I am not making a case here for the wisdom or value of all our traditional communities: some taught basely and many more, inadequately; many, too, behaved badly in more than one respect. I am
arguing that the private order formed a vital part of our political
life, that it is increasingly fragmented and unstable, and that political
wisdom counsels us to strengthen and rebuild it, hopefully in ways
that will enhance the virtues and minimize the vices of the older private order. And, in relation to equality, political memory was not
the least of those virtues.

Nowhere do we appear in a worse light than in our tendency to
equate memory with nostalgia. To estrange the past and the dead
prevents us from truly learning the lesson of our own mortality.
Mourning and remembering, we come closer to that truth, and in
the sadness of the sense of loss, find joy in the discovery that other
persons, alike but not identical to those we have lost, can be found
to replace them. Reminding us that we, too, can be replaced—a powerful but painful testimony to human equality—nature offers us the

consoling knowledge that love and worth are abundant.[71] Stable communities make that lesson easier, for they have memories that may include us, guaranteeing that our unique identities will not be altogether lost. If we are troubled by the knowledge that all memory, too, fades with time, we may consider the mystery that knowledge of equality hints at: if our nature yearns for a love and worth more perfect than even that which abounds in nature, it may be that it *is* our nature to seek a love and a worth beyond nature itself.

[71] Jacques Maritain, *Ransoming the Time* (New York: Scribner's, 1941), pp. 14–18; see also Freud, *Works*, 14:293, 307, 13:60 ff., 156, and 18:134–35.

Slavery and the Moral Foundations of the American Republic

Herbert J. Storing

IT is refreshing," said one of the dissenters in the case of *Dred Scott* v. *Sandford*, "to turn to the early incidents of our history and learn wisdom from the acts of the great men who have gone to their account."[1] It is a common opinion today, however, that, admirable as the American Founders may be in other respects, in their response to the institution of Negro slavery their example is one to be lived down rather than lived up to. A good expression of this opinion has recently come from the distinguished American historian John Hope Franklin. We need to face the fact, Franklin contends, that the Founders "betray[ed] the ideals to which they gave lip service." They failed to take an unequivocal stand against slavery. They regarded "human bondage and human dignity" as less important than "their own political and economic independence." They spoke "eloquently at one moment for the brotherhood of man and in the next moment den[ied] it to their black brothers." They "degrad[ed] the human spirit by equating five black men with three white men." The moral legacy of the Founders is shameful and harmful. "Having created a tragically flawed revolutionary doctrine and a Constitution that did *not* bestow the blessings of liberty on its posterity, the Founding Fathers set the stage for every succeeding generation of Americans to apologize, compromise, and temporize on those principles of liberty that were supposed to be the very foundation of our system of government and way of life."[2]

This view of the American Founding—that the Founders excluded the Negroes from the "rights of man" expressed in the Declaration of Independence and sanctioned slavery and Negro inferiority in the Constitution—is a view that the radical Abolitionists, from whom John Hope Franklin descends, share with their pro-slavery antago-

[1] *Scott* v. *Sandford* 19 How 393, 545 (1857) (Justice McLean).
[2] "The Moral Legacy of the Founding Fathers," *University of Chicago Magazine*, Summer 1975, pp. 10–13.

nists. Indeed, one of the best, and surely most authoritative, expressions of this view came in the opinion of Chief Justice Taney in the famous Supreme Court case of *Dred Scott* v. *Sandford* in 1857, in which the Supreme Court, for the second time in its history, held an act of Congress unconstitutional, and in which Taney tried to secure once and for all the place of slavery under the Constitution. I want to examine Taney's carefully worked-out reasoning, for there one can confront most clearly what is today the dominant opinion about the Founders and slavery.

Dred Scott was a slave owned by a Doctor Emerson, a surgeon in the United States Army. In 1834 Scott was taken by his master from Missouri to Rock Island, Illinois, where they lived for about two years, and from there to Fort Snelling in the federal "Louisiana territory;" where they lived for another couple of years before returning to Missouri. On Emerson's death Scott tried to purchase his freedom from Mrs. Emerson. Failing in that, he sued in the Missouri courts for his freedom, on the ground that he had become free by virtue of his residence in a free state and a free territory. He won in the lower court, but the decision was reversed on appeal. The Supreme Court of Missouri, abandoning eight Missouri precedents and departing from the then almost universal adherence of Southern courts to the principle "once free, always free," held that, whatever his condition in Illinois and in federal territory, Scott was a slave upon his return to Missouri.

On Mrs. Emerson's remarriage, Scott became the property of her brother, John Sandford, a citizen of New York; and this enabled Scott to sue for his freedom in federal court under the provision of the Constitution that gives federal courts jurisdiction in cases between citizens of different states. He lost in the lower court and appealed to the Supreme Court, which in 1857 finally handed down its opinion—or rather its opinions, for all nine justices expressed their opinions, most at considerable length. I will be concerned here only with the opinion "of the court" given by Chief Justice Taney.

Taney held, in the first place, that because he was a Negro, Scott was not and could not be a citizen of the United States (whether he was free or not) and could therefore not sue in the federal courts on the grounds he had chosen. (I pass over Taney's dubious assumption that for a citizen of a state to be entitled to sue under the diversity clause he must establish citizenship of the United States.) Taney held, in the second place, that the federal act under which Scott claimed freedom, the Missouri Compromise Act of 1820 outlawing

slavery in the northern part of the Louisiana Purchase, was unconstitutional: for Congress to prohibit slavery in federal territory was
to deprive slave-owning citizens who might move into that territory
of their property without due process of law.

These two holdings are the conclusions of two lines of argument,
one concerning the status of Negroes and the other concerning the
status of slavery, that provide my two themes. Taney emphasized
throughout his opinion that he was merely giving effect to the Constitution. It was not his business to read into the Constitution the
more favorable views toward the Negro that had emerged since the
time of the Founding. Actually, as Lincoln correctly argued, opinion
about Negroes had hardened rather than softened in the seventy
years since the adoption of the Constitution.[3] But more important
is the fact that Taney's reading of the Constitution and the views
of the Founders was wrong, except perhaps in one very important
respect.

Taney takes up first the question of Negro citizenship, then the
question of Negro slavery; but it will be clearer if I reverse the order
and look first at slavery. According to Taney, the Founders assumed
the legitimacy of slavery; and back of that was a universal opinion
of the inferiority of the Negro race.[4] Negroes "had for more than a
century before been regarded as beings of an inferior order; and
altogether unfit to associate with the white race, either in social or
political relations; and so far inferior, that they had no rights which
the white man was bound to respect; and that the negro might justly
and lawfully be reduced to slavery for his benefit." "No one thought,"
Taney said, "of disputing" such opinions. Negroes "were never
thought of or spoken of except as property."

Only on such a basis, it seemed to Taney, could the framers of the
Declaration of Independence be absolved from utter hypocrisy.
They *said* that "all men are created equal and are endowed by their
Creator with certain unalienable rights." Yet they were, many of
them, slaveholders; and they certainly did not destroy slavery. But
there was no hypocrisy, because the writers of the Declaration "perfectly understood the meaning of the language they used, and how
it would be understood by others; and they knew it would not, in
any part of the civilized world, be supposed to embrace the negro

---

[3] "The Dred Scott Decision," Speech at Springfield, June 26, 1857, in *Abraham
Lincoln: His Speeches and Writings*, ed. Roy P. Basler (New York: World Publishing Co., 1946), p. 359.

[4] *Scott* v. *Sandford* 19 How 407–10 (1857).

race, which, by common consent, had been excluded from civilized governments and the family of nations, and doomed to slavery." The men of that age (that is, the white men) simply did not regard Negroes as included among the "all men" who are, according to the Declaration of Independence, "created equal"; and, Taney concluded, "no one misunderstood them."

This whole argument—and I repeat, it is identical to the common view today—is a gross calumny on the Founders. The truth is almost the exact opposite of Taney's account. The Founders understood quite clearly that Negroes, like men everywhere, were created equal and were endowed with unalienable rights. They did not say that all men were actually secured in the *exercise* of their rights or that they had the power to provide such security; but there was no doubt about the *rights*. Far from it being true that "negroes were never thought of except as property," not only Negroes but slaves were very frequently spoken of and treated as persons. All of the Constitutional provisions relating to slaves, for example, refer to them as persons. And while slaves were typically deprived of *civil* rights, they were regarded as persons under criminal law. As rational and, to some degree, morally responsible human beings, they were held capable of committing crimes, and they were protected by the law—in principle and surprisingly often in practice—against crimes committed against them. In the first three or four decades of our history, the injustice of slavery was very generally acknowledged, not merely in the North but in the South and particularly in Southern courts.

Since this is likely to be unfamiliar territory to most readers, let me give a couple of examples.

In 1820 the Superior Court in Mississippi was confronted with the question, there being no positive legislation covering the matter, whether the killing of a slave was murder under the common law.[5] The Court held that it was; and this was the usual view of Southern courts that considered this question. The Mississippi judge began by emphasizing that "because individuals may have been deprived of many of their rights by society, it does not follow that they have been deprived of all their rights." The slave "is still a human being, and possesses all those rights, of which he is not deprived by the positive provisions of the law. . . ." Since the common law definition of murder is the taking away the life of a reasonable creature with malice aforethought and since a slave is a reasonable being, such a killing of a slave is murder.

[5] *State* v. *Jones* 1 Miss 83 (1820).

Slavery is the creature, Southern as well as Northern judges said again and again, of positive law only; it has no support in natural law or in transcendent principles of justice. Yet slavery existed; it was lawful in the Southern states. Even when the judges were giving effect to the positive law of slavery (which they had a clear duty to do), they typically acknowledged the injustice of the institution.

In a Supreme Court case fifteen years before *Dred Scott, Prigg* v. *Pennsylvania* (1842), the Supreme Court upheld the constitutionality of the Fugitive Slave Act of 1793, which implemented the fugitive slave clause of the Constitution; the Court held that this federal power was exclusive, thereby invalidating state "personal liberty laws," which had been passed in a number of Northern states to try to give greater protection than the federal law provided to Negroes claimed as fugitive slaves.[6] The opinion was written by a strong antislavery man, Joseph Story, and many of Story's friends wondered how he could make such a decision. Story replied that his first obligation was to the law but that, in any case, he thought his opinion a great "triumph of freedom."[7] It was a triumph of freedom mainly because, while upholding the Fugitive Slave Law, Story took the opportunity to stress that slavery is a mere creature of positive law and has no support in natural law. "The state of slavery is deemed to be," in Story's words, "a mere municipal regulation, founded upon and limited to the range of the territorial laws." That means that the presumption is always against slavery, even while provisions of the positive law protecting slavery are being enforced.

The same view was common in the South. Indeed, contrary to Taney's claim that no one questioned the legitimacy of slavery, nothing was more common than Southern judges giving public utterance to the excruciating agony of trying to reconcile the law that protected slavery with the principle of justice that condemns it. One of the most interesting of these cases is an 1820 North Carolina case, *State* v. *Mann*, where the court held that a master cannot commit a legal battery upon his slave.[8] The court had held earlier that a white person could be punished for assault and battery against someone else's slave.[9] But the law cannot protect the slave, Judge Ruffin held, against his master, even in case of a wanton, cruel, senseless beating. Ruffin was offered by counsel the analogy of parent and child or

6 *Prigg* v. *Pennsylvania* 16 Pet 539, 611 (1842); cf. Taney's different view, 628.

7 William W. Story, ed., *Life and Letters of Joseph Story* (Boston: Charles C. Little and James Brown, 1851), 2:390ff.

8 *State* v. *Mann* 13 N.C. 263 (1829).

9 *State* v. *Hale* 9 N.C. 582 (1823).

master and apprentice, where the authority of the superior is limited and supervised by law. He reluctantly, but surely correctly, rejected the analogy on the ground that the end of these relations is the good and happiness of the child or the apprentice, whereas in U.S. slavery the end is nothing but the profit of the master. It is the wrongness of slavery that makes it impossible to limit it. "We cannot allow the right of the master to be brought into discussion in the courts of justice." To question that right is to deny it, and that cannot be the business of a judge in a slave state. "The slave, to remain a slave, must be made sensible that there is no appeal from his master. . . ." "I most freely confess sense of the harshness of this proposition; I feel it as deeply as any man can; and as a principle of moral right every person in his retirement must repudiate it. But in the actual condition of things it must be so. There is no remedy. . . . It constitutes the curse of slavery to both the bond and free portion of our population. But it is inherent in the relation of master and slave."

I should add that twenty years later, nevertheless, Ruffin upheld a conviction of murder in the case of an especially brutal, but probably not premeditated, killing by a master of his own slave.[10]

Another kind of case that was common in the Southern courts was like *Dred Scott*; it arose where a person who had been a slave but who had been taken to reside in a free state and then returned to a slave state sued in the courts of the latter for his freedom. As I have said, in such a case the Southern courts held (at least until the 1840s or 1850s) that such a person was free. Once the chains of slavery enforced by positive law are broken, they can never be restored.

A slave, Lydia, was taken in 1807 by her master from Missouri to free Indiana, where he registered her as his servant under Indiana's gradual emancipation law. He sold his right to her but when her new master brought her back to Missouri, the court there upheld her claim to freedom.[11] The rights of her master had been destroyed in Indiana, "and we are not aware of any law of this state which can or does bring into operation the right of slavery when once destroyed." Can it be thought, the judge asked, that "the noxious atmosphere of this state, without any express law for the purpose, clamped upon her newly forged chains of slavery, after the old ones were destroyed? For the honor of our country, we cannot for a moment admit, that the bare treading of its soil, is thus dangerous, even to the degraded African."

10 *State* v. *Hoover* 4 Dev & Bat (N.C.) 365 (1839).
11 *Rankin* v. *Lydia* 2 AK Marshall (Ky.) 470 (1820).

The American Founders and their immediate descendants, North and South, not only believed in but emphasized the wrongness of slavery, at the same time that they wrestled with the fact of slavery and the enormous difficulty of getting rid of it. It was a fact; it seemed for the time being a necessity; but it was a curse—the curse of an unavoidable injustice.

It is true, as Taney said, that Negroes were thought to be inferior to whites; but it is not true that this was thought to justify slavery. In a famous section of his *Notes on the State of Virginia*, published in 1784, Thomas Jefferson reflected on Negroes and Negro slavery in terms which are today generally found offensive and which are in consequence usually distorted and misunderstood.[12] Proceeding in the spirit of the eighteenth-century student of natural history, and emphasizing the shameful lack of systematic study of this subject, Jefferson examined the differences between the races. He thought that the blacks "participate more of sensation than reflection." He judged them inferior to whites in physical beauty, in reason, and in imagination, though in many physical attributes and in what he called "endowments of the heart," or the "moral sense," they are equal. Jefferson did conclude that this inferiority was an obstacle to Negro emancipation; but the reason was not that it makes Negroes less entitled to liberty than whites or that their enslavement is in some way just—Jefferson emphatically and consistently held the contrary. He would have agreed fully with Lincoln's view that "in some respects [a Negro woman] certainly is not my equal, but in her natural right to eat the bread she earns with her own hands without asking leave of anyone else, she is my equal, and the equal of all others."[13] Negro inferiority hindered emancipation in Jefferson's view, not because it justified slavery, but because it increased the difficulty of knowing how to deal with Negroes, once freed. Before pursuing this, however, we need to return to Taney's defense of slavery in the Constitution.

Taney held that Congress cannot prohibit slavery in federal territory: "an Act of Congress which deprives a citizen of the United States of his liberty or property, merely because he came himself or brought his property into a particular Territory of the United States, and who had committed no offense against the laws, could

---

12 *Notes on the State of Virginia*, Query 14, Adrienne Koch and William Peden, eds., *The Life and Selected Writings of Thomas Jefferson* (New York: Modern Library, 1944).

13 "The Dred Scott Decision," *Lincoln* (Basler ed.), p. 360.

hardly be dignified with the name of due process of law." Nor, Taney contended (and this is crucial and the point on which Taney abandoned both federal and state precedents) is there any difference between property in slaves and other property. In fact, he said, "the right of property in a slave is distinctly and expressly affirmed in the Constitution."[14] These words are striking: if one had to think of two adverbs that do *not* describe the way the Constitution acknowledged slavery, he could not do better than "distinctly and expressly."

No form of the word *slave* appears in the Constitution, and one would not know from the text alone that it was concerned with slavery at all. Today's beginning law students, I am told, are generally not aware that there are three provisions of the Constitution relating to slavery. This is testimony to the skill with which the Framers wrote. Some concessions to slavery were thought to be necessary in order to secure the Union, with its promise of a broad and long-lasting foundation for freedom; the problem was to make the minimum concessions consistent with that end, to express them in language that would not sanction slavery, and so far as possible to avoid blotting a free Constitution with the stain of slavery. Frederick Douglass described it this way:

> I hold that the Federal Government was never, in its essence, anything but an anti-slavery government. Abolish slavery tomorrow, and not a sentence or syllable of the Constitution need be altered. It was purposely so framed as to give no claim, no sanction to the claim, of property in man. If in its origin slavery had any relation to the government, it was only as the scaffolding to the magnificent structure, to be removed as soon as the building was completed.[15]

"Scaffolding" catches the intention exactly: support of slavery strong enough to allow the structure to be built, but unobtrusive enough to fade from view when the job was done.

Let us look at the provisions. Article I, Sec. 2(3) provides, in a masterpiece of circumlocution: "Representatives and direct Taxes shall be apportioned among the several States which may be included within this Union, according to their respective Numbers, which shall be determined by adding to the whole Number of free Persons, including those bound to Service for a Term of Years, and excluding Indians not taxed, three fifths of all other Persons." "All other Per-

14 19 How 450–51 (1857).

15 "Address for the Promotion of Colored Enlistments," July 6, 1863, in *The Life and Writings of Frederick Douglass*, ed. Philip S. Foner (New York: International Publishers, 1950), 3:365.

sons" are slaves. Thus in counting population for purposes of determining the number of representatives and also apportioning land and poll taxes, five slaves count as three free persons. What this provision signifies in principle is extremely complex, and I will not exhaust the matter here.[16] The question came up in the Constitutional Convention in the course of a debate over whether numbers or wealth is the proper basis of representation. That issue was resolved, or avoided, by use of Madison's suggestion that numbers are in fact a good index to wealth. In the case of slaves, however, that is not so clear, partly because the productivity of slaves is thought to be lower than that of free men, so some kind of discount seemed appropriate. This line of reasoning is supported by recalling that the three-fifths rule originated under the Articles of Confederation as a way of apportioning population for purposes of laying requisitions on the states. Suggestions that the three-fifths rule implies a lack of full humanity in the slave, while not without some basis, are wide of the main point. The three-fifths clause is more a way of measuring wealth than of counting human beings represented in government; wealth can claim to be the basis for apportioning representation and is of course the basis for apportioning direct taxes. Given the limited importance of direct taxation, the provision was understood to be a bonus for the Southern slave states. That gives the common argument against the three-fifths clause an unusual twist. While it may be that the provision "degrades the human spirit by equating five black men [more correctly, five slaves] with three white men," it has to be noted that the Southerners would have been glad to count slaves on a one-for-one basis. The concession to slavery here was not in somehow paring the slave down to three-fifths but in counting him for as much as three-fifths of a free person.

Regarding the second Constitutional provision relating to slavery, Justice Tancy said, "the right to trade in [slave property], like an ordinary article of merchandise and property, was guaranteed to the citizens of the United States, in every State that might desire it, for twenty years."[17] Clearly this is a major concession to slavery. It protects not merely an exiting slave population but the creation of new slaves. Practically, it allowed a substantial augmentation of the slave population and thus, of course, of the slave problem. Yet the concession is less than Taney suggests. Even on the basis of Taney's

16 See Donald L. Robinson, *Slavery in the Structure of American Politics, 1765–1820* (New York: Harcourt Brace Jovanovich, 1971), chaps. 4, 5.
17 19 How 451 (1857).

account, one might wonder why the slave trade is guaranteed only to those citizens "in every State that might desire it" rather than to all citizens; and one would surely ask why this guarantee was limited to twenty years. These qualifications suggest that there is something that is *not* ordinary about this particular article of merchandise and property. When we look at the clause itself, this suggestion is re-enforced. The clause reads: "The Migration or Importation of such Persons as any of the States now existing shall think proper to admit, shall not be prohibited by the Congress prior to the year one thousand eight hundred and eight, but a tax or duty may be imposed on such Importation, not exceeding ten dollars for each Person" (Art. I, sec. 9[1]). We note that the form is not a guarantee of a right but a postponement of a power to prohibit. Moreover we see, what Taney neglects to point out, that the postponement of federal power to prohibit applies only to the states "now existing." We have here, apparently, a traditional or vested right or interest which is to be preserved for a time but which Congress need not allow to spread to new states. The clause, fairly interpreted, gives a temporary respite to an illicit trade; the presumption was that Congress would, after twenty years, forbid this trade (as it would not and perhaps could not prohibit trade in ordinary articles of merchandise), and in fact Congress did so.

Finally, to quote Taney again, "the government in express terms is pledged to protect [slave property] in all future times, if the slave escapes from his owner."[18] Here is another major concession. It is a clear case of a new legal right of slavery—there was nothing like it under the Articles of Confederation. It amounts, moreover, to a kind of nationalization of slave property, in the sense that everyone in a free state has an obligation to assist in the enforcement, so far as fugitive slaves are concerned, of the institution of slavery. It is not surprising that this clause turned out to be the most intensely controversial of the three provisions dealing with slavery. Yet it was hardly noticed in the Northern ratification conventions. The fugitive slave clause in the Constitution, like its model in the Northwest Ordinance which outlawed slavery in the Northwest Territory, was the price of a broader freedom. And the price was grudgingly, at least narrowly, defined. Here are what Taney called "plain words —too plain to be misunderstood": "No Person held to Service or Labour in one State, under the Laws thereof, escaping into another, shall, in Consequence of any Law or Regulation therein, be dis-

18 19 How 451–54 (1857).

charged from such Service or Labour, but shall be delivered up on Claim of the Party to whom such Service or Labour may be due" (Art. IV, sec. 2[3]). Whether or not these words are plain, they were carefully chosen.[19] The suggestion for such a provision was first made in the Constitutional Convention on 28 August by Pierce Butler and Charles Pinckney of South Carolina, who moved "to require fugitive slaves and servants to be delivered up like criminals." Following some discussion (in which, incidentally, Sherman equated "a slave or servant" and "a horse" for the purpose of limiting the slaveowner's claim), the motion was withdrawn, to be replaced the next day by the following version: "If any person *bound to service or labor* in any of the U——States shall escape into another State, he or she shall not be discharged from such service or labor, in consequence of any regulations subsisting in the State to which they escape, but shall be delivered up to the person *justly claiming* their service or labor," which was agreed to.[20] This was later revised by the Committee on Style to something close to the final version: "No person *legally held to service or labour* in one state, escaping into another, shall in consequence of regulations subsisting therein be discharged from such service or labour, but shall be delivered up on claim of the party to whom such service or labour *may be due.*" Thus the Committee on Style withdrew from the master the claim that he "justly claimed" the services of his slave, acknowledging only that the slave's labor "may be due." On 15 September, the Committee on Style's description of a slave as a "person legally held to service or labour" (already probably a narrowing of the previous and morally more comprehensive description, "bound to service or labour") was objected to by some who, in Madison's words, "thought the term (legal) equivocal, and favoring the idea that slavery was legal in a moral view." Thus "legally" was struck out and "under the laws thereof" inserted. Supposing that a concession to return fugitive slaves had to be made, it is hard to see how it could have been made in any way that would have given less sanction to the idea that property in slaves has the same moral status as other kinds of property.

The Founders did acknowledge slavery, they compromised with it. The effect was in the short run probably to strengthen it. Perhaps

19 The following deliberations are reported in Max Farrand, ed., *The Records of the Federal Convention of 1787*, 4 vols. (New Haven: Yale University Press, 1911–37), 2:443, 453–54, 601–2, 628.

20 The emphases here and throughout this paragraph are mine.

they could have done more to restrict it, though the words of a Missouri judge express what the Founders thought they were doing and, I think, probably the truth. "When the States assumed the rights of self-government, they found their citizens claiming a right of property in a miserable portion of the human race. Sound national policy required that the evil should be restricted as much as possible. What they could, they did."[21] "As those fathers marked it," Lincoln urged on the eve of the Civil War, "so let it be again marked, as an evil not to be extended, but to be tolerated and protected only because of and so far as its actual presence among us makes that toleration and protection a necessity."[22] Slavery was an evil to be tolerated, allowed to enter the Constitution only by the back door, grudgingly, unacknowledged, on the presumption that the house would be truly fit to live in only when it was gone, and that it would ultimately be gone.

In their accommodation to slavery, the Founders limited and confined it and carefully withheld any indication of moral approval, while they built a Union that they thought was the greatest instrument of human liberty ever made, that they thought would lead and that did in fact lead to the extinction of Negro slavery. It is common today to make harsh reference to the irony of ringing declarations of human rights coming from the pens of men who owned slaves. But I think that Professor Franklin is wrong when he says that "they simply would not or could not see how ridiculous their position was." They saw it all right, and they saw better than their critics how difficult it was to extricate themselves from that position in a reasonably equitable way. But they saw, too, a deeper irony: these masters knew that they were writing the texts in which their slaves would learn their rights.

Having, I hope, rescued the Founders from the common charge that they shamefully excluded Negroes from the principles of the Declaration of Independence, that they regarded their enslavement as just, and that in their Constitution they protected property in man like any other property, I must at least touch on a deeper question, where they do not come off so well. But at this deeper level the problem is not that they betrayed their principles, the common charge; the problem lies rather in the principles themselves. That very principle of individual liberty for which the Founders worked

21 *Winny* v. *Whitesides* 1 Mo Rep 472 (1824).

22 "Address at Cooper Institute," New York, February 27, 1860, in *Lincoln* (Basler ed.), p. 526.

so brilliantly and successfully contains within itself an uncomfortably large opening toward slavery. The principle is the right of each individual to his life, his liberty, his pursuit of happiness as he sees fit. He is, to be sure, subject to constraints in the pursuit of his own interests because of the fact of other human beings with similar rights. But are these moral constraints or merely prudential ones? Locke says that under the law of nature each individual ought, as much as he can, "to preserve the rest of mankind" "when his own preservation comes not in competition."[23] Each individual is of course the judge of what his own preservation does require, and it would be a foolish man, an unnatural man, who would not, under conditions of extreme uncertainty, give himself every generous benefit of the doubt. Does this not tend to mean in practice that each individual has a right to pursue his own interests, as he sees fit and as he can? And is there not a strong tendency for that "as he can" to become conclusive? In civil society, indeed, each of us gives up the claim of sovereign judgment for the sake of the milder, surer benefits of a supreme judge. Even in that case there is a question whether the first principle does not remain that one may do what one can do. The Founders often described the problem of civil society as resulting from that tendency. In any case, regarding persons outside civil society, there is a strong implication that any duty I have to respect their rights is whatever residue is left after I have amply secured my own.

Now, in the case of American slavery, especially in the South at the time of the writing of the Constitution, there clearly was a conflict between the rights of the slaves and the self preservation of the masters ."[W]e have a wolf by the ears," Jefferson said, "and we can neither hold him, nor safely let him go. Justice is in one scale, and self preservation in the other."[24] Only an invincible naiveté can deny that Jefferson spoke truly. But the deeper issue, as I think Jefferson knew, is the tendency, under the principles of the Declaration of Independence itself, for justice to be reduced to self-preservation, for self-preservation to be defined as self-interest, and for self-interest to be defined as what is convenient and achievable. Thus the slave owner may resolve that it is necessary to keep his slaves in bondage for the compelling reason that if they were free they would kill him; but he may also decide, on the same basic principle, that

23 John Locke, *Two Treatises of Government*, Book 2, chap. 2, section 6.
24 Thomas Jefferson to John Holmes, April 22, 1820, Jefferson, *Selected Writings* (Koch and Peden, eds.), p. 698.

he must keep them enslaved in order to protect his plantation, his children's patrimony, his flexibility of action, on which his preservation ultimately depends; and from that he may conclude that he is entitled to keep his slaves in bondage if he finds it convenient to do so. All of this presumes of course that he *can* keep his slaves in bondage. Nor does it in any way deny the right of the slave to resist his enslavement and to act the part of the master if he can. This whole chain of reasoning is a chilling clarification of the essential war that seems always to exist, at bottom, between man and man.

Hobbes

American Negro slavery, in this ironic and terrible sense, can be seen as a radicalization of the principle of individual liberty on which the American polity was founded. Jefferson wrote in his *Notes on the State of Virginia* of the demoralization of the masters caused by slavery and its threat to the whole institution of free government. Masters become tyrants and teach tyranny to their children (and, incidentally, to their slaves). Even more important, slavery, through its visible injustice, tends to destroy the moral foundation of civil society. "And can the liberties of a nation be thought secure when we have removed their only firm basis, a conviction in the minds of the people that these liberties are of the gift of God? That they are not to be violated but with His wrath? Indeed I tremble for my country when I reflect that God is just; that his justice cannot sleep forever; that ... an exchange of situation [between whites and blacks] is among possible events; that it may become probably [*sic*] by supernatural interference! The Almighty has no attribute which can take side with us in such a contest." [25] I do not think that Jefferson was literally concerned with divine vengeance, but he was concerned with the underlying tension—so ruthlessly exposed in the institution of Negro slavery—between the doctrine of individual rights and the necessary moral ground of any government instituted to secure those rights.

Let me proceed, more briefly, to my second theme, Negro citizenship. Justice Taney was wrong in his claim that the Founding generation excluded Negroes from the principles of the Declaration of Independence. But he was not wrong in his claim that the Founders excluded Negroes from that "We the People" for whom and whose posterity the Constitution was made. Or rather, he was wrong in detail but right fundamentally.

Taney's reasonable contention was that citizens of the United States in 1787—the "People" by and for whom the Constitution was

25 *Notes on the State of Virginia*, Query 18, ibid., pp. 278–79.

made—were all those people who were then citizens of the states. He went on to claim that Negroes were not then citizens of any states and are therefore forever excluded from United States citizenship. But it was easy to show, as Justice Curtis did, that free Negroes were citizens in many of the states; and Taney's argument excluding Negroes from United States citizenship collapses. In this matter Taney is simply wrong; but he had a better case at a deeper level. The way to this level is through the privileges and immunities clause, which was Taney's real concern here, even though it was not involved in the legal dispute. This clause provides that "the Citizens of each State shall be entitled to all Privileges and Immunities of Citizens in the several States." Taney said that the Southern states cannot be presumed to have agreed to a Constitution that would give any Northern state the power to make citizens of free blacks, who could then go to Southern states, claim there all of the privileges and immunities of citizens, and by their agitation and example disrupt the whole police system on which the maintenance of slavery, and the preservation of the white South, depended. The privileges and immunities clause was the knife by which Northern freedom cut into the South, as the fugitive slave clause was the knife by which Southern slavery cut into the North. And it could be said of the privileges and immunities clause that the South did agree, as the North agreed to the fugitive slave clause, even if it did not anticipate all the consequences; and that the bargain should be kept. But the deeper question is whether the Constitution was really meant to provide for a large-scale racially mixed polity. Here I think Taney was right, for although the answer is less clear than he says, it is nevertheless a fairly resounding no.

The position of most American statesmen from the time of the Declaration of Independence through the Civil War was well expressed by Jefferson in his autobiography: "Nothing is more certainly written in the book of fate, than that these people are to be free; nor is it less certain that the two races, equally free, cannot live in the same government."[26] And in his *Notes on the State of Virginia* Jefferson gave perhaps the best explanation of this widely held view.[27] He gives an account of a scheme he had helped draft for reforming the laws of Virginia. Included in that plan was a provision for the emancipation of slaves, to be followed by their colonization to some suitable place, "sending them out with arms, implements of

[26] "Autobiography," ibid., p. 51.
[27] Query 14, ibid., pp. 255–62.

household and of the handicraft arts, seeds, pairs of the useful domestic animals etc., to declare them a free and independent people, and extend to them our alliance and protection, till they have acquired strength." At the same time, it was proposed that vessels be sent to other parts of the world for an equal number of white emigrants. Jefferson naturally anticipated the question, Why not leave the free blacks where they were and save the expense of resettling them and securing replacements? His answer can be collected under three heads. The first obstacle was the race prejudice of the whites—deep, aggressive, and invincible. Second was the blacks' sense of the injustice done to them, a sense sure to be kept alive by new injuries. Third were the natural differences between the races and particularly the actual and probably inherent inferiority of the blacks in certain respects that affect crucially the quality of civil society.

The first and second causes seemed to Jefferson and his generation to insure that there would never be that sense of fellow feeling and mutual trust between the races that forms the indispensable social basis of civil society. The third (supposed Negro inferiority) expressed a concern not with the bare possibility but with the quality of civil life. Many of the advocates of Negro rights, Jefferson said, "while they wish to vindicate the liberty of human nature, are anxious also to preserve its dignity and beauty. Some of these, embarrassed by the question, 'What further is to be done with them?' join themselves in opposition with those who are actuated by sordid avarice only." Race prejudice, a tangled history of injustice, natural differences suggesting Negro inferiority—these are not promising materials for civil society.

These early American statesmen (including, by the way, many blacks) may have been wrong, as most of us would think today, in believing that a long-term biracial society was unfeasible and undesirable. They surely did not in fact provide any real alternative in their American Colonization Society and its minute settlement in Liberia. But we are likely to be too quick to assume that in trying to get rid of both slavery and Negroes they were being simply hypocritical or unprincipled. We have lost sight of the crucial difference between the two questions I am discussing: the question of freedom and the question of citizenship. To concede the Negro's right to freedom is not to concede his right to United States citizenship. And, on the other hand, to deny his right to United States citizenship is not to affirm that he is justly enslaved. There is nothing contradictory in arguing that while the Negroes have a human right to be free, they do not have a human right to be citizens of the United States. This distinction, which is today muddled inadvertently, was deliberately muddled by Stephen Douglas, and probably by Taney also. The former, Lincoln said in his magnificent speech on the *Dred Scott* decision, "finds the Republicans insisting that the Declaration of Independence includes ALL men, black as well as white; and forthwith he boldly denies that it includes negroes at all, and proceeds to argue gravely that all who contend it does, do so only because they want to vote, and eat, and sleep, and marry with negroes. He will have it that they cannot be consistent else. Now I protest against that counterfeit logic which concludes that, because I do not want a black woman for a *slave* I must necessarily want her for a *wife*. I need not have her for either, I can just leave her alone."[28]

Of course the problem was that while an individual could "leave the Negro alone," the American polity could not. Unless there was to be a permanent class of underlings, Negro emancipation had to imply either political and social equality of the races in the United States or separation of the races into distinct polities. For Lincoln, as for nearly all American statesmen up to his time, only the latter seemed to hold any promise for the long-term viability and quality of the American polity. In advocating a policy of emancipation and colonization, the Founders may have been cold or unwise or inequitable, but they were not acting contrary to the principles of the Declaration of Independence. To put the point differently, American Negroes may have had a valid claim to United States citizenship (I think they did); but it was a claim depending on particular circumstances and history (and thus discussable on such grounds) quite distinct from their claim to freedom, which depended upon nothing but their humanity.

The American Founders would have done their work better, it is now generally thought, if they had seen the need for, and responded to, the challenge of a multi-racial, heterogeneous, open society. Instead, they toyed with unrealistic schemes of colonization, temporized with racism and racial segregation, delayed justice for blacks unconscionably long, sanctioned second-class citizenship. They "set the stage," in John Hope Franklin's terms, "for every succeeding generation of Americans to apologize, compromise, and temporize on those principles of liberty that were supposed to be the very foundation of our system of government and way of life."[29]

28 "The Dred Scott Decision," *Lincoln* (Basler ed.), p. 360.
29 *University of Chicago Magazine*, Summer 1975, p. 13.

What might one of the thoughtful Founders say in response to these charges and in the light of present-day circumstances in the United States?

First, I think he would be amazed at the degree to which blacks and whites have progressed in making a civil society together. I think he would frankly admit that he would never have expected anything like the degree of harmony, mutual trust and toleration, and opportunity for blacks that have been achieved in the United States at the bicentennial of our beginning. At the same time, on closer inspection, he might wonder whether even the elementary question of whether the races can live together in peace has yet been settled beyond doubt. Are the races so well bonded that long-term economic depression or large-scale war (fought perhaps mainly by black American soldiers against black or yellow enemies) could not still tear them apart?

Moreover, in defense of his "temporizing" with racism and segregation and injustice, our Founder might ask what else he could have done? What, he might slyly ask our generation, has been your most successful (perhaps your only successful) large-scale integration program? Surely the desegregation in the United States military forces. That example is interesting in two respects. First the success seems increasingly problematical, as festering racial antagonism and the worrisome prospect of an all-black army, or infantry, suggest. Second, to the extent that it is a success, why was that possible? Because an army is an army. But a political democracy is not an army. It rests on and is severely limited by opinion, which cannot be commanded. Prejudice—arbitrary liking and trust and, of course, also disliking and mistrust—is inherent in political life, and its role is greater as the polity is more democratic. To criticize a Jefferson or a Lincoln for yielding to, even sharing in, white prejudice is equivalent to demanding either that he get out of politics altogether—and leave it to the *merely* prejudiced—or that he become a despot.

Regarding the quality of civil life, as distinct from its bare possibility, our Founder might say much. He might point to the extraordinary vulgarity and triviality of American popular culture, to the difficulty that America has in generating any high culture of its own, to the superficiality of social bonds and community values. And he might ask whether these oft-observed and deplored characteristics of American civil life are not connected with its attempt to be all things to all men, with its attempt to embrace the most extreme heterogeneity, so that it can be nothing much to any of them.

Finally, however, I think our Founder might be intrigued, if not altogether persuaded, by the prospect of a free society consisting not merely of a huge aggregation of individuals but of diverse ethnic and religious and other groups. He would be interested in the possibility of a civil society, viable yet capable of exploring and exemplifying diverse significant human possibilities. He would see the point, I think (especially if he had read his Tocqueville), of criticisms by Negroes like W. E. B. Du Bois of the Declaration of Independence itself for a radical individualism that cuts each man off from his fellows and from God. While he would be skeptical, I think he would be interested in exploring the world into which Du Bois offers a window, a world that is built (perhaps more than Du Bois realized) on our Founders' principles and institutions, but that is nevertheless quite different from anything they imagined.

[I]f . . . there is substantial agreement in laws, language and religion; if there is a satisfactory adjustment of economic life, then there is no reason why, in the same country and on the same street, two or three great national ideals might not thrive and develop, that men of different races might not strive together for their race ideals as well, perhaps even better, than in isolation. Here, it seems to me, is the reading of the riddle that puzzles so many of us. We are Americans, not only by birth and by citizenship, but by our political ideals, our language, our religion. Farther than that, our Americanism does not go. At that point, we are Negroes, members of a vast historic race that from the very dawn of creation has slept, but half awakening in the dark forests of its African fatherland. We are the first fruits of this new nation, the harbinger of that black to-morrow which is yet destined to soften the whiteness of the Teutonic to-day. We are that people whose subtle sense of song has given America its only American music, its only American fairy tales, its only touch of pathos and humor amid its mad money-getting plutocracy. As such, it is our duty to conserve our physical powers, our intellectual endowments, our spiritual ideals; as a race we must strive by race organization, by race solidarity, by race unity to the realization of that broader humanity which freely recognizes differences in men, but sternly deprecates inequality in their opportunities of development.[30]

Reflecting on thoughts like these and on present circumstances in the United States, our Founder might concede that the huge problem of racial heterogeneity, which his generation saw but could not master, may show the way to deal with another problem, which they did not see so clearly, the political and moral defects of mere in-

[30] "The Conservation of the Races," Washington, 1897, in *What Country Have I? Political Writings by Black Americans*, ed. Herbert J. Storing (New York: St. Martin's Press, 1970), pp. 82–83.

dividualism. He would surely point out that the foundation of this new polity is the old one; and he might wryly observe that his own principle of racial separation is, after all, an essential element in the new polity of racial and ethnic diversity. But I think he would concede, finally, that while in his heart of hearts he had thought that he and his generation had finished in its essentials the task of making the American polity, there is after all work still to be done.

Contributors

BENJAMIN R. BARBER is Professor of Political Science at Rutgers University and the author of seven books including *Superman and Common Men* (1971), *The Death of Communal Liberty* (1974), *Liberating Feminism* (1975), and the novel *Marriage Voices* (1981). His most recent book is *Strong Democracy*, published in 1984. Barber was for ten years the editor of *Political Theory*, and has held fellowships from the Guggenheim Foundation, the Fulbright Council, and the American Council of Learned Societies. He is currently working on a book called *Theater in the City of Man*, based on his 1984 Loyola Lectures, a project on Rousseau, Tocqueville, and Modernity, and a second novel.

WALTER BERNS is John M. Olin Distinguished Scholar in Constitutional and Legal Studies at the American Enterprise Institute and professorial lecturer in the Department of Government, Georgetown University. He is the author of, *Freedom, Virtue, and the First Amendment* (1957), *The First Amendment and the Future of American Democracy* (1976), *For Capital Punishment: Crime and the Morality of the Death Penalty* (1979), *In Defense of Liberal Democracy* (1984), joint author of *Essays on the Scientific Study of Politics* (1962); editor of *Constitutional Cases in American Government* (1963); and author of several articles in the Public Affairs Series, among them, "Beyond the (Garbage) Pale, or Democracy, Censorship, and the Arts," in *Censorship and Freedom of Expression* (1971). He has written numerous articles for legal and political science journals.

JAMES W. CEASER is Associate Professor of Government at the University of Virginia. Among his books are *Presidential Selection* (1979), *Reforming the Reforms* (1979), and *American Government, Origins, Institutions and Public Policy* (1984).

JOSEPH CROPSEY is Professor of Political Science at the University of Chicago. His special field is history of political philosophy. He is the author of *Polity and Economy* and *Political Philosophy and the Issues of Politics*, coeditor with the late Leo Strauss of *History of*

Political Philosophy, and editor of *Ancients and Moderns* and of *Hobbes's Dialogue between a Philosopher and a Student of the Common Laws of England.*

ROBERT A. DAHL is the Sterling Professor of Political Science at Yale University, where he has served on the faculty since 1946. He was the recipient of the Woodrow Wilson Prize, 1963, the Talcott Parsons Prize, 1977, the James Madison Prize, 1978, and has served as President of the American Political Science Association. Among the most important of his many books are: *A Preface to Democratic Theory* (1956), *Who Governs?* (1961), *Modern Political Analysis* (1963), *Political Oppositions in Western Democracies* (1966), *After the Revolution?* (1970), and *Size and Democracy* (1973).

MARTIN DIAMOND (1919–1977) was the Leavey Professor of the Foundations of American Freedom at Georgetown University. He also taught at Northern Illinois University, Claremont McKenna College, and the University of Illinois. Among his publications are "The Revolution of Sober Expectations," (in *America's Continuing Revolution*), *The Democratic Republic: An Introduction to American National Government,* and *The Founding of the Democratic Republic.* He wrote extensively on American political thought, federalism, American institutions, and on the teaching of politics.

ROBERT A. GOLDWIN is Resident Scholar and Director of Seminar Programs at the American Enterprise Institute for Public Policy Research in Washington, D.C. He has been Special Consultant to the President of the United States and Advisor to the Secretary of Defense. His fields of study include American political thought and political philosophy. He is the author of "John Locke," in *History of Political Philosophy* (1963). His edited books include *Political Parties in the Eighties* (1980), *Bureaucrats, Policy Analysts, Statesmen: Who Leads?* (1980), *How Democratic Is the Constitution?* (1980), and *How Capitalistic Is the Constitution?* (1982).

RICHARD HOFSTADTER (1916–1970) was a noted American historian and Professor of History at Columbia University. He received a Pulitzer Prize for history in 1956 for *The Age of Reform.* In addition, he authored *Social Darwinism in American Thought, 1860–1915, The American Political Tradition,* and edited *Great Issues in American History: A Documentary Record.*

ROBERT HORWITZ is Professor of Political Science and the Director of the Public Affairs Conference Center at Kenyon College. His special fields of interest include political philosophy, civic education, and public policy formation. He is the editor of and contributor to *The Moral Foundations of the American Republic*, coeditor of *Modern Political Ideologies* and *Civic Education in the United States*, and coauthor of *John Locke's Questions concerning the Law of Nature*. He has contributed chapters to *History of Political Philosophy, Representation and Misrepresentation*, and *Land Tenure in the Pacific*, and has published numerous research monographs, as well as articles and reviews in professional journals.

WILSON CAREY MCWILLIAMS is Professor of Political Science, Rutgers University. Among his publications are *The Idea of Fraternity in America* (1973), "Democracy and the Citizen," in R. Goldwin and W. Schambra, eds., *How Democratic is the Constitution?* (1980), and "The Bible in the American Political Tradition," in M. Aronoff, ed., *Religion and Politics* (1984).

WILL MORRISEY is an Associate Editor of *Interpretation: A Journal of Political Philosophy*. Author of *Reflections on De Gaulle: Political Founding in Modernity* (1983) and *Reflections on Malraux: Cultural Founding in Modernity* (1984); his articles and reviews have appeared in many newspapers and scholarly journals. He has contributed to Gerald Levin, ed., *Short Essays: Models for Composition* (1983). While serving as an aide to New Jersey State Senator S. Thomas Gagliano he has been working on a book-length study of moral relativism.

HERBERT J. STORING (1928–1977) was the Robert Kent Gooch Professor of Government at the University of Virginia. He also taught at the University of Chicago, Northern Illinois University, and Colgate University. Among his publications are *The Complete Anti-Federalist; Essays on the Scientific Study of Politics; What Country Have I? Political Writings by Black Americans*. He also wrote in the areas of American political thought, constitutional law, and public administration.

GORDON S. WOOD, Professor at Brown University since 1969, has also taught at the University of Michigan and at Harvard University. His publications include *The Creation of the American Re-*

public, 1776–1787 (1969), which was nominated for the National Book Award for History and Biography in 1970 and received the Bancroft and John H. Dunning Prizes in 1970, *Representation in the American Revolution* (1969), and *The Rising Glory of America, 1760–1820* (1971).

MICHAEL P. ZUCKERT is Congdon Professor of Political Science at Carleton College. He has published reviews and articles in a wide range of political science journals. He has written extensively on John Locke and on the liberal tradition of political philosophy in general.

Index

Library of Congress Cataloging-in-Publication Data
Main entry under title:

The Moral foundations of the American Republic.

    Includes index.
    1. United States—Politics and government—Addresses,
essays, lectures. 2. Political ethics—United States—
Addresses, essays, lectures. 3. United States—Moral
conditions—Addresses, essays, lectures. I. Horwitz,
Robert H.
JK39.M67 1986   320.973   85-17772
ISBN 0-8139-1081-1
ISBN 0-8139-1082-x (pbk.)